INTERNATIONAL LEGAL ASPECTS OF FEDERALISM

IVAN BERNIER

Professeur Agrégé, Department of Public Law,
Université Laval, Québec

ARCHON BOOKS

1973

Library of Congress Cataloging in Publication Data

Bernier, Ivan.
International legal aspects of federalism.

Bibliography: p.
1. Federal government. 2. International law. I. Title.
JX4005.B45 1973   341.26   73-2713
ISBN 0-208-01384-9

© Longman Group Limited 1973

First published 1973 by Longman Group Limited, London
and in the United States of America as an Archon Book
by The Shoe String Press, Inc., Hamden, Connecticut.

Printed in Great Britain by
Northumberland Press Limited
Gateshead

CONTENTS

PART TWO

FEDERALISM AND EVOLVING
INTERNATIONAL LAW

CHAPTER 5

THE IMPACT OF THE FEDERAL MODEL ON
INTERNATIONAL LAW

CHAPTER 6

THE IMPACT OF FEDERAL LAW ON INTERNATIONAL LAW

CHAPTER 7

GENERAL CONCLUSION

PREFACE

FEDERALISM raises numerous problems for international law. Some of them, such as the problems of personality, responsibility and immunity, are old and have been the subject of many studies. Others are more recent and need further investigation: examples are the apparent incapacity of federal states to participate fully in the development of international law and the questionable influence played by federal decisions in certain fields of international law. The object of this thesis is to take a global look at these problems.

The first part, entitled 'Federalism and Traditional International Law', deals with the problems of personality, responsibility and immunity in federal states. More specifically, it examines whether a number of alleged rules of international law concerning federal states are truly based on the practice of states and whether they conform to such general principles of international law as those of sovereignty, consent and recognition.

The second part, entitled 'Federalism and Evolving International Law', studies first the impact of federal structures on international law—to what extent they are an obstacle to the development of international law, the existing remedies to the division of competence in federal states, the significance of federalism as a model for international integration—and second the impact of federal law on international law.

The conclusion will show that federalism and international law are two systems whose inter-relationship, best described as one of attraction-repulsion, cannot be ignored.

In its original form, this work was submitted as a thesis for the degree of Doctor of Philosophy at the University of London in 1969. It was subsequently revised and partially re-written so as to bring within its compass the problems raised by autonomous states in international law. It was also brought up to date to January 1971. The task of revising the original work was facilitated by a grant from the Canada Arts Council.

I wish to express my gratitude to Professor D. H. N. Johnson, Professor of International Law and Air Law at the University of London, under whose constant guidance and encouragement this study emerged. My thanks are also due to Professor S. A. DeSmith, for his invaluable advice on constitutional law matters, and to Dr Philippe Evans and Professor Anthony Hooper who patiently read through the manuscript and advised on correct English usage. Finally, I wish also to express my gratitude to my wife, Lise, without whose loyal devotion and fortitude throughout, this work could not have been completed.

ACKNOWLEDGEMENTS

We are indebted to The World Press Private Ltd. for permission to reproduce extracts from *Treaties and Federal Constitutions— Their Mutual Impact* by R. C. Ghosh.

ABBREVIATIONS

ABAJ	=	*American Bar Association Journal*
AC	=	Appeal Cases (United Kingdom)
AJCL	=	*American Journal of Comparative Law*
AJIL	=	*American Journal of International Law*
All E.R.	=	All England Law Reports
Ann. fr. dr. int.	=	*Annuaire français de droit international*
BYIL	=	*British Yearbook of International Law*
CIIA	=	Canadian Institute of International Affairs
CYIL	=	*Canadian Yearbook of International Law*
Can. Bar. Rev.	=	*Canadian Bar Review*
Can. JEPS	=	*Canadian Journal of Economics and Political Science*
CLR	=	Commonwealth Law Reports
Cmd. Cmmd.	=	*Command Papers (United Kingdom)*
DLR	=	Dominion Law Reports
HR	=	*Hague Recueil: Académie de droit international, Recueil de cours*
ICAO	=	International Civil Aviation Organization
ICJ	=	International Court of Justice, Reports
ICLQ	=	*International and Comparative Law Quarterly*
JCLIL	=	*Journal of Comparative Legislation and International Law*
J. dr. int.	=	*Journal du droit international*
Öster. Zeit für öff. Recht	=	*Osterreichische Zeitschrift für öffentliches Recht*
PCIJ	=	*Permanent Court of International Justice*
RIAA	=	*United Nations Reports of International Arbitral Awards, 1948–*
Rev. dr. int. lég. comp.	=	*Revue de droit international et de législation comparée*
RGDIP	=	*Revue générale de droit international public*
SCR	=	Supreme Court Reports (Canada)
Univ. Toronto LJ	=	*University of Toronto Law Journal*
U.S.	=	United States Reports
Zeit. für aus. öff. Recht und Völk.	=	*Zeitschrift für ausländisches öffentliches Recht und Völkerrecht*

CHAPTER 1

INTRODUCTION: INTERNATIONAL LEGAL PROBLEMS OF FEDERALISM

HISTORICALLY, international law responded to the appearance of federal states by ignoring their constitutional characteristics and assimilating them to other sovereign states. This lack of interest was in part caused by the fact that international law itself was not traditionally concerned with the field of activities normally entrusted to the member states of a federation. With the widening of the scope of international law, it became difficult to ignore the characteristic features of federal states. Gradually, at first in bilateral treaties and then in multilateral instruments, provisions taking into consideration the particular problems of federal states were included. Then in recent years, the advantages of wider economic union and the necessity of more effective cooperation in all fields have resulted in the increasing use in international law of federal techniques and solutions.

In spite of this historical development, few attempts have been made so far to analyse in a comprehensive manner the international legal problems of federalism. Most textbooks of international law refer briefly to federal states, more often than not to make the point that federations normally absorb the international personality of their subdivisions and that federal governments must answer for the international delicts of their member states. Occasionally, questions are raised as to 'the effect of the federal system upon the capacity of federal States to contract and give effect to international obligations and to contribute, by their effective participation, to the development of International Law in matters requiring concurrent action of States'.[1] More recently, the realization of the European Communities has given rise to a number of studies relating to the impact of the federal model on international law. But very little is known about the nature of the relationship that exists between federalism and international law.

This is rather surprising in view of the fact that the continuing

---

[1] Oppenheim, *International Law*, 8th edn, ed. i, Lauterpacht, 1955, p. 179.

evolution of this relationship may have an important bearing on the future development of international law. Friedmann's warning 'that the extent of the structural changes in international relations in our time requires a far more basic reorientation of our thinking in international law'[2] takes here its full significance. The object of this work is precisely to determine what kind of relationship exists at present between federalism and international law.

In order to achieve a better understanding of the general topic, it may be useful to begin with a brief examination of the meaning of federalism. Having done that, we shall then discuss the international legal problems that are more often associated with federalism.

The meaning of federalism

In a recent study, A. H. Birch suggests that federalism, as a concept, 'has no fixed meaning: its meaning in any particular study is defined by the student in a manner which is determined by the approach which he wishes to make to his material'.[3] This is true to a certain extent. But before venturing on a new definition of federalism, it may be in order to examine some of the meanings given to the term by the more recognized authors on the subject.

Birch himself distinguishes four different approaches to the study of federalism. The first and most influential one is the institutional approach of Wheare.[4] In essence it is a comparative study of four governmental systems generally considered as federal. Wheare interprets federalism as a 'method of dividing powers so that the general and regional governments are each, within a sphere, co-ordinate and independent'.[5] Among the essential requirements of federal governments he includes the necessity that neither the central nor the regional governments should control independently the process of amendment, and the existence of an impartial body to interpret the meaning of the division of powers. But Wheare insists perhaps too much on the complete independence of the general and regional governments from each other. This leads him to dismiss numerous states generally considered as federal, at least from the point of view of international law.[6]

---

[2] Friedmann, *The Changing Structure of International Law*, 1964, p. 3.
[3] Birch, 'Approaches to the study of federalism', 14 *Political Studies* (1966), 15.
[4] Wheare, *Federal Government*, 4th edn, 1963.
[5] *Ibid.*, p. 10.
[6] See below, pp. 5-6.

A totally different approach has been proposed by Friedrich.[7] According to him, federalism must be seen as a process

> by which a number of separate political organizations, be they states or any other kind of associations, enter into arrangements for working out solutions, adopting joint policies and making joint decisions on joint problems. Or, reversely, it is the process through which an hitherto unitary political community, as it becomes differentiated into a number of separate and distinct political communities, achieves a new organization in which the differentiated communities, now separately organised, become capable of working out separately and on their own those problems they no longer have in common.[8]

The merit of Friedrich's approach is that it stresses the dynamic character of federalism. It is particularly helpful in the study of such atypical entities as the European Communities. However, Friedrich does not tell us whether there are any stages in the process which can and must be distinguished. Surely there are differences between a mere alliance and a federal state.[9]

The other two approaches to federalism mentioned by Birch are those of Livingston and Riker. Livingston's view is that:

> The essential nature of federalism is to be sought for, not in the shadings of legal and constitutional terminology, but in the forces —economic, social, political, cultural—that have made the outward forms of federalism necessary.... The essence of federalism lies not in the constitutional or institutional structure but in the society itself. Federal government is a device by which the federal qualities of the society are articulated and protected.[10]

This approach emphasizes another aspect of federalism: the decisive part played by social forces in the moulding of federal institutions. But it is not too helpful in deciding whether a government is federal or not, and as Birch points out, when Livingston 'gets down to specific examples his analysis has the same kind of institutional basis as Wheare's'.[11]

Riker interprets federalism as a bargain between prospective national governments for the purpose of aggregating territory, the better to lay taxes and raise armies.[12] Then he goes on to specify

---

[7] See Friedrich, *Man and his Government, an empirical theory of politics,* 1963, chapter 32; by the same author, 'International federalism in theory and practice', in Plischke, ed., *Systems of Integrating the International Community,* 1964, pp. 117–55.

[8] Friedrich, in Plischke, ed., pp. 126–7.

[9] According to Friedrich, the federalizing process 'may indeed commence in the forming of a League', *ibid.,* p. 128.

[10] Livingston, *Federalism and Constitutional Change,* 1956, pp. 1–2.

[11] Birch, 14 *Political Studies* (1966), p. 18.

[12] Riker, *Federalism: origin, operation, significance,* 1964, p. 11.

when a constitution must be considered as federal; the rule for identification is:

> A constitution is federal if (1) two levels of governments rule the same land and people, (2) each level has at least one area of action in which it is autonomous, and (3) there is some guarantee (even though merely a statement in the constitution) of the autonomy of each government in its own sphere.[13]

Riker's theory of federalism as a bargain between different governments is really a historical interpretation of the bringing into being of federations. More important, for present purposes, is the definition he gives of a federal constitution; it differs from the federal principle enunciated by Wheare in that it puts much less emphasis on the autonomy of the general and regional governments. Riker, from this point of view, is typical of a growing number of scholars who want to do away with what is considered to be a too narrow approach to federalism.

In 1955 already, Birch himself had suggested a modification of Wheare's definition which stressed, not so much the independence between the federal and regional governments, as their coordinate status.[14] But to other writers, this was still unsatisfactory. In 1961, impressed by the growing interdependence between central and regional authorities within federations, M. J. C. Vile proposed a new definition of federalism which significantly altered that of Wheare. According to Vile:

> Federalism is a system of government in which central and regional authorities are linked in a mutually interdependent political relationship; in this system a balance is maintained such that neither level of government becomes dominant to the extent that it can dictate the decisions of the other, but each can influence, bargain with, and persuade the other. Usually, but not necessarily, this system will be related to a constitutional structure establishing an independent legal existence for both central and regional governments, and providing that neither shall be legally subordinate to the other. The functions of government will be distributed between these levels (exclusively, competitively, or co-operatively), initially perhaps by a constitutional document, but thereafter by a political process, involving where appropriate the judiciary; in this process the political interdependence of the two levels of government is of the first importance in order to prevent one level absorbing all effective decision-making power.[15]

As an example of the kind of interrelationship existing between federal and state politics in the United States, Vile mentioned the

[13] *Idem.*
[14] Birch, *Federalism, Finance and Social Legislation*, 1955, p. 291.
[15] Vile, *The Structure of American Federalism*, 1961, p. 199.

field of foreign affairs where, in his view, 'the States have, from time to time throughout American history, exerted considerable political influence'.[16]

Vile's definition of federalism was soon approved by a number of authors, including Riker, Friedrich, May and, it would seem, Wheare himself.[17] The only opposition has come from writers who, sticking to the original definition of federalism proposed by Wheare, have suggested the use of a new concept in order to account for the changes that have taken place in traditional federations: they speak of 'quasi-federalism'. Thus for Aiyar: 'Since we have defined the federal principle rigidly, we must limit the term "quasi-federal" to a constitution that maintains the constitutional autonomy only in name.'[18] But this is just another way of saying that the practice of federalism has changed over the years: instead of modifying the definition of federalism so as to make it conform to that practice, Aiyar prefers to say that true federalism is gradually disappearing.[19]

Having thus surveyed the various approaches to federalism, it is possible now to draw a fairly clear picture of what federalism is. Formally, it would appear to exist when the following features may be found in a political entity: (1) a division of powers between a central and regional governments; (2) a certain degree of independence between central and regional governments; (3) direct action on the people by the central and regional governments; and (4) some means of preserving the constitutional division of powers. In its practical functioning, federalism is characterized essentially by the political interdependence of the central and regional authorities. In the background, there are numerous other factors—sociological, political, economic—that may explain the existence of such characteristic features in federal entities. But in deciding whether or not a particular state may be classified as federal, they cannot be of much help.

Such is, then, the meaning of federalism. In the present study, however, the question arises whether it is practicable to distinguish between entities that are truly federal, and others that claim to be federal but are not. Although it is often said that the South American federations and the Soviet Union are federal only in name, the fact is that the constitution of these states has been used either as

---

[16] *Ibid*, p. 194.
[17] See May, *Federalism and Fiscal Adjustment*, 1969, pp. 10–11, where the author cites the relevant authorities.
[18] Aiyar, *Federalism and Social Changes*, 1961, p. 9.
[19] For a criticism of this view, see Dudley, 'The Concept of Federalism', 1 *The Nigerian Journal of Economic and Social Studies* (1963).

an excuse for not fulfilling international obligations, or, as in the case of the Soviet Union, for claiming multiple representation in international organizations. Obviously, the present study would be incomplete if it did not deal with such problems.

This brings us back to the remark made previously by Birch: that the meaning of federalism 'in any particular study is defined by the student in a manner which is determined by the approach which he wishes to make to his material'.[20] In the present case, it is clear that a loose interpretation of federalism must be adopted if useful results are to be achieved. Therefore, all states that claim to be federal will be accepted as such in this study; but a greater degree of caution will be exercised in the analysis of situations involving entities that are federal only in name.

Federalism and international law

Having thus defined federalism, it becomes easier to understand why traditional international law refused at the outset to differenti-ate between federal states and other types of sovereign states. Recognition of the division of competence inherent in federal states would have meant a serious encroachment on one of the most basic principles of international law, that of state sovereignty. How-ever, this unyielding attitude soon gave rise to a number of problems.

The international legal problems traditionally associated with federal states are those of personality, responsibility and immun-ity. There exists in fact a vast body of literature on these problems. But not all the difficulties have yet been solved. For example, al-though there is little doubt in international law about the status, rights and duties of the federal state, the same cannot be said about the status, rights and duties of the component states. So, in a recent textbook, one discovers that in the case of com-ponent states exercising international capacities, 'such capacities are *probably* exercised as agents for the union, even if the acts concerned are done in the name of the component state';[21] one also finds that 'the extent to which member states of federations and provinces of other types of state can claim immunity is un-settled'.[22] Such problems are not merely academic. In 1958, the Government of Quebec complained, in the midst of a controversy

[20] See above, p. 2.
[21] Brownlie, *Principles of Public International Law*, 1966, pp. 54–5 (my italics).
[22] *Ibid.*, p. 284.

with the federal authorities of Canada, that it was 'high time a study in depth be made on this question of international agreements and of the international relations of the Provinces'.[23]

What appears to be lacking in the existing studies is a clear idea of how the division of internal sovereignty within a federation accords, not only with the basic principle of state sovereignty, but also with such other principles as those of consent and recognition. A surprising number of theories have been put forward regarding the international status, responsibility and immunity of subdivisions of federal states. Each pretends to be based on some acknowledged principle of international law; but each arrives at a different result. In such circumstances one is justified in asking: do any of these theories actually conform to the international practice of states?

Unfortunately, older works on the subject too often rely on deductive speculations, an unacceptable approach to international law. Thus, in a 1910 book entitled *De l'influence de la forme fédérale dans les relations de droit international*, the author explains:

> Nous aurions voulu pouvoir appliquer à cette étude la méthode inductive.... Cela eut été plus scientifique, mais ce n'eut été logique qu'en apparence. Il ne peut en effet être question de chercher une théorie de l'Etat fédéral au point de vue international. Elle est faite depuis longtemps. Elle est toute simple. Elle est parfaite parce qu'elle ne peut être autrement et les principes qui y sont affirmés sont indiscutables parce qu'ils sont l'expression de la logique même.[24]

Even in recent and more scholarly works, the importance of the international practice of states is not always recognized. Most writing on the international status of member states of federations is founded on purely constitutional law considerations. If it is mentioned that certain member states of federations have concluded international agreements with foreign powers, no attempt is made to find out whether these powers in such circumstances considered the member states as subjects of international law. So it will be the first aim of this study to determine more precisely what impact federalism has had on the traditional rules of international law.

The result of this enquiry will afford a clearer understanding of the fundamental relationship that exists between classical federalism and classical international law. But both federalism and international law, while still retaining their basic characteristics, are

---

[23] *The Government of Quebec and the Constitution*, Office of Information and Publicity of Quebec, 1968, p. 86.

[24] Mommeja, 'De l'influence de la forme fédérale dans les relations de droit international', thesis, Bordeaux, 1910, p. 6.

involved in a process of change. In 1931, in a book entitled *The Foreign Relations of the Federal State*, R. Stoke pointed out that federal constitutions often had the effect of preventing federal governments from undertaking international obligations in fields beyond their legislative competence; he also showed that in certain circumstances this led to the inclusion of special provisions in international agreements.[25] But Stoke considered that the real obstacle in the conduct of federal foreign relations was 'a tenacious localism' and concluded that 'if this spirit could be banished by a greater "international-mindedness", the legal differences between federal and unitary states in the management of the international relations would be of little significance'.[26] This last conclusion was perhaps a little optimistic.

In a book published in 1961, R. C. Ghosh examines anew the impact of federal constitutions on the foreign policy of federal states.[27] More forcibly than Stoke, Ghosh establishes that such constitutions, in so far as they affect the capacity of federal states to contract and give effect to international obligations, have a negative impact on the development of international law. He also enquires into the devices that federal governments adopt 'to promote Federal-State co-operation in the making and implementation of treaties, and for the protection of the rights of the member-States'.[28] His study ends with a warning that classical federalism may well be incompatible with the future growth of international law.[29]

But if this is exact, how can it be explained that federalism seems to hold an attraction for international law. Speaking about federations, Reuter declared in 1958: 'Moreover these structural relations, which grew out of exceptionally favourable circumstances, are "models" for the future development of societies which are not yet so advanced.'[30] Since the end of the First World War, a vast number of projects for international federations have been put forward; at the same time, federalist movements have sprouted up in almost every part of the world. More recently, the realization of the European Communities has been hailed as an important step towards the United States of Europe—'a notable advance and, in some respects, a new phase in the evolution of international law.'[31] All this suggests that an objective assessment of the impact of the

[25] Stoke, *The Foreign Relations of the Federal State*, 1931, pp. 175 ff.
[26] *Ibid.*, p. 231.
[27] Ghosh, *Treaties and Federal Constitutions: Their Mutual Impact*, 1961, pp. 233 ff.
[28] *Ibid.*, p. vii.
[29] *Ibid.*, p. 308.
[30] Reuter, *International Institutions*, 1958, p. 180.
[31] Friedmann, p. 96.

federal model on international law should include a study of the extent to which it has influenced the theory and practice of international integration and the significance of this for international law.

In addition to this enquiry, it would be profitable to determine the precise impact of federal law on international law. In Basdevant's *Dictionnaire de la terminologie du droit international,* one finds under 'federal State':

> Bien qu'institution de droit public interne, l'Etat fédéral intéresse le droit international, d'une part, en ce qu'il fait surgir certaines questions particulières concernant les traités et la responsabilité internationale, d'autre part, en ce que l'on a parfois cherché, pour la solution de certaines questions, p. ex. des questions de limites, à faire jouer l'analogie entre l'ordre international et l'ordre fédéral.[32]

There is some disagreement as to whether decisions reached in disputes between member states of federations are of any use for the determination of international law. But very little has been done to find out to what extent such decisions have influenced the development of international law.

Such is the background against which must be assessed the impact of federalism on international law. Having regard to what has just been said, the present study will take the following form: the first part will cover federalism and traditional international law and will include three chapters dealing with the problems of personality, responsibility and immunity in federal states; the second will be concerned with federalism and evolving international law and it will examine first, the impact of federal structures on international law and in turn, the impact of federal law on international law.

---

[32] Basdevant, *Dictionnaire de la terminologie du droit international,* 1960, p. 267.

PART ONE

FEDERALISM AND TRADITIONAL INTERNATIONAL LAW

CHAPTER 2

FEDERALISM AND INTERNATIONAL PERSONALITY

International personality is generally defined as the capacity to be a bearer of rights and duties under international law.[1] Thus, in the *Injuries* case, the International Court of Justice found that the United Nations Organization constituted an international person because it was capable of possessing international rights and duties.[2] However, it has been pointed out with reason that 'this definition, though conventional is unfortunately circular since the *indicia* referred to depend on the existence of a legal person'.[3] If international personality is the capacity to be a bearer of rights and duties under international law, one must necessarily refer to international law in order to apprehend the meaning of international personality. But the usual definition of international law is that of a body of rules accepted as legally binding by sovereign states and other international subjects.[4] So, it is not clear in the last resort which entities, apart from sovereign states, are entitled to be considered as subjects of international law.

The difficulty becomes immediately obvious when one considers the situation of federal states in international law. The federation itself is universally considered as a sovereign state, enjoying full international competence as well as full international personality.[5] But the situation of the member states is not so clear. The disagreement among those who have written on the subject is very deep. Ghosh, for example, considers that 'it is not possible for member-

---

[1] See Anzilotti, *Cours de droit international public*, 1929, i, 121; Guggenheim, *Lehrbuch des Völkerrechts*, 1948, i, 161; Kelsen, *The Law of the United Nations*, 1950, p. 329; Schwarzenberger, *A Manual of International Law*, 4th edn, 1960, i, 47; Brownlie, *Principles of Public International Law*, 1966, p. 52. On international personality in general see, Mosler, 'Réflexions sur la personnalité juridique en droit international public', in *Mélanges Henri Rolin*, 1964, pp. 228 ff; O'Connell, 'La personnalité en droit international', 67 *RGDIP* (1963), 5–43; Castro-Rial, 'Considérations sur la personnalité internationale', 4 *Revue hellénique dr. int.* (1951), 29 ff.

[2] *Reparation for Injuries Suffered in the Service of the United Nations*, Advisory Opinion (1949) *ICJ Rep.* 174.

[3] Brownlie, p. 52.

[4] See for instance Schwarzenberger, i, 1.

[5] See below, pp. 29–30.

States of a Federal State to be recognized as International Persons for the simple reason that they are neither full nor half-sovereign entities, that is, they are not "States" in the sense in which the term is used in International Law.'[6]

Other international law writers, such as Bernhardt, O'Connell and Steinberger, take the contrary view, that member states of federations endowed with a limited international competence may become to a certain extent subjects of international law.[7] Some authors have revised their opinions on the subject. Bora Laskin, for instance, after asserting in 1964 that international law required federal states 'to present but one face to the community of nations,'[8] evidenced in 1969 a more cautious approach when he wrote that a federal state had 'one juridical personality (subject to constitutional and international arrangements to the contrary)'.[9]

The same divergence of opinion is to be found in the discussions of the International Law Commission over the question of treaty-making by members of a federal state. In the 1953 Report on the Law of Treaties prepared by Lauterpacht, the view is expressed that treaties concluded by member states of federations 'are treaties in the meaning of international law'.[10] But in the Fitzmaurice Report of 1958, it is stated that in so far as the component states of a federal union 'are empowered or authorized under the constitution of the union to negotiate or enter into treaties with foreign countries, even if it is in their own name, they do so as agents for the union which, as alone possessing international personality, is necessarily the entity that becomes bound by the treaty and responsible for carrying it out.'[11]

In his Report of 1962, Waldock adopted a different attitude. He recognized that 'if the constitution of a federation or Union confers upon its constituent States power to enter into agreements directly with foreign States, the constituent State normally exer-

---

[6] Ghosh, *Treaties and Federal Constitutions: Their Mutual Impact*, 1961, p. 84.

[7] Bernhardt, *Der Abschluss völkerrechtlicher Verträge im Bundesstaat, Eine Untersuchung zum deutschen und ausländischen Bundesstaatsrecht*, 1957, pp. 18-24; O'Connell, *International Law*, 1965, i, 318; Steinberger, 'Constitutional subdivisions of states or unions and their capacity to conclude treaties, Comments on Art. 5 para. 2 of the ICL's 1966 Draft Articles on the Law of Treaties', 27 *Zeitschrift für ausländisches öffentliches Recht und Völkerrecht* (1967), 411 at 416.

[8] Laskin, 'Some international legal aspects of federalism: the experience of Canada', in *Federalism and the New Nations of Africa*, Currie, ed., 1964, p. 391.

[9] Laskin, *Canadian Constitutional Law*, rev. 3rd edn, 1969, p. 290.

[10] *Yearbook of the International Law Commission*, 1953, ii, 139.

[11] *Yearbook of the International Law Commission*, 1958, ii, 24.

cises this power in the capacity only of an organ of the federal State or Union, as the case may be.'[12] But he acknowledged two exceptions to this. Member states of a federation, he suggested, must be considered as international subjects if they become members of the United Nations or if they are recognized, by the federal state and other contracting states, to possess an international personality of their own.[13] In the final Draft Articles on the Law of Treaties adopted in 1965 by a narrow majority of 7 to 3 with four abstentions, Article 5(2) provided that: 'States members of a federal union may possess a capacity to conclude treaties if such capacity is admitted by the federal constitution and within the limits there laid down.'[14]

In 1966 the General Assembly of the United Nations resolved to convene an international conference of plenipotentiaries to prepare a convention on the Law of Treaties, using as a starting point the draft articles prepared by the International Law Commission.[15] At the first session of the United Nations Conference on the Law of Treaties, which was held in Vienna from 26 March to 24 May 1968, Article 5(2) of the draft articles encountered serious opposition. By making capacity dependent solely upon the provisions of the federal constitution, argued a number of representatives, Article 5, paragraph 2, risked being interpreted on the one hand 'as an invitation to outside States to purport to interpret the constitution of a federal State',[16] and on the other hand as an abdication of international law 'in favour of internal constitutional law—and that in the fundamental role of establishing what subjects of law were empowered to act'.[17] However, an amendment to delete paragraph 2 of Article 5 was rejected by 45 votes to 38, with 10 abstentions.[18]

In 1969, at the second session of the United Nations Conference on the Law of Treaties held in Vienna from 9 April to 21 May, Article 5(2) came up again for discussion. Following a vigorous attack led by federal states, paragraph 2 was finally rejected by 66

---

[12] *Yearbook of the International Law Commission*, 1962, ii, 36.
[13] *Idem.*
[14] General Assembly, Official Records: Twenty-first session, Supplement no. 9 (A/6309/Rev.1), p. 10; see *Yearbook of the International Law Commission*, 1965, ii, 160 (Art. 3 (2)).
[15] General Assembly Resolution 2166 (XXI) of 5 December 1966.
[16] United Nations Conference on the Law of Treaties, First session, Vienna, 26 March–24 May 1968, Official Records, p. 62 (Doc. A/CONF. 39/11) The remark was made by Mr Wershof of Canada. For a summary of the discussion on the subject, see Stanford, 'United Nations Law of Treaties Conference: first session', 19 *Univ. Toronto LJ* (1969), 59 at 60-1.
[17] *Ibid.*, p. 67 (Mr Jiminez de Arechaga of Uruguay).
[18] *Ibid.*, pp. 68-9.

votes to 28, with 13 abstentions.[19] In the opinion of the majority, the rule found in paragraph 2 was not only unsatisfactory from a legal viewpoint—reference was made again to the danger of undue intervention in the affairs of a state and the lack of importance given to international recognition—but the rule was also beyond the scope of the convention itself, which was intended to deal solely with treaties between independent states.[20] It was the general feeling that without affecting the capacity of member states of federations to conclude international treaties, and therefore their capacity to become subjects of international law to a degree, the deletion of Article 5, paragraph 2, would serve to avoid what McNair J. in *Sayce v. Ameer of Bahawalpur* termed 'the difficult question of the status of component parts of a State federation.'[21] In other words, the Conference did not reject the possibility that member states of federations could become subjects of international law, but, finding the subject too controversial and not properly within the scope of the Convention, it preferred not to pronounce on it. As the representative of New Zealand explained earlier in 1968, Article 5(2) 'was only the incomplete fragment which had survived the International Law Commission's extensive debates on the intractable subject of international personality and State capacity, debates which had ranged far beyond the scope of the law of treaties.'[22]

The problem of the status of member states of federations epitomizes in a sense the difficulties of identifying those subjects of international law which are not sovereign states. It is not in itself a problem that is bound to arise very often. Yet, new and similar situations may be created in the future where the same problem will have to be faced again. As early as 1954 the suggestion was made that a provision clarifying the question of international personality in the constitution of an eventual European Federation would have

> 'not only theoretical importance in solving a long standing dispute on the subject among writers on federalism, but also ... have important practical consequences, e.g., with respect to their representation in international organizations, their privileges and im-

[19] United Nations Conference on the Law of Treaties, Second Session, provisional Summary Record of the Eighth Plenary Meeting, Vienna, 28 April 1969, pp. 15-16 (Doc.A/CONF.39/SR.8).
[20] The various arguments put forward on this subject at the second session of the Conference are summarised in Stanford, 'The Vienna Convention on the Law of Treaties', 20 Univ. Toronto LJ (1970), 18 at 29-31.
[21] (1952) 1 All ER 326 at 331.
[22] United Nations Conference on the Law of Treaties, First session, Vienna, 26 March–24 May 1968, Official Records, p. 60 (Doc. A/CONF. 39/11).

munities in other States, and their international responsibility.'[23]

However, such a suggestion implies, like Article 5(2) of the International Law Comission's Draft Articles on the Law of Treaties, that a mere constitutional law provision may be sufficient to solve important problems of international law. This has yet to be demonstrated.

In order to clarify the situation, it may be useful to consider in the first place the various theories which have been put forward concerning the status of federal unions and their member states. Each theory will subsequently be confronted with the practice of states. First to be examined will be those theories based on the concept of sovereignty; second, those that consider international competence to be the true criterion of international personality. The enquiry will be completed by a study of the role of recognition in the determination of international personality, with particular reference to federations.

Sovereignty as a criterion of international personality in federal states

THEORETICAL CONSIDERATIONS

Many writers attempt to solve the problem of international personality in federal states by referring to sovereignty. Among them, three main tendencies may be distinguished. In some cases, sovereignty is considered as divisible and so international personality is regarded as capable of belonging in part to the central state and in part to the member states. Other writers consider sovereignty to be indivisible and attribute it, and therefore also international personality, either to the central state or to its member states. Finally, it is sometimes argued that sovereignty, in federal states, is located concurrently in the central body and in its parts, each of them enjoying complete international personality.[24]

Divided sovereignty

The doctrine of the divisibility of sovereignty, in relation to federal

[23] Sohn and Shafer, 'Foreign affairs', in Bowie and Friedrich, *Studies in Federalism*, 1954, p. 241.
[24] For an exhaustive bibliography on this subject, see Kunz, *Die Staatenverbindungen*, 1929, pp. 599 ff. See also Hallmayer, 'Die völkerrechtliche Stellung der deutschen Länder nach dem Bonner Grundgesetz', inaugural dissertation, Tübingen, 1954, pp. 4-5.

states, can be traced back to *The Federalist* papers which appeared in America between 1787 and 1788.[25] It was popularized by De Tocqueville, an observer of American political life,[26] and formulated in legal terms by Waitz, a German jurist.[27] According to Waitz, individual sovereign states entering into a federal pact were giving up a part of their sovereignty to a new entity, the federal state. Although divided, sovereignty itself was not qualitatively affected; quantitatively, of course, it was no longer the same as certain subject matters were taken away from it. In the resulting situation, the central state and the member states were independent of each other within their respective spheres of competence. But Waitz did not go so far as to claim that the member states were endowed with international personality to the relative extent of their sovereignty.[28]

Such a claim, however, has been put forward recently by Ross.[29] His view is that sovereignty 'is merely another term for self-government.'[30] Having interpreted it in this way, he adds: 'It is correct to say that "sovereignty" (self-government) is the element which is determining for the position of a state as subject of International Law (a subject of international obligations).'[31] Thus, in the case of federations, the central state and the member states are self-governing within their respective spheres of jurisdiction. Therefore, not only the central state but also the member states are subjects of international law.[32] But Ross openly admits that his theory 'differs from the prevailing view which would only regard the member state as an international person in so far as it has preserved competence to act in external affairs by sending and receiving envoys, concluding treaties, etc.'. This, he explains, 'is due to an unwarranted confusion of the terms capacity for duty and capacity for action'.[33]

A different view of the theory of divisible sovereignty is adopted by Oppenheim.[34] For him, only external sovereignty must be taken into account for the determination of international personality. Thus, when the whole field of external relations in a federal state

---

[25] See *The Federalist: A Commentary on the Constitution of the United States: being a collection of essays written in support of the Constitution,* 1787, ed. H. Cabot Lodge, 1886.
[26] De Tocqueville, *De la démocratie en Amérique,* 1835.
[27] Waitz, *Grundzüge der Politik,* 1862, pp. 43–5.
[28] *Ibid.,* p. 43.
[29] Ross, *A Text-Book of International Law,* 1947.
[30] *Ibid.,* p. 36.
[31] *Idem.*
[32] *Ibid.,* p. 100.
[33] *Ibid.,* p. 101.
[34] Oppenheim, *International Law,* 8th edn, ed. Lauterpacht, 1955, i, pp. 175-7.

belongs to the central government, the member states are deprived of external sovereignty and, therefore, of international personality. But where a partial international competence is retained by them, they enjoy a corresponding external sovereignty and are, to that extent, international subjects. This view is apparently shared by Hay.[35] After suggesting that external sovereignty should be seen 'as *supreme power* over specific subject matter', he adds that such an approach would 'explain more adequately than does classic doctrine the participation in the international legal community of constituent parts of states or federations.'[36]

Undivided sovereignty

Numerous writers have challenged the theory that sovereignty in federal states is divided and belongs in part to the federal state, in part to the member states. The first to do so were Calhoun and von Seydel.[37] For them, sovereignty was indivisible and could only belong to the member states. Most federations, they argued, are based on a treaty between sovereign states. If the treaty subsists, this means that the member states have retained their sovereignty; the federation then is in reality a confederation. If on the other hand the treaty is replaced by a constitutional act, sovereignty is entirely transferred to the central state; the federation is then in reality a unitary state. Their own view was that a treaty of federation could not be replaced purely and simply by a constitutional act. Its very disappearance would put an end to the obligations of the member states with the result that they would be bound only morally by the constitutional act. Therefore, the treaty subsists, the member states enjoy full international sovereignty and the central state is merely their agent.

However, this theory never gained much acceptance among other writers. Those who agree that sovereignty is indivisible generally consider that it is possessed exclusively by the federation. This view, which originated with Zorn,[38] was developed by Borel and Le Fur.[39] The crucial point, according to Borel, is that the federa-

---

[35] Hay, *Federalism and Supranational Organizations*, 1966.

[36] *Ibid.*, p. 73, note 205.

[37] Calhoun, *A Discourse on the Constitution and Government of the United States*, in *The Works of John C. Calhoun*, ed. R. C. Cralle, 1858, i, 111-406; von Seydel, 'Der Bundesstaatsbegriff', 28, *Zeitschrift für die gesammte Staatswissenschaft* (1872), 185–256.

[38] Zorn, 'Neue Beiträge zur Lehre vom Bundesstaat', *Hirth's Annalen des deutschen Reiches*, 1884, pp. 453–83.

[39] Borel, *Etudes sur la souveraineté de l'Etat fédératif*, 1886; Le Fur, *L'Etat fédéral et la confédération d'Etats*, 1896; see also Mouskheli, *La théorie juridique de l'état fédéral*, 1931.

tion can determine freely its own competence. This is evidenced by the power of federal organs to modify the federal constitution without the unanimous consent of the member states.[40] It is also evidenced by the fact that federal legislation prevails over the legislation of member states.[41] Therefore, Borel concluded, sovereignty in a federation must be said to belong exclusively to the federal state. The arguments of Le Fur are exactly the same.[42] But neither Borel nor Le Fur concluded from this that member states of federations cannot enjoy international personality. Both of them admitted that, in so far as these member states are endowed with international competence, they must be considered as international subjects.[43] Their own conclusion is simply that they cannot be considered as states in the sense of international law.

Some years later, however, the theory of the supremacy of the central state over the member states led Verdross and Kunz to different conclusions.[44] Their basic assumption is that sovereignty means simply 'international immediacy' (Völkerrechtunmittelbarkeit).[45] Thus, they argue, it is important to distinguish between states in the sense of international law and states in the sense of municipal law. The former are immediately subordinated to international law and they can be deprived of their competence only by a procedure of international law; whereas states in the sense of municipal law are not immediately subordinated to international law and a procedure of municipal law can deprive them of their competence. Since the member states in a federation can be individually deprived of their competence without their consent—as a rule they do not have an individual right of veto in the amending process[46]—they are not directly subordinated to international law. The federation itself, on the other hand, cannot be deprived of its competence otherwise than by an international procedure; consequently, it is a full subject of international law. But then, contrary to Verdross, Kunz goes on to say that even if the member states retain a limited international competence, this does not mean that they are limited subjects of international law; for such competence is simply dele-

---

[40] Borel, p. 117.
[41] *Ibid.*, p. 66.
[42] Le Fur, pp. 590-5.
[43] Borel, p. 97; Le Fur, p. 762.
[44] Verdross, *Die Verfassung der Völkerrechtsgemeinschaft*, 1926, p. 101; Kunz, Die *Staatenverbindungen*, 1929, pp. 537 ff; by the same author also, 'Une nouvelle théorie de l'Etat fédéral', 11 *Rev. dr. int. lég. comp.* (1930) 835.
[45] See Kunz, 11 *Rev. dr. int. lég. comp.* (1930), 845.
[46] See on this question, Livingston, *Federalism and Constitutional Change*, 1956.

gated to them and can easily be abolished by federal legislation.[47]

The only problem was to explain how in certain cases federal legislation could be declared by the courts to be invalid and unconstitutional. The difficulty was perceived by Kelsen who proposed an ingenious solution to this problem. In the footsteps of Austin and Haenel,[48] Kelsen argues that there are three different legal orders in a federal state.[49] Two of them, the legal order of the central state and the legal order of the member states, are coordinate; the third, typified by the constitutional court and the constituent organs, stands above these two. Such a structure, he affirms, is the only way to explain how acts of the member states as well as acts of the central state can be declared unconstitutional. But Kelsen admits that since 'the organs of the federation are at the same time organs of the total community ..., the federation is usually not distinguished, as a partial community, from the federal state, as the total community'.[50] In the end, he reaches more or less the same conclusion as Kunz as regards the international status of member states of federations. He writes, on this point:

> The centralization in the field of foreign affairs may not be complete; the component States may have some competence left in this respect, for instance, the power to conclude treaties with third States in certain limited fields. Then they may be considered as subjects of international law, with a restricted personality. But since the component states have this competence in accordance with the federal constitution, the organs of the component States, in concluding treaties within the competence conferred upon them by the federal constitution, may also be considered as indirect organs of the federal state; hence, the international person concluding these treaties may be considered to be the federal state acting, in certain respects, through a component state.[51]

Recently, the theory that member states of federations cannot be recognized as international persons because they are neither full nor half-sovereign entities, that is, they are not states in the sense of international law, has been taken up by Ghosh.[52] His arguments are similar to those of Kunz. He writes:

[47] Kunz, 'Une nouvelle théorie...', pp. 873-4. Verdross considers on the contrary that member States of federations exercising a limited international competence are subjects of international law to a degree; see below, p. 33.

[48] Austin, *The Province of Jurisprudence Determined etc.*, 1832, Weidenfeld and Nicolson, 1965, pp. 245–51; Haenel, *Studien zum deutschen Staatsrecht*, 1873, i, 63.

[49] Kelsen, 'Die Bundesexekution, ein Beitrag zur Theorie und Praxis des Bundesstaates' in *Festgabe für Fleiner*, 1927, pp. 127-87; see also by the same author, *Principles of International Law*, 2nd edn, 1966, p. 262.

[50] Kelsen, *Principles of International Law*, p. 262.

[51] *Ibid.*, pp. 260–1.

[52] Ghosh, *Treaties and Federal Constitutions: Their Mutual Impact*, 1961, pp. 74–85.

> They are integral parts of a single State and govern under the paramountcy of a Constitution which determines their competence but which they cannot individually alter or amend. On the other hand, their powers, including their limited capacity to conclude certain classes of treaties, may be curtailed by a constitutional amendment without their unanimous consent.... In case of conflict between their laws and federal law, both made in pursuance of the Constitution, federal laws prevail.[53]

From this he concludes that their limited power to conclude treaties, and the occasional application of international law for the settlement of disputes between them, 'are completely ineffective to induce the members of the Family of Nations to recognize their claim to international personality'.[54]

Concurrent sovereignty

A more unusual view of where sovereignty lies in federal states was put forward by Nawiasky in 1920.[55] For him, indivisible sovereignty was also an essential characteristic of the state. Since a federation was a state composed of states, he argued, sovereignty necessarily resided in all of them. In other words, the relationship between these states was one of coordination rather than of subordination. He explained the division of competence between the member states and the central state by *renvois* from one sovereignty to another. Thus, when the competence of the member states was modified by the federal state, it could not be in violation of their sovereignty: for the federal state itself was acting in accordance with the will of the member states. As for international personality, it was purely a question of international competence. If the member states had charged the central government with the exclusive conduct of international relations, then only the federation itself enjoyed international personality. If the member states had retained a limited international competence, then they were to that extent subjects of international law.[56]

After the Second World War Nawiasky's theory was adopted and transformed by the Soviet theoreticians of international law. In a recent textbook published by the Academy of Sciences of the USSR it is stated that the Soviet Union is a sovereign state, but that 'this state of affairs does not reduce or qualitatively affect the sovereignty and independence of each Union Republic'.[57] The

[53] *Ibid.*, pp. 84–85.
[54] *Ibid.*, p. 85.
[55] Nawiasky, *Der Bundesstaat als Rechtsbegriff*, 1920.
[56] *Ibid.*, p. 49.
[57] *International Law*, an undated publication of the Academy of Sciences of the USSR, p. 91.

sovereignty of the USSR, it is explained, is based on the sovereign rights of its constituent Union Republics. From this, it is concluded that the member states as well as the central state are full subjects of international law.[58] A more detailed examination of the question appears in the *Soviet Yearbook of International Law* for 1963.[59] According to Professor P. Y. Nedbailo, and V. A. Vassilenko, the basic fact is that 'in present-day conditions, a state is a subject of international law on the basis of its sovereignty which is the keystone of international law'.[60] They then go on to explain that not only the Soviet Union but also the member republics of the Soviet Union are fully sovereign states and therefore subjects of international law. They write:

> The union of the republics in the USSR took place on the basis of a treaty. And it is well known that the voluntary conclusion of an equal and mutually advantageous treaty, far from limiting, strengthens sovereignty, being a striking expression of it, because in this case the interests of a state are not limited but on the contrary fully met.
> The formation of the USSR by the Soviet Republics is a supreme manifestation of their sovereignty, and not a renunciation of it. This is a form of preserving it by delegating definite rights to the USSR. The exercise of these rights by the USSR, in whose organs all the republics are represented, serves as a reliable protection of the sovereignty of the republics.[61]

Regarding the sovereignty of the Soviet Union itself, they add:

> The USSR possesses sovereignty because it is an expression of the sovereignty of the Union Republics. The sovereignty of the USSR is a result of the sovereign will of the Republics; they have created it and its supreme power by free, voluntary and sovereign agreement. The sovereignty of the USSR, consequently, is based on the sovereignty of the Union Republics; without the sovereign Republics there would not be a sovereign Union of Soviet Socialist Republics either.[62]

In conclusion, they declare that 'the attempts of bourgeois jurists to interpret the fact that the Union Republics do not maintain diplomatic relations with foreign states as evidence that the Republics are not full subjects of international law' are doomed to failure. For 'the question *how* the Union Republics exercise the rights they possess by virtue of their status of sovereign and full subjects of

[58] *Ibid.*, p. 92.
[59] Nedbailo and Vassilenko, 'Soviet Union Republics as subjects of international law' *Soviet Yearbook of International Law* (1963), pp. 105–8 (summary in English).
[60] *Ibid.*, p. 105.
[61] *Ibid.*, pp. 106–7.
[62] *Ibid.*, p. 107.

international law is not a question of law. It is a question of practical expediency, which fully depends on the sovereign will of a Republic'.[63]

Similar views were again expressed in 1968 and 1969, at the first and second session of the United Nations Conference on the Law of Treaties. In stating their support for a provision recognizing the capacity of members of a federal union to conclude treaties if that capacity were admitted by the federal constitution, the representatives of the Soviet Union, Byelorussia and the Ukraine reaffirmed that the USSR constituted a single state while at the same time comprising fifteen sovereign republics. Those republics, they explained, 'had freely formed the Union and, in so doing, had not relinquished their sovereignty. Their sovereignty was confirmed by the USSR Federal Constitution and also by the separate constitutions of the federated republics. Within the framework of the Union, each republic had all the attributes of a sovereign State and enjoyed full sovereign rights.'[64]

THE PRACTICE OF STATES

The constitutional practice

From a purely constitutional law point of view, it is possible to show that some of the theories set out above are not in accordance with the facts. Calhoun's and Seydel's opinion that sovereignty in a federal union is possessed exclusively by the member states, for instance, is implicitly condemned by many decisions of the American Supreme Court. In *United States v. Curtiss-Wright Export Corporation*, a case relating to the powers of the federal government in respect of external affairs, the Supreme Court declared: 'As a member of the family of nations, the right and power of the United States in that field are equal to the right and power of the other members of the international family. Otherwise, the United States is not completely sovereign.'[65] In *Mackenzie v. Hare*, the same Court asserted that, 'As a Government, the United States is invested with all the attributes of sovereignty'.[66] In *New York v. United States*, it was held that 'the States on entering the Union surrendered some of their sovereignty'.[67] More recently, in *Cooper*

[63] *Ibid.*, p. 108.

[64] United Nations Conference on the Law of Treaties, Provisional Summary Record of the Eighth Plenary Meeting, Vienna, 28 April 1969, p. 2 (UN Doc. A/conf. 39/SR.8).

[65] 299 US 304 at 318 (1936).

[66] 239 US 299 at 311 (1915).

[67] 326 US 572 at 594 (1946).

v. Aaron, the Supreme Court has denounced the doctrine of nullification put forward by the Southern States to prevent racial integration in the schools.[68] This doctrine, developed by Calhoun, was based on the belief that the state party to a federal compact had a right to judge for itself whether the compact had been violated; it followed naturally from the view that a federal constitution was a compact between separate, independent sovereignties.[69] The Court declared in its decision:

> No state legislator or executive or judicial officer can war against the Constitution without violating his undertaking to support it. Chief Justice Marshall spoke for a unanimous Court in saying that: 'If the legislatures of the several states may, at will, annul the judgments of the courts of the United States, and destroy the rights acquired under those judgments, the Constitution itself becomes a solemn mockery.'[70]

Calhoun and von Seydel argue, moreover, that a treaty of federation cannot be replaced purely and simply by an internal act. This also is not in accordance with the constitutional practice of states. In *D.D. Cement Co. v. Commissioner of Income Tax,* an Indian decision of 1955, it was held that the Covenant under which the ruler of Zind and seven other rulers agreed to integrate their territories into a new State to be known as Patiala and East Punjab States Union was a treaty, and as such not enforceable by a municipal court. The Court said more specifically:

> It [the Covenant] embodies the terms on which the Rulers agreed and decided to unite or federate and bring into existence a new International Persona (*sic*). This is one of the circumstances under which a State personality breaks or ceases to exist and the results in such a case are not materially different from those which flow when a sovereign State cedes to or is subjugated by another sovereign State.[71]

Clearly, the doctrine of Calhoun and Seydel cannot be accepted.

Serious doubts can also be expressed about the validity of Borel's and Le Fur's view that constitutional sovereignty in a federation belongs exclusively to the federal state. Their argument is that the federal organs can amend at will the federal constitution and that federal law always prevails over State law. But this is true only to a limited extent. In 1908, Dicey wrote: 'A federal state derives its

[68] 358 US 1 (1958).
[69] See in particular on this subject: Miller and Howell, 'Interposition, nullification and the delicate division of powers in a federal system', 5 *Journal of Public Law* (1956), 1–89.
[70] 358 US 1 at 18 (1958).
[71] *D.D. Cement Co. v. Commissioner of Income Tax, All India Rep.* (1955) Pepsu 3: 49 *AJIL* (1955), 573.

very existence from the constitution, just as a corporation derives its very existence from the grant which creates it. Hence every power, legislative, executive or judicial, whether it belongs to the nation or to the individual States, is subordinate to and controlled by the constitution.'[72] The mistake of Borel and Le Fur is that they confuse federal supremacy with constitutional supremacy.

In many federations, neither the central authority nor the states, acting alone, can change the constitution at will.[73] In the United States, for instance, three-fourths of the states must cooperate with two-thirds of Congress to amend the Constitution.[74] In Switzerland constitutional amendments must be approved by a majority of the electors voting in a referendum and by a majority of the electors voting in a majority of the cantons.[75] In Australia, amendments must be passed by both houses of parliament and approved by a majority of the states and a majority of the Commonwealth electorate.[76] In Canada it is not even clear how much provincial consent 'is requisite before the Dominion parliament may ask the United Kingdom parliament to legislate and before that parliament may itself feel free to accede to the request'.[77]

In other federations, such as Germany or India, a two-thirds majority in the two houses of the national legislature is all that is required for a constitutional amendment. But this does not mean that the federal authorities in these States can amend the constitution at will. In Germany, members of the upper house are also members of the governments of the *Länder* and all the members from one *Land* must cast their votes in a solid state block.[78] In India, amendments dealing with the distribution of powers require ratification by a majority of the states.[79] Obviously, it is impossible to conclude that the federal government in a federation is always competent to determine its own jurisdiction.

Similar remarks can be made with respect to the claim that national law always prevails over state law. Acts of the federal government as well as of the state governments may be declared unconstitutional. The argument of Borel and Le Fur that since the Supreme Court is always a federal organ, it is the will of the federa-

---

[72] Dicey, *Introduction to the Study of the Law of the Constitution*, 7th edn., p. 140.
[73] See Stoke, *The Foreign Relations of the Federal State*, 1931, p. 10.
[74] Article V of the American Constitution.
[75] Article 118–123 of the Swiss Constitution.
[76] Article 128 of the Australian Constitution.
[77] Wheare, *Federal Government*, 4th edn., 1963, p. 214. See more generally on this subject Livingston, ch. 2.
[78] See Livingston, pp. 288–9.
[79] Article 368 of the Indian Constitution.

tion that prevails, reflects a rather poor opinion of the independence of the judiciary.[80] However, it is true that in case of conflict between state law and federal law, both made in pursuance of the Constitution, federal law usually prevails.[81] Thus, in Australia, Article 109 of the Constitution provides that 'when a law of a State is inconsistent with a law of the Commonwealth, the latter shall prevail and the former shall, to the extent of the inconsistency, be invalid'. In the United States, Chief Justice Marshall declared in *Cohens v. Virginia*: 'The constitution and laws of a State, so far as they are repugnant to the constitution and laws of the United States, are absolutely void.'[82] In Canada, it is also accepted that in the event of collision between a federal law and a provincial law, each valid under the Constitution, the federal law prevails.[83] But there is one article in the Canadian Constitution which appears to give priority to provincial law. According to Article 94A of the British North America Act: 'The Parliament of Canada may make laws in relation to old age pensions and supplementary benefits, including survivor's and disability benefits irrespective of age, but no such law shall affect the operation of any law present or future of a provincial legislature in relation to any such matter.'[84] Thus, it is only in particular circumstances that federal law prevails over state law.

Now if the legislation of the federal government may be declared unconstitutional, and if the federal organs cannot unilaterally determine their own competence, it is inexact from a constitutional law point of view to speak of federal supremacy. For this reason, the theory of Borel and Le Fur must be rejected. But Borel and Le Fur themselves, as already seen, did not conclude from the alleged supremacy of the federal state that the component parts could not enjoy international status. This was the particular conclusion of Kunz. In so far as he argues from the constitutional superiority of the federal state over the member states, his view must, of course, be rejected. Kelsen suggested more correctly that only the constituent organs, those which could amend at will the constitution, were sovereign.[85] He added that since these organs were at the same time the organs of the federation, the federation, as a partial community, was usually not distinguished from the federal state, as the

[80] Borel, p. 66; Le Fur, pp. 590–5.
[81] As argued more rightly by Ghosh, p. 85.
[82] 6 Wheaton 264.
[83] *AG for Ontario v. AG for Canada* [1896] AC 348.
[84] Originally enacted by the BNA Act 1951, 14–15 Geo VI, c. 32 (UK).
[85] See above, p. 21.

total community.[86] This view, as will be seen below, reflects adequately the practice of states; but it does not justify his conclusion that the member states can only act in the international sphere as agents of the federal government.

Another theory which is difficult to reconcile with constitutional reality is that put forward by Nawiasky and officially adopted by the Soviet Union. Among Soviet publicists it is unanimously accepted that the various republics as well as the Union are fully sovereign. Yet, Article 15 of the Constitution of the USSR asserts that the 'sovereignty of the Union Republics is limited only in the sphere defined in Article 14 of the Constitution'. One would be justified in concluding from this that the republics are not fully sovereign. However, according to Nedbailo and Vassilenko, 'This formulation of Article 15 cannot be qualified otherwise than an inapt expression of the legislator, because it does not reflect the true content of the Constitution, does not correspond to its spirit and letter and also to the nature of relations between the Soviet Socialist Republics as states of qualitatively new, and higher type'.[87] There are other provisions of the Soviet Constitution which tend to show that the member republics are not fully sovereign. Article 20, for instance, provides that if a divergence exists between a law of a Union Republic and a law of the Union, the Union law prevails. According to Article 67, moreover, every decision or order of the Union Cabinet is binding throughout the territory of the USSR. The supremacy of the federal government is clearly illustrated also by the power of the Union Praesidium to annul, and the authority of the Union Council of Ministers to suspend, decrees and orders of the Republican Council of Ministers (Articles 49 f and 69).[88] On the whole, it is quite obvious that the relations between the Republics and the relations between the Republics and the Union are not governed by international law but by constitutional law.[89]

It may be argued that Article 35 of the Soviet Constitution, which recognizes the right of the Republics to secede from the federation, guarantees them full sovereignty.[90] But doubts have been raised as to their actual right to secede. In the West, there is a general tendency to agree with Wheare that: 'the one modern

[86] Kelsen, *Principles of International Law*, p. 262.
[87] Nedbailo and Vassilenko, 'Soviet Union Republics as subjects of international law', *Soviet Yearbook of International Law* (1963), 106.
[88] Aspaturian, 'The theory and practice of Soviet federalism' 12 *The Journal of Politics* (1950), 37.
[89] Verdross, 'Die Völkerrechtssubjektivität der Gliedstaaten der Sowjetunion', 1 *Österreichische Zeitschrift für öffentliches Recht* (1946), 216.
[90] See Calvez, *Droit international et souveraineté en URSS*, 1953, p. 9.

government claiming to be federal which grants a right to secede, the USSR, is the one where the exercise of the right is least likely to be permitted'.[91] For Soviet lawyers, however, this attitude simply 'reflects the desire of the imperialists to limit the circle of Socialist states, subjects of international law, which play a progressive role in international relations'.[92]

The international practice

Turning to international law, it becomes even more obvious that many of the theories enunciated previously have no relevance to the practice of states. The views based on the divisibility of sovereignty, those of Ross, Oppenheim and Hay in particular, are not easy to reconcile with this practice.

In international relations, federal states are universally regarded as fully sovereign entities, notwithstanding any limitations imposed by their constitution; as a result they enjoy complete international personality. The participation of federal States as sovereign entities in international relations is an indisputable fact. They have declared war and made peace; they conclude treaties of alliance, commerce, establishment, etc.; they send and receive diplomatic envoys and they are members of all kinds of international organizations. In the *de Brissot* case, the United States–Venezuela Arbitral Tribunal spoke of 'the sovereignty of the United States of Venezuela'.[93] In *Ville de Genève v. Consorts de Civry*, the Paris Court of Appeal held that only the Swiss federation, and not the various cantons, could claim to be a sovereign power in international relations.[94] In *Feldman v. Etat de Bahia*, the Court of Appeal of Brussels declared: 'la souveraineté absolue et complète, au point de vue du droit international, n'appartient qu'aux Etats-Unis du Brésil'.[95]

Further evidence regarding the sovereign status of federal states in international relations can be found in the debates of the International Law Commission on the Law of Treaties. At the 666th meeting of the Commission, held in June 1962, the Drafting Com-

---

[91] Wheare, p. 87; Similarly, Aspaturian talks in this case of 'a so-called right to secession' and quotes Stalin as saying that 'of course none of our republics would actually raise the question of seceding from the USSR': see V. Aspaturian, 'The theory and practice of Soviet federalism', 12 *The Journal of Politics* (1950), pp. 35–6.

[92] Nedbailo and Vassilenko, p. 106.

[93] *De Brissot*, in Moore, *International Arbitrations*, iii, 2971.

[94] *Ville de Genève v. Consorts de Civry*, 1894, *Dalloz*, ii, 515.

[95] *Feldman v. Etat de Bahia*, 1908, *Pasicrisie Belge*, part ii, 56; see also 26 *AJIL* (1932), Official Documents, p. 484.

mittee proposed a redrafted Article 3 which contained the following provision: 'In a federal state, the capacity of the federal state and its component states to conclude treaties depends on the federal constitution.' Mr Briggs (United States) who opened the discussion proposed that the provision should be deleted because it seemed to suggest that the capacity of the United States to conclude treaties 'depended on the Constitution of the United Sates, whereas it was based on international law'. Mr Verdross (Austria) suggested instead that the provision should be retained but made applicable only to the subdivisions of the federal state. As he explained: 'Only the member states of such a federal state were subject to any limitations in respect of treaty-making; the federal state itself was a sovereign state and as such possessed the full capacity to conclude treaties under international law.' This suggestion was supported by MM Tunkin, Bartos, Waldock, Ago, Yasseen and de Luna. Mr Amado thought for his part that the provision should be adopted as drafted, as he considered that the test of the capacity of a component state of a federal state was its sovereignty.[96] Other members of the Commission, like Mr Briggs, considered that the provision should be deleted completely. Mr Verdross's amendment was put to the vote and was adopted by 9 votes to 7, with 3 abstentions. The provision as amended became Article 5 (2) of the Draft Articles on the Law of Treaties adopted in 1966.

When Article 5 (2) came before the UN Conference on the Law of Treaties in 1968 and 1969, certain representatives pointed out that since the federal union rather than the political subdivision was designated as a sovereign state under international law, there was no reason to retain a provision dealing with the capacity of member states of federations in a convention intended to deal exclusively with treaties between sovereign states. As already seen, this consideration subsequently played a fundamental role in the decision to delete the second paragraph of Article 5 which referred to the capacity of member states of federal unions to conclude treaties if that capacity were admitted by the constitution and within the limits there laid down.[97]

Thus there can be no doubt that the capacity of federal states in international law, and therefore their international status, is a direct function of their sovereignty. The situation of the member states is different. Their capacity in international relations does not derive from their sovereignty but from the federal constitution. If the federal constitution grants them a limited international com-

[96] *Yearbook of the International Law Commission*, 1962, i, 240–1, 243.
[97] See above, p. 15.

petence, it does not necessarily mean that they enjoy a corresponding international personality. Many writers deny that a mere constitutional law provision, without the complement of international recognition, can dictate the solution of an international law problem.[98] Nor is it clear that because the international competence of the member states depends on the federal constitution they can never enjoy international personality. The theory of Kunz, Kelsen and Ghosh that member states of federations exercising a limited international competence normally act in such circumstances as agents of the federal state has never been demonstrated to be true.[99] All we can say at this stage is that such entities cannot claim the status of an international person on the basis of their sovereignty.

It may be objected of course that if member states of federations do enter into treaty relations with foreign states, this constitutes sufficient evidence that they possess at least a limited international sovereignty and a corresponding personality. In the *Wimbledon* case, the Permanent Court of International Justice has made it clear that the right of entering into agreements is an attribute of sovereignty.[100] However, such an argument fails in practice. That entities not really sovereign can be endowed with treaty-making power was acknowledged in 1949 by the International Court of Justice when it recognized the international personality of the United Nations. Furthermore, a number of non-sovereign entities had previously exercised treaty-making power. The British Dominions and India, for example, became members of the League of Nations at a time when they were not yet sovereign.[101] In a like manner, the former Federation of Rhodesia enjoyed a limited treaty-making power, but certainly not sovereignty.[102] The real meaning of the expression used by the Permanent Court in the *Wimbledon* case is simply that the exercise of treaty-making power by sovereign states, far from constituting a surrender of their sovereignty, is in fact an attribute of this sovereignty.

[98] This, for instance, is the opinion of Hallmayer, 'Die völkerrechtliche Stellung der deutschen Länder nach dem Bonner Grundgesetz', diss. Tübingen, 1954, pp. 11–13. For further reference, see below, pp. 80–81.

[99] See above, pp. 20–21.

[100] *Wimbledon* Case (1923) *PCIJ*, ser. A, no. 1, p. 25.

[101] See Lewis, 'The international status of the British self-governing Dominions', 3 *BYIL* (1922–3), 21 at 31 ff; Baker, 'Le statut juridique actuel des Dominions britanniques dans le domaine du droit international' *HR* 19 (1927), 247.

[102] See Advisory Commission on the Review of the Constitution of the Federation of Rhodesia and Nyasaland, Report, Appendix VII, p. 75 (Cmnd 1150, 1960). See Palley, *The Constitutional History and Law of Southern Rhodesia 1888–1965*, 1966, p. 724.

It may also be pointed out that Ukraine and Byelorussia, as members of the United Nations, enjoy the 'sovereign equality' guaranteed to states members by Article 2(1) of the Charter. But it does not necessarily follow, as suggested by Yakemtchouk, that Ukraine and Byelorussia are sovereign entities.[103] Two other non-sovereign states, India and the Philippine Commonwealth, were made original members of the United Nations; the latter became an independent Republic only in 1946, and the former did not exist as a sovereign state before 1947.[104] Thus, it is clear that entities other than sovereign states 'may be recognized solely for the purpose of membership in inter-governmental agencies'.[105] Article 2(1) of the Charter simply establishes the obligation of the members of the United Nations to consider other members as sovereign equals for the purposes of the Organization.[106] Even Yakemtchouk admits that the sovereignty of Ukraine and Byelo-russia in certain areas is problematical: according to Article 51 of the Charter, they have the right of self-defence; but under the Soviet Constitution, questions of war and peace are reserved to the exclusive jurisdiction of the Union.[107]

In the end, it must be admitted that federal states in presentday international law are universally considered sovereign states enjoying full international personality.[108] But this leaves open the question of the international status of their member states. None of the theories based on sovereignty seriously helps to clarify this problem. They are either in disagreement with international law or with constitutional law. The theory that approaches most closely actual practice is that of Kelsen. It is difficult to disagree with him when he asserts that constitutional sovereignty in a federation ultimately lies with the constituent organs, but that foreign states, for reasons of simplicity, identify sovereignty with the federal government. But there is no evidence to support Kelsen's suggestion that member states of federations exercising a limited international competence may be considered indirectly as agents of the federal government. In order to clarify this problem it is necessary

[103] Yakemtchouk, *L'Ukraine en droit international*, 1954, pp. 42 ff.
[104] As pointed out by Kelsen, *The Law of the United Nations*, 1950, p. 60.
[105] Aufricht, 'Principles and practices of recognition by international organizations', 43 *AJIL* (1949), 679 at 703.
[106] See Dolan, 'The member republics of the USSR as subjects of the law of nations', 4 *ICLQ* (1955), 629 at 635.
[107] Yakemtchouk, p. 50; the Article of the Soviet Constitution to which he refers is Article 14(b).
[108] See Mosler, 'Die völkerrechtliche Wirkung bundesstaatlicher Verfassungen', in *Festschrift R. Thomas*, 1950, p. 172.

to examine the role of international competence as a criterion of personality in federal states.

International competence as a criterion of personality in federal states

THEORETICAL CONSIDERATIONS

Among earlier writers on federalism, international competence was often considered as the true criterion of international personality. Borel, for instance, wrote:

> En vérité, la personnalité internationale tient à la compétence internationale. Pour l'Etat souverain, cette compétence découle naturellement du seul fait de son existence comme Etat; pour toutes les autres collectivités non-souveraines ... membres d'un Etat fédératif ou provinces d'un Etat unitaire—elle repose uniquement sur la volonté de l'Etat souverain.[109]

Le Fur, who shared this view, considered the proposition that the very nature of a federation prevented the member states from becoming international persons as highly questionable.[110] Jellinek, Laband and Triepel also considered that member states of federations enjoying international competence could become international subjects.[111]

After the First World War, in 1926 Verdross expressed the opinion that subdivisions of federal states exercising international competence were partial subjects of international law.[112] The vast majority of German writers who wrote on this subject in the following years also agreed with him. These included Döhring, Baumbach, Stützel, Strupp, Korte and Klein.[113] In 1949 the International Court of Justice clearly recognized the link between international competence and international personality in the *Reparation for*

---

[109] Borel, *Etudes sur la souveraineté l'Etat fédératif*, 1886, p. 97.

[110] Le Fur p. 763; see also Mouskhéli, pp. 278–9.

[111] Jellinek, *Die Lehre von den Staatenverbindungen*, 1882, pp. 307–11; Laband, *Deutsches Reichsstaatsrecht*, 1912, p. 216; Triepel, *Völkerrecht und Landesrecht*, 1899, p. 367.

[112] Verdross, Die Verfassung der Völkerrechtsgemeinschaft, 1926, p. 125.

[113] Döhring, *Das Gesandtschaftsrecht der deutschen Einzelstaaten unter der Verfassung von Weimar*, 1928, pp. 7–18; Baumbach, *Die unmittelbare völkerrechtliche Handlungsfähigkeit der deutschen Einzelstaaten in Vergangenheit und Gegenwart*, 1928, pp. 8 ff; Stützel, *Die völkerrechtliche Handlungsfähigkeit des Einzelstaates im Bundesstaate*, 1929, pp. 14–24; Strupp, *Eléments du droit international public*, 2nd edn, 1930, 267; Korte, *Grundfragen der völkerrechtlichen Rechtsfähigkeit und Handlungsfähigkeit der Staaten*, 1934, pp. 146–7; Klein, *Die mittelbare Haftung im Völkerrecht* 1941, pp. 170–3.

Injuries case. This was enough to convince a majority of international law writers that member states of federations could become international subjects to a degree.[114] The prevailing view now seems to be that 'as long as the component units retain a general right to enter into direct relations with foreign States, their international personality will continue to exist.'[115]

There are, however, three arguments against this, all of which have already been mentioned. The common denominator of all three is that member states of federations exercising a limited international competence do so as agents for the federal government.

The first argument stems from Sir Gerald Fitzmaurice's suggestion that in so far as the component states of a federal union

> are empowered or authorized under the constitution of the union to negotiate or enter into treaties with foreign countries, even if it is in their own name, they do so as agents for the union which, as alone possessing international personality, is necessarily the entity that becomes bound by the treaty and responsible for carrying it out.[116]

This view is also shared by such writers as Castro-Rial and Ghosh.[117] But the argument of Sir Gerald is difficult to understand. He seems to regard the member states as agents rather than as international subjects because they are supposedly not responsible for the treaties into which they enter. Yet, at the same time he argues that they are not responsible because they lack international status. In a number of specific instances, admittedly, federal states have been held responsible for the international torts of their component units; but in all these cases, the member states concerned had no recognized international competence. In the absence of any evidence that member states of federations cannot be held responsible for their own treaties, the conclusion must be reached that Sir Gerald's argument is a circular one in that he takes for granted what he sets out to prove. Like the representative of Italy at the second session of the UN Conference on the Law of Treaties, he seems to consider that member states of a federal

---

[114] See for instance Huber, *Le Droit de conclure des traités internationaux*, 1951, p. 76; Guggenheim, *Traité de droit international public*, 1953, i, 305–6; Bernhardt, *Der Abschluss völkerrechtlicher Verträge im Bundesstaat*, 1957, pp. 18–24; Mosler, in *Mélanges Henri Rolin*, p. 228; Steinberger, 'Constitutional subdivisions of states or unions and their capacity to conclude treaties', 27 *Zeitschrift für ausländisches öffentliches Recht und Völkerrecht* (1967), 411 at 416.

[115] Sohn and Shafer, 'Foreign affairs', in Bowie and Friedrich, p. 240.

[116] *Yearbook of the International Law Commission*, 1958, ii, 24.

[117] Castro-Rial, 'Considérations sur la personnalité internationale,' 4 *Revue hellénique de droit international* (1951), 29; Ghosh, p. 82.

union, by definition, are not subjects of international law.[118]

It may also be argued that member states of federations exercising a limited international competence do so as agents for the federal government because their competence is a delegated one that can always be abolished by federal legislation. This was precisely the view adopted by Kunz.[119] But this argument again cannot be accepted as valid. The competence of the member states in effect derives from the constitution and not from federal legislation. The federal government itself is bound by the constitution and cannot modify it at will.[120] In theory, therefore, if a delegation of competence exists in the field of external affairs, it cannot be from the federal government to the member states.

Perhaps Kelsen puts forward the only valid way of arguing that member states of federations exercising a limited international competence may do so as agents for the federal government. As explained previously, Kelsen admits that member states of federations endowed with the power to conclude treaties with third states 'may be considered as subjects of international law, with a restricted personality.'[121] But then he goes on to suggest that 'since the component States have this competence in accordance with the federal constitution, the organs of the component States, in concluding treaties within the competence conferred upon them by the federal constitution, may also be considered as indirect organs of the federal State'.[122] What Kelsen says, in other words, is that member states of federations exercising limited international competence need not be considered subjects of international law. Unfortunately, he is not too explicit when suggesting that they may be viewed indirectly as organs of the central government. In order to understand his meaning, one must necessarily refer to his own peculiar theory of the federal state.

Kelsen sees three different orders within a federal union: the first is the legal order of the member states, the second is the legal order of the federation considered as a partial community and the third is the legal order of the federal state considered as the total community of the member states and the federation.[123] Within this framework, it is theoretically possible to argue that the member states, in the same way as the federation, enjoy a degree of

---

[118] Conférence des Nations Unies sur le droit des traités, Deuxième session, Compte rendu analytique provisoire de la septième séance plénière, Vienne, 29 avril 1969, p. 14 (Doc. A/CONF. 39/SR. 7).
[119] See above, pp. 20–21.
[120] See above, pp. 26–27.
[121] Kelsen, *Principles of International Law*, pp. 260–1.
[122] *Idem.*
[123] See above, p. 21.

competence delegated to them by the constituent organs of the total community. But as Kelsen himself points out, in international relations 'the federation is usually not distinguished, as a partial community, from the federal State, as the total community'.[124] This being the case, it must be admitted that the same confusion may arise in the case of member states of federations exercising a limited international competence; the grant of external competence made to them by the constituent organs may easily be assimilated to a delegation of competence from the federal government. In this sense, Kelsen's claim that member states of federations exercising some international competence may be considered indirectly as agents of the federal government is fully justified. What remains to be seen is whether it actually conforms to the international practice of states.

THE PRACTICE OF STATES

In the written statement presented by the Government of the United Kingdom in the *Reparation for Injuries* case, the view is expressed that:

> while all sovereign independent States are international persons, it does not follow that there are no international persons other than sovereign independent States. On the contrary it is now widely admitted that such personality, in a greater or lesser degree (and if not for all, at any rate for some, purposes), may be possessed by other entities or organisms such as ... Federations of the kind where the constituent members themselves retain a measure of international personality side by side with that possessed by the Federation as a whole.[125]

In subsequent pages, a survey will be undertaken of the various federations where the member states enjoy a limited international competence in order to ascertain more precisely the international status of these states. This survey will be completed by a study of the international status of other entities whose situation is somewhat analogous to that of member states of federations, such as autonomous states endowed with a limited international competence.

The German Federal Empire of 1871

The Imperial Constitution of 1871 contained no specific provision

---

[124] Kelsen, *Principles of International Law*, p. 262.
[125] *Reparation for Injuries Suffered in the Service of the United Nations*, ICJ (1949), Pleadings, Oral Arguments, Documents, p. 26.

concerning the right of the member states to deal with foreign countries. But the presumption was that they had retained this right, except to the extent that it was vested exclusively in the federal union.[126] According to Article 11 of the Constitution, the *Reich* was authorized to conclude alliances and other treaties with foreign Powers; political treaties in particular were reserved to the exclusive competence of the Imperial Government. Under Article 4, moreover, commercial treaties and consular relations fell exclusively within the jurisdiction of the federal authorities. In other fields, the member states were considered as competent, in so far as they had the necessary legislative competence to implement their treaty obligations and as long as the Imperial Government itself had not concluded a treaty on the same subject.[127]

In practice, the member states made relatively frequent use of their treaty-making power, particularly in the fields of extradition, double taxation and frontier relations.[128] In order to find out whether such treaties were treaties of the member states or treaties of the *Reich*, it may be useful to look more closely at one of them. In the Convention of Extradition of 1875 between Bavaria and Russia, the first striking point is that it is signed by the Plenipotentiary of Bavaria and the Minister for Foreign Affairs of Russia without any reference whatsoever to the federal government of Germany.[129] Then, the first Article of the Russian Note begins: 'Le Gouvernement Impérial de Russie s'engage à livrer au Gouvernement Royal de Bavière...' Similarly, Article 1 of the Bavarian Note provides that 'Le Gouvernement Royal de Bavière s'engage à livrer au Gouvernement Impérial de Russie...' In the remaining articles, the two governments similarly deal with each other on a footing of equality. So, it would seem that the Government of Bavaria was not acting on behalf of the federal authorities of Germany.[130]

Another indication that treaties entered into by the member

---

[126] See Hallmayer, pp. 19–21.

[127] See Bernhardt, *Der Abschluss völkerrechtlicher Verträge im Bundesstaat*, 1957, pp. 109–11.

[128] For the period extending from 1871 to 1914, de Martens, *Nouveau recueil général de traités*, mentions 13 agreements between Baden and Switzerland, 3 between Baden and Austria-Hungary, 4 between Bavaria and Austria, one between Bavaria and Russia, one between Bavaria and Italy, one between Bavaria and Switzerland, 6 between Prussia and The Netherlands, 2 between Prussia and Austria, one between Prussia and Russia, 2 between Saxony and Austria, 2 between Wurttemberg and Austria.

[129] De Martens, *Nouveau recueil général* (hereafter cited as *NRG*) II, vol. xi, 594.

[130] A similar argument is made by Beisswingert, 'Die Einwirkung bundesstaatlicher Kompetenzverschiebungen auf völkerrechtliche Verträge', dissertation, 1960, Munich, pp. 49–50.

states did not concern the federal state as such is the existence of federal treaties in which the Imperial Government agrees that certain engagements entered into by its member states are binding on it also. In 1879, for instance, the German Government entered into an agreement with Switzerland whereby it recognized as valid the Convention of frontier delimitation concluded one year before between Baden and Switzerland.[131] If Baden had acted as agent of the central government, such recognition would obviously not have been necessary.[132]

It would seem also that the treaties concluded by the member states before the formation of the Empire in 1871 remained in force subsequently in so far as they were not superseded by federal treaties. In *Terlinden v. Ames*, the Supreme Court of the United States declared, concerning a treaty of extradition of 1852 with Prussia: 'We do not find in this Constitution [of the Germanic Empire] any provision which in itself operated to abrogate existing treaties or to affect the status of the Kingdom of Prussia in that regard. Nor is there anything in the record to indicate that outstanding treaty obligations have been disregarded since its adoption.'[133] In its opinion, the Court relied heavily on the fact that in 1899, the Imperial Foreign Office had transmitted to the United States chargé at Berlin a memorial on German extradition practice which stated: 'In so far as by-laws and treaties of the Empire relating to the extradition of criminals, provisions which bind all the states of the union have not been made, those States are not hindered from independently regulating extradition by agreements with foreign States, or by laws enacted for their own territory.'[134] The Court further relied on the case *Re Thomas* in which the continued existence of an extradition treaty between the United States and Bavaria was called into question. In this case, Mr Justice Blatchford, then District Judge, said:

> It is further contended on the part of Thomas, that the convention with Bavaria was abrogated by the absorption of Bavaria into the German Empire. An examination of the provisions of the Constitution of the German Empire does not disclose anything which indicates that then existing treaties between the several States composing the confederation called the German Empire, and foreign countries, were annulled, or to be considered as abrogated.... In the present case the mandate issued by the Government of the United States shows that the convention in question

---

[131] See de Martens, *NRG*, II, vol. 4, 433.
[132] Such a view is shared by Triepel, *Droit international et droit interne*, 1920, p. 364, n. 1.
[133] *Terlinden v. Ames*, 184 US 270, 285 (1920).
[134] *Ibid.*, 285–6.

is regarded as in force both by the United States and the German Empire, represented by its envoy, and by Bavaria, represented by the same envoy.[135]

In 1917, in *Stern Jacob dit Julius*, the Civil Tribunal of the Seine similarly held regarding the Bancroft Treaties of 1868 between the United States and the German States, that:

> à défaut de dénonciation des traités de 1868, et bien qu'ils aient pour objet la matière réservée de la nationalité, les Etats qui composent l'Empire Allemand et dont la personnalité persiste doivent observer les conventions diplomatiques qu'ils ont passées et que maintiennent, non pas une disposition du droit interne allemand, mais les principes du droit public international.[136]

Although these various cases cover only a very limited aspect of the problem of treaty succession in federal states,[137] they do show that in certain circumstances the member states of the German Federal Empire were accepted by foreign states as limited subjects of international law.

Even more conclusive evidence that the member states of the German Federal Empire of 1871 were accepted as international subjects by foreign Powers may be found in the Preamble of the Treaty of Versailles. The last paragraph of the Preamble provides that: 'From the coming into force of the present treaty the state of war will terminate. From that moment and subject to the provisions of this Treaty official relations with Germany, and with any of the German States, will be resumed by the Allied and Associated Powers.'[138] From this it must be inferred that official relations existed before the war between the member states of Germany and foreign powers.

The Weimar Republic

Under the Weimar Constitution of 1919, the right of the *Länder* to conclude treaties with foreign states was explicitly recognized According to Article 78 of the Constitution, the conduct of foreign affairs was exclusively in the hands of the federal government, but the *Länder* could, with the assent of the federal government,

---

[135] *Ibid.*, 287–8.

[136] *Stern Jacob dit Julius, Tribunal civil de la Seine*, 1 Chambre, 1917, *Revue Darras*, 1918, p. 436.

[137] See O'Connell, 'State succession and the effect upon treaties of entry into a composite relationship', 39 *BYIL* (1963), 54 ff.

[138] After the First World War, France maintained for a while a representative in Bavaria, arguing that the Preamble of the Treaty of Versailles gave her right to do so. See Thilo, *Problem der staats-und völkerrechtlichen Stellung Bayerns*, 1930, pp. 13 ff.

make treaties with foreign states on matters which fell within their own legislative competence. On the other hand, the wording of Article 78 implied that they were no longer competent to maintain permanent legations in foreign countries. However, they could still send special plenipotentiaries abroad and Bavaria was allowed, by exception, to maintain diplomatic relations with the Holy See.[139]

In practice, the *Länder* concluded only a limited number of agreements with foreign states.[140] But it must be borne in mind that Germany remained a federal state only until 1934, when it was transformed into a unitary state by the Nazi regime.[141] During this short period, it seems that the member states continued to be considered as limited subjects of international law by foreign powers. Until 1934, for instance, it was the States of Württemberg and Bavaria which were represented on the European Commission for the River Danube—'and not Germany *qua* Germany'.[142] In a Note from the British Foreign Office to the German Ambassador in London, dated February 1935, it was explained that the plurality of German representatives was due to the fact that 'the two German States were treated as separate entities'.[143] But with the unification of Germany, Württemberg and Bavaria disappeared 'altogether as international entities'.[144] The British Government decided therefore that only one German representative should sit in the future on the European Commission for the River Danube.

It was also the view of the German Government that until 1934 the member states enjoyed international personality. Shortly after the passage of the law reorganizing the German Empire, a senior official of the German Ministry of Justice stated that, since the international personality of the states had disappeared, the *Reich* could be affected by their treaties only as legal successor.[145] This view was upheld in 1936 by the Supreme Court of Germany:

> The extradition treaties of France with the German States are extinguished as a consequence of the law of January 30, 1934, regulating the reorganization of the German Empire (German Statutes, 1934, Part I, 75), because Germany has become a unitary state by virtue of this statute and the German States have ceased

[139] See Bernhardt, pp. 111–20; Hallmayer, pp. 23–5; Jean Huber, p. 73.
[140] One treaty between Württemberg and Austria, de Martens, *NRG*, III, xx, 513; one concordat between Prussia and the Holy See, *ibid.*, vol. xxi, 58 and another between Bavaria and the Holy See, *ibid.*, vol. xxviii, 13 and 25; and finally, one treaty between Prussia and Austria, *ibid.*, vol. xviii, 189.
[141] *Reichgesetzblatt*, 1934, i, 75.
[142] Note from the French Ministry for Foreign Affairs to the German Embassy in Paris, League of Nations, 16 *Official Journal* (1935), 1664.
[143] *Ibid.*, p. 1666.
[144] *Ibid.*, p. 1667.
[145] See O'Connell, 39 *BYIL* (1963), 108.

to exist in their capacity as international legal subjects, so that the extradition treaties which they have entered into are extinguished.[146]

Thus, in view of the evidence, it must be admitted that between 1919 and 1934, the member states of Germany enjoyed international personality.[147]

Modern Germany

In 1949 Germany adopted a federal Constitution for the third time. Under Article 32 of this Constitution, which reproduces closely Article 78 of the Weimar Constitution, the conduct of external relations belongs to the *Bund*, with the qualification that the *Länder* may, with the consent of the federal government, enter into treaties with foreign states on matters which fall within their own legislative competence. According to Article 59 (1) moreover, the federal president represents the Federation in its international relations. Together with Article 73 (1), which states that the Federation has the exclusive power to legislate on foreign affairs as well as defence, this provision is generally interpreted to mean that the *Länder* are not allowed to maintain permanent representation in foreign countries; but it is generally agreed that they may send *ad hoc* representatives in order to conclude particular agreements.[148] Finally, Article 59 (2) provides that 'treaties which regulate the political relations of the Federation or relate to matters of federal legislation require the consent or participation, in the form of a federal law, of the bodies competent in any specific case for such federal action'. This particular provision, read in conjunction with Article 32, appears to exclude political treaties from the field of external competence of the *Länder*.[149]

A controversy exists as to whether the treaty-making power of the *Länder* is exclusive or concurrent. Certain authors consider that the federal government has a concurrent competence to sign international treaties concerning matters within the jurisdiction of the *Länder*; their view is based more particularly upon the general

[146] 31 *AJIL* (1937), 739–40.
[147] Also of this opinion: Baumbach, pp. 18–46; Elben, *Die Staatsverträge Württembergs mit nichtdeutschen Staaten*, 1926, p. 19; Thilo, p. 13 ff.
[148] Bernhardt, pp. 121 ff; Hallmayer, pp. 27–31; Rudolf, 'Internationale Beziehungen der deutschen Länder', 13 *Archiv, des Völkerrechts* (1966), 53; Leisner, 'A propos de la répartition des compétences en matière de conclusion des traités dans la République Fédérale d'Allemagne', *Ann. fr. dr. int.* (1960) 291 ff.
[149] Leisner, *loc. cit.*, p. 298.

language of Article 32 (1), 59 (2) and 73 (1).[150] Other authors, on the contrary, restrict the federal treaty-making power to the fields of jurisdiction belonging properly to the *Bund*; they emphasize the limitative character of Article 32 (3) and the fact that the *Länder* are not bound in principle to implement federal treaties dealing with subject matters within their exclusive field of competence.[151] Both categories of writers refer to the legislative history of Article 32 as evidence in support of their view.[152] However, as will be seen in a subsequent chapter, a practical solution to this difficulty was found in 1957, when the *Länder* agreed to let the federal government undertake international obligations in matters within their competence, but subject to specific conditions.[153]

Another problem concerns the effect of the federal consent on the validity of the treaties entered into by the member states. In view of the fact that third states parties to these agreements are not informed of the consent given by the federal government, it would seem that the absence of such consent is of no particular significance for the international validity of such treaties. In the *Port of Kehl* case, the Federal Constitutional Court declared that the consent required from the federal government was a purely internal matter.[154] This is also the view of a majority of German constitutional law writers.[155] In the absence of federal consent,

---

[150] Grewe, 'Die auswärtige Gewalt der Bundesrepublik', 12 *Veröffent-lichungen der Vereinigung deutscher Staatsrechtslehrer* (1954), 165; Menzel, 'Die auswärtige Gewalt der Bundesrepublik' *ibid.*, p. 206; Haas, 'Abschluss und Ratifikation internationaler Verträge', 78 *Archiv des öffentlichen Rechts* (1952) 382; Kölble, 'Auslandsbeziehungen der Länder? *Die öffent-liche Verwaltung* (1965) p. 145.

[151] Leisner, 6 *Ann. fr. dr. int.* (1960), p. 291; Leisner, 'The Foreign Rela-tions of the Member States of the Federal Republic of Germany', 16 *Univ. Toronto LJ* (1966), p. 346; Kraus, 'Die Zuständigkeit der Länder der Bundes-republik Deutschland zum Abschluss von Kulturabkommen mit auswär-tigen Staaten nach dem Bonner Grundgesetz', 3 *Archiv des Völkerrechts* (1951/52), 421; Bernhardt, pp. 154 ff. Maunz, *Deutsches Staatsrecht*, 9th edn, 1959, pp. 269 ff; Hallmayer, p. 31; Rudolf, 'Internationale Beziehungen der deutschen Länder', 13 *Archiv. des Völkerrechts* (1966), 65–6.

[152] According to Kölble (p. 148), for instance, the legislative history of Article 32 supports the view that the federal Government possesses a com-prehensive treaty-making power. The same argument is used by Leisner, 6 *Ann. fr. dr. int.* (1960), 302, and Weiser, 'La conclusion d'accords inter-nationaux par les Etats fédérés allemands, suisses et autrichiens', in Brossard, Patry et Weiser, *Les Pouvoirs extérieurs du Québec*, 1967, pp. 127–9, in order to demonstrate that the federal treaty-making power is restricted to the field of jurisdiction belonging properly to the *Bund*.

[153] See below, p. 199.

[154] *Entscheidungen des Bundesverfassungsgerichts*, 1953, 2, 370.

[155] See for instance von Mongoldt und Klein, *Das Bonner Grundgesetz*, 2nd edn, 1964, ii, 794; Maunz and Durig, *Grundgesetz, Kommentar*, 1964, Art 32, no. 56; Leisner, 6 *Ann. fr. dr. int.* (1960), 307; *contra*: Hallmayer, p. 59; Rudolf, p. 70.

however, it is agreed that the member states have no legal power to give internal effect to their treaties.[156]

In practice, the member states of Germany have not made frequent use of their treaty-making power. As pointed out by Leisner:

> The system of the Lindau Convention seems to have confined the Länder to the conventional settlement of border questions: production of electric power, water police and fishing regulations on border rivers and lakes, maintenance of border bridges, common national parks and the annually-renewed agreement on free intercourse of shepherds on the border mountains of Bavaria and Austria as well as the conventions on salt mines between the same states.[157]

These are almost the only examples one can find of such agreements. But again, to the extent that the *Länder* have entered into treaty relations with foreign countries, it would seem that they must be considered as subjects of international law.

Some indication of this may be found in the Austrian-Bavarian treaties of 1950 for the production of hydroelectric power. The two agreements signed in Munich on the same day contain provisions for the formation of a board of arbitrators in case of disputes between the two parties. Article 13 of the first agreement adds:

> If the Arbitral Board cannot come to a decision for any reason or if within a period of six months from the appointment of the umpire no decision has been delivered, either of the two Parties can institute the settlement of the dispute by diplomatic means or can appeal to the Arbitral Tribunal under Section 27 of the Treaty.[158]

It is submitted that such reference to the settlement of disputes by diplomatic means or by appeal to an arbitral tribunal is justified only by considering the Austrian-Bavarian treaties of 1950 as international agreements between equal partners.

Further evidence of the international status attained by some of the member states of Germany is to be found in the fact that, in 1954, the Swiss Federal Council admitted that Switzerland was legally obliged not to cancel a concession on the River Rheinau, the granting of which had required the assent of Baden-Württemberg in accordance with a treaty of 1879 between the two governments.[159] The question of pecuniary compensation in particular

---

[156] Maunz and Durig, Art 32, no. 57; Hallmayer, p. 54; Rudolf, p. 69.
[157] Leisner. 'The foreign relations of the Member States of the Federal Republic of Germany', 16 *Univ. Toronto LJ* (1966), 346, 356.
[158] Berber, *Rivers in International Law*, 1959, p. 269.
[159] Feuille fédérale, i (1954), 739–43. See also 12 *Annuaire suisse de droit international* (1955), 180–91.

was envisaged by the Council in the fellowing terms:

> Pour ce qui est des dommages-intérêts qu'il y aurait lieu de payer au pays de Bade-Wurtemberg, nous nous bornons à relever que ce pays a déjà annoncé qu'il réclamerait une indemnité en cas de retrait de la concession. Il a en outre laissé clairement entendre que cette indemnité ne serait pas limitée au montant des taxes de concession et des redevances non perçues, mais qu'elle devrait aussi comprendre la réparation du dommage économique subi par le pays.[160]

More recently, in 1959, Switzerland proposed to the Government of Baden-Württemberg a revision of the fishery agreement of 1897 for Untersee and the Rhine. The Federal Council took the view that fishery was a *Land* competence and proceeded to deal directly with Baden-Württemberg, without communicating first with the federal authorities of Germany.[161] Such a line of conduct on the part of Switzerland would be difficult to understand if Baden-Württemberg was not considered as a separate entity.[162]

In 1953, the Federal Constitutional Court of Germany itself acknowledged in the *Port of Kehl* case that the *Länder* could become subjects of international law. It declared:

> The provisions of the Constitution concerning international treaties apply only to treaties with foreign States and subjects of international law which are to be assimilated to foreign States. So far as concerns the Contracting Parties on the German side, these are the Federal Republic and the Länder.[163]

By distinguishing between the federal Republic and the *Länder* as contracting parties to international treaties, the Court implicitly recognized that both of them could become subjects of international law.[164]

Switzerland

Article 8 of the Swiss Constitution delegates to the Confederation 'The sole right to declare war and conclude peace, and to make

---

[160] 12, *Annuaire suisse de droit international* (1955), 186–7.

[161] Beisswingert, p. 90; also mentioned by O'Connell 39 *BYIL* (1963), 115.

[162] Beisswingert, pp. 93–4, considers that this agreement may still be interpreted as a treaty of Switzerland with an organ of the German Government competent according to the Constitution. But he has no doubt that Baden-Württemberg was recognized by Switzerland as an international subject in the 1954 incident concerning the Rheinau concession.

[163] 1953 *International Law Reports*, p. 407 at 408.

[164] This is also the opinion of a majority of German writers. See for instance, Leisner, *Ann. fr. dr. int.* (1960) 293; Rudolf, p. 53 ff; Beisswingert, p. 94.

alliances and treaties, particularly customs and commercial treaties with foreign States'.[165] According to Article 9, the cantons retain the right to conclude treaties with foreign states with respect to matters of public economy, frontier relations and police. Taken in conjunction, these two Articles are interpreted in practice to mean that the cantons have a concurrent power to sign international agreements dealing with matters under cantonal jurisdiction.[166] Among Swiss constitutional lawyers, the prevailing view nowadays seems to be that the federal treaty-making power is unlimited.[167]

As regards the cantonal power to negotiate treaties with foreign states, Article 18 of the Constitution provides:

1. Official relations between a canton and a foreign government or its representatives take place through the intermediary of the Federal Council.
2. Nevertheless, upon the subjects mentioned in Article 9 the canton may correspond directly with the inferior authorities or officials of a foreign State.

Therefore, a canton desiring to make a treaty with a foreign government must ask the Federal Council to take the necessary steps. Even in matters of a minor administrative nature it must obtain the approval of the federal authorities before actually signing an agreement.[168] If the Federal Council objects, the matter is taken up by the Federal Assembly in accordance with Article 85 (5) of the Constitution and its decision is final.

Since 1848, when Switzerland became a federation, the cantons have concluded a fairly large number of international agreements on matters such as judicial assistance, double taxation and frontier relations.[169] Moreover, it would seem that the treaties concluded by them before 1848 remained in force after that date. In 1862, Switzerland informed France that the Federal Constitution had not affected existing treaties.[170] Such treaties, according to the Swiss Federal Tribunal, were not to be confused with those of

[165] See Aubert, *Traité de droit constitutionnel suisse*, 1967, i, 255–61; Looper, 'The treaty power in Switzerland', 7 *American Journal of Comparative Law* (1958), 178 ff; Bernhardt, *Der Abschluss völkerrechtlicher Verträge im Bundesstaat*, p. 52–62.

[166] Aubert, i, 258; see also the opinion expressed by the federal Department of Justice and Police, 14 *Annuaire suisse de droit international* (1957), 128–9.

[167] *Ibid.*, pp. 257–8; Bernhardt, p. 59.

[168] Article 102 (7) of the Constitution.

[169] See Aubert, p. 260 where the author mentions a certain number of these agreements. See also Morin, 'La conclusion d'accords internationaux par les provinces canadiennes à la lumière du droit comparé', 3 *Canadian Yearbook of Int. Law* (1965), 163. But cantonal activity in the field of foreign affairs has become less and less important with the years.

[170] *Feuille fédérale* (1862), ii, 227.

the Confederation. In 1892, in the case of *In re Schmid*, it declared concerning a treaty between the Canton of Argovie and the Great Duchy of Baden: 'Such treaties of the individual cantons with foreign States to be sure are not federal treaties but cantonal treaties.'[171] Therefore, it would seem that to the extent that the cantons conclude treaties with foreign states in their own name, they must be considered as subjects of international law. This was also the view held by Professor Basdevant in 1931. Speaking on behalf of France in the *Austro-German Customs Union* case, he declared: 'La personnalité juridique internationale, le pouvoir de conclure un traité, peut appartenir à des corps politiques qui ne sont pas indépendants—le cas s'est présenté pour les cantons suisses et pour les Dominions.'[172]

On the other hand, it is difficult to decide whether treaties concluded by the Federation on behalf of the cantons are federal or cantonal treaties. Morin suggests, in such cases, that it is necessary to examine the form and the content of each particular treaty.[173] In the treaty of 1946 between the Swiss Confederation and the United Nations, the federation is declared to act for the Canton and Town of Geneva; the conferment of powers is said to be permanent so that the United Nations can 'at all times approach the Swiss Confederation with a view to the settlement of any question arising between it and the Geneva authorities'.[174] There is no mention anywhere of a necessary ratification by the Canton of Geneva which, in relation to this agreement, does not play any meaningful international role.

However, in the exchange of notes of 1958 between Canada and Switzerland, acting on behalf of the Canton of Vaud, it is provided that the agreement is to enter into force upon ratification by the Parliament of the Canton of Vaud.[175] Again, in the exchange of notes of 19 December 1959, between the Ambassador of Switzerland in the United Kingdom and the Acting High Com-

---

[171] The original text reads: 'Allerdings sind solche Verträge einzelner Kantone mit ausländischen Staaten nicht Staatsverträge der Eidgenossenschaft, sondern von den Kantonen ...'; *Entscheidungen des schweizerischen Bundesgerichts*, vol. 18, p. 198 at 203 (1892).

[172] *Austro-German Customs Union*, PCIJ, ser. C, no. 53, p. 423 (1931). This was also Huber's opinion in 1909; he wrote then: 'The legal personality of the Cantons in international law has not been taken away by the Federal Constitution. The Cantons can acquire rights and duties by treaties with foreign nations about specified matters ...': Huber, 'The Intercantonal Law of Switzerland (Swiss Interstate Law)', 3 *AJIL* (1909), 78. See also Schwarzenbach, 'Staatsverträge der Kantone mit dem Ausland', dissertation, Zurich, 1926.

[173] Morin, p. 164.

[174] *UN Treaty Series*, vol. 1, 154 at 160.

[175] See Morin, *loc cit.*, p. 165.

missioner for New Zealand in the United Kingdom, reference is made to the desire expressed by the competent authorities of the Canton of Vaud 'to abrogate the Declaration signed at Berne on August 27, 1872, between the Federal Council of the Swiss Confederation, acting in the name of the Canton of Vaud, and the Government of Her Britannic Majesty, relating to the succession or legacy duties to be levied on the property of a citizen or subject of either of the two Contracting Parties'. The two Notes are drafted in such a way as to constitute a new agreement 'between the Government of New Zealand and The Federal Council of the Swiss Confederation acting in the name of the Canton of Vaud terminating the Declaration of 27 August 1872, as far as it applies to the relations between the Canton of Vaud and New Zealand, and coming into force on the day of its approval by the Conseil d'Etat of the Canton of Vaud'.[176] Similarly, the earlier treaty of 1923 between the German Reich and the Swiss Confederation was to take effect only if accepted by the Canton and Town of Basle and to become defunct upon denunciation by the same Canton and Town of Basle. Other cantons could accede to the treaty but their denunciation would be limited to their own territory.[177] In these various instances, it may still be justified to speak of cantonal treaties. But then, as one author puts it, 'the subject is a nice one for the theoretical ingenuity of jurists'.[178]

The United States of America

Under Article I, Section 10, Clause 1, of the United States Constitution, the States are forbidden to enter into any 'treaty, alliance or confederation'. But Clause 3 goes on to say that 'no State shall, without the consent of Congress ... enter into any Agreement or Compact with another State, or with a foreign Power ...' Article II, Section 1, then confers treaty-making power on the President in very general terms and only makes specific provision for the valid ratification of treaties. Finally, Article VI provides that 'all Treaties made, or which shall be made under the Authority of the United States, shall be the Supreme Law of the Land'.

These various provisions have always been interpreted by the Supreme Court of the United States to mean that responsibility for the conduct of foreign relations rests exclusively with the

[176] The exchange of notes is quoted in International Law Association, *The Effect of Independence on Treaties*, 1965, pp. 60–1.

[177] *League of Nations Treaty Series*, vol. xxvii, p. 41.

[178] Looper, 'The treaty power in Switzerland, 7 *American Journal of Comparative Law* (1958), p. 178 at 187.

Federal Government.[179] But as Attorney-General Wickersham
pointed out in an advice to the Secretary of State in 1909, Article
1, Section 10, necessarily implies that an agreement or compact
'might be entered into between a foreign Power and a State, to
which Congress shall have given its consent'.[180] What is meant
by 'agreement' or 'compact' is not clear. The view advanced by
Justice Storey in *Kansas v. Colorado* was that a 'treaty' relates to
political matters whereas an 'agreement' relates to 'mere private
rights of sovereignty'.[181] In *Holmes v. Jennison*, Chief Justice
Taney held that the term 'agreement' included 'every agreement,
written or verbal, formed or unformed, positive or implied, by the
mutual understanding of the parties'.[182] In *Virginia v. Tennessee*
the Supreme Court held that Article I, Section 10, did not apply
to agreements concerning such minor matters as adjustments of
boundaries, which have no tendency 'to increase and build up
the political influence of the contracting states, so as to encroach
upon or impair the supremacy of the United States'.[183] Nevertheless, it remains difficult to distinguish clearly the two categories and
certain writers consider more simply that 'any compact to which
Congress gives its assent should be deemed an "agreement" falling within the permitted class of transactions'.[184]

In practice, there exist very few agreements between states and
foreign jurisdictions of the type requiring the consent of Congress.
In some instances, permission to enter into direct relations
with foreign governments was refused by the federal authorities.
Thus, concerning the possibility of a compact between Florida
and Cuba for the promotion of trade, the Department of State
stated in 1937 that 'the Department's policy in regard to promotion of commerce with foreign countries and the negotiation of
commercial treaties does not contemplate the conclusion of special
agreements or pacts between separate states and foreign governments even if the consent of Congress to such special agreements

[179] See *Constitution of the United States Annotated*, Senate Document
39, 88th Congress, 1st Session (1963), p. 374; *United States v. Arjona*, 120
US 479 (1887); *United States v. Curtiss Wright Export Corp.* 299 US 304
(1936). *Zacherning v. Miller* 389 US 429, 432 (1968).
[180] 27 *Official Opinion of the Attorneys-General of the United States* 327
(1909).
[181] *Kansas v. Colorado*, 185 US 125, 140 (1902).
[182] 14 Pet. 540, 572 (1840).
[183] 148 US 503, 518 (1893).
[184] Dumbauld, *The Constitution of the United States*, 1964, pp. 249–50;
Frankfurter and Landis, 'The Compact clause of the Constitution—A
Study in Interstate Adjustments', 34 *Yale Law Journal* (1925), 685 at 695.
See further on this subject Weinfeld, 'What did the framers of the Federal
Constitution mean by "Agreements or Compacts"?' 3 *University of Chicago
Law Review* (1936), 453–64.

could be obtained'.[185] In 1936, a similar attitude had been adopted regarding an arrangement between California and the Mexican territory of Baja California for reciprocal exemption of commercial motor vehicles from registration and payment of fees.[186] More recently, Congress has indicated that it would not approve the participation of the provinces of Ontario and Quebec in the Great Lakes Compact entered into by the riparian American states in 1955; the reason given was that, with provincial participation, the states parties to the agreement would be entering the field of international relations.[187] Yet, in other circumstances, Congress has authorized compacts open to accession by Canadian provinces: examples are the North-Eastern Forest Fire Protections Compact of 1949 and the Interstate Civil Defence Compact of 1951.[188] For some time, the Canadian Government refused to let the Provinces become parties to these agreements.[189] In January 1970, however, following official demands to this effect by the Provinces of Quebec and New Brunswick, it proceeded to an exchange of notes with the Government of the United States in order to give international legal effect to adhesion by Quebec and New Brunswick to the Northeastern Interstate Forest Fire Protection Compact.[190]

Many of the compacts effectively entered into by the American States with foreign jurisdictions relate to the construction and maintenance of international bridges and highways. In 1958 the Department of State of the United States wrote to the Ambassador of Canada to the United States that:

> In accordance with your request and in implementation of the understanding reached at meetings held by representatives of the Government of Canada and the United States and the State of New York, I have the honour to confirm the passage of (1) a law of the State of New York, entitled ..., and (2) An Act of Congress, approved on August 14, 1957, entitled 'Joint Resolution granting the consent of Congress to an agreement or compact between the State of New York and the Government of

[185] Hackworth, *Digest of International Law*, v., 25.

[186] *Idem.*

[187] See US, Congress, Senate, Subcommittee of Committee on Foreign Relations, *Hearings, The Great Lakes Basin*, 84th Cong., 2nd Sess., 1956, pp. 6–8, 14, 17, 31–2.

[188] See Sohn and Shafer, 'Foreign Affairs', in Bowie and Friedrich, *Studies in Federalism*, pp. 291–2; Zimmermann and Wendell, *The Interstate Compact since 1925*, 1951, p. 71.

[189] See Morin, pp. 159–60; Rand, 'International agreements between Canadian Provinces and foreign states', 25 *University of Toronto, Faculty of Law Review* (1967), p. 77.

[190] Canada, Department of External Affairs, Press Release no. 6, 29 January 1970, see further below, p. 51.

Canada providing for the continued existence of the Buffalo and Fort Erie Authority, and for other purposes.'[191]

In 1960 an agreement was entered into by Her Majesty the Queen in Right of Ontario as represented by the Minister of Highways with the State of Minnesota as represented by its Commissioner of Highways for the construction of a bridge over the Pigeon River.[192] In 1962 the Province of Manitoba negotiated a similar compact with the State of Minnesota concerning an international highway.[193] In 1963 the Government of Canada itself concluded an agreement with the state of Alaska to keep open a portion of the Haynes 'cut-off' road in British Columbia during the winter.[194] Finally, an informal Quebec–Louisiana Agreement on Cultural Cooperation has recently been concluded and made public within the text of a joint communiqué issued in September 1969.[195]

There is no clear authority on whether it is the federal government or the individual state that is bound by an agreement entered into by a state with a foreign jurisdiction. Given that Congress usually reserves for itself 'the right to alter, amend or repeal' a resolution granting its consent to an agreement between a state and a foreign jurisdiction.[196], it would seem that the federal government must be considered as the real party to such agreements. This view is reinforced by the fact that most of the agreements mentioned above were preceded by consultations between the federal authorities of the United States and Canada. Mention has already been made of an exchange of notes between these two countries regarding the Buffalo and Fort Erie Bridge Authority. Similar consultations took place before the conclusion of the Canada–Alaska agreement.[197] Another example was the proposal of the State of Maine and the Province of New Brunswick to construct an international bridge at Milltown on the St Croix River. In this case also, the State Department asked for an expression of Canadian views on the subject.[198] Furthermore, in

[191] 1958 *Canadian Treaty Series*, 10.
[192] See Delisle, 'Treaty-making power in Canada' in *Ontario Advisory Committee on Confederation, Background Papers and Reports*, 1967, p. 140; see also Rand, p. 79.
[193] See Rand, p. 80; but the compact does not appear to have come yet into force: see below note 198.
[194] See *House of Commons Debates* (Canada), 1963, vi, 5448.
[195] Rodgers, 'Conclusion of Quebec–Louisiana Agreement on Cultural Co-operation', 64 *AJIL* (1970), p. 380.
[196] See *Public Law*, no. 145, approved on 14 August 1957, 85th Congress, Sess. 1, 71 Stat. 367.
[197] See *House of Commons Debates* (Canada) 1963, v, 4397.
[198] See *Federalism and International Relations*, a White Paper prepared by the Honourable Paul Martin, Secretary of State for External Affairs, Ottawa, 1968, p. 27; in the case of the agreement between Manitoba and

the press release issued by the Department of External Affairs of Canada in January 1970 announcing an exchange of notes between Canada and the USA for the purpose of permitting Quebec and New Brunswick to join the Northeastern Interstate Forest Fire Protection compact, it is clearly specified that this exchange of notes was essential to give effect to such an agreement.[199] The safest conclusion, it would seem, is that the states of the American Union are not presently subjects of international law. Such a conclusion is in accordance with Article 4 of the Montevideo Convention, to which the United States is a party, which provides that 'a federal State constitutes a single international person'.[200]

Canada

The only provision of the British North America Act, 1867, referring to foreign or external affairs is Section 132, which reads as follows: 'The Parliament and Government of Canada shall have all powers necessary or proper for performing the obligations of Canada or of any Province thereof, as part of the British Empire, towards foreign countries, arising under treaties between the Empire and such foreign countries.' However, Section 132 lost all significance when Canada became an international subject and acquired its own treaty-making power. This was made clear by the Privy Council in the *Labour Conventions* case.[201] But at the same time, the problem arose of locating such power within Canada.

There are two different theories on this subject: both of them were exposed in the *Labour Conventions* case. In the judgment of the Supreme Court of Canada, Duff C.J. and Davis and Kerwin J.J. held that:

> As regards all such international arrangements, it is a necessary consequence of the respective positions of the Dominion executive and the provincial executives that this authority resides in the Parliament of Canada. The Lieutenant-Governors represent the Crown for certain purposes. But, in no respect does the Lieutenant-Governor of a province represent the Crown in

Minnesota, there is no evidence that preliminary consultations took place between the Canadian and American Government and as a matter of fact the agreement has not yet come into force: see Lissitzyn, 'territorial entities other than independent states in the law of treaties', 125 (HR (1968), 1 at 26.

[199] See above, p. 49, note 190.

[200] See Malloy, *Treaties, Conventions, International Acts, Protocols and Agreements between the US and Other Powers*, iv, 4807. For a different view, see Tizzitzyn, pp. 29–32.

[201] *Attorney-General for Canada v. Attorney-General for Ontario* [1937], AC 326 at 350.

respect of relations with foreign Governments.[202]

On the other hand, the Government of Ontario argued before the Privy Council that:

> There are no grounds whatever for saying that the parties to advise His Majesty in matters relating to the jurisdiction of the Provinces have in some way come to be the Dominion Ministers. The Province has the right to advise the Crown in matters where its legislative powers apply. Ontario has a right to enter into an agreement with another part of the British Empire or with a foreign State.[203]

But the Privy Council itself found it unnecessary to deal with this question. It insisted that it was expressing no opinion upon where the prerogative right of making treaties in respect of Canada was vested.[204]

In recent years, the claim of the Province of Quebec to an international status of its own has given new impetus to discussions on this subject. In 1968, the Canadian Government published a White Paper dealing with *Federalism and International Relations* and another dealing with *Federalism and International Conferences on Education*.[205] In February 1969 the Quebec Government produced a Working Paper on *Foreign Relations*, in which the legal position of the federal authorities was challenged.[206] Meanwhile numerous writers have joined the controversy. Probably the best way of clarifying the question is to examine in turn the positions of the Canadian and Quebec Governments and to make reference to the supporting arguments of writers.

The attitude of the Canadian Government is based almost exclusively on the delegation of the prerogative powers of the Crown

---

[202] *References re: The Weekly Rest in Industrial Undertakings Act, The Minimum Wages Act and the Limitation of Hours of Work Act* [1936], SCR 461 at 488.

[203] [1937] AC 326 at 333.

[204] *Ibid.*, pp. 348–9. Commenting on the fact that the Privy Council did not challenge the opinion of Justices Duff, Davis and Kerwin, McWhinney says: 'Why on earth, of course, should the Privy Council have bothered to do so, simply to strike down an *obiter dictum*?'; McWhinney, 'Canadian federalism, and the Foreign Affairs and Treaty Power. The impact of Quebec's "Quiet Revolution"', 7 *The Canadian Yearbook of International Law* (1969), p. 3 at 7.

[205] *Federalism and International Relations* (note); *Federalism and International Conferences on Education*, A supplement to *Federalism and International Relations*, Honourable Mitchell Sharp, Secretary of State for External Affairs, Ottawa, 1968.

[206] Constitutional Conference Continuing Committee of Officials, *Working Paper on Foreign Relations*, Notes prepared by the Quebec Delegation, Quebec, 5 Feb. 1969.

in right of Canada to the Governor-General in 1947.[207] Part of Clause 2 and Clause 3 of the Letters Patent which affected the delegation read as follows:

> II. And We do hereby authorize and empower Our Governor General, with the advice of Our Privy Council for Canada or of any members thereof or individually, as the case requires, to exercise all powers and authorities lawfully belonging to Us in respect of Canada. (...)
> III. And We hereby authorize and empower our Governor General to keep and use Our Great Seal of Canada for sealing all things whatsoever that may be passed under Our Great Seal of Canada.[208]

Since the treaty-making power in the British Commonwealth is essentially a prerogative power of the Crown, the conclusion is reached that the foreign affairs power is now exercised by the Governor-General in Council. The Canadian Government supports this with the opinion of Chief Justice Duff of the Supreme Court of Canada in the *Labour Conventions* case.[209] Finally, it is argued that 'the powers of the Federal Government as set forth in the British North America Act are not such as to support the view that the Queen's external prerogatives developed (*sic*) upon the lieutenant-governors of the provinces'.[210] The Canadian Government mentions as evidence the fact that, through the exercise of the power of disallowance, it can make it impossible for the provinces to perform any treaty which requires legislation.

The argument based on the delegation of royal prerogative to the Governor-General has been taken up by a number of Canadian constitutional law writers. Szablowski, for instance, writes:

> If there still existed any doubt as to the federal government's exclusive authority to make treaties irrespective of subject matter, this delegation of royal prerogative to the Governor General seems to have intended to extinguish it once and for all. Consequently, the Governor General-in-Council possesses now exactly the same power, in scope and extent, to issue full powers and to ratify treaties as does the Queen; hence, the Canadian Government is legally free to make international agreements involving matters that come within the legislative jurisdiction of the provinces.[211]

---

[207] *Federalism and International Relations*, pp. 13–14.
[208] *Letters Patent Constituting the Office of Governor General of Canada, Effective Oct. 1, 1947*: for the full text, see Kennedy, 'The Office of the Governor-General in Canada', 7 *Univ. Toronto L. J.* (1947–48), 474.
[209] See above, pp. 51–52.
[210] *Federalism and International Relations*, p. 15.
[211] Szablowski, 'Creation and implementation of treaties in Canada', 34 *Can. Bar Rev.* (1956), 28, 32.

Other writers sharing similar views include Grenon,[212] Chef-fins,[213] Morris[214] and Delisle.[215] Recently, however, a new line of argument in support of the exclusive treaty-making power of the federal government has been suggested.

In a paper presented in 1965 to the Ontario Advisory Committee on Confederation, Professor Laskin, as he then was, writes: 'The *British North America Act* limits provincial legislative power territorially; a provincial legislature must confine its valid enactments to operation within the boundaries of the province.'[216] Then he raises the question whether a province 'may, so to speak, reach out to deal with a foreign government' and seems to suggest that 'the admitted prohibition against provincial extraterritorial legislative power means a correlative prohibition against provincial extra-territorial executive power'. [217] But this view is not borne out by the rest of his argument. Laskin declares that the provinces had no treaty power in the colonial period and that the release by the British Government of legal and political control over Canadian affairs invited recognition of Canada as the spokesman for Canada in international affairs. He adds that, under general international law, 'only one juridical personality can be recognized in a federal state'.[218] But having accepted that 'the distribution of legislative power between Parliament and the provincial legislatures involves a correlative distribution of the accompanying executive or pre-rogative power',[219] Laskin finds it difficult to reconcile his theory with the fact that the legislative power to implement treaty obligations is divided in Canada between the federal and provincial governments. He simply asserts that 'a grant of legislative power to implement domestically the obligations undertaken in international negotiations is not necessarily a concession of international status', giving, as an example, the fact that colonial legislatures were empowered to carry into effect by local legislation the inter-

[212] Grenon, 'De la conclusion des traités et de leur mise en oeuvre au Canada', 40 *Can. Bar Rev.* (1962), 151, at 153.
[213] Cheffins, 'The negotiation, ratification and implementation of treaties in Canada and Australia', 1 *Alberta Law Review* (1955–61), 312.
[214] Morris, 'The treaty-making power: a Canadian dilemma', 45 *Can. Bar Rev.* (1967), 478 at 482–4.
[215] Delisle, 'Treaty-making Power in Canada' in *Ontario Advisory Committee on Confederation, Background Papers and Report,* 1967, p. 115 at 132.
[216] Laskin, 'The Provinces and international agreements', in *Ontario Advisory Committee on Confederation, Background, Papers and Report,* 1967, p. 101 at 105.
[217] *Ibid.,* p. 106.
[218] *Ibid.,* p. 108.
[219] *Ibid.,* p. 103.

national commitments made by Great Britain on their behalf.[220]

The basic position of the Government of Quebec may be stated as follows: there is no constitutional authority to support any exclusive federal treaty-making power, judicial evidence suggesting on the contrary that the provinces can make treaties with regard to matters within their legislative capacities.

At the beginning of its *Working Paper on Foreign Relations*, the government of Quebec reminds us forcibly that 'Quebec is not the first province to seek a measure of international capacity'.[221] Already the Attorney-General for Ontario had suggested before the Privy Council in the *Labour Conventions* case, that his Province had 'a right to enter into an agreement with another part of the British Empire or with a foreign State'.[222] The Quebec Government makes it clear also, before discussing the constitutional problem, that there is no objection in international law to a member state of a federation concluding international agreements, quoting in support Article 5 of the International Law Commission's Draft Articles on the Law of Treaties.[223]

Then follows an examination of the argument put forward by the federal government. This argument, it is said, rests entirely on the *Labour Conventions* case of 1937, or more precisely on the opinion of some of the Supreme Court Judges in this case.[224] The Quebec Government points out that the subsequent decision of the Privy Council removed any character of judicial authority from the opinion expressed by these judges.[225] Examining the argument based on the Letters Patent issued to the Governor-General in 1947, Quebec argues that the language of these letters cannot prevail over the Constitution itself. Reference is made for this view to the case of *St George's Church v. Cougle and Mayes*, a decision of 1878 holding that, even though the Governor-General's Letters Patent invested him with control over church benefices, this, in the light of the Canadian Constitution, was null and void and that this power should in fact be exercised by the Lieutenant-Governor.[226] In this way, the conclusion is reached that the 1947 Letters Patent 'cannot prevent provincial governments from exer-

---

[220] *Ibid.*, p. 104.
[221] Constitutional Conference Continuing Committee of Officials, *Working Paper on Foreign Relations*, Notes prepared by the Quebec Delegation, Quebec, 5 February 1969, p. 4.
[222] See above, p. 52.
[223] *Working Paper on Foreign Relations*, pp. 13–14.
[224] *Ibid.*, p. 15.
[225] See above, p. 52.
[226] *Working Paper on Foreign Relations*, p. 17; the case is mentioned in 13 *New Brunswick Reports* 96 (1870).

cising executive powers corresponding to their legislative competence'.[227]

Finally, the Quebec Government mentions two judicial decisions leading to the conclusion that the provinces can make treaties with regard to matters within their legislative capacities. In the first of these cases, that of *The Liquidators of the Maritime Bank of Canada v. The Receiver-General of New Brunswick*, it was held that the British North America Act, 1867, had not severed the connection between the Crown and the Provinces, the relation between them being the same as that which subsists between the Crown and the Dominion in respect of the executive and legislative powers.[228] In the second case, that of *Bonanza Creek Gold Mining Company Limited v. The King*, the Privy Council went so far as to say that 'executive power is in many situations which arise from the statutory Constitution of Canada conferred by implication in the grant of legislative power, so that where such situations arise the two kinds of authority are correlative. It follows that to this extent the Crown is bound and the prerogative affected.'[229] In conclusion, the Government of Quebec suggests that any new constitution should make this power clear and beyond doubt.[230]

Further support in favour of Quebec's position may be found in a recent article published in 1968 by Giroux.[231] After arguing that the Letters Patent of 1947 must be considered to have delegated the treaty-making power to the federal and provincial governments —in accordance with the *Bonanza Creek* decision of 1916—the author challenges the contention that the powers of the federal government, as set forth in the British North America Act, indicate that the Queen's external prerogatives did not devolve upon the lieutenant-governors of the provinces.[232] Against this contention he cites a unanimous decision of the Supreme Court in which Taschereau J. held that:

The framers of our Constitution have reserved to the Governor-General in Council the necessary authority to interfere, in a certain way, in provincial matters, but the exercise of these powers, contemplated to be for the better government of the provinces, does not modify the legal status of the provincial

[227] *Idem.*
[228] [1892] AC 437 at 442.
[229] [1916] 1 AC 566 at 587.
[230] *Working Paper on Foreign Relations*, p. 19.
[231] Giroux, 'La capacité internationale des provinces en droit canadien', 9 *Les Cahiers de droit* (1967–68), 241.
[232] *Ibid.*, pp. 252–61.

executives, and does not purport to make them act, on behalf
of the Federal authority.[233]

Giroux concludes that the federal and provincial executives are
each sovereign within their respective spheres of competence. He
also rejects the argument of extraterritoriality suggested by Laskin
on the grounds that extraterritorial legislation is rarely needed to
implement international agreements.[234]

Another line of argument in support of Quebec's position was
suggested in 1965 by Mr Gérin-Lajoie, then Minister of Education
of the province. In an interview to the Montreal newspaper *Le
Devoir* on 1 May 1965, Mr Gérin-Lajoie established a distinction
between treaties, usually dealing with political problems, and
ententes, concerning matters of less importance.[235] According to
him, Quebec had the right to make *ententes* with foreign states.
What he had in mind, apparently, was a distinction such as that
existing in the United States between treaties on the one hand, and
agreements or compacts on the other hand. In Canada, the decision
of the Supreme Court in *Attorney-General for Ontario v. Scott*
may appear at first sight to support the contention of Mr Gérin-
Lajoie: a distinction was made in this case between mere arrangements and treaties between states.[236] But what the Court meant by
arrangements was different from what Mr Gérin-Lajoie had in
mind. The Court declared:

> A treaty is an agreement between states, political in nature, even
> though it may contain provisions of a legislative character which
> may, by themselves or their subsequent enactment, pass into
> law. But the essential element is that it produces binding effects
> between the parties to it. There is nothing binding in the scheme
> before us. The enactments of the two legislatures are comple-
> mentary but voluntary; the application of each is dependent on
> that of the other: each is the condition of the other; but that
> condition possesses nothing binding to its continuance.[237]

Unless Mr Gérin-Lajoie by *ententes* meant non-binding agreements, which does not appear to be the case, there is no ground
for distinguishing between 'treaties' and *ententes* in Canadian constitutional law.

Recently, however, a compromise solution has been proposed
by McWhinney who uses as a starting point the very distinction
made in *Attorney-General for Ontario v. Scott* between inter-

---

[233] *Ibid.*, p. 263; Giroux refers to the case of *The King v. Carroll*, [1948]
SCR 126 at 131
[234] *Ibid.*, pp. 265–6.
[235] *Le Devoir*, Montreal, 1 May 1965, p.5.
[236] *Attorney-General for Ontario v. Scott* [1956] SCR 137.
[237] *Ibid.*, p. 142.

national treaties and non-binding agreements. According to McWhinney, the Canadian provinces have not only the right to enter into non-binding agreements with foreign entities but indeed have done so on many occasions. Discussing more particularly the cultural agreements concluded between France and Quebec, he says:

> By the same token, I cannot see why the Dominion should be upset if Quebec or any other province should wish to make cultural or cultural exchange agreements directly with other countries, as Quebec has in fact done with France. The essence of such agreements is that they rest on goodwill, and mutual, reciprocal benefit, for their effectiveness: one does not go to law over them.[238]

Such a view, however, does not conform entirely with the actual practice. It is true that the Canadian provinces, nowadays, often enter into administrative arrangements of an informal character with foreign jurisdictions. A good example on the point would be the numerous reciprocal agreements on motor vehicle registration entered into with American states.[239] Such arrangements are generally not regarded as subject to the provisions of international law and as a matter of fact they often speak of privileges rather than of rights.[240] However, this does not preclude the existence of other agreements that may be intended to have effect under international law.

Indeed, on a number of occasions the federal government has intervened purportedly to give international legal effect to agreements between Canadian provinces and foreign jurisdictions. The intervention of the federal authorities usually takes the form of an exchange of notes with the government of the foreign states concerned, the terms of which give assent to the understanding reached by the province.[241] It has been seen, for instance, that in 1960 Ontario concluded an agreement with Minnesota concerning a bridge over the Pigeon River.[242] Another agreement relating to the construction of an international bridge was concluded in 1968 between New Brunswick and Maine.[243] More recently, Quebec

[238] McWhinney, 'The constitutional competence within federal systems for international agreements', in Ontario Advisory Committee on Confederation, *Background Papers and Reports*, 1967, p. 154.
[239] In 1969, Quebec alone had 12 such agreements signed with various American states.
[240] The existence of such informal arrangements is openly recognized by the federal government. *Federalism and International Organizations*, p. 26.
[241] *Federalism and International Relations*, p. 32.
[242] See above, pp. 50–51.
[243] See Rand, 'International Agreements between Canadian Provinces and Foreign States', 25 *University of Toronto, Faculty of Law Review* 1967, pp. 78–9; see also Lissitzyn, 'Territorial entities in the law of treaties', 125 *HR*, 1968, pp. 24–8.

and New Brunswick have joined the North-eastern Interstate Forest Fire Protection Compact.[244] Each of these agreements was especially authorized by Act of Parliament[245] and each was preceded by an exchange of notes with the Federal Government of the United States.[246] Now, according to the Canadian government:

> The exchange of notes gives international legal effect to the arrangements between the province and the foreign entity, but does not involve the province itself acquiring international rights or accepting international obligations.[247]

This point of view finds some corroboration in a Report prepared by the Ontario Department of Highways concerning a proposed international bridge at Kingston. The Report reads:

> An international bridge requires close co-operation and agreement between the two sovereign states. The respective governments of Canada and the United States have sole jurisdiction in respect of international obligations entered into on behalf of their nations and thus the Government of Canada must sanction by legislation any undertaking which necessitates an agreement with the United States or an agency thereof.[248]

The inescapable conclusion, it would seem, is that any binding agreement with a foreign entity to which a province is a party must not be interpreted as meaning that the province itself acquires international rights and duties and thereby becomes a subject of international law.

However, since 1965, this point of view has been challenged by the Government of Quebec. On 27 February 1965, a France-Quebec Educational *Entente* was concluded.[249] On the same day, an exchange of notes took place between the French Chargé d'affaires in Ottawa and the Canadian Secretary of State for External Affairs, in which the Canadian Government informed the French Government that the *entente* met with its concurrence.[250] But the Quebec Government adopted the position that the *entente* constituted an international agreement between France and Quebec. In a speech

---

[244] For New Brunswick, see Order-in-Council 70–231 dated 8 April, 1970, authorizing the Minister of Natural Resources to enter into arrangements with the North-eastern Forest Fire Protection Commission. The agreement itself was signed on 9 June 1970. For Quebec, see Order-in-Council 2496 dated 27 August 1969. The agreement was signed on 23 September 1969, and entered into force on 29 January 1970.

[245] See Rand, *op. cit.*, p. 80.

[246] See *Federalism and International Relations*, pp. 26–7.

[247] *Ibid.*, p. 32.

[248] Delisle, p. 140.

[249] English translation in 1 *Education Weekly, A Department of Education Bulletin* (1965) 199–202 (Province of Quebec).

[250] *Federalism and International Relations*, p. 27.

before the consular corps of Montreal, on 12 April 1965, Mr Gérin-Lajoie, who had signed the *entente* for Quebec, spoke of the desire of the province to acquire an international status of her own.[251] Shortly afterwards, on 23 April, the Secretary of State for External Affairs made a public statement on the subject.[252] He declared that Canada had only one international personality, since only sovereign states could be members of the international community; the provinces could discuss detailed arrangements with foreign states, but formal international agreements were left to the federal power. To make this clearer a new cultural agreement was concluded between France and Canada on 17 November 1965; notes exchanged on the same day gave a general right to the provinces to make *ententes* with the French Government on the subjects covered by the Agreement.[253] On 24 November 1965, a second France-Quebec cultural agreement was signed; no mention was made in it of the framework agreement of 17 November 1965, though the prior assent of the federal government was again obtained.[254] As pointed out by Fitzgerald, whereas the earlier *entente* referred only to 'delegations', the later one referred to 'contracting parties'; and while the earlier one was styled as an *entente* between 'France' and the 'Province of Quebec', the later one was described as being between the 'Government of France' and the 'Government of Quebec.'[255]

The next step in this confrontation took the form of the creation by the Quebec Government in April 1967 of a Department of Intergovernmental Affairs divided into three branches: a Branch for Relations Abroad, a Quebec Delegations Service and a Federal-Provincial and Interprovincial Affairs Branch.[256] In August 1967, following the visit of General de Gaulle to Canada, M. Gorse, the French Information Minister, remarked that Quebec enjoyed a 'beginning of international personality' and that its *ententes* with France had 'the validity of treaties'.[257] In February 1968, at the invitation of Gabon, Quebec attended the enlarged Conference of Education Ministers from French-speaking countries in Africa and Malagasy, held in Libreville. When the Conference resumed in Paris in April 1968, Quebec was again represented.[258] This led to

[251] *Le Devoir*, Montreal, Wednesday, 14 April 1965, p. 5.
[252] 17 *External Affairs* (1965), 306.
[253] 17 *External Affairs* (1965), 514–17.
[254] *Ibid.*, p. 521–3.
[255] FitzGerald, 'Educational and cultural agreements and ententes: France, Canada and Quebec—birth of a new treaty-making technique for federal states?', 60 *AJIL* (1966), 529 at 534.
[256] See *Annuaire du Québec/Quebec Yearbook*, 1968–69, pp. 58–9.
[257] *Herald Tribune*, Paris, Tuesday, 1 August 1967, p. 2.
[258] *Working Paper on Foreign Relations*, p. 11.

the publication by the Federal Government of a White Paper on *Federalism and International Conferences on Education*, in which it reasserted its position that only Canada as a whole could participate in international conferences.[259] In January 1969 Quebec took part in the second meeting of the Conference on Education in Kinshasa. This time Canada was also invited. Both delegations joined at the place of meeting to form one Canadian 'representation'. However, Quebec had her name put separately on the list of delegations and her flag was displayed in appropriate places.[260] A similar arrangement prevailed at the Conference of *la Francophonie* which took place in February 1969 in Niamey, Niger.[261]

Further difficulties arose at that time over the bilateral arrangements of the province with France concerning satellite communication programmes. In a statement issued on 31 January 1969, Mr Sharp, Minister of External Affairs, made it 'clear that the Quebec Government should have consulted the Trudeau Administration before disclosing its plans for a joint communications, satellite programme and including it in a "letter of intent" to the government of another country'.[262] Later during the year, on 2 July, the Governments of Quebec and Gabon signed what was described as their 'first entente of co-operation' involving a small teacher-student exchange.[263] Asked whether the agreement was approved by the Canadian Government, Mr Trudeau, the Canadian Prime Minister, replied that without having studied the specific exchange, he had been informed by Quebec authorities that the Gabonese Minister of Education's interpretation was 'that no agreement or treaty was involved but a mere exchange between both governments.'[264]

A peak in the political tug-of-war between Quebec and Canada over the question of external relations was reached in October 1969 with the incident now known as *l'affaire de Lipkowski*. M. Jean de Lipkowski, Secretary of State for Foreign Affairs in the French Government, visited Quebec from 9 to 16 October on the invitation of M. Marcel Masse, Quebec Minister of Intergovernmental Affairs.[265] Although he had been invited by the federal government to include a visit to Ottawa in his itinerary, he chose

[259] *Federalism and International Conferences on Education*, p. 8.
[260] *Working Paper on Foreign Relations*, pp. 11 and 24–5.
[261] *Le Devoir*, Montreal, Tuesday, 18 February 1969, p. 1.
[262] *The Times*, London, 1 February 1969, For the complete text of his declaration, see *Le Devoir*, Montreal, 1 February 1969, p. 9.
[263] Canadian Institute of International Affairs, *Monthly Report on Canadian External Relations*, vol. viii, nos 7–8 (July-August 1969), p. 219.
[264] *Idem*.
[265] The incident is reported in the CIIA *Monthly Report*, vol. viii, no. 10 (October 1969), pp. 252–3. See also Bonenfant, 'Les relations extérieures du Québec', 1 *Etudes Internationales* (1970), 81–3.

to ignore the invitation. The press generally interpreted this gesture as a deliberate 'snub' to the Canadian Government. The incident itself, however, was not of much significance; its importance derives from a series of statements made by Mr Trudeau, M. Masse and M. de Lipkowski himself. The debate was touched off by M. de Lipkowski's remark to the effect that the cultural agreement between France and Canada authorized the France-Quebec satellite project 'en raison du fait que la constitution de 1867 était muette—et pour cause—sur les télécommunications, et que, d'autre part, le projet franco-québécois a une vocation culturelle et éducative, matières qui relèvent de la compétence des provinces'.[266] Mr Trudeau later chided M. de Lipkowski for having offered an interpretation of the Canadian constitution and added that the matter in itself was not important but: 'It is important if it is an indication that the French Government intends following a policy, we feel, of making it harder for Canada to remain united. Because of this we are asking France to discuss with us procedures whereby in the future ministers of that Government will come to Canada.'[267] Mr Trudeau went so far as threatening to denounce the France-Canadian cultural agreement. Later, M. Masse intervened in the debate to defend the statements made by M. de Lipkowski. Eventually, following a meeting in Brussels between M. Schumann, the French Foreign Minister, and Mr Sharp, Secretary of State for External Affairs of Canada, the dispute was resolved amicably.

Since then noticeable progress has been made in discussions between Quebec and Ottawa over external affairs matters. On 17 February 1970, the Secretary of State for External Affairs announced that Canada would send a delegation headed by the Quebec Minister of State for Education, M. Jean-Marie Morin, to the first 1970 meeting of the Conference of Ministers of Education of French-speaking countries of Africa and Madagascar.[268] The same pattern had been used with success at the previous meeting of the Conference held in Paris in December 1969.[269] On 3 March 1970, Mr Sharp and M. Masse announced that the Federal Government and the Government of Quebec had agreed to work together on the implementation of an economic and social development project in Morocco in which Canada had undertaken to participate at the request of the Moroccan government.[270]

---

[266] Bonenfant, *ibid.*, p. 82.
[267] The CIIA, *Monthly Report*, no. 10 (October 1969), 254.
[268] CIIA, *International Canada* (replacing *Monthly Report*), vol. I, no. 2 (February 1970), 31.
[269] CIIA, *Monthly Report* ..., viii, no. 12, December 1969, p. 324.
[270] 22 *External Affairs* (1970), 101.

On 12 March 1970, following protracted negotiations between Quebec and Ottawa over the composition of the Canadian delegation to the March 1970 Niamey conference, the purpose of which was the creation of an Agency for technical and cultural cooperation among French-speaking countries, an agreement was reached whereby one delegation was to represent Canada as a whole, the provinces retaining a right of veto on subject matters within their exclusive jurisdiction. In case of disagreement, the delegation was to abstain. The text of the treaty establishing the proposed Agency was to be signed by the chairman of the delegation in the name of Canada, followed by the signature of the provincial delegates.[271] During the Conference itself, the admission of non-sovereign states to the proposed Agency was discussed. A Cameroon proposal to allow Quebec as well as other non-sovereign states to become members of the Agency while reserving signature of the founding Charter to sovereign states was rejected by the Canadian government. In the end, an agreement was reached over the following text:

> Dans le plein respect de la souveraineté et de la compétence internationale des Etats membres, tout gouvernement peut être admis comme gouvernement participant aux institutions, aux activités et aux programmes de l'Agence, sous réserve de l'approbation de l'Etat membre dont relève le territoire sur lequel le gouvernement participant concerné exerce son autorité et selon les modalités convenues entre ce gouvernement et celui de l'Etat membre.[272]

Thus, even though Quebec could not become a member state of the Agency, it could nevertheless be admitted as a participating government under conditions to be fixed between the Province and the Federal Government and with the consent of the latter. Those conditions were fixed in a later document agreed upon by the two governments on 1st October 1971.[273]

It is against such a background that the international status of the Canadian provinces must be assessed. On the one hand there is the affirmation of the Federal Government that Canada has only one international personality and the tacit acquiescence of most of the provinces with this. On the other hand there is the recent claim of Quebec to a limited international personality of her own and her direct dealings with foreign states. The dispute illustrates per-

[271] CIIA, *International Canada*, vol. i, no. 3 (March 1970), pp. 59–61. See also Bonenfant, 'Les relations extérieures du Québec', 2 *Etudes internationales* (1970), 86–90.
[272] Art. 3(3) Charte de l'agence de coopération culturelle et technique; see *Etudes internationales*, Juin 1970, no. 2, p. 96.
[273] Canada, Department of External Affairs, Press Release no. 74, 1st October 1971.

fectly the difficulty of defining in clear terms on what basis member states of federations may be considered as subjects of international law. Article 5 (2) of the International Law Commission's Draft Articles on the Law of Treaties—which stated that 'States members of a federal union may possess a capacity to conclude treaties if such capacity is admitted by the federal constitution and within the limits there laid down'—was not really acceptable. In referring to the federal constitution as a criterion of international capacity in member states of federations, not only did it fail to specify what the term 'constitution' means—the written document or the constitutional practice—but it did not say what happens when there is disagreement in the federation as to what the constitutional law on the subject is.[274] Indeed, this is one of the main reasons why the provision was dropped at the second meeting of the United Nations Conference on the Law of Treaties in 1969.[275]

The role played by recognition in a situation of this sort is not entirely clear either. The fact that certain states have dealt directly with Quebec may be interpreted as evidence that the Province enjoys a limited international status. But such dealings may also be qualified as undue intervention by foreign governments in the internal affairs of a sovereign state. This was the attitude adopted by the Canadian authorities when Gabon invited Quebec to the Conference on Education in Libreville: to all intent and purposes, diplomatic relations between Canada and Gabon were suspended.[276] It was also the attitude adopted by Germany in 1920 when France sent a permanent representative to Munich; under the Weimar Constitution, the member states had no right of legislation and the conduct of France was judged as an intrusion in German internal affairs.[277] In international law as in constitutional law, one must recognize that the status of Quebec raises difficulties which have perhaps more to do with politics than with law.

The Soviet Union

In the Soviet Union, the constitutional texts are clear. Article 18(a) provides that the member republics have the right 'to enter into direct relations with foreign states and to conclude agreements and exchange representatives with them'. In the eyes of the Soviet

---

[274] That such difficulties could arise was clearly foreseen by Steinberger in 1967; see Steinberger, p. 417.
[275] See above, pp. 15–16.
[276] *The Times*, London, 6 March 1968, p. 7.
[277] See Thilo, pp. 16–22; see also Mosler, 'Die völkerrechtliche Wirkung bundesstaatlicher Verfassungen' p. 161.

theoreticians of international law, this is sufficient to establish the international personality of the member republics.[278] But among Western jurists doubts are entertained as to the true constitutional practice in the USSR. Dolan, for instance, points out that no republic has yet taken advantage of the right to exchange diplomatic officers with foreign countries and that British and American approaches to enter into diplomatic relations with Ukraine and Byelorussia were rebuffed.[279] Dobrin, for his part, writes that the Commissariat for Foreign Affairs of each Republic stands in relation to the Commissariat for Foreign Affairs of the Union 'as a subordinate to a superior'.[280] Ghosh comments that 'it does not require a logician to prove that the USSR is a very highly centralised Federation'.[281]

Yet, following the Yalta Agreements of 1942, not only the Soviet Union but also Ukraine and Byelorussia became original members of the United Nations in 1945.[282] Politically, it cannot be doubted that the purpose of the membership of Ukraine and Byelorussia in the United Nations was to give larger representation to the USSR.[283] Legally, the fact remains that the two Republics assumed thereby international rights and duties. Like all other members of the United Nations, they were also made parties to the Statute of the International Court of Justice.[284] Ukraine and Byelorussia are presently members of the International Atomic Energy Agency, the International Labour Organization, UNESCO, the World Health Organization, the Universal Postal Union, the International Telecommunications Union and the World Meteorological Organization.[285] They have ratified a certain number of international agreements such as, for instance, the 1958 Geneva Convention on the High Seas.[286] Finally, their delegations in New York are separately located and they are comparable in size with the delegations of other small nations.[287] Their international status is then,

---

[278] See Krylov, 'Les notions principales du droit des gens', 70 *HR* (1947), 407, 458; see also above, pp. 22–24.
[279] Dolan, pp. 629, 631; see also Yakemtchouk, *L'Ukraine en droit international* 1954, p. 37.
[280] Dobrin, 'Soviet federalism and the principle of double subordination', 30 *The Grotius Society's Transactions* (1945), 283.
[281] Ghosh, pp. 81–2.
[282] See Yakemtchouk, pp. 30–41.
[283] See Dolan, p. 629; Jean Huber, p. 75.
[284] Article 93 of the UN Charter.
[285] According to the *Statesman Yearbook*, 1966–67.
[286] *UN Treaty Series*, vol. 450, p. 82.
[287] See Aspaturian, *The Union Republics in Soviet Diplomacy*, 1960, pp. 172–3.

not surprisingly, generally recognized.[288] The question remains whether, in the absence of recognition, they would be accepted as international subjects. The same question must be posed for all member states of federations.

Comparison with autonomous states

Autonomous states by definition are entities that enjoy a certain degree of self-government but have not yet attained sovereign independence. This general description excludes such former international protectorates as Morocco, which was considered by the International Court of Justice as a sovereign state having delegated part of its competence to a foreign power, and other independent states such as Liechtenstein or Western Samoa, which have voluntarily assigned their international competence to another sovereign state for reasons of efficiency.[289] The expression, on the other hand, embraces various entities such as the British Dominions and the vassal states of the Ottoman Empire, all of which belong to the past, and former colonies which have today opted for a form of statehood in association with the mother country, such as Surinam and certain countries in the West Indies.

Autonomous states have in common with member states of federations the fact that they cannot claim international status on the basis of their sovereignty. Also, autonomous states like member states of federations sometimes enjoy a limited competence to conclude certain types of international agreements. In such cases, the question may be asked whether the exercise of their limited treaty-making power makes them subjects of international law. At first sight, it would seem that the rules of international law applicable to them in such circumstances must be the same as those applying to member states of federations. But the only way to be sure is to consider the practice of states.

The earliest example of autonomous states enjoying some degree of external competence are those of vassal states such as Egypt, Bulgaria and South Africa. While still a vassal state of Turkey, Egypt could conclude commercial and postal treaties with foreign states without the consent of the suzerain; the same applied to

---

[288] See Verdross, 'Die Völkerrechtssubjectivität der Gliedstaaten der Sowjetunion', p. 218; Yakemtchouk, p. 42; Jean Huber, p. 75; Halsjczuk, 'Les états fédéraux face au droit international', 13 *Öst. Zeit. öff. Recht* (1964), 307-17.

[289] See in general on this subject: Colliard, 'La collectivité autonome en droit international public et dans la pratique de la charté de l'O.N.U.', *Ann. fr. dr. int.* (1958), p. 7 ff.

Bulgaria, which could conclude treaties regarding railways, posts and the like.[290] In addition, both were permitted to send and receive consuls as diplomatic agents.[291] In 1899 Egypt went so far as to sign a treaty with Great Britain concerning the establishment of a co-protectorate over the Sudan, a gesture which clearly exceeded its international competence.[292] As for the former Republic of South Africa, it could, under the Convention of 1884, conclude treaties of all kinds with other states, provided Great Britain did not interpose a veto within six months after receiving a copy of the draft treaty. Furthermore, it was absolutely independent with regard to treaties concluded with the neighbouring Orange Free State. In the *Robert E. Brown* case, the British-United States Claims Arbitral Tribunal held that, to the extent that the South African Republic maintained its own international personality before the Boer War, it remained internationally responsible for any illegal acts and omissions attributable to it.[293] In the light of such examples, it seems justified to conclude that vassal states, even though they were not formally independent, could enjoy some international status insofar as they possessed the capacity to deal with foreign states.

Putting aside the case of vassal states, the first official mention of autonomous or self-governing states in an international agreement is to be found in the Covenant of the League of Nations. Article 1 (2) declared that any fully self-governing state, dominion or colony could become a member of the League if its admission were agreed to by two-thirds of the Assembly and provided it was willing to abide by its international obligations under the Covenant. As a result of this provision, included in the Covenant at the request of Great Britain, the British Dominions and India joined the Organization in 1919 as original members, thereby becoming bearers of rights and duties under international law. Some Dominions even accepted special international duties: Australia, New Zealand and South Africa, as mandatory states, were directly responsible to the League of Nations.[294] Yet the British Dominions and India at that time were not sovereign states. Before 1919, indeed, the British Empire for purposes of international law was considered as a unitary state. According to an author writing on

---

[290] Oppenheim (8th edn), i. 190; see also Guggenheim, *Traité de droit international public*, i, 60, n. 5.

[291] Oppenheim (8th edn) i, 191.

[292] See below, p. 117.

[293] *Robert E. Brown (US) v. Great Britain*, 6 RIAA, 120 at 131; see also Schwarzenberger, *International Law*, i, (3rd edn, 1957), p. 625.

[294] See *South West Africa Cases (Merits), ICJ Rep.* (1966), p. 29.

the position as it was before 1914: 'The control exercised by the Imperial Government over Dominion legislation, judicial appeals, and, in particular, over foreign policy, debarred the Dominions from making any assertion of international personality.'[295] However, the end of the First World War brought a change in the constitutional theory of the Empire. A first indication came when the Dominion representatives were allowed to participate in the Peace Conference. As a next step, each Dominion signed the Treaty of Versailles separately on its own behalf, directly below the British signature. In 1923 Canadian representatives for the first time negotiated and signed a treaty without British participation.[296] In spite of such developments foreign states continued to consider the Dominions as dependencies of Great Britain. General Herzog, Prime Minister of South Africa, asserted in a 1926 speech that a declaration emanating from London was absolutely necessary to convince foreign states that the Dominions were, for purposes of international law, independent states.[297] A declaration to this effect was made at the Imperial Conference of 1926 whereby the Dominions and the United Kingdom were termed 'autonomous Communities within the British Empire, equal in status, in no way subordinate one to another in any aspect of their domestic or external affairs'.[298] Practically, this amounted to a recognition of the international law sovereignty of the Dominions. In 1931 the Statute of Westminster gave legal effect to certain aspects of the resolution passed by the 1926 Imperial Conference.[299]

Even though they were not yet sovereign, the Dominions became in 1919 subjects of international law. Their international personality was founded solely on their recognized international competence. In the words of Sir W. H. Moore: 'The Dominions were international persons in that they were entities in relations with other States, and were recognized both by Great Britain and foreign States.'[300] Most international law writers seem to agree with this view.[301]

---

[295] Lewis, 3 *BYIL* (1922–23), 21, at 28.

[296] The Halibut Fisheries Treaty concluded with the United States on 2 March 1923; see further Castel, *International Law* (1965), 116.

[297] See Baker 'Le statut juridique actuel des Dominions britanniques dans le domaine du droit international', 19 *HR* (1927), 349.

[298] Scott, 'The British Commonwealth of Nations', 21 *AJIL* (1927). 99.

[299] *Revised Statutes of Canada*, 1952, vi, 265.

[300] Moore, 'The Dominions and Treaties', 8 *Journal of Comparative Legislation and International Law* (1926), p. 35.

[301] See Pilotti, 'Les Unions d'états', 24 *HR* (1928), 514; Lewis, p. 33; Baker, p. 339; B. Keith, 'The international status of the Dominions', 5 *Journal of Comparative Legislation and International Law* (1923), p. 165; Hall's *International Law*, 8th edn, ed. Pearce Higgins, 1924, p. 35.

Other examples of autonomous states endowed with some degree of international competence date from after the Second World War. Perhaps the most significant is that of the Federation of Rhodesia and Nyasaland, which existed from 1953 to 1963. It was largely self-governing internally, and, particularly after 1957, enjoyed a wide freedom in the conduct of its external affairs. The Federation Constitution stipulated that the Federation was competent with regard to:

> the implementation of treaties, conventions and agreements with, and other obligations towards countries or organisations outside the Federation affecting the Federation as a whole or any one or more of the Territories, whether entered into
> (i) either before or after the date of the coming into force of this Constitution, by Her Majesty, or by Her Majesty's Government in the United Kingdom on behalf of the Federation or any of the Territories; or
> (ii) after the said date, by the Federation with the authority of Her Majesty's Government in the United Kingdom; or
> (iii) before the said date, by any of the Territories with the said authority.[302]

Further to this implementation power, the Federation was also declared competent to conclude certain classes of treaties by the device of entrustment. In 1957 the Federation was granted a large measure of autonomy when the United Kingdom Government 'agreed to entrust responsibility for external affairs to the Federal Government to the fullest extent possible consistent with the responsibility which Her Majesty's Government must continue to have in international law so long as the Federation is not a separate international entity'.[303] The specific terms of the document provided that the Federation might enter into agreements with any foreign country subject to potential United Kingdom obligations and also provided that the Federation could acquire in its own right membership in international organizations whose statutes permitted the Federation to join.

In practice, the powers granted to the Federation were but the continuation of those which had been accorded previously to the self-governing colony of Southern Rhodesia.[304] Thus, prior to Federation, Southern Rhodesia had already become in its own right a signatory to the General Agreement on Tariffs and Trade as well as

[302] 1953 Statutory Instrument no. 1199, Order in Council adopted under the Rhodesia and Nyasaland Federation Act (1953), 1–2 Eliz. II, c. 30. See also Fawcett, *The British Commonwealth in International Law*, 1963, p. 31.
[303] See E. Lauterpacht 'The contemporary practice of the United Kingdom in the Field of International Law—Survey and Comments, IV', 6 *ICLQ* (1957), 506.
[304] See Millar, *The Commonwealth and the United Nations*, 1967, p. 93.

to a certain number of multilateral treaties.[305] Once the Federation came into existence, its international activity intensified on two fronts—the exercise of its treaty-making power and its right to participate as a member or associate of certain international agencies. On its own initiative, the Federation entered into a large number of agreements with different countries both on a multilateral and bilateral level. In general these conventions related to trade and commerce or regional affairs.[306] In all cases no mention whatsoever is made of United Kingdom authorization. The Federation moreover replaced Southern Rhodesia as contracting party to the General Agreement on Tariffs and Trade. In this capacity, it acknowledged 'the rights and obligations of Southern Rhodesia and of the UK... in respect of Northern Rhodesia and Nyasaland ... as rights and obligations of the Federation of Rhodesia and Nyasaland.'[307] It became a member of such organizations as the International Telecommunications Union, the World Meteorological Organization, and the World Health Organization and an associate member of the Food and Agriculture Organization.[308] Obviously, the fact that the Federation of Rhodesia and Nyasaland was not a sovereign state did not prevent it, during its brief existence, from acquiring rights and duties under international law.

Between 1958 and 1963, the date of its entry into the Federation of Malaysia, Singapore enjoyed a status comparable in some ways

[305] For GATT, see *UN Treaty Series*, vol. 55, p. 194. See also 'Agreement between the Governments represented at the Bermuda Telecommunications Conference', *UN Treaty Series*, vol. 9, p. 102.

[306] The following is a list of multilateral and bilateral treaties entered into by the Federation between 1953 and 1963. Multilateral Agreements: 'International Convention to Facilitate the Importation of Commercial Samples and Advertising Materials', (1956) *UN Treaty Series*, vol. 236, p. 397; 'Phyto-Sanitary Convention for Africa South of the Sahara', (1956) *UN Treaty Series*, vol. 249, p. 46; 'Agreement for the Establishment of the Commission for Technical Cooperation in Africa South of the Sahara', (1959) *UN Treaty Series*, vol. 330, p. 121; 'International Wheat Agreements, 1959 and 1962', (1960 and 1962) *UN Treaty Series*, vol. 343, p. 168 and vol. 444, p. 3; 'Union Convention of Paris (1883) for the Protection of Industrial Property', (1959) *UN Treaty Series*, vol 343, p. 369; 'International Coffee Agreement', (1963), *UN Treaty Series*, vol. 469, p. 169; 'Commonwealth Telegraphs Agreement 1963', (1964) *UN Treaty Series*, vol. 500, p. 294. Bilateral Agreements: Trade agreements were entered into with the following countries. Australia, (1956) *UN Treaty Series*, vol. 226, p. 216; Canada, (1961) *UN Treaty Series*, vol. 392, p. 27; Portugal, (1960) *UN Treaty Series*, vol. 354, p. 137; South Africa, (1957) *UN Treaty Series*, vol. 267, p. 272 and (1960) *UN Treaty Series*, vol. 376, p. 217; South Africa, 'Air Service between Vilanculos and Johannesburg', (1956) *UN Treaty Series*, vol. 255, p. 318; Netherlands, 'Agreement on Migration', (1957) *UN Treaty Series*, vol. 263, p. 382; South Africa, 'Extradition Agreement', (1963) *UN Treaty Series*, vol. 458, p. 59.

[307] See *UN Treaty Series*, vol. 321, p. 263; fourteen other protocols were ratified in a similar fashion: see *UN Treaty Series*, vol. 226, p. 342.

[308] *United Nations Yearbook*, 1963, p. 791.

to that of the Federation of Rhodesia and Nyasaland. Under the terms of its Constitution Singapore was granted self-government, while the United Kingdom remained officially responsible for external affairs and defence. However, Article 73 (1) of the Constitution authorized the Singapore Government to handle all matters relating to trade and cultural relations with foreign states, with the proviso that the scope of this responsibility was to be defined by a subsequent entrustment communication.[309]

The extent of Singapore's responsibility was defined by a communication on 6 July 1959, and included any agreements of purely local concern with the Federation of Malaya, Sarawak, North Borneo and Brunei, multilateral or bilateral agreements with other countries on the treatment of goods and finally, multilateral agreements involving membership of international organizations which Singapore would be allowed to join.[310]

In practice, a survey of treaties and agreements concluded by Singapore up to 1963 reveals that in most cases they were negotiated and signed exclusively by plenipotentiaries of the Singapore Government, although the United Kingdom is generally mentioned in the title as acting on behalf of Singapore.[311]. Each agreement also takes note of the specific United Kingdom authorization or entrustment by means of formulae such as: 'The Government of the State of Singapore with the authority and consent of the Government of the United Kingdom...',[312] or 'Whereas the Singapore Government is a party to this Agreement with the assent of Her Majesty's Government in the United Kingdom...'.[313]

Singapore's participation in international organizations was not very extensive. Immediately before joining the Federation of Malaysia in 1963, it was listed as a member of the World Meteorological Union and as an associate member of the International

---

[309] *State of Singapore Act*, 1958 (6–7 Eliz. II, c. 59) and the Singapore (Constitution) Order in Council, 1958, Statutory Instrument No. 1956. See also E. Lauterpacht, 'The contemporary practice of the United Kingdom in the field of international law-survey and comment, VII', 8 *ICLQ* (1959), 146–47.

[310] See E. Lauterpacht, 'The contemporary practice of the United Kingdom in the field of international law-survey and comment, IX', 10 ICLQ (1961), 576–7.

[311] See for instance the Basic Arrangements on Trade and Economic Relations Concluded between the United Kingdom (on behalf of Singapore) and Indonesia: *UN Treaty Series*, vol. 443, p. 255.

[312] Convention between the Government of the United Kingdom (on behalf of the State of Singapore) and Japan for the avoidance of double taxation, *UN Treaty Series*, vol. 420, p. 75.

[313] Agreement between Australia and the United Kingdom (on behalf of the State of Singapore) concerning the provision of treatment in Singapore hospitals for Asian residents of Christmas Island, *UN Treaty Series*, vol. 472, p. 158.

Telecommunications Union and the Economic Commission for Asia and the Far East (ECAFE). Its participation in the Universal Postal Union was still under the heading 'Whole of the British Overseas Territories...'.[314] By comparison with the Federation of Rhodesia and Nyasaland, Singapore exercised its external competence in only a limited manner. Yet, according to one writer, Singapore by 1963 had already achieved some international legal status.[315]

Among autonomous states presently in existence, none is of real significance for the present enquiry. In most instances, they enjoy internal self-government but are totally deprived of any external competence: such is the case of Puerto Rico,[316] the Netherlands Indies[317] and the Cook Islands.[318] In some instances, although external competence has been delegated within limits to the autonomous state, it has never been used in practice. This is the particular situation of the Associated West Indian States.

The West Indies Act of 1967 groups into association with Great Britain the colonial territories of Antigua, Dominica, Grenada, St Kitts–Nevis–Anguilla, St Lucia and St Vincent.[319] The Act provides that the Associated States shall in general be responsible for internal affairs, whereas external affairs and defence are reserved to the United Kingdom.[320] However, at the constitutional conferences which preceded the passing of the Act Heads of Agreement were reached on Defence and External Affairs which provided that 'The United Kingdom Government will from time to time by despatch define the extent to which the Government of the Territory will have authority to act in the field of external relations'.[321] A draft despatch annexed to the report of the Constitutional Conferences set out the extent to which the United Kingdom was prepared to delegate external competence to the Islands. Among other things, they could apply for full or associate membership in those special-United States and any international organization of which the United Kingdom was a member. They could conclude bilateral or

---

[314] See *United Nations Yearbook*, 1963, pp. 657 and 792.

[315] Keith, 'Succession to bilateral treaties by seceding states', 61 *AJIL* (1967), 521 at 527.

[316] See Cabranes, 'The status of Puerto Rico', 16 *ICLQ* (1967), 531.

[317] See Van Panhuys, 'The international aspects of the reconstruction of the Kingdom of the Netherlands in 1954', 5 *Netherlands International Law Review* (1958), 1.

[318] See Broderick, 'Associated statehood—a new form of decolonization', 17 *ICLQ* (1968), 368 at 390–2.

[319] 1967 UK Statutes, c. 4.

[320] For a general analysis of the Act, see Broderick, 'Associated statehood —a new form of decolonization', 17 *ICLQ* (1968), 368.

[321] See Broderick, p. 376.

multilateral agreements with foreign states relating to the treatment of goods, immigration and emigrant labour schemes, as well as agreements of a purely local concern with any member of the British Commonwealth or any British Colony in the Caribbean area. They could also conclude agreements for technical and financial assistance with any member of the British Commonwealth, the United States and any international organization of which the United Kingdom was a member.[322] An entrustment of external affairs in such terms was made in February 1967 to the government of each associated state on the condition that they agree to inform the Government of the United Kingdom in advance of their intention to enter into relations with foreign states.[323] Since then, however, the Associated States have not made much use of their delegated international competence. According to Broderick, they have not yet achieved status in international law; but 'Given a desire on the part of the Associated States themselves, some of the international organizations, and the encouragement of the Secretary-General of the United Nations, an evolution to some degree of international personality on the part of the Associated States can be expected in time.'[324]

To sum up, then, there is little doubt that non-sovereign entities such as autonomous states may in certain circumstances become bearers of rights and duties under international law. When the Federation of Rhodesia and Nyasaland replaced Southern Rhodesia as party to the General Agreement on Tariffs and Trade, it acknowledged the rights and obligations of Southern Rhodesia and of the UK, in respect of Northern Rhodesia and Nyasaland, as rights and obligations of the Federation.[325] The advisory commission charged by the British Government to review the constitution of the Federation concluded that the status of the latter fell short of that of a full international person because it was not an independent sovereign state.[326] Implicitly this meant that the Federation did enjoy some international status.

A more general conclusion would be that 'a dependent territory may be said to have international personality to the extent of its

---

[322] *Ibid.*, p. 377.

[323] *Idem.*

[324] *Ibid.*, p. 397. In 1968, Antigua signed with Barbados, Guyana, Trinidad and Tobago the Agreement setting up the Caribbean Free Trade Association (7 *International Legal Materials* (1968), 935). Later during the year, Dominica, Grenada, St Kitt's–Nevis–Anguilla, St Lucia and St Vincent joined the Association.

[325] See above, p. 70.

[326] Advisory Commission on the Review of the Constitution of the Federation of Rhodesia and Nyasaland, *Report,* Appendix VII, Possible Constitutional Changes, p. 75 (Cmnd 1150, UK).

capacity to enter into international relations'.[327] In 1962, the various states members of the United Nations were invited to comment on the first 29 Draft Article on the law of Treaties. Concerning Article 5, which dealt with the capacity of states to conclude treaties, the Government of the United States observed that 'where a colony or other subordinate jurisdiction has been entrusted with authority to conduct its foreign relations with respect to certain matters, or to conclude a particular agreement, the new law of treaties should not preclude commitments entered into by it from constituting valid international agreements'.[328] Therefore, it maintained, 'so far as such a colony or entity is entrusted with a measure of authority by the parent State in the conduct of its foreign relations, it necessarily becomes "a subject of international law" for the purpose of paragraph 1 of the present Article'.[329] Such a conclusion, however, is not exact. If foreign states refuse to deal with a dependent territory endowed with a measure of international competence, then the latter obviously cannot be regarded as a subject of international law. It is safer, and certainly more exact, to say that a dependent territory, like a member state of a federation, may, but not necessarily will, become a subject of international law to the extent of its capacity to enter into international relations. This leaves open the problem of the role of recognition in the determination of international personality.

Recognition as a condition of international personality in federal states

The specific role of recognition in the determination of international personality is a subject of disagreement among international lawyers. Some of them argue that recognition has a constitutive effect and is the essential condition of international personality;[330] other writers consider that recognition is merely declaratory, international personality being primarily a question of fact.[331] As O'Connell says: 'For every ounce of practice the con-

[327] Fawcett, *The British Commonwealth in International Law*, 1963, p. 143.
[328] *Yearbook of the International Law Commission*, 1965, ii, 17.
[329] *Idem.*
[330] Anzilotti, i, 161; Oppenheim, *International Law*, 8th edn, i, 125; Kelsen, 'Recognition in international law, theoretical observations', 35 *AJIL* (1941), 605; Schwarzenberger, *International Law*, 3rd edn, i, 89 and 132–4.
[331] Cavaré, *Le Droit international public positif*, 1951, p. 297; Brownlie, p. 84; O'Connell, *International Law*, 1965 i, 140; Starke, *An Introduction to International Law*, 6th edn, 1967, pp. 128–9.

stitutivist can put in the scales the declaratory theorist can add his ounce.'[332]

On the whole, however, there appears to be a sizeable majority of writers in favour of the declaratory theory of recognition. In 1936, the Institut de droit international pronounced itself in favour of the declaratory view by a majority of 30 members to 1, with 3 abstentions.[333] Although certain compromise solutions have been proposed, they have never really gained acceptance.[334]

Judicial decisions on the subject tend to be contradictory. If the municipal tribunals of newly created states have generally looked on recognition as the mere acknowledgment of their existence in fact and in law,[335] municipal courts of recognizing states have tended to consider it as decisive in matters of international status.[336] As for arbitral tribunals, their attitude has been one of open support for the declaratory theory of recognition; but serious consideration was given by them to actual acts of recognition.[337] The World Court, in contrast, adopted a more prudent stand. In the case of *Certain German Interests in Polish Upper Silesia*, it found that Poland was not a Contracting Party to the Armistice Convention because Germany had never recognized it as a belligerent,[338] but the problem was treated as one of conventional international law rather than as one of international status. In the *Reparation for Injuries* advisory opinion, the Court found itself faced with the question of the international status of the United

---

[332] O'Connell, *International Law*, i, 141.

[333] *Annuaire de l'Institut de droit international*, 1936, ii, 175, 301.

[334] Lauterpacht, *Recognition in International Law*, 1947, p. 74, adopts the constitutive theory, but asserts that there is an obligation on other states to recognize. For a strong criticism of that view, see Kunz, 'Critical remarks on Lauterpacht's *Recognition in International Law*', 44 *AJIL* (1950), 713. For other compromise solutions, see Chen, *The International Law of Recognition*, 1951, pp. 32 and 46.

[335] See *Ware v. Hylton*, 1 US (3 Dall.) 199, 224; *Rights of Citizenship (Establishment of Czechoslovak State) Case*, Annual Digest 1919–22, case no. 5; for other instances, Chen, p. 90.

[336] See *Duff Development Co. Ltd v. Government of Kelantan*, [1924] AC 797; the rule expressed in that case is not so much an acknowledgement of the constitutive theory of recognition but is rather the result of an act of judicial self-limitation.

[337] In *Deutsche Continental Gas-Gessellschaft v. Polish State*, *Tribunaux Arbitraux Mixtes*, vol. ix, p. 336 at 344, it was held that: 'The recognition of a State is not constitutive but merely declaratory'. See also *Lay & Marcus v. German Empire & Deutsche Ostafrikanische Bank AG*, *Tribunaux Arbitraux Mixtes*, III, 998 at 1008. But commenting on the *Deutsche Continental Gas-Gesselleschaft v. Poland* decision, Schwarzenberger points out that: 'Though professing to base its decision on the declaratory doctrine of recognition, the Tribunal mainly relied on the assertion of a German act of *de jure* recognition of Poland in November 1918': Schwarzenberger, *International Law*, vol i, 3rd edn, p. 134.

[338] (1926) *PCIJ*, A/7, p. 28.

Nations vis-à-vis non-member states; its answer was that: 'Fifty States, representing the vast majority of the members of the international community, had the power, in conformity with international law, to bring into being an entity possessing objective international personality, and not merely personality recognized by them alone.'[339] Thus, in the eyes of the Court, recognition was not, strictly speaking, constitutive of international personality; yet, to a large extent, it remained an essential requirement of international status.

In conventional international law, the 1933 Convention of Montevideo and the Charter of Bogota of 1948 are also of interest.[340] Both are multilateral agreements signed by the Latin American States and the United States and they contain identical provisions on the question of recognition. In the first place, the political existence of the state is said to be independent of recognition by the other states; pre-recognition rights of self-defence and internal freedom are derived from this *de facto* existence.[341] Furthermore, the recognition of a state is described as 'the acceptance of the personality of the other with all the rights and duties determined by international law'.[342] The result is that non-recognized states enjoy a basic international status but must be recognized in order to become full subjects of international law.

Considering the evidence, it would seem that neither the constitutive nor the declaratory view of recognition fully accounts for the practice of international law. The former ignores the compelling force of reality,[343] the latter does not pay sufficient attention to the individualistic character of international law.[344] It appears more exact to regard international personality as resulting from the interplay of the principles of effectiveness and recognition.[345] Such a view at least allows for some basic rights in non-recognized sovereign entities while stressing at the same time the important role of recognition in matters of international personality.[346]

---

[339] (1949) *ICJ Rep.*, p. 185.
[340] Convention of Montevideo: see Hudson, *International Legislation*, vi, 620; Charter of Bogota: see Briggs, *The Law of Nations*, 2nd edn, p. 101.
[341] Article 3 of the Convention of Montevideo and 9 of the Charter of Bogota.
[342] Article 6 of the Montevideo Convention and 10 of the Charter of Bogota.
[343] See on this subject De Visscher, 'Observations sur l'effectivité en droit international public', 62 *RGDIP* (1958), 601.
[344] See Schwarzenberger, *A Manual of International Law*, 4th edn, i, 8.
[345] See Reuter, *Droit international public*, 1963, p. 94.
[346] See *Preparatory Study Concerning a draft declaration on the rights and duties of States*, UN Secretary General, 1948 (Doc. A/CN.4/2), p. 55. See also the correspondence between the Spanish and British Governments on

THE RECOGNITION OF THE FEDERAL STATE

In 1906, the opinion was expressed by John Bassett Moore that:

> There can be no reason for refusing to recognize a federated state,
> formed by the union of recognized states, such as the German
> Empire in 1871, and the North German Confederation in 1866;
> or as Switzerland in 1848, after the confederation of states became
> a federated State. For those States, being sovereign, had the in-
> contestable right to bind themselves together by a federal bond.
> It was a matter which concerned them, and did not concern
> third Powers.[347]

The right of sovereign states to bind themselves by a federal bond
is undeniable. What is less clear is whether other subjects of international law are bound to accept the new entity.

In the case of Switzerland, there is clear evidence that the pro-
jected transformation of the confederation into a federation, around
1847–48, became a subject of concern for foreign powers. As early
as in 1845, the British Foreign Secretary, the Earl of Aberdeen,
claimed that the destruction of the confederal bond would require
the assent of the powers, in view of their 1815 guarantee of the
Swiss neutrality.[348] In 1848, after the Sunderbund war had come
to an end, France, Austria, Prussia and Russia sent a note to the
confederal Diet in which they pointed out that the Swiss neutrality
guaranteed in 1814–15 was based upon the respect of the
sovereignty of the Cantons and the maintenance of a confederal
state.[349] The Diet answered that the rights of Switzerland as a
nation did not depend upon its internal organization, and took
pains to reassure the powers concerned that Switzerland intended
to remain a strictly neutral state.[350] The government of the new
state came into existence in September 1848, and soon all Powers
except Russia recognized it.[351]

On the other hand, there is no evidence that the German Federal
Empire of 1871 was expressly recognized by foreign states on its
formation. Indeed, the creation of the North German Confederation in 1866 was not even announced to foreign states.[352] Bismarck

the subject of the Spanish Colonies, in Smith, *Great Britain and the Law
of Nations*, 1932–5, i, 122 and 167. In 1820, before it had recognized Chile,
the Government of the USA settled some difficulties with the *de facto*
state by way of a transaction: see the *Macedonian* Case, in Lapradelle-
Politis, *Recueil des arbitrages internationaux*, ii, 182 at 215–7.

[347] Moore, *International Law Digest*, i, 72.
[348] See Imlah, *Britain and Switzerland 1845–1860*, 1966, p. 15 and p. 181.
[349] See de Martens, *NRG*, vol. ii, p. 68 and 85.
[350] *Ibid.*, p. 91.
[351] Imlah, p. 40.
[352] See Bruns, *Fontes Juris Gentium*, 1932. Ser. B, Sec. I, Tom. i, para. i,
p. 143, no. 467.

justified such an attitude by declaring that the significance of the *Bund* in international relations depended not on recognition but on its actual power and importance.[353] In his view, the Confederation was powerful enough to make recognition unnecessary. Similarly, it would seem that the transformation of the American Confederation into a federal state in 1787 was accepted by foreign Powers as a matter of fact.[354]

Thus, as far as concerns federations formed by the union of sovereign states, past examples tend to show that recognition is merely declaratory. In the case of federations formed by the decentralization of unitary sovereign states, the problem of recognition as such does not arise: the change from a unitary to a federal constitution remains a purely internal matter. The situation is more or less the same in the case of colonial federations: the problem of recognition only arises when they leave the colonial empire to become independent.

THE RECOGNITION OF MEMBER STATES OF FEDERATIONS

In the doctrine of international law, it is remarkable that a number of publicists, opposed in principle to the constitutive view of recognition, accept it as valid in relation to non-sovereign entities. Among them mention may be made of Waldock and Briggs, whose views on the subject can be found in the discussions of the International Law Commission,[355] and Berezowski, who wrote on non-sovereign subjects of international law.[356] Judicial decisions also suggest that recognition is essential for non-sovereign states to become subjects of international law. In *Jolly v. Mainka*, for instance,

---

[353] *Ibid.*, p. 144. Bismarck declared exactly: 'Ich kann mich mit dieser Argumentation insoweit einverstanden erklären, als wir allerdings einer ausdrücklichen Anerkennung des Bundes nicht bedürfen. Der Bund ist eine vollendete Tatsache, und seine Konstituierung lediglich Sache der Mitglieder selbst. Die Bedeutung, welche der Bund im europäischen Staatsleben hat, hängt nicht von einer ausgesprochenen Anerkennung, sondern von seiner faktischen und realen Macht und dem Gewicht ab, welches er selber in die europäische Wagschale zu legen vermag.'

[354] A possible explanation for this may be found in the opinion expressed by Justice Sutherland, in *United States v. Curtiss-Wright Export Corporation*, that 'the States severally never possessed international powers': 299 US 304 at 317. This would mean that even before the United States became a federation, it constituted a single state from the point of view of international law. But see Quarles, 'The Federal Government: as to foreign affairs are its powers inherent as distinguished from delegated?', 32 *Georgetown L.J.* (1944), 375.

[355] See *Yearbook of the International Law Commission*, 1962, i, 59 (Briggs) and ii, 36 (Waldock).

[356] Berezowski, 'Les sujets non souverains du droit international', 65 *HR* (1938), 1, 24.

Evatt J. held, concerning the right of Australia to become party to the Treaty of Versailles and the Covenant of the League of Nations, that 'a refusal by foreign States to recognize any separate personality in a Dominion would leave them quite outside the family of nations'.[357] As for protectorates, it was decided in the *Spanish Zone of Morocco Claims* that the delegation of competence and responsibility which they involve cannot affect third states without their acquiescence.[358] Finally, the Advisory Commission on the Review of the Constitution of the Federation of Rhodesia and Nyasaland concluded in 1960 that the Federal Government could assume international commitments and participate in international negotiations only to the extent to which the United Kingdom Government was prepared to authorize them and other states were prepared to treat with them.[359]

According to certain jurists, however, the international law capacity, and presumably the international personality, of member states of federations is essentially a constitutional law matter. Thus, Morin argues that, if the member states are constitutionally endowed with international competence, 'le droit des gens ne peut alors que s'incliner et reconnaître la capacité ou l'incapacité internationale des Etats-membres'.[360] This also appears to be the opinion of Kröneck. After asserting that member states of federations are subjects of international law if they have the capacity to possess international rights and duties,[361] he adds that this capacity does not depend on recognition but rather constitutes a prerequisite of recognition.[362] Attorney-General Cushing of the United States also asserted, many years ago, that the international competence of individual members of federal systems depended upon the constitution of the system.[363]

More recently, the International Law Commission seems to have adopted a similar view. In its Draft Articles on the Law of Treaties the international capacity of the member states of a federal union was made to depend on the federal constitution.[364] But several members of the Commission criticized Article 5 (2) 'for not giving

[357] *Jolly v. Mainka*, 49 *Commonwealth Law Reports* (1933), 242, 282.
[358] 2 *RIAA* 615, 648.
[359] Advisory Commission on the Review of the Constitution of the Federation of Rhodesia and Nyasaland, Report, Appendix VII, Possible Constitutional Changes p. 75 (Cmnd 1150—UK).
[360] Morin, p. 147.
[361] Kröneck, 'Die völkerrechtliche Immunität bundesstaatlicher Gliedstaaten vor ausländischen Gerichten', dissertation, Munich, 1958, p. 143.
[362] *Ibid.*, p. 145.
[363] See Deener, *The United States Attorneys General and International Law*, 1957, pp. 183–4.
[364] See above, p 15.

enough prominence to the role of international law on the capacity of States members of federal unions to conclude treaties'.[365] Already in 1962 Sir Humphrey Waldock had made it clear that in his view states members of a federation could become subjects of international law only if their personality were recognized both by the constitution of the federation and by other contracting state or states.[366] Similar views were again expressed by a number of states at the 1968 and 1969 sessions of the United Nations Conference on the Law of Treaties.[367]

A majority of international lawyers, on the other hand, admit that member states of federations must be recognized in order to become subjects of international law. Some of them, like Klein, Redslob and Bernhardt, consider this recognition to be included in the recognition of the federal state itself.[368] Mosler adopts an intermediate position. He asserts that the recognition of the member states is, as a rule, implicitly included in that of the federal state. However he recognizes that, in certain circumstances, foreign states can object to the federal allocation of international competence, especially if it impairs the existing status of the federal state.[369] Finally, certain writers, such as Sørensen, Dolan and Hallmayer make individual recognition of member states an essential condition of their international personality.[370]

The practice of states conforms most closely to the views of Sørensen, Dolan and Hallmayer. Thus, although Article 14 (e) of the Soviet Constitution gives to each Republic the right to enter into direct relations with foreign states, only Ukraine and Byelorussia were accepted as members of the United Nations. According to Kröneck, this does not mean that recognition is essential for member states of federations in order to become subjects of international law; on the contrary it may be interpreted as a sign that

---

[365] As pointed out by Mr Jimenez de Arechaga, representative of Uruguay, at the 894th meeting of the International Law Commission: *Yearbook of the International Law Commission*, 1966, i, part 2, p. 339. Mr Tunkin replied that 'the agreement reached in the Commission had certainly not been that the capacity of member States of federal unions to conclude treaties depended upon rules of international law or was restricted thereby. The capacity depended solely on the constitution of the federal union and could only be limited by the provisions of that constitution': *idem*.

[366] *Yearbook of the International Law Commission*, 1962, ii, 37.

[367] In particular by the representatives of Switzerland and Uruguay in 1968, and the representatives of Canada, India, Uruguay, Australia, and Cyprus in 1969.

[368] Klein, *Die mittelbare Haftung im Völkerrecht*, 1941, p. 170; Redslob, *Traité de droit des gens*, 1951, p. 122; Bernhardt, *Der Abschluss völkerrechtlicher Verträge im Bundesstaat*, p. 21, see also Rudolf, pp. 54–6.

[369] Mosler, in *Festschrift R. Thoma*, 129 at 161–3.

[370] Dolan, p. 636; Sørensen, 'Principes de droit international public', 101 *HR* (1960), 1 at 134–5; Hallmayer, p. 13.

the member Republics of the Soviet Union already had the capacity to possess international rights and duties.[371] However, in the light of what happened subsequently in 1947, his interpretation must be rejected. In that year, the Baltic States, who had been members of the International Telecommunication Union before 1940, were deprived of their vote on the ground that they had lost their international standing upon becoming members of the Soviet Union.[372] The same states which had accepted Ukraine and Byelorussia as members of the United Nations refused to recognize on this occasion the international status of the Baltic Republics.

The practice of states also indicates that the member states of the American union do not presently enjoy any effective international status.[373] Therefore, one must agree with Hallmayer that recognition of the United States did not imply recognition of their member states as subjects of international law.[374] The subdivisions of the American federation may enjoy a potential international status, but their claim to international personality fails in practice. In view of the evidence, it must be acknowledged that constitutional provisions are not enough to grant international status to member states of federations.[375]

Conclusion

To sum up, the position of international law on the subject of international personality in federal states is as follows. In so far as such states are recognized as sovereign members of the international community, they enjoy full international personality. The fact that their internal competence is limited to some extent does not affect in any way their international status. As for member states, their claim to international personality as sovereign entities

---

[371] Kröneck, p. 144.

[372] *Documents of the International Telecommunication Conference at Atlanta City*, 1947; Bern, Bureau of the ITU, 1948, minutes of the second plenary session, 18–19 July 1947.

[373] See above, pp. 47–51.

[374] Hallmayer, pp. 12–13.

[375] As one writer puts it, 'It is not enough for a federal constitution to proclaim that all its members have treaty-making power. Other states must be prepared to recognize that they have that power. Otherwise, a federal constitution could merely assert that all its members have full treaty-making power and insist, for example, that they all be members of the United Nations or some other international body. It is clear that other states would have to recognize the status which the federal constitution describes and be willing to treat with such states in that manner before the constitutional assertion of such powers could be regarded as creating a genuine international status' (see Gotlieb, *Canadian Treaty-Making*, 1968, p. 32).

fails entirely. But it does not follow that they cannot enjoy international personality. If the federal constitution grants them the right to deal separately with foreign states and such states agree to deal with them, then they are subjects of international law.[376] If on the other hand the constitution is not clear as to the right of the member states to deal with foreign jurisdictions, and if at the same time there is no agreement within the federation itself on this point, then it is the duty of foreign states to abstain from intervening in the internal affairs of the federation.[377] In practical terms, this means that they must ignore the member states and deal exclusively with the federal government, since only the latter by virtue of its sovereignty is presumed to be competent in international law. All this is in accordance with the fundamental principles of sovereignty, consent and recognition.

[376] This was also the conclusion reached by Stutzel in 1927. He wrote: Aus der Natur des Bundesstaates nicht notwendig die Negierung der völkerrechtlichen Handlungsfähigkeit des Einzelstaates folgt' and added that the problem of the international status of each member state was 'eine Frage seiner Kompetenz und der Anerkennung durch die Staatengemeinschaft': Stutzel, 'Die völkerrechtliche Handlungsfähigkeit der Einzelstaaten im Bundesstaat', dissertation, Munich, 1927, p. 19.

[377] This was the attitude adopted by Austria, Canada, Sweden, Switzerland, Ethiopia, Italy, Tanzania, United States, Germany, Brazil, India and the Republic of Vietnam at the 1968 and 1969 sessions of the United Nations Conference on the Law of Treaties: see UN documents A/Conf. 39/11, A/Conf. 39/SR.7 and A/Conf. 39/SR.8.

CHAPTER 3

FEDERALISM AND INTERNATIONAL RESPONSIBILITY

'IT is a principle of international law, and even a general conception of law, that any breach of an engagement involves an obligation to make reparation.'[1] Behind this fundamental principle of responsibility lie a number of more specific rules. Generally speaking, there must be an act or omission contravening an international obligation, this act or omission must cause some injury and above all it must be imputable to a subject of international law.[2] Various tests have been evolved to determine in which circumstances different activities were imputable to a state. Following the division of powers prevailing in most states, acts of the legislature, of the executive and of the judiciary have been separately examined.[3] Inevitably, federal states with their typical division of competence have been the object of particular attention.

On the authority of certain decisions, federal states are considered by most international law writers as responsible for the acts or omissions of their component units. The usual argument is that a sovereign state cannot evade its international obligations for mere reasons of constitutional law. It is also, sometimes, added that component states of federations not being international subjects cannot be held internationally responsible. However, there are some aspects of this responsibility which are not altogether clear.

It is debatable, for instance, whether a federal state is responsible 'for all acts of its States which might give rise to claims by foreign government'.[4] In a number of instances federal states have been

---

[1] *Case Concerning the Factory at Chorzow*, Merits, 1928 *PCIJ*, ser. A, no. 17, p. 29; see also *Spanish Zone of Morocco Claims* (1924), 2 *RIAA*, p. 615.
[2] *Phosphates in Morocco*, Preliminary Objections, 1938 *PCIJ*, ser. A/B, no. 74, p. 28.
[3] Regarding acts of the legislature, see the *Shufeldt Claim* (1930), 2 *RIAA*, p. 1079; regarding acts of the executive, see the *Massey Claim* (1927) 4 RIAA, p. 155; finally, regarding acts of the judiciary, see the *Chattin Claim*, 4 *RIAA*, pp. 282.
[4] *Hyacinthe Pellat Claim, Annual Digest*, 1929–30, Case no. 90; the decision is reported in French in 5 *RIAA*, p. 534.

held not responsible for the contracts of their component units. But more important than this, there is the fact that the member states of certain federations can undertake their own international obligations. If, as argued by Garcia-Amador in 1956, imputability depends upon who is the subject of the obligation,[5] then a federal state obviously does not have to answer for the international obligations of its member states, unless of course the existence of a rule of international law to the contrary is established. A particular difficulty arises when a political subdivision of a federal state undertakes international obligations in excess of its competence. Among international lawyers, there is a tendency to consider any such agreement concluded by a member state as absolutely void. But the few instances to be found in international practice contradict their view.

It may also be of interest to examine what happens when a federal state is held responsible for the conduct of one of its member states. In a claim for compensation, the matter is relatively simple. But when the claim requires the federal state to take action beyond its competence, the matter becomes more complex. Short of amending the constitution, reparation may be impossible. How federal states have reacted in such circumstances merits, therefore, further consideration.

In order to clarify these various problems, it is necessary to re-examine the whole question of responsibility in federal states. Such an enquiry, it is hoped, will constitute a useful step towards the clarification of the rules of international law concerning the responsibility of states for subordinate governments. It was only in 1965, after all, that O'Connell complained that the whole topic of state responsibility for subordinate governments was largely unexplored.[6]

The responsibility of the federal state as a sovereign entity

Basically, the problem of the responsibility of a federal state for its member states is one of conflict between municipal law and international law. Its solution, therefore, must be sought first of all in the decisions of the World Court dealing with this question. In the *Case Concerning Certain German Interests in Polish Upper Silesia*, the Permanent Court of international Justice established that, 'From the standpoint of International Law and of the Court

[5] *Yearbook of the International Law Commission*, 1956, ii, 185.
[6] O'Connell, *International Law*, 1965, ii, 1046.

which is its organ, municipal laws are merely facts'.[7] In a later case, a natural consequence of this was brought to light: 'A State,' declared the Court, "cannot adduce as against another State its own Constitution with a view to evading obligations incumbent upon it under international law or treaties in force.'[8] In a third case, the Court went so far as to indicate what solution was to be given in case of conflict between international law or municipal law. 'A State which has contracted valid international obligations' it said, 'is bound to make in its legislation such modifications as may be necessary to ensure the fulfilment of the obligations undertaken.'[9] However, the World Court itself has never had occasion to apply these principles in circumstances involving federal states.

International tribunals, on the other hand, have had many such opportunities. In *The Montijo* arbitration of 1875, one of the problems raised was whether the Federal Government of Colombia could decline responsibility for damage caused by a member state to American citizens whose treaty rights had been invaded.[10] The Umpire pointed out, at the outset, that the treaty was made with the federal government and not with the member states; from this, he deduced that the former was responsible for its execution. Then, he went on to examine the difficulty raised by the fact that the federal government was constitutionally prohibited from intervening in the domestic disturbances of the states. In such a case, he declared, 'a treaty is superior to the constitution, which latter must give way. The legislation of the Republic must be adapted to the treaty, not the treaty to the laws'.[11]

A few years later, in the *de Brissot* case, the problem of the responsibility of a federal state for its member states was again raised.[12] Mr Findlay, the Umpire, examined at length the argument that the United States of Venezuela was not responsible for the conduct of one of its separate independent states, Apure. He held that:

> Whatever may be the relations *inter se* between the constituent parts of a federative body, admitted as such into the family of nations, they can play no part in determining the liability of the body by its own distinctive name to other nations for wrongs

[7] *Case Concerning Certain German Interests in Polish Upper Silesia*, Merits, (1926), 1926 *PCIJ*, ser. A, no. 7, p. 19.

[8] *Treatment of Polish Nationals in Danzig*, Advisory Opinion (1932), 1932 *PCIJ*, ser. A/B, no. 44, p. 24.

[9] *Exchange of Greek and Turkish Populations*, Advisory Opinion (1925) 1925 *PCIJ*, ser. B, no. 10, p. 20.

[10] *The Montijo*, in Moore, *International Arbitrations*, ii, 1421.

[11] *Ibid.*, p. 1440.

[12] *De Brissot*, in Moore, *International Arbitrations*, iii, 2949 ff.

inflicted by any of the parts or within the domestic jurisdiction of the same.[13]

Then he went on to explain his decision. He said:

> Apure has no flag recognized among the national flags of the world; she has no power to make war on other nations; she can make no treaties, and she can break none; and as far as her relations with foreign powers are concerned her existence is completely veiled in the sovereignty of the United States of Venezuela, which, by the necessity of the status, must be responsible in any proper case for whatever is done within the limits of its jurisdiction.[14]

Finally, Mr Findlay concluded that 'Venezuela could not be excused because Apure was not liable, but only because she was not responsible herself'.[15]

In the *Davy Case*, which came before the Great Britain–Venezuela Mixed Claims Commission in 1903, the Commissioner for Venezuela urged that the respondent Government was not responsible for the acts of its member states because of the federal character of the Venezuelan Government and the limitations thereby attached to its action.[16] Plumley, Umpire, declared in answer to this:

> Internationally, the National Government is solely responsible for the proper safeguarding of the rights and interest of foreigners, resident or commorant, within its territory. No diplomatic relations exist except as between the respective nations as such. The responsibility in a given case being admitted the duties attaching must be performed, or satisfactory atonement made. Great Britain can not deal with the State of Bolivar. The national integrity of the respondent Government alone would prevent it. Hence the nation itself, in its representative character and as a part of its governmental functions, must meet the complaint and satisfy it.[17]

The view that a federal state is responsible for the acts or omissions of its member states also prevailed in the *Tribolet* claim,[18] the *Mallen* claim,[19] the *Youmans* claim[20] and the *de Galvan* claim[21], all decided under the General Claims Convention of 1923 between the United States and Mexico.[22] Article 1 of the

---

[13] *Ibid.*, p. 2971.
[14] *Idem.*
[15] *Idem.*
[16] *Davy Case*, 9 *RIAA*, 467.
[17] *Ibid.*, p. 468.
[18] *Jesus Novarro Tribolet et al.*, 4 *RIAA*, 598.
[19] *Francisco Mallen*, 4 *RIAA*, 173 at 177.
[20] *Thomas H. Youmans*, 4 *RIAA*, 110 at 116.
[21] *De Galvan*, 4 *RIAA*, 273.
[22] 4 *RIAA*, 11.

Convention implicitly accepted that the acts of the component units in both federations would be attributable to the central governments. In the *Tribolet* claim, however, such responsibility of the federal state for its political subdivisions was declared to be not only in conformity with the General Claims Convention, but also in accordance with general international law.[23]

Federal courts themselves have occasionally acknowledged the responsibility of a federal government for the conduct of member states contravening the international obligations of the federation. A curious example of this is the opinion rendered by the Supreme Court of Canada in *Re Ownership of Off-shore Mineral Rights*.[24] In declaring that the Province of British Columbia could not claim the right to explore and exploit, or claim legislative jurisdiction over, the resources of the continental shelf, the Court gave the following reasons, among others:

> Canada is the sovereign State which will be recognized by international law as having the rights stated in the Convention of 1958, and it is Canada, not the Province of British Columbia, that will have to answer the claims of other members of the international community for breach of the obligations and responsibilities imposed by the Convention.[25]

This brought from one writer the comment that the Court made the equation, fatal in Canadian constitutional law, 'between jurisdiction at the international law level in relation to foreign countries, and jurisdiction (in a federal state) at the internal or municipal law level as between the federal government and the governments of the member-states or provinces'.[26] But then the Canadian Court may have been influenced to some extent by a similar kind of reasoning used, perhaps more justifiably, by the Supreme Court of the United States in three decisions dealing exactly with the same problem.[27] Be that as it may, one gets the impression that the international responsibility of federal authorities for their member states is more readily (and more profitably) accepted at the municipal rather than at the international law level.

The diplomatic practice of states offers even more examples of federal states being held internationally responsible for the conduct of their political subdivisions. Thus, following riots which took

[23] 4 *RIAA*, 601.
[24] 65 *DLR* (2d), 353 (1968).
[25] *Ibid.*, p. 380.
[26] McWhinney, Canadian Federalism, and the Foreign Affairs and Treaty Power. The Impact of Quebec's "Quiet Revolution"', 7 *CYIL* (1969), 3 at 19.
[27] *United States v. California*, 332 US 19, *per* Black J. at 29; *United States v. Texas*, 339 US 707, *per* Douglas J. at 719; *United States v. Louisiana*, 339 US 699, *per* Douglas J. at 704.

place at New Orleans in 1851 and in which the Spanish Consulate was raided and other Spanish places of business destroyed, the Government of Spain asked for redress from the Government of the United States, although it was clear that the State of Louisiana was primarily responsible for the maintenance of civil order.[28] In 1875 the American Government asserted the responsibility of the national Government of Brazil for the destruction of the property of an American citizen by lawless persons, acting with the admitted connivance of provincial authorities.[29] In 1909 the United States were again held responsible for riots against Greeks in South Omaha (Nebraska).[30] In 1922, Germany accepted responsibility for the failure of the Bavarian Government in October and November 1922 to prevent attacks upon the members of the Inter-Allied Control Commission.[31]

In the face of the evidence, there can be no doubt that a federal state is responsible for the conduct of its member states. But how far does this responsibility extend? In 1929, in the *Hyacinthe Pellat* claim, a French-Mexican Mixed Claims Commission held that, inasmuch as it was contended that the Mexican federation was not responsible for the acts of one of its states, 'the argument would disregard the principle of international (often called indirect) responsibility of a federal state for all acts of one of its states which might give rise to claims by foreign governments'.[32] The decision dealt with a claim by a French citizen to recover, *inter alia*, certain sums of money alleged to be due to him under compulsory loans levied in 1913 by the then revolutionary government of the Mexican State of Sonora. But if the claim had been for sums of money lent by voluntary contract instead of forced loans, would the rule enunciated by the Commission have applied?

In principle, it seems that a federal state does not have to answer for the public or private contracts of its member states. In *Rosenstein v. Etat Allemand*, it was held that the State of Hamburg, having a legal personality of its own, could not by its contracts give rise to the responsibility of the German State.[33] In the *Florida Bond* cases, the State of Florida was considered as exclusively responsible for the payment of bonds issued in its own name.[34] In

---

[28] Moore, *International Law Digest*, vi, 812.
[29] Moore, *International Law Digest*, vi, 816.
[30] See 23 *AJIL, spec. supp.* (1929), 192.
[31] See Strupp, *Wörterbuch des Völkerrechts und der Diplomatie*, ii, 247–8.
[32] *Hyacinthe Pellat*, 5 *RIAA*, 534; *Annual Digest*, 1929–30, case no. 90.
[33] *Rosenstein v. Etat Allemand*, 1927, *Tribunaux Arbitraux Mixtes*, vii, 121 at 123.
[34] *Florida Bond Cases*, in Moore, *International Arbitrations*, iv, 3594.

the case of *Francis Nolan v. Mexico*, a claim for a reward promised by the State of Sinaloa was turned down by the Umpire on the grounds that it did not involve a question which came within the cognizance of the commission: 'it was a sort of contract, which the claimant voluntarily entered into with the State of Sinaloa', and for which the Mexican Government could certainly not be held responsible.[35]

In exceptional circumstances, a federal state may have to answer for the contracts of its member states. In the *Bolivar Railway Company* Case, a British-owned railway company had carried some freight on the orders of the State of Lara, a member state of the Venezuelan Federation.[36] No payment having been made, Great Britain sought in this arbitration to obtain satisfaction from the federal government of Venezuela. The latter denied its responsibility on the grounds that the officials of the State of Lara had no authority to make accounts chargeable to the National Government without a special order to that effect. The Umpire held that in a case where the 'relation of the several States to the National Government is of such intricate character, apparently so intimate that it becomes difficult to discriminate rightfully between the two',[37] a federal state has to answer for the conduct of its member state. Such responsibility also arises when the central government of a federation has interests in a contract concluded by one of its subdivisions. This occurs when there is '(1) an immediate connexion of the Federal government with the contract as a participant therein; or (2) an assumption thereof or of liability therefor; or (3) a connexion therewith as beneficiary, whether in the inception or as beneficiary of the performance, in whole or in part; or (4) some direct Federal interest therein'.[38] In all other circumstances, the responsibility of the federal government 'is no more called for than in the case of contractual obligations of private individuals or corporations'.[39]

As far as concerns delictual acts of member states, there does not appear to be any limit to the responsibility of the federal state for its subdivisions. But certain cases are less clear than others. In

---

[35] *Francis Nolan v. Mexico*, in Moore, *International Arbitration*, iv, 3484.
[36] *Bolivar Railway Company*, 9 *RIAA*, 445, at 449–50.
[37] *Ibid.*, p. 450.
[38] *Cayuga Indians Claim*, 6 *RIAA*, 173 at 188.
[39] Schwarzenberger, *International Law*, 1957, i, 627. In *The Montijo*, the Umpire expressed his disagreement with the view that the debts incurred to foreigners by the separate States of Venezuela were private in their character and therefore could not give rise to the responsibility of the Union. But the debts in question were of a delictual rather than contractural character. See Moore, *International Arbitration II*, 1441–2

1927, the Province of Quebec imposed a succession duty on stock belonging to the Bank of Montreal and registered under the by-laws of that Bank in New York.[40] The executor of the estate of an American citizen paid the duty under protest and sought reimbursement in the courts of Quebec. The shares were held not to be subject to the duty and reimbursement with interest was decreed.[41] The case went on appeal to the Court of King's Bench,[42] and from there to the Supreme Court of Canada.[43] In both instances, judgment was given against the Province of Quebec. Special leave to appeal was subsequently refused by the Judicial Committee of the Privy Council.[44] The Province, finally, accepted to pay the duty, but declined payment of the interest. The case was taken up by the Department of State of the United States which presented the claim of its national to the Canadian Government. The latter replied that 'it was not prepared to admit responsibility under the existing rules of international law for the liabilities of the Province of Quebec'.[45] However, to avoid any suggestion that it was responsible for a denial of justice, Canada proposed to have the matter decided by an arbitral tribunal. Shortly after it changed its mind and made an *ex gratia* payment in order, allegedly, to avoid the costs of arbitration.

Was the Canadian Government really justified in declining responsibility for the liability incurred by the Province of Quebec? It may be argued, on the one hand, that the judiciary had done its duty and that Canada was not bound by the debts of the Province. On the other hand, it may also be argued that the absence of legal machinery capable of forcing Quebec to pay the interest claimed amounted in the circumstances to a denial of justice. Looking more closely at the case, it cannot be doubted that the second solution is the correct one. The refusal of the Quebec Government to pay the interest awarded by the courts may be assimilated to the non-execution of a judgment by the executive branch of a state. Now in a number of cases international tribunals have held that such conduct on the part of the executive constitutes a denial of justice.[46] The only defence that Canada could have raised against

---

[40] *Robert Fulton Cutting* Case, Hackworth, *Digest of International Law*, v, 561.
[41] *Cutting v. The King* (1930), 2 *DLR* 297.
[42] 51 Que. K.B., 321.
[43] (1932) 3 *DLR* 273.
[44] *Weekly Notes* 1933, pt I, p. 2.
[45] Hackworth, *Digest of International Law*, v. 562.
[46] *Montano* case, Moore, *International Arbitrations*, ii, 1630, 1634; *Fabiani* case, *ibid.*, v, p. 4878 at 4893, 4907; see also Borchard, *The Diplomatic Protection of Citizens Abroad*, 1915, pp. 199 and 339.

this would have been the limitations imposed by the constitution of the country. As already seen, however, 'a State cannot adduce as against another State its own constitution with a view to evading obligations incumbent upon it under international law.[47] Therefore, one must conclude that Canada was indeed responsible for Quebec's refusal to pay.

So far, it has been seen that a federal state must answer for the international torts of its political subdivisions as well as for their acts or omissions contravening its treaty obligations. But can one go further and assert that a federal state is responsible for the international obligations undertaken by its member states? According to the doctrine of international law, this would appear to be a separate problem.

One of the topics examined by the Institut de droit international at its session of Neuchatel, in 1900, was that of state responsibility for mob violence.[48] Article 4 of the *Règlement*, adopted by a majority of members, provided that:

> Le gouvernement d'un Etat fédéral composé d'un certain nombre de petits Etats, qu'il représente au point de vue du droit international, ne peut invoquer, pour se soustraire à la responsabilité qui lui incombe, le fait que la constitution de l'Etat fédéral ne lui donne sur les Etats particuliers ni le droit de contrôle, ni le droit d'exiger d'eux qu'ils satisfassent à leurs obligations.[49]

The text of this Article raised no comments and was adopted unanimously. It is, therefore, difficult to elaborate on it. But it would seem from its wording that the problem of member states dealing directly with foreign states was not envisaged.

In 1927, at its meeting of Lausanne, the Institut de droit international considered the topic of state responsibility for injuries done in their territory to the person or property of foreigners.[50] Again the question of the responsibility of a federal state for its political subdivisions came up for examination. The conclusion was reached that: 'A federal State is responsible for the conduct of the individual States, not only if it is contrary to its own international obligations, but also if it is contrary to the international obligations incumbent upon those States.'[51] This time, the formulation used left no doubt as to the responsibility of a federal state for acts of its member states contravening their own inter-

---

[47] *Treatment of Polish Nationals in Danzig*, Advisory Opinion (1932), 1932 *PCIJ*, Series A/B 44, p. 24.
[48] *Annuaire de l'Institut de droit international*, 1900, p. 233.
[49] *Ibid.*, p. 255.
[50] *Annuaire de l'Institut de droit international*, 1927, i, p. 455.
[51] The translation is taken from 22 *AJIL* (1928), spec. supp., p. 331–2.

national obligations. But it did not specify whether this responsibility was direct or vicarious.

Two years later, in 1929, a draft convention prepared by the Harvard Law School appeared on the same subject of state responsibility for injuries to foreigners.[52] Article 3 of the project stated that:

> A state is not relieved of responsibility because an injury to an alien is attributable to one of its political subdivisions, regardless of the extent to which the national government, according to its constitution, has control of the subdivision. For the purposes of this article, a dominion, a colony, a dependency, a protectorate, or a community under mandate, which does not independently conduct its foreign relations, is to be assimilated to a political subdivision.[53]

Article 8 (b) specified that a state was not responsible if an injury to an alien resulted from the non-performance of a contractual obligation owed by a political subdivision to an alien, apart from responsibility because of a denial of justice.[54] In the comments attached to Article 3, it was explained that 'to the extent that the dependent government or community does not independently conduct its foreign relations, the protecting or controlling state must assume responsibility for violations of international law with respect to aliens committed by the dependent government or community'.[55] Whether this meant that member states of federations dealing directly with foreign powers were responsible for their own engagements, it is not quite clear.

The two studies undertaken by the Institut de Droit International in 1927 and by the Harvard Law School in 1929 were in anticipation of the League of Nations Codification Conference of 1930 which was to consider among other topics that of the responsibility of states for injuries done in their territory to the person or property of foreigners. In connection with this project, the League of Nations itself sent a questionnaire to all its members inviting them to give their opinion on different points of law and one of the questions concerned the responsibility of federal states for their political subdivisions.[56] The general view of the members, in answer to it, was that responsibility fell on the state which represented the offending state in its relations with third parties.[57]

[52] 23 *AJIL* (1929), spec. supp. p. 131.
[53] *Ibid.*, p. 145
[54] *Ibid.*, p. 168.
[55] *Ibid.*, p. 145.
[56] League of Nations, *Conference for the Codification of International Law, Bases of Discussion*, 1929, iii, 121 (Doc. C. 75, M.69).
[57] *Ibid.*, pp. 121–4.

Some answers simply stated that a federal state was responsible for the acts of its member states.[58] Switzerland acknowledged exclusive responsibility for all acts of its component units, including presumably acts of the latter contravening their own international obligations.[59] Germany on the contrary, declined responsibility for the acts of its member states contrary to their own international obligations.[60]

Following these remarks, a basis of discussion was worked out.[61] In essence, it reproduced the view commonly held that a state entrusted with the conduct of the foreign relations of one or more states was responsible for damage suffered by foreigners on the territories of such states. In 1930, at the Codification Conference the various delegations were invited to comment on this. Finland remarked that some dependent states were or could become members of the League.[62] As such, it argued, they had to acknowledge individual responsibility. The Finnish Delegation suggested in consequence an amendment which read in part as follows: 'A common or central government may be invested with power to conduct the foreign relations of several States in such a way that the responsibility for damage suffered by foreigners in the territory of any one of the States devolves upon that government alone.'[63] The final text adopted by the Conference states more simply that 'a State cannot avoid international responsibility by invoking its municipal law'.[64] Thus, the issue of the responsibility of a federal state for its political subdivisions acting as subjects of international law was ultimately shelved.

In 1953, at its eighth session, the General Assembly of the United Nations adopted a resolution requesting the International Law Commission to undertake, as soon as the Commission considered it advisable, the codification of the principles of international law governing state responsibility.[65] In 1955 the International Law Commission complied with this request and named F. V. Garcia-Amador Special Rapporteur.[66] The latter produced his first report

---

[58] *Ibid.*, p. 123 (Answer of Italy).
[59] *Ibid.*, p. 123–4.
[60] *Ibid.*, 121.
[61] *Ibid.*, p. 124 (Basis of discussion no. 23).
[62] League of Nations, *Acts of the Conference for the Codification of International Law*, 1930, Minutes of the Third Committee (LN. v, 1930, 17), 212.
[63] *Idem.*
[64] *Ibid.*, p. 236.
[65] General Assembly, Eighth Session, 1953, Resolution 799 (VIII).
[66] *Official Records of the General Assembly*, 10th Session, Supp. No. 9, par. 33.

in 1956.[67] Among other things, he declared that imputability depended on who was the direct subject of the obligations.[68] Thus, he argued, political subdivisions of states and semi-sovereign entities, in so far as they have the capacity to contract international obligations directly, can be active subjects of responsibility.[69] But, of course, as he pointed out, a state could never plead the provisions of its municipal law for the purpose of repudiating the responsibility arising out of the breach of one of its international obligations.[70] Concluding his report, he declared that the topic of international responsibility was too broad and suggested a more gradual approach dealing first of all with the responsibility of states for damage caused to the persons or property of aliens.[71]

In his second report, the Special Rapporteur narrowed his research to the field of acts and omissions involving the responsibility of states for damage caused to aliens.[72] He also decided not to deal with cases of international responsibility arising out of acts or omissions of political subdivisions; according to him, the responsibility of a federal state for its member states presented no serious difficulty.[73] In 1961, however, he reversed his decision and in a revised draft included the following provision: 'The acts or omissions of political subdivisions, whatever their internal organization may be and whatever degree of legislative, judicial or administrative autonomy they enjoy, shall be imputable to the State'.[74]

Did he mean by this that a federal state has to answer for the acts or omissions of its member states contravening their own international obligations? Apparently not, for in his comments he declared it to be a well established rule that acts or omissions of political subdivisions contravening the international obligations of the state were imputable to the state.[75] This seems to indicate that he was not concerned with acts or omissions of member states contravening their own international obligations.

In 1962, Mr Amador left the Commission, and as his reports had not been discussed or approved by the Commission, the question arose whether the subject should not be taken up *ex novo*. At its

[67] *Yearbook of the International Law Commission*, 1956, ii, 173 (Doc. A/CN.4/96).
[68] *Ibid.*, p. 219 (Basis of discussion no. II, para 1).
[69] *Ibid.*, p. 220 (Basis of discussion no. II, para. 2).
[70] *Ibid.*, p. 220 (Basis of discussion no. II, para. 3).
[71] *Ibid.*, p. 221.
[72] 1957, *Yearbook of the International Law Commission*, ii, 104 (Doc. A/CN.4/106).
[73] *Ibid.*, p. 108.
[74] 1961 *Yearbook of the International Law Commission*, ii, 48 (Doc. A/CN.4/134, add. 1).
[75] *Ibid.*, p. 52.

637th meeting, on 7 May 1962, the Commission decided to set up a Sub-Committee on State Responsibility to study the scope of a new approach to the topic.[76] The Sub-Committee reported in 1963 and recommended that the Commission should give priority to the definition of the general rules governing the international responsibility of the states.[77] It also recommended that the question of the responsibility of subjects of international law other than states should be left aside.[78] This suggestion, approved by the Commission, effectively excluded from its consideration problems arising out of acts or omissions of states members of a federation contravening their own international obligations.

Among international lawyers, the lack of consensus is immediately evident. Most of them agree that acts or omissions of political subdivisions which contravene the international obligations of the federal state are imputable to that state. They differ, however, in their appreciation of the federal state's responsibility for acts or omissions of its political subdivisions contrary to their own international obligations. Some of them consider the federal state directly and exclusively responsible for the fulfilment of these obligations.[79] Others, like Triepel, prefer to speak of an indirect and subsidiary responsibility of the federal state.[80]. Finally, writers such as O'Connell do not reject the possibility that member states of federations may be exclusively responsible for the fulfilment of their own international obligations.[81] Thus, even among international lawyers, considerable uncertainty exists as to the responsibility of a federal state for the conduct of its subdivisions acting as subjects of international law.

It is then far from clear whether a federal state is responsible, under customary international law, for the fulfilment of international obligations undertaken by its member states. When reference is made to the responsibility of federal states for their member states, what is meant basically is that acts or omissions of political subdivisions contravening the international obligations of the federal state are imputable to the latter. This follows from the view that a state 'cannot evade its responsibility by invoking its muni-

---

[76] *Yearbook of the International Law Commission,* 1962, i, 45 and ii, 191.
[77] *Yearbook of the International Law Commission,* 1963, ii, 227–59.
[78] *Ibid.,* p. 228, note 2.
[79] See for instance Accioly, 'Principes généraux de la responsabilité internationale, d'après la doctrine et la jurisprudence', 96 *HR* (1959), 349 at 388–91.
[80] Triepel, *Völkerrecht und Landesrecht,* 1899, p. 368.
[81] O'Connell, *International Law,* 1965, i, 318.

cipal law'.[82] On the other hand, the undertaking of international obligations by member states themselves appears to raise separate issues.

Before focusing our attention more closely on this problem, it remains to examine the legal consequences arising when a federal state is held responsible for the acts or omissions of its political subdivisions. The basic duty, of course, is to make reparation, but this may take different forms.[83] In most cases, the federal state will be asked to make pecuniary reparation. In some instances, it may be required to make such modifications to its legislation as are necessary to ensure the fulfilment of its international obligations.

In the *Hawaiian Claims*,[84] which arose out of alleged mistreatment of some Englishmen by Hawaiian police, Attorney General Griggs of the United States put forward an ingenious theory concerning the responsibility of a central government in a federal state for claims against the regional or state governments. He stated that:

> If there is a distinct and independent civilized government, potent and capable within its territorial limits, conducted by a separate executive, not acting as the mere representative by appointment of the distant central administration, I perceive no reason to doubt that such government rather than the central authority should respond out of its separate assets to any valid claim upon it, whether accruing in the past, presently accruing or to accrue in the future.[85]

And he went on:

> It is beyond question that a claim on foreign behalf against a State or Territory of the Union would be presented through, rather than to, the State Department; that is, it would be presented to the local and not to the Federal Government, and finally be adjusted and recognized or denied by the former, although the Federal Government is the international representative, and in various ways, short of coercion of a State—as unnecessary, ordinarily, as it is impossible—admits a certain liability.[86]

The tribunal disallowed the Claims against the United States, but not on the grounds argued by Griggs.[87]

However, a subsequent incident which arose in 1934 in Australia

[82] This is the view adopted in the final report of the League of Nations Codification Conference of 1930: see above p. 000.
[83] *Case Concerning the Factory at Chorzow*, Merits, 1928, *PCIJ*, A-17, p. 28.
[84] Nielsen's *Report* (GB–US, 1910) pp. 85–161.
[85] See Deener, *The US Attorneys General and International Law*, 1957, p. 320.
[86] *Ibid.*, p. 320.
[87] *Ibid.*, p. 321.

would appear to give countenance to Griggs' theory. In January of that year, serious riots against Greek, Yugoslav and Italian immigrants took place in Western Australia.[88] Shortly after this, claims for indemnity were made upon the Commonwealth Government on behalf of Italy, Yugoslavia and Greece. The attitude of the Commonwealth to the claims by the three countries was thus stated in the Commonwealth Parliament: 'The responsibility for the preservation of law and order, and as a consequence, the liability for the payment of compensation for any loss sustained in cases of civil disturbances were matters for the Government of Western Australia'.[89] Thereupon, the claims made by the consuls on behalf of their nationals were directed to the Government of Western Australia who handled them until a satisfactory solution was reached.[90]

In fact, it makes little difference, from the point of view of international law, whether a claim for indemnity is presented to the federal government, or through the federal government to the states. The important point is that foreign powers are not obliged to take into consideration the constitutional difficulties of federal states. In the case of *Jesus Rodriguez v. Brazil*, decided by the *Tribunal Arbitral Brasileiro-Boliviano*, the Umpire held Brazil responsible for the action of local authorities of the State of Amazonas, but ignored the request of the Brazilian arbitrator that he save the rights of the nation to require the State of Amazonas to indemnify it for paying the claim.[91] The internal problems of federations, in other words, did not concern the tribunal. But of course, if foreign powers have no objection, they are free to negotiate their claims for indemnity with the member states themselves.

Federal states may also be required to make in their legislation such modifications as are necessary to ensure the fulfilment of their international obligations. As was said in the *Montijo* Arbitration, 'the legislation of the Republic must be adapted to the treaty, not the treaty to the laws'.[92] But this, in a federation, is not always easy.

In most cases, the federal government has the constitutional power to give effect to its treaty obligations. Sometimes, this power results from a judicial interpretation of the constitution. In the United States, for instance, the Supreme Court has relied upon

---

[88] See Evatt, 'International responsibility of states in the case of riots or mob violence', 9 *Australian Law Journal* (1935), Supp., p. 9 ff.

[89] *Ibid.*, p. 10.

[90] *Ibid.*, p. 12.

[91] Ralston, *The Law and Procedure of International Tribunals*, Supplement to 1926 rev. edn, 1936, p. 174.

[92] *The Montijo*, Moore, *International Arbitrations*, ii, 1440.

Article VI of the constitution—which declares that all treaties made under the authority of the United States 'shall be the supreme law of the land'—to hold that Congress has the power to implement a Canadian–US treaty, the subject matter of which was beyond the normal legislative powers of the federal government.[93] In the *Curtiss-Wright* case,[94] it was asserted that the right and power of the United States in the field of international relations were equal to the right and power of the other members of the international family.[95] In Australia, similar results have been reached through the judicial interpretation of the 'External Affairs' clause of the constitution.[96] Sometimes, the power to implement treaties is made explicit in the federal constitution itself. In India, for instance, Article 253 of the Constitution stipulates that:

> Notwithstanding anything in the foregoing provisions of this Chapter, Parliament has power to make any law for the whole or for any part of the territory of India for implementing any treaty, agreement of convention with any other country or countries or any decision made at any international conference, association or other body.[97]

In Austria, the federal Constitution specifies that the provinces 'are obliged within the limits of their independent competence to take such measures as are necessary for the execution of international treaties.'[98] In case of failure to do so, the competence to enact the necessary legislation passes to the federation.

In certain federations, however, the federal government is not in a position to ensure the fulfilment of all its treaty obligations. This is the case with Canada, for example. In 1937, in the *Labour Conventions* case, the Privy Council decided that international obligations undertaken by the federal government over subjects belonging to the Provinces could not be implemented internally without the cooperation of the latter.[99] The decision was arrived at without any consideration of the responsibility of the federal government in international law. More recently, in 1957, the Constitutional Court of Germany adopted a similar attitude. In the *Reichskonkordat* case, it held that:

---

[93] *Missouri v. Holland*, 252 US 416 (1920).
[94] *US v. Curtiss-Wright Export Corporation*, 299 US 304 (1936).
[95] Although certain decisions vaguely refer to possible limitations of the federal government's treaty power (*Geofroy v. Riggs*, 133 US 258, 267 (1890) and *Reid v. Covert*, 354 US 1, 16–17 (1957)) no treaty has ever been held unconstitutional in the United States: see below, chapter 5, pp. 160–161.
[96] *The King v. Burgess*, ex parte Henry, 55 *CLR* 608 (1936).
[97] Basu, *Shorter Constitution of India*, 3rd edn, 1960, pp. 478–9.
[98] Article 16 of the Austrian Constitution.
[99] *Attorney-General for Canada v. Attorney for Ontario* [1937] AC 326.

Legal obligations deriving from an international treaty which is binding upon a federal State can create legal duties for its constituent States only in accordance with the provisions of constitutional law... We need not consider the question whether the German Federal Republic is liable to the Holy See for the acts of a *Land* which are contrary to the provisions of the Concordat.[100]

In both cases, the international obligations undertaken were not fulfilled.

The very fact that a federal government is empowered to give effect to its treaty obligations does not mean that it can ensure the fulfilment of other types of international obligations. In 1841 a person named McLeod was arrested by the police of New York and charged with the murder of certain people killed in the destruction of the *Caroline*, an American ship sent to help revolutionaries in Canada;[101] his case was taken up by Great Britain who argued that the destruction of the *Caroline* was an act of state and demanded his immediate release. The federal government was unable to accede to this demand, arguing that the case was pending in a State Court; but it made similar situations thenceforth impossible by extending the federal *Habeas Corpus* Act to such cases. In 1880 Secretary of State Evarts answered a Chinese request for the arrest and punishment of all those who had participated in an attack on certain Chinese at Rock Springs, Colorado, in the following words:

I need only remind you that the powers of direct intervention on the part of this Government are limited by the Constitution of the United States.... It will thus be perceived that so far as the arrest and punishment of the guilty parties may be concerned, it is a matter which, in the present aspect of the case, belongs exclusively to the government and authorities of the State of Colorado.[102]

In 1891 some Italian nationals were lynched in New Orleans.[103] The government of the United States refused at first to be held responsible for this, saying that the matter was strictly within the competence of the State of Louisiana. Later, pressed by Italy, it agreed to pay damages. But it never acceded to the Italian demand for the punishment of the offenders; only Louisiana could do this.

In some cases, a federal government legally empowered to give

---

[100] *International Law Reports*, 1957, p. 592 at p. 594.
[101] Moore, *Digest of International Law*, vi, 261.
[102] See Moore, *Digest of International Law*, vi, pp. 820–1.
[103] See Donot, *De la responsabilité de l'Etat fédéral à raison des actes des États particuliers*, 1912, pp. 55–68.

effect to its treaty obligations may find it impossible in practice to do so. In 1894 a treaty was made between Japan and the United States, which prescribed equality of treatment for Japanese citizens in America.[104] Some years later the school authorities of San Francisco decided that Japanese children would be admitted only to special schools. This was clearly in violation of the treaty of 1894, and Japan complained about it to the federal government. Because education was a subject reserved to the states, the latter could only try to persuade the school authorities to modify their decision. In the end, the school authorities yielded, but only after Japan had agreed to limit the immigration of Japanese subjects to the United States.

The fact must be recognized that federal governments cannot always make in their legislation such modifications as may be required to ensure the fulfilment of their international obligations. This is especially the case when these modifications imply an amendment to the constitution. In almost every federation, as already seen, the process of amending the constitution is different from that of amending the ordinary laws of the federation.[105] In Switzerland and Australia, an amendment to the constitution requires the consent of a majority of electors voting in a majority of the states.[106] In the United States, an amendment must be ratified either by the legislature of three-fourths of the states, or by conventions in three-fourths of the states.[107] In Canada it even requires an Act of the British Parliament.[108] In view of this, it is not surprising that federal governments prefer to default on their international obligations rather than try to amend the constitution. Sometimes, federalism and international law are simply not reconcilable.[109]

The result is that, in certain cases, foreign powers may find it preferable to deal directly with those member states of federations which are endowed with a degree of international competence. In 1965, for instance, the Holy See entered into treaty relations with the *Land* of Lower-Saxony after the latter had violated with im-

---

[104] See Donot, 68–88.
[105] See Wheare, *Federal Government*, 4th edn., 1963, p. 209 ff; Livingston, *Federalism and Constitutional Change*, 1956.
[106] Swiss Constitution; arts. 118–123; Australian Constitution: art. 128.
[107] United States Constitution, article 5.
[108] See Gérin-Lajoie, *Constitutional Amendment in Canada*, 1950.
[109] See Looper, 'Federal state clauses in multilateral instruments', 32 *BYIL* (1955–56), 162 at 203. The problems arising out of the division of competence in federal States are examined at pp. 152–171; a study of existing remedies follows at pp. 171–202.

punity the *Reich* Concordat of 1933.[110] It then becomes important
to know who is responsible for the fulfilment of the obligations
undertaken, the member state or the federation?

The responsibility of the member states as subjects of international law

Political subdivisions of federal states become internationally obligated primarily through their international agreements.[111] As the
obligations are assumed in their own name and in their own interest, they should normally be held exclusively responsible for their
fulfilment. It is a well-known rule of international law that international agreements bind only the contracting parties. In the case
of the *Free Zones of Upper Savoy and the District of Gex*, the
Permanent Court of International Justice held that Article 435 of
the Treaty of Versailles was not binding on Switzerland since the
latter was not a party to this Treaty.[112] In order to hold a federal
state responsible for the international engagements of its subdivisions, therefore, one must prove that a special rule of international
law to that effect exists.

There are no international decisions stating explicitly that a
federal state must answer for the international obligations of its
member states. However, no international tribunal has ever dealt
with claims arising out of the non-fulfilment of their international
obligations by political subdivisions of states. In the *Montijo*
arbitration, the Umpire made it clear that he was dealing with
obligations of the central state and not with obligations of the
separate states of the Union. He said: 'As regards the first point
it cannot be denied that the treaties under which the residence of
foreigners in Colombia is authorized, and their rights during such
residence defined and assured, are made with the general government, and not with the separate States of which the Union is
composed.'[113] But considering the question of responsibility, he
added:

[110] See *Herder-Korrespondenz*, April 1965, p. 292; see also: Lucien-Brun,
'Une nouvelle étape dans le droit concordataire', *Ann. fr. dr. int.* (1965), p.
113; Rousseau, 'Commentaires sur le concordat entre le St-Siège et la Basse-
Saxe', 69 *RGDIP* (1965), 768.
[111] If such subdivisions have foreign delegations accredited to them,
then obligations under customary international law also arise: see Triepel,
Droit international et droit interne, 1920, p. 363.
[112] *Free Zones of Upper Savoy and the District of Gex*, Judgment (1932),
1932 *PCIJ*, A/B 46, p. 141.
[113] Moore, *International Arbitrations*, ii, 1439.

In the event, then, of a violation of a treaty stipulation, it is evident that a recourse must be had to the entity with which the international engagements were made. There is no one else to whom application can be directed. For treaty purposes the separate States are non-existent; they have parted with a certain defined portion of their inherent sovereignty, and can only be dealt with through their accredited representative or delegate, the federal or general government.[114]

Implicitly, this meant that member states of federations competent to deal directly with foreign powers and to undertake international obligations in their own name were responsible for the fulfilment of such obligations. In the *de Brissot* case, a similar attitude was adopted. Among other reasons for holding that the member states of Venezuela could not be held responsible for their breaches of international law, Mr Findlay, Umpire, pointed out that they could make no treaties, and could break none.[115]

Proceeding by analogy, the conclusion that member states of federations have to answer for their own international engagements may be drawn from the *Brown* case, which examined the relation of suzerainty between Great Britain and South Africa. In the course of the decision, the following remarks were made:

[U]nder the 1884 Convention it is plain that Great Britain as suzerain, reserved only a qualified control over the relations of the South African Republic with foreign powers. The Republic agreed to conclude no 'treaty or engagement' with any State or nation other than the Orange Free State, without the approval of Great Britain, but such approval was to be taken for granted if the latter did not give notice that the treaty was in conflict with British interests within six months.... The relation of suzerain did not operate to render Great Britain liable for the acts complained of.[116]

It may be argued that these remarks do not apply to member states of federations. Verdross, for instance, refuses to see a parallel between the situation of South Africa in 1895, which he equates with that of a protected state, and the situation of member states of federations.[117] In the first case, he says, two distinct territories exist; in the second case, there is only one. This means that a foreign power cannot retaliate against a member state of a federation without affecting the federal state itself; with a protected state, on the contrary, this is possible. The argument, however, suffers from a serious weakness. It ignores the fact that foreign powers

[114] *Ibid.*, ii, 1439–40.
[115] Moore, *International Arbitrations*, iii, 2971.
[116] *Robert E. Brown (US) v. Great Britain*, 6 *RIAA*, 120 at 131.
[117] Verdross, 'Theorie der mittelbaren Staatenhaftung', 1 *Österreichische Zeitschrift für Offentliches Recht* (1946) 388. at 402 and 413.

are free to refuse recognition to member states of federations whose international status, as defined by the relevant constitutional texts, involves exclusive responsibility for their acts, in the same way as they are free to refuse recognition to protected states whose international status, as defined by the relevant international agreements, leaves them with a limited responsibility for their conduct.[118] Foreign powers that choose deliberately to deal with member states of federations, when they are aware that there will be no recourse against the federal state, cannot change their mind subsequently and hold such federal state responsible. Even if one accepts the validity of Verdross's argument, it still remains that there are no international decisions suggesting, explicitly or implicitly, the responsibility of a federal state for the international engagements of its political subdivisions.

The practice of states offers a little more evidence of the existence of such a responsibility. There are some indications that the Imperial Government of Germany accepted responsibility for the treaties of extradition of its member states. In 1892, it was stated before the *Reichstag* that the *Reich* was responsible for a denial of extradition by a member state notwithstanding the fact that the matter was regulated by a treaty of the latter.[119] Such responsibility, however, resulted more from a deliberate choice of the German authorities than from an international duty imposed on them. This, at least, is what emerges from a declaration of the State Secretary for Internal Affairs made on 12 June 1900, before the *Reichstag*, in which he stated that if an individual State of the Empire used its external competence in a manner detrimental to the security of the Empire, the Imperial Government had the right and duty to intervene.[120]

It would seem also that the complaints of foreign states bound by treaties of extradition with the member states of Germany were addressed to the Imperial Government.[121] Yet, in other instances, similar complaints were addressed directly to the individual states concerned. In 1901 the survival of a bankruptcy treaty with Baden was contested in Switzerland on the grounds that it was not respected by the Courts of Baden. The Swiss Federal Council raised the question at the intergovernmental level and reported in 1902 that Baden and Switzerland were in agreement that the treaty was

---

[118] *Spanish Zone of Morocco Claims* (1924), 2 *RIAA*, 615 at 648–9.

[119] See Schoen, 'Die völkerrechtliche Haftung der Staaten aus unerlaubten Handlungen', 10 *Zeitschrift für Völkerrecht* (1917–18), Supp, 2, p. 104, n. 8.

[120] See Pohl, 'Die Zuständigkeitsverteilung zwischen Reich und Ländern im Auslieferungswesen', 14 *Zeitschrift für Völkerrecht* (1927–28), 1, 9.

[121] See Triepel, *Droit international et droit interne*, 1920, p. 357, n. 3.

still in force.[122] As for the claims of the member states against foreign powers, they were sometimes presented by a representative of the federal government acting also as representative of the member state concerned.[123] In other circumstances, they were transmitted directly to the foreign power: in May 1879, the Minister of Justice and Foreign Affairs of Baden communicated directly with the Swiss Government demanding that a stop be put to certain works being done in Lake Constance because they were in contradiction with the treaty rights of Baden.[124]

On the whole, it seems that the individual States of Germany were directly responsible for their international engagements, but that, at the same time, the Imperial Government, in view of its acknowledged control over their external activity, had to answer in a subsidiary way for their breaches of international law. It is difficult to conclude from this that federal states are responsible in all cases for the international engagements of their member states.

The comparison with the international practice relating to autonomous states leads to more or less similar conclusions. The case of the former Federation of Rhodesia and Nyasaland in particular is interesting. As already seen, the Federation had received a wide delegation of external affairs power from the United Kingdom, but subject to certain reservations consistent with the United Kingdom's 'ultimate responsibility'.[125] Despite this situation, the United Kingdom refused in 1958 all responsibility for an incident in the Federation which involved certain Indian diplomats, considering it 'properly' an affair between India and the Federation.[126] The precise motives for this attitude are unknown. But it has been pointed out with reason that as Commonwealth countries approach independence, the responsibility of the United Kingdom for their external relations 'becomes attenuated, sometimes almost to the vanishing point'.[127]

In the normal case, however, it would seem that each time the United Kingdom has entrusted autonomous states with a limited

---

[122] See *Feuille Fédérale*, 1902, 3, 859, and Beisswingert, 'Die Einwirkung bundesstaatlicher Kompetenzverschiebungen aus völkerrechtliche Verträge under besonderer Berücksichtung der deutschen Entwicklung', 1960, unpublished thesis, Munich, p. 32. In its report, the Swiss Federal Council declared: 'Um diese Zweifel zu heben, haben wir uns direkt an die badische Regierung gewendet und die bestimmte Auskunft erhalten, dass dieselbe den genamten Staatsverträge zur Zeit als in Kraft befindlich noch betrachtet.'

[123] See *Terlinden v. Ames* (1902), 184 US 270.

[124] See Doka, *Der Bodensee im internationalen Recht*, 1927, p. 89, n. 217.

[125] See above, p. 69.

[126] See Fawcett, *The British Commonwealth in International Law*, 1963, p. 114.

[127] *Idem.*

degree of external competence, it retained ultimate responsibility for their external relations. To be more precise, the autonomous state assumed direct responsibility for its international commitments, while the United Kingdom remained vicariously responsible for its undertakings. The Federation of Rhodesia and Nyasaland, for example, assumed direct responsibility, as a contracting party of GATT, for obligations arising from the treaty itself as well as certain protocols.[128] Yet, the Monckton Commission charged to review the constitution of the Federation noted in 1960 the ultimate responsibility of the United Kingdom with regard to such undertakings.[129] Similarly, the 1959 letters entrusting a limited external competence to the autonomous State of Singapore contained specific reference to the United Kingdom's ultimate responsibility:

> 3. Her Majesty's Government in the United Kingdom, in view of their general responsibility for the external affairs of Singapore, will be informed by the Singapore Government of the initiation and progress of any proposals or negotiations...
> Since in international law ultimate responsibility rests with Her Majesty's Government in the United Kingdom...[130]

But does this mean that a sovereign state must answer in all cases, directly or indirectly, for the international dealings of its territories? Writing about the participation in various international organizations of Surinam, the Netherlands Antilles and New Guinea, all members of the Kingdom of the Netherlands, Van Panhuys asserted in 1958 that it entirely depended 'on the contents of the treaty whether, apart from the rights and obligations of the Countries, the Kingdom as a whole remains responsible—either directly or vicariously—for the fulfilment of some or all of the treaty obligations incumbent on the Countries'.[131] This passage appears to confirm the conclusions already reached concerning federal states. The existence of an absolute rule is not affirmed, it being left to the interested parties to settle among themselves the question of responsibility. However, Van Panhuys does not indicate the criteria which should be applied in determining whether or not the sovereign state is responsible.

As far as federal states are concerned, the decisive factor, in

---

[128] *United Nations Treaty Series*, vol. 226, p. 342; *UN Treaty Series*, vol. 321, p. 263.

[129] Cmnd 1150 (UK), p. 75.

[130] Lauterpacht, 'The contemporary practice of the United Kingdom in the field of international law—survey and comments, IX', 10 *ICLQ* (1961), 577.

[131] Van Panhuys, 'The international aspects of the reconstruction of the Kingdom of the Netherlands in 1954', 5 *Netherlands International Law Review* (1958) 1 at 25.

each particular instance, appears to be the federal constitution itself. This will be exemplified by the following incident. The international shipping treaty of 1868 concerning Lake Constance obliged the riparian states to maintain necessary installations for the security of navigation. In 1957 the installations in the German ports had become inadequate and Switzerland complained about it to the German riparians Baden-Württemberg and Bavaria, and finally, in May 1957, to the foreign ministry in Bonn. The Note acknowledged the difficulties concerning the internal distribution of powers in the German Constitution, and complained that no one was certain who, on the German side, was to be regarded as the other party to the treaty, and therefore responsible for maintaining the installations. The Swiss position was one of indifference towards the question of conflict of functions, but one of concern that Swiss rights should seemingly be impaired.[132]

Such an attitude is very close to the one adopted by the German Government in 1929 in its answer to the League of Nations questionnaire. It declared first of all that 'in the case of a union of States, the co-existence of several subjects of international law should not cause a claim to remain in suspense'.[133] Then, it added that responsibility could only be established according to the circumstances of the case. The decisive factor was the manner in which, within the union, the various subjects of international law decided who was responsible for foreign affairs. In Hungary's answer, a similar link was also established between international responsibility and international competence.[134]

Switzerland's answer to the same questionnaire is sometimes relied upon as evidence that a federal state is responsible for the international engagements of its member states.[135] In short, it said that a state was liable for unlawful acts committed by political entities which depended on it, or whom it represented. Thus, according to Article 10 (1) of the Swiss Constitution, the official relations between the Cantons and foreign governments were maintained through the Federal Council; this had always been interpreted to mean that the Confederation was solely responsible for acts contrary to international law committed by a Canton. But the Swiss answer implied that political subdivisions able to communi-

---

[132] See Beisswingert, p. 89; these facts are also related in O'Connell, 'State succession and Entry into a composite Relationship', 39 *BYIL* 1963, p. 115.

[133] League of Nations, *Conference for the Codification of International Law*, 1929, Bases of Discussion, iii, 121.

[134] *Ibid.*, p. 122.

[135] See Verdross, 'Theorie der mittelbaren Staatenhaftung'. 21 *Zeitschrift für öffentliches Recht* (1941), 283 at 287.

cate directly with foreign states were personally responsible for the fulfilment of their own international obligations. It is a mistake, therefore, to rely upon it to prove that a federal state is responsible for the international dealing of its member states.

In determining whether or not the political subdivisions of a federal state are responsible for their own international engagements, it is also important to consider the attitude adopted by foreign states. It has been stated in the previous chapter that the decision to accept Ukraine and Byelorussia as original members of the United Nations was prompted more by political reasons than by an objective consideration of the federal structure of the Soviet Union. Nevertheless, as members of the United Nations, Ukraine and Byelorussia have assumed international obligations of their own; if they do not fulfil these, sanctions such as expulsion or suspension can be applied directly against them.[136] This means that they are individually responsible for their conduct as members of the United Nations. Such responsibility, however, can be explained only in terms of their recognition by the other members of the United Nations.

In certain treaties between member states of federations and foreign powers, provisions are included for the creation of an international tribunal to which disputes concerning the treaty are referred. Thus the Austrian–Bavarian Treaties of October 1950 relating to the diversion of common waters provide for the reference of disputes between the two parties to an arbitral tribunal whose decision is final.[137] Similar provisions can be found in Article 22 of the Treaty of 1950 between Luxembourg and the State of Rhine-Palatinate.[138] In such instances, any responsibility of the federal state for the international engagement of its member state is excluded in practice.[139] But a solution of this type obviously requires the assent of the foreign power concerned.

To turn now to the doctrine of international law, one must distinguish between three different tendencies. Certain writers, such as Donot, Accioly, Fitzmaurice and Ghosh, consider that a federal

---

[136] See Kelsen, *The Law of the United Nations*, 1950, p. 710.

[137] The text of the relevant articles may be found in Berber, *Rivers in International Law*, 1959, p. 268, n. 26.

[138] See Bernhardt, *Der Abschluss völkerrechtlicher Verträge im Bundesstaat*, 1957, p. 171, n. 693.

[139] In theory, the problem of the responsibility of the federal state for its member state could still arise if the decision of the arbitral tribunal was not executed. But in view of Article 25 of the Constitution of the Federal Republic—which provides that the general rules of international law form part of the federal law and that 'they take precedence over the laws and directly create rights and duties for the inhabitants of the federal territory'—the possibility of this happening in practice is remote.

state is responsible for the obligations undertaken by its member states because the latter have no standing in international law.[140] In other words, the obligations are undertaken in the name of the member states, but they are in fact obligations of the federal state itself. However, this view must be rejected, as the overwhelming evidence shows that member states of federations may indeed become subjects of international law.[141] Furthermore, the reasoning of these writers is not very convincing. Donot, for instance, asserts that a federal state is responsible in all circumstances for the conduct of its member states because they enjoy no international status; but in the last pages of his work, he adds: 'Il en est ainsi, non seulement lorsque les Etats particuliers n'ont aucune personnalité internationale, auquel cas il est bien évident que l'Etat fédéral seul peut être mis en cause, mais encore lorsque ces Etats possèdent une certaine personnalité internationale, laquelle est toujours très restreinte.'[142] This contradicts the very basis of his argument. Similarly, Ghosh speaks of the sole and exclusive responsibility of the federal state for its member states, and then goes on to say: 'Where the member-States have limited treaty-making power, foreign nations invariably hold the Federal Government ultimately, if not immediately, responsible for breaches of their treaty obligations.'[143] In such circumstances, apparently, Ghosh is not certain that the federal state is solely and exclusively responsible for its member states.

In 1937 Starke also wrote that member states of federations and vassal states had no status which enabled them to act internationally; this, in his opinion, meant that the federal state and the protector state could claim to stand internationally for them.[144] In the sixth edition of his *Introduction to International Law*, published in 1967, he again declares: 'The Federal State and the protecting State are responsible for the conduct respectively of the State Member and the protected State, inasmuch as in the realm of foreign affairs they alone are recognized as having capacity to enter into relations with other States.'[145] But what would Starke

---

[140] Donot, p. 102; Accioly, 'Principes généraux de la responsabilité d'après la doctrine et la jurisprudence', 96 *HR* (1959), pp. 388–91; Fitzmaurice, *Yearbook of the International Law Commission*, 1958, ii, 24; Ghosh, *Treaties and Federal Constitutions: their mutual impact*, 1961, p. 82.

[141] See above, chapter 2, pp. 36–47.

[142] Donot, p. 102. For a similar criticism of Donot's reasoning, see Klein, *Die mittelbare Haftung im Völkerrecht*, 1941, p. 172, note 35.

[143] Ghosh, p. 82.

[144] Starke, 'Imputability in international delinquencies', 19 *BYIL* (1938), 104 at 116.

[145] Starke, *An Introduction to International Law*, 6th edn, 1967, p. 255.

say if certain member states of federations or protected states were recognized as having the capacity to enter into international relations with other states? Should not his reasoning lead him to the conclusion that in such circumstances they are responsible for their own engagements?

A second group of publicists does not deny that member states of federations can assume their own international obligations, but considers nevertheless the federal state responsible for such obligations. They do not always agree among themselves, however, as to the basis of this responsibility.

The most usual argument is that foreign powers have no means of coercion against member states of federations as such. The first publicists to use this approach were German writers commenting on the German Constitution of 1871. Laband, von Kirchenheim, von Sarwey and Haenel, for instance, all agreed that the Government of the *Reich* had a duty to intervene in a dispute between a member state and a foreign power, because only the *Reich* had the right to wage war.[146] This meant that the individual states had no means of enforcing their rights against foreign powers, and that foreign powers could not use force against the member states without involving the federal government. In other words, the individual states of Germany had no active or passive right of action on the international plane.

The argument of the German constitutionalists was taken up by Triepel in 1899.[147] He recognized that the individual states of Germany were directly responsible for their own international engagements, but claimed that there was also an indirect responsibility of the federal state for such engagements. He reasserted that member states of federations had no active or passive right of action on the international plane and that foreign powers as a result could not obtain the respect of their rights without involving the federal state itself. Triepel referred for this view to the opinion of Laband, von Sarwey, Haenel and von Kirchenheim, and also to that of Gaupp, *Civilprozessordnung*, ii, 3rd edn, p. 318, n. 10.[148] Apart from a passing reference to the fact that complaints made by foreign powers bound by treaties of extradition with the member states were addressed to the Imperial Government,[149] he did

---

[146] Haenel, *Deutsches Staatsrecht*, 1892, i, 554; Laband, *Staatsrecht des deutschen Reiches*, 3rd edn, 1895, i, 640; von Kirchenheim, *Lehrbuch des deutschen Staatsrechts*, 1887, p. 432; von Sarwey, *Staatsrecht des Königreichs Württemberg*, 1883, ii, p. 88.

[147] Triepel, *Völkerrecht und Landesrecht*, 1899, trans. into French, *Droit international et droit interne*, 1920.

[148] Triepel, *Völkerrecht und Landesrecht*, pp. 367–8.

[149] *Ibid.*, p. 360, note 4.

not give any practical example of this responsibility. In 1917 Schoen came to similar conclusions. He referred to the view of Triepel, Laband and Haenel, mentioning also the admission by the Secretary of State for Internal Affairs in 1892 that the Imperial Government was responsible for denials of extradition by the member states.[150]

In his study on the subject of indirect responsibility in international law, published in 1941, Klein also accepted that a federal state was indirectly responsible for the international dealings of its member states.[151] He showed that this was the general view of the doctrine of international law—mentioning in the process the names of Triepel and Schoen and those of numerous other writers[152]— and went on to prove that it was also the attitude adopted in the practice of international law. He referred for this to the *McLeod* case, the *Youmans* case, the *Pellat* case, the *Mallen* case as well as to the diplomatic incident which followed the lynching of Italian nationals in New Orleans.[153] But none of these instances concerned member states of federations endowed with international personality. It cannot, therefore, be said that he proved that a federal state had to answer for the international dealings of its member states.

The flaw in Klein's argument was immediately denounced by Verdross. In his article entitled 'Theorie der mittelbaren Staatenhaftung', also published in 1941, he rejected as mistaken the examples of indirect responsibility mentioned by Klein.[154] But Verdross did not deny that a federal state was indirectly responsible for the international engagements of its member states. He mentioned as evidence of this the answer of Switzerland to the League of Nations questionnaire.[155] Germany's point of view, he admitted, was to the contrary but, according to him, it reflected neither the established practice nor the opinion of most German publicists.[156] He also referred, by analogy, to the 1871 Strousberg incident between Germany and Turkey. This concerned a contract between a German citizen and the vassal state of Romania. Strous-

---

[150] Schoen, 'Die völkerrechtliche Haftung der Staaten aus unerlaubten Handlungen', 10 *Zeitschrift für Völkerrecht* (1917), supp. 2, p. 104.
[151] Klein, pp. 127 and 194 ff.
[152] *Ibid.*, pp. 195-7.
[153] *Ibid.*, pp. 201-9.
[154] Verdross, 'Theorie der mittelbaren Staatenhaftung', 21 *Zeitschrift für öffentliches Recht* (1941), 283 at 288; the article is reproduced more or less in the same form in 1 *Österreichische Zeit für öff. Recht* (1946), 388.
[155] Verdross, 21 *Zeit. für öff Recht* (1941), p. 287.
[156] *Ibid.*, p. 287-8.

berg's claim was taken up by Germany and presented to Turkey, the suzerain state. The immediate answer of Turkey was that the matter concerned Romania only. The reply from Germany was dictated by Bismarck himself; he declared that there was no way of communicating directly with Romania, that coercion could not be used against the vassal state without involving Turkey and concluded that Turkey had to answer for its vassal state. But in the end, the matter was solved between the original parties, Strousberg and Romania.[157]

Satisfied that there existed a rule of international law obliging federal states to answer for the international dealings of their political subdivisions, Verdross then undertook to find a theoretical explanation for this. He rejected first of all what he called the 'representation theory', which asserts that a state is responsible for the conduct of another state which it represents externally; in the case of a member state of federation dealing directly with foreign powers, there was obviously no question of representation.[158] He also rejected the 'control theory' enunciated in the *Brown* case for reasons already discussed.[159] Verdross settled in the end for the 'interference theory' used by Bismarck to declare Turkey responsible for its vassal state Romania. He admitted, however, that the prohibition against the use of force contained in Article 2 of the United Nations Charter made his theory obsolete in practice and concluded that federal states might cease to be indirectly responsible in the future for the international engagements of their member states.[160]

Since the last war, other international law writers have used the interference theory to explain that a federal state is responsible in a subsidiary way for the international obligations undertaken by its member states.[161] Most of them, in fact, simply refer with

[157] *Ibid.*, p. 302; the incident is discussed more fully in the 1946 version of Verdross's article (1 *Österreichische Zeit. für öff. Recht* (1946) pp. 399–400.
[158] *Ibid.*, p. 302.
[159] *Ibid.*, p. 299; see above, p. 102.
[160] Verdross, 1 *Österreichische Zeit. für öff. Recht* (1946) pp. 416–17. He said more specifically: 'Die praktische Bedeutung dieser Theorie ist jedoch dadurch wesentlich reduziert worden, dass durch die Charter der Vereinten Nationen nicht nur der Krieg, sondern auch die militärische Repressalie völkerrechtlich verboten sind. Andere Repressalien, die der verletzte Staat auf seinem eigenen Gebiete duchführt, können aber in der Regel gegen einen als Völkerrechtssubjekt anerkannten Gliedstaat ergriffen werden, ohne in die Zuständigkeit des Gesamtstaates einzugreifen. Daher kann die Frage der mittelbaren Haftung dieses Staates für den schuldigen Gliedstaat kaum mehr aktuell werden.'
[161] Hallmayer, 'Die völkerrechtliche Stellung der deutschen Länder nach dem Bonner Grundgesetz', dissertation, Tübingen, 1954, p. 74; Kröneck, 'Die völkerrechtliche Immunität bundesstaatlicher Gliedstaaten vor aus-

approval to the writings of Verdross, Klein, Schoen and Triepel on the subject. But, recently, a new approach to the problem has been suggested.

In his 1963 book entitled *Das völkerrechtliche Delikt in der modernen Entwicklung der Völkerrechtsgemeinschaft*, Ingo von Munch examines at length the question of the responsibility of a federal state for its member states. In his opinion, there can be no doubt that a federal state is responsible for the international engagements of its member states. He finds evidence for this in the various answers to the League of Nations questionnaire, in the results of official and private codification conferences and in the fact that most international lawyers agree with this view.[162] The real problem for him concerns the nature of this responsibility: is it a direct or indirect responsibility, a cumulative or a joint and several responsibility?

Von Munch acknowledges that since the last war, at least, there is no instance of a federal state being held responsible for the international wrong of a member state acting within its international competence.[163] Reviewing the interference theory of Verdross, Schoen and Triepel, he rejects it as not convincing. According to him, some of the individual states of the German Federal Empire were represented abroad and this made it possible for foreign powers to use coercion against them without affecting at the same time the Empire as a whole.[164] Other considerations like the dependent character of the member states or the origin of the federation are not judged more rewarding. Von Munch then enumerates four solutions that he considers possible: an exclusive responsibility of the federal state, a cumulative responsibility of the federal state and the member states, a primary responsibility of the federal state and a subsidiary responsibility of the member states or, vice versa, a primary responsibility of the member states and a subsidiary responsibility of the federal state. In favour of the first solution, he mentions the findings of the various codifica-

---

ländischen Gerichten', dissertation, Munich, 1958, p. 154; Beisswingert, 'Die Einwirkung bundesstaatlicher Kompetenzverschiebungen auf völkerrechtliche Verträge under besonderer Berücksichtung der deutschen Entwicklung', dissertation, Munich, 1960, pp. 54–5; Mallmann, 'Völkerrecht und Bundesstaat', in Strupp iii. Schlochauer, *Wörterbuch des Völkerrechts*, 1962, p. 648.

[162] Von Munch, *Das völkerrechtliche Delikt in der modernen Entwicklung der Völkerrechtsgemeinschaft*, 1963, p. 242.

[163] *Ibid.*, p. 243; see also Hallmayer, p. 75 who writes: 'Ein praktischer Fall für diese mittelbare Haftung eines Bundesstaates für einen Gliedstaat ist bis jetzt noch nicht vorgekommen.'

[164] Von Munch, p. 244.

tion conferences which dealt with the subject of state responsibility: there is no mention in them of a possible responsibility of the member states for their own international obligations. But he admits that apart from the 1927 resolution of the Institut de droit international, there is no indication that such conferences had considered the particular case of member states undertaking their own international obligations.[165] Von Munch, therefore, is not convinced that a federal state is exclusively responsible for the conduct of its member states acting as subjects of international law. He also rejects the idea of a cumulative responsibility because he cannot find any legal justification for this. In the end, he opts for a primary responsibility of the member states and a subsidiary responsibility of the federal state on the grounds that it is the most rational solution.[166] In his view, it is only natural that political subdivisions acting as subjects of international law should answer directly for the breach of their international engagements; as for the federal state, it is indirectly responsible for letting them act as subjects of international law.

However, von Munch's argument is open to question. He reasons that a federal state is responsible for the international engagements of its member states because this is the view held by most international law writers, whilst not accepting himself any of their usual arguments. He refers to the findings of various codification conferences, but admits that they probably had very little to do with international obligations undertaken by member states. He also mentions the answers to the League of Nations questionnaire, and most of these asserted that a state was responsible for the conduct of another state which it represented externally; but such a situation obviously does not arise when a member state of federation deals directly with foreign powers—as Verdross himself admitted.[167] For these reasons von Munch's argument is not entirely convincing.

There is a third category of writers who accept that a federal state does not necessarily have to answer for the international engagements of its member states. In 1915, for instance, Borchard declared that the responsibility of a central government for its political subdivisions depended generally upon the extent to which the political subdivisions were constitutionally deprived of independent international personality.[168] Similarly, one can read in the eighth edition of Oppenheim's work that:

[165] *Ibid.*, p. 247–8.
[166] *Ibid.*, p. 249.
[167] See above, p. 111.
[168] Borchard, *The Diplomatic Protection of Citizens Abroad*, 1915, p. 201.

the circumstances of each case decide whether the delinquent [subordinate State] has to account for its neglect of an international duty directly to the wronged State, or whether it is the full sovereign State (suzerain, federal or protectorate-exercising State), to which the delinquent State is attached, that must bear a vicarious responsibility for the delinquency.[169]

Reuter, for his part, wrote in 1958, that it was possible to recognize in member states of federations an international status sufficient to make them responsible for their own delinquencies.[170] In 1960, Schwarzenberger asserted that a federation was responsible for the wrong of its subordinate unit 'to the extent to which the latter's international personality has ceased to exist'.[171] A similar point of view was again put forward in 1965 by O'Connell who declares: 'The federal government may or may not be responsible for breaches of international law committed by the States, depending upon whether or not the latter retain sufficient international competence.'[172]

To sum up, there is no convincing evidence to prove that federal states always remain responsible for the international engagements undertaken by their member states. The only seemingly convincing argument in support of this view is the so-called 'interference theory' adopted by Triepel, Schoen, Klein and Verdross. But Triepel and Schoen based their view exclusively on the practice prevailing in Imperial Germany—not necessarily that operating elsewhere. Schoen, for his part, relied on decisions involving member states of federations completely deprived of international status, and so did not really prove his point. Verdross, finally, referred to Switzerland's answer to the League of Nations questionnaire and also mentioned, by analogy, the Strousberg incident. As already seen, however, the exclusive responsibility of Switzerland for the international engagements of its member states was based on the fact that official relations between them and foreign governments were conducted through the federal Council.[173] In other words, Switzerland adopted the representation theory, the validity of which in the case of member states dealing directly with foreign powers was denied by Verdross himself. As for the Strousberg incident which he mentioned, it concerned a vassal state with which Germany, on the admission of Bismarck, could not communicate directly. If Romania had had a permanent representation in

---

[169] Oppenheim, *International Law*, 8th edn, ed. Lauterpacht, p. 339–40.
[170] Reuter, *Droit international public*, 1958, p. 153.
[171] Schwarzenberger, *A Manual of International Law*, i, 167.
[172] O'Connell, *International Law*, 1965, i, 318.
[173] See above, pp. 106–107.

Germany—in the same way as most German states at that time had permanent representations abroad—Bismarck would not have been compelled to address himself to Turkey. As von Munch points out, moreover, he could have threatened the use of sanctions against such representation. In any case, there is little point in taking the argument further, since Verdross himself admits that the interference theory is now obsolete.

What the evidence really suggests is that the responsibility of a federal state for the international obligations undertaken by its political subdivisions depends basically on the international status of the latter. This in turn depends on the prescriptions of the federal constitution and the attitude adopted by foreign powers towards the member states. If, as in Switzerland, the constitution does not permit official relations between member states and foreign powers, then the federal government is exclusively responsible for the international engagements of its member states. If, on the other hand, the federal constitution allows direct communications between member states and foreign powers, as did the German constitution of 1871, then the member states are directly responsible for their own international engagements. This corresponds to the attitude implicitly adopted in the *Montijo* and *de Brissot* arbitrations, and to the express attitude of Switzerland vis-à-vis the member states of Germany. It also accords with the answer of the German Government to the League of Nations questionnaire as well as with the theory adopted by most other states—namely the representation theory.

Whether or not the federal state is indirectly responsible for the international dealings of its subdivisions depends on the extent of the control that it exercises over their activity. If the member states enjoy a more or less independent international competence according to the constitution, and foreign powers agree to deal with them in full knowledge of this fact, then no indirect responsibility of the federal state arises. This view is supported by the decision of the arbitral tribunal in the *Brown* case. If, on the other hand, the federal state exercises a certain control over the external activity of its member states, as was obviously the case under the German Constitution of 1871, then an indirect responsibility of the federal state is justified.

However, foreign powers dealing with member states of federations are free to renounce any recourse that they might have against the federal state itself by agreeing to refer their claims to an arbitral tribunal. This they have done in a certain number of instances. Naturally, they remain free also not to enter into agreements with the member states of a federation when they are aware that the federal state has no control over their external activity and will not accept indirect responsibility for such agreements.

International responsibility in cases of excess of competence

A federal state is considered in international law as a sovereign entity, and is always presumed to be competent. With member states of federations, however, the situation is different. They are derived subjects of international law and their capacity as subjects depends on the extent of their international competence. Acting beyond this competence, they no longer act as subjects of international law. Therefore, it would seem, as concluded by Lauterpacht in 1953, that

> a treaty concluded by a member state in disregard of the constitution of the Federation must also be considered as having been concluded in disregard of the limitations imposed by international law upon its treaty-making power. As such it is not a treaty in the contemplation of international law. As a treaty, it is void. Moreover, as unlike in the case of protected States a State member of a Federation is not *prima facie* a subject of international law, it would seem that there is in this case no question of the treaty being merely voidable at the option of the Federal State.[174]

However, this remains to be proved.

In December 1945, the *Land* Governments of Vorarlberg and Tyrol, two member States of the Austrian federation, concluded a trade agreement with Switzerland.[175] They did so in clear violation of Article 10 (1), sub-paragraph 3, of the Austrian Constitution which vests the treaty-making power exclusively in the hands of the Federation. However, the treaty was not considered as a complete nullity. It remained valid until August 1946, when the Federal Government concluded a new trade agreement with Switzerland on behalf of Austria as a whole. The treaties of Vorarlberg and Tyrol were denounced by the *Land* Governments themselves, upon the suggestion of the central authority.

A second instance relates to a treaty concluded between Austria and Slovenia concerning the movement of Austrian tourists in Yugoslavia—a treaty whose provisions were to be extended to

---

[174] Lauterpacht, Report on the Law of Treaties, *Yearbook of the International Law Commission* (1953), ii, 139.
[175] See Seidl-Hohenveldern, 'Relation of international law to internal law in Austria', 49 *AJIL* (1955), 451 at 474.

Croatia.[176] By a Note addressed to the Austrian Government, the Yugoslav Government explained that while Slovenia and Croatia had a very large measure of autonomy, they were not subjects of international law. The Yugoslav Government agreed to conclude a treaty to the same effect binding Yugoslavia, and the matter was settled to the satisfaction of both countries.

There seems to be no other example of a member state of federation acting beyond its international competence. An interesting analogy, however, is provided by the Convention of 1899 between Great Britain and Egypt.[177] Egypt at that time was a vassal State of Turkey. By two firmans of 1879 and 1892 respectively, it had been authorized to conclude treaties of commerce and customs agreements with foreign states. But the Convention of 1899 concerned the establishment of a co-protectorate over Sudan. Quite clearly, Egypt was not competent to deal with such a matter. Nevertheless, the Convention remained in force for many years.

In the doctrine of international law, there is a strong tendency to consider as absolutely void any treaty concluded by a member state in excess of its international competence. In 1917, for instance, Schoen wrote that it was the duty of foreign powers concluding treaties with constitutional subdivisions of states to make sure that the latter had the necessary competence to deal with them.[178]. Otherwise, they might find themselves relying on an invalid treaty, with no remedy either against the federal state or the subdivisions themselves. In his 1926 dissertation dealing with agreements of Swiss cantons with foreign states, W. Schwarzenbach asserted that such agreements always had to be approved by the Federal Council; this approval created a presumption that the agreement was valid and that the federal state was responsible for the obligations undertaken. If the approval was lacking, however, there was no treaty at all and no responsibility of the federal state.[179] The point of view of Klein, in 1941, was that no responsibility could arise from a treaty entered into by a member state in excess of its international competence.[180] There was no direct responsibility of the federal state because the engagement was not its own; there was no indirect responsibility either, because the

---

[176] This incident is mentioned by Bartos in *Yearbook of the International Law Commission*, 1964, i, 229.

[177] See Despagnet, 'Chronique des faits internationaux', 6 *Rev. gén. dr. int. pub.* (1899), 169 at 191; see also Guggenheim, *Traité de droit international public*, 1953, i, 60, n. 5.

[178] Schoen, pp. 104–5.

[179] Schwarzenbach, 'Staatsverträge der Kantone mit dem Ausland', dissertation, Zurich, 1926, p. 129.

[180] Klein, pp. 176 ff.

member state could not be said to have acted on the basis of a delegated competence. As for the member state, having acted in excess of its international competence, it could not be considered as a subject of international law in these circumstances and consequently would not be held internationally responsible. More recently, in 1953, Cavaré repeated that a federal state was not bound to answer for the international engagements undertaken by its member states in excess of their external competence, as such engagements were not valid.[181]

In Strupp-Schlochauer's *Wörterbuch des Völkerrechts*, published in 1962, the question is examined again by Mallmann who concludes that member states acting in excess of their international competence do not undertake valid international obligations.[182] But he also raises the question of the good faith of the foreign powers dealing with the member states; in his view, if the member states require the assent of the federal government to bind themselves by treaties, it is to be expected that these foreign powers make sure this assent is given. The only writer to express an opinion based rather on the practice of states is Seidl-Hohenveldern.[183] Referring to the Conventions of 1945 between Switzerland and the Governments of Vorarlberg and Tyrol, he declares that even if a member state concludes a treaty with a third state without the necessary competence, the third state can rely on that treaty. But he does not say whether the federal state or the member state is responsible for its fulfilment.

On the whole, it cannot be doubted that capacity to conclude a treaty is a prerequisite for the validity of an agreement entered into by a member state of federation. In Article 5 (2) of the International Law Commission's draft articles on the law of treaties, it was clearly specified that: 'States members of a federal union may possess a capacity to conclude treaties if such capacity is admitted by the federal constitution and within the limits there laid down".[184] Although this provision was dropped eventually from the Convention adopted by the United Nations Conference on the Law of Treaties, at no stage was the close relationship existing between the capacity of member states to conclude treaties and the federal constitution put in doubt. Therefore, it may be stated confidently that an engagement undertaken by a member state with-

---

[181] Cavaré, *Le Droit international public positif*, 1953, i, 372–3.
[182] Mallmann, in Strupp-Schlochauer, iii, p. 647.
[183] Seidl-Hohenveldern, 'The legal personality of international and supranational organizations', 21 *Revue égyptienne de droit int.* (1965), 35, at 60.
[184] General Assembly, Official Records, Twenty-first session, Supp. no. 9, p. 10.

out the necessary capacity is not valid. But is it absolutely void or simply voidable? Most writers consider that it is absolutely void. Yet, as Seidl-Hohenveldern pertinently pointed out, the practice of states does not bear this out. The treaties of Switzerland with Vorarlberg and Tyrol retained their validity until denounced at a later date. Similarly, the Convention of 1899 between Great Britain and Egypt was applied for a number of years, despite the fact that Egypt lacked the competence to sign such a treaty. Lastly, if the treaty between Austria and Slovenia was never really applied, this is because it was immediately denounced by Yugoslavia. Therefore, it would seem that an agreement concluded by a member state of federation in excess of its international competence is not absolutely void, but only voidable.

The rules of international law applicable here seem to be those of good faith and estoppel.[185] If a federal union has approved a treaty concluded by one of its member states without the necessary competence, 'under international law it would be inadequate if such transgression of constitutional competences could be invoked against the validity of the component member's consent to be bound by the treaty.'[186] Similarly, it would seem that a third power who contracts with a member state in full knowledge of its lack of competence must be estopped from contesting the validity of the agreement concluded by them. If both the federal state and the third power were aware of the transgression of constitutional competence and have not denounced it, then there is no reason to doubt the validity of the agreement.

The question of responsibility now remains to be considered. The problem, as will be perceived, arises only when the treaty concluded by a member state in excess of its competence is not denounced by the federal state or third power party to it. Otherwise, no treaty exists and no question of responsibility arises. However, if the treaty is held to be valid, the following solution must prevail. Inasmuch as the member state has dealt directly with a foreign power, and has undertaken valid international obligations, it must answer for these. As for the federal state, its intervention in validating the treaty of its member state makes it indirectly responsible for the fulfilment of the obligation undertaken. This

---

[185] See Bowett, 'Estoppel before international tribunals and its relation to acquiescence', 33 *BYIL* (1957), 176; MacGibbon, 'Estoppel in international law', 7 *ICLQ* (1958), 468

[186] Steinberger, 'Constitutional subdivisions of states or unions and their capacity to conclude treaties', 27 *Zeit. für ausländisches öffentliches Recht und Völkerrecht* (1967), 427. See also Schwarzenbach, p. 129.

is in accordance with the conclusions reached previously concerning international agreements of member states.

Conclusion

The same principles which, as we have seen, govern the question of international personality in federal states, namely those of sovereignty, consent and recognition, are also applicable to the solution of the problem of international responsibility in federal states. The first question that was examined concerned the plea of constitutional lack of competence sometimes raised by these states as an excuse for not fulfilling their international obligations. Being universally accepted as sovereign subjects of international law, they must answer for the acts or omissions of their component units in the same way as if they were unitary states. But this does not mean that they can always fulfil the international duties arising from such responsibility. In certain circumstances, particularly when giving satisfaction to foreign states involves a modification of the constitution, federal governments find themselves unable to act.

A different problem arises when the member states of a federation are allowed to deal separately with foreign powers and undertake international obligations in their own name. Then the latter will normally be held responsible for the fulfilment of their international obligations. If the federal government, by virtue of the constitution, retains a limited control over their international dealings, it would seem that it must answer indirectly for their acts or omissions contrary to international law. If, on the other hand, the member states act in complete independence of federal authorities, and this is known to the other state concerned, then it would seem that the federal government does not have to answer at all for them.

Finally, if the member states, in concluding agreements with foreign states, exceed their external competence, the federal government may denounce the agreement and in this case it becomes null and void. If the federal government regards the agreement as valid, and the other contracting party has no objection, then the treaty remains in force and the federal state as well as the member states are responsible for its execution.

CHAPTER 4

FEDERALISM AND INTERNATIONAL IMMUNITY[1]

The question whether member states of federations are entitled to immunity in international law does not appear as yet to have received a satisfactory answer. In 1932 a research undertaken by the Harvard Law School found that not enough cases had arisen in practice to justify the conclusion that any rule of international law had come into practice concerning the position of political subdivisions of states in the courts of another state.[2] The same research concluded that this was a very serious problem and that its importance was increasing with the growth in the number of federal states.[3]

In 1949 a survey of international law prepared by the Secretary General of the United Nations for the benefit of the International Law Commission stressed the necessity 'of making precise and uniform the rules relating to the jurisdictional immunities of not fully sovereign States such as protectorates or member States of federal States'.[4] The International Law Commission never carried out this suggestion. Indeed, it managed in its study of the law relating to diplomatic and consular immunities to steer clear of the difficulty raised by member states of federations. The Commission considered that the problem was intimately linked to their rights of legation and that the latter was purely a question of constitutional law.[5]

Among international law writers, there seem to be two different ways of looking at the problem of the international immunity of political subdivisions of states. In 1958 F. J. Kröneck,

[1] By 'international immunity' is understood here all those exceptions from the laws and jurisdiction of a State that are based on a norm of international law: see *Asylum Case (Judgment), ICJ*, 1950, p. 284.
[2] 26 *AJIL* (1932), supp., p. 483.
[3] *Idem.*
[4] *Survey of International Law in Relation to the Work of Codification of the International Law Commission*, Memorandum submitted by the Secretary General, United Nations, General Assembly. International Law Commission, 1949, p. 33 (Doc. A/CN.4/1/Rev.1).
[5] See *Yearbook of the International Law Commission*, 1957, i, 9–10. (Doc. A/CN.4/91 and 98).

dealing specifically with this question, suggested that political sub-divisions of states should be granted immunity in so far as they act as subjects of international law.[6] Similarly, according to certain authors, the right of legation possessed in the past by individual states of the German Empire carried with it the benefit of international immunity; for these writers such immunities were a necessary consequence of the possession of an international status.[7] On the other hand, a different approach was taken by Sucharitkul in 1959. In this view:

> State practice on the whole seems to suggest that, in order to be entitled to State immunity, an entity must establish that it is either a sovereign State or one of its recognized agencies, and that political subdivisions of a foreign State such as member States of a federal union and part-sovereign States such as protected States which still lack full external sovereignty are apparently in danger of falling between two stools.[8]

Sucharitkul considers that international immunity belongs only to sovereign states and their recognized agencies. Kröneck, on the other hand, admits that non-sovereign entities which are recognized as subjects of international law may also be entitled to immunity. To decide which of the two views is correct, it is necessary to re-examine the subject of the international immunity of member states of federations.

The lack of immunity of member states of federations as sovereign entities

It is now an accepted rule of international law that a sovereign state is entitled to immunity before the national courts of foreign countries. The *locus classicus* for this theory is the judgment of the United States Supreme Court in the *Schooner Exchange v. McFadden* case, where Marshall C.J. declared that:

> This full and absolute territorial jurisdiction being alike the attribute of every sovereign, and being incapable of conferring extra-territorial power, would not seem to contemplate foreign sovereigns nor their rights as its objects. One sovereign being in no respect amenable to another; and being bound by obligations

---

[6] Kröneck, 'Die völkerrechtliche Immunität bundesstaatlicher Glied-staaten vor ausländischen Gerichten', dissertation, Munich, 1958, ch. 7.

[7] See Sech, *Das Gesandtschaftsrecht der deutschen Einzelstaaten*, 1911, pp. 102 and 113; also Windisch, *Die völkerrechtliche Stellung der deutschen Einzelstaaten*, 1913, pp. 27 and 34.

[8] Sucharitkul, *State Immunities and Trading Activities in International Law*, 1959, p. 106.

of the highest character not to degrade the dignity of his nation, by placing itself or its sovereign rights within the jurisdiction of another, can be supposed to enter a foreign country only under an express licence, or in the confidence that the immunities belonging to his independent sovereign station, though not expressly stipulated, are reserved by implication, and will be extended to him.[9]

This being the case, it is clear that federal states which are accepted in international law as sovereign entities are legally entitled to immunity. But what happens in the case of member states of a federal union? Must immunity be denied to them because they lack external sovereignty? Are they not entitled to immunity if they have retained their internal sovereignty? Or should immunity perhaps be granted to them as agencies of sovereign states? Each of these possibilities must be examined separately, bearing in mind that the existence of sovereignty may not be the only justification for according immunity to a state.

EXTERNAL SOVEREIGNTY

A certain number of international law writers claim that international immunity may be granted only to those states which are externally as well as internally sovereign. Tenékidès, for instance, asserts that:

L'immunité de juridiction, qu'elle touche à l'indépendance des Etats ... ou à leur souveraineté..., n'est qu'un privilège des Etats jouissant de la plénitude de leur souveraineté.... Les Etats à souveraineté réduite et à personnalité internationale amoindrie, tels les *Etats protégés* et les *Etats fédérés*, ne sauraient en bénéficier.[10]

He consequently disapproves of a French decision which granted immunity to the protected State of Morocco when it was clear that the Sultan had abdicated his external sovereignty.[11] Even more ambiguously, Batiffol declares that: 'Les Etats qui peuvent se prévaloir de l'immunité sont ceux qui, étant souverains, entretiennent des relations diplomatiques avec la France. Les Tribunaux français sont donc compétents à l'égard d'un Etat fédéré, l'union fédérale ayant seule la personnalité internationale.'[12] Batiffol,

[9] The *Schooner Exchange v. McFadden*, (1812) 7 Cranch 116, 137; see also Sucharitkul, pp. 12–13.
[10] Ténékidès, 'L'immunité de juridiction des Etats étrangers', 38 *RGDIP* (1931), 608 at p. 613–14.
[11] *Idem*; Ténékidès refers to the case of *Morocco v. Laurens*, 56 *Clunet* (1929), 716; the decision was later affirmed by the Court of Cassation *Annual Digest*, 1933–34, case no. 64.
[12] Batiffol, *Droit international privé*, 1967, p. 783.

curiously, seems to equate sovereignty with international personality. His view is close to that of Sucharitkul who affirms that national courts have generally held autonomous entities to be amenable to the local jurisdiction 'on the ground that they lack international personality and external sovereignty'.[13]

But why this double reference to external sovereignty and to international personality? It is essential to examine the cases referred to by these writers in order to learn more about their views. The earliest case mentioned by them is that of *Ville de Genève v. Consorts de Civry* decided in 1894.[14] The Paris Court of Appeal held in this case that immunity could be claimed neither by the City of Geneva nor by cantons of Switzerland but only by the Swiss Confederation. The Court said more particularly:

> Dans ses rapports avec les puissances étrangères, en effet, elle seule [the Swiss Confederation] peut se prévaloir de la qualité de puissance souveraine, ayant seule, à l'exclusion des divers Etats cantonaux qui la composent, des représentants accrédités auprès des gouvernements étrangers et auprès de laquelle seule ces gouvernements sont diplomatiquement représentés.[15]

Commenting on the decision, Audinet suggested in 1895 that what the Court really meant was that immunity from jurisdiction belonged only to those states endowed with a distinct international existence.[16] He added that, although member states in most federations were deprived of international status, they could well be recognized in particular instances as subjects of international law and enjoy international immunity; as an example, he mentioned the case of the member states of Germany. A different point of view was put forward by Pillet in 1895 in a note appended to the report of the case.[17] Whilst approving the judgment on other grounds, he claimed that the refusal of immunity for the reasons given was not only in conflict with the view the French court had taken of the status of semi-sovereign states, but also ignored the fact that a constituent state in a federation could be as much the organ of the federal government as was an administrative authority created by a unitary or centralized state.[18] The case was also made the

---

[13] Sucharitkul, p. 106.
[14] Cour d'appel, Paris, 1894, 1894 *Dalloz*, II, 513; affirmed by the Court of Cassation Paris, 1895, *Dalloz*, I, 344.
[15] 1894 *Dalloz*, II, 515.
[16] Audinet, 'L'incompétence des tribunaux français à l'égard des États étrangers et la succession du Duc de Brunswick', 2 *RGDIP* (1895), 385 at 391.
[17] *Sirey*, 1896, I, 225.
[18] *Sirey*, 1896, I, 226; see also: Hamson, 'Immunity of foreign states: the practice of the French courts', 27 *BYIL* (1950), 293, 320 ff.

subject of a report by the Swiss Federal Council to the Federal Assembly.[19] The latter reiterated the view of the Swiss Government that the French courts had no jurisdiction because the canton of Geneva was a sovereign political entity.

In view of these comments, the significance of the decision in *Ville de Genève v. Consorts de Civry* should not be overestimated. It would be wrong, for instance, to conclude from this case that member states of federations have no right to immunity because they lack external sovereignty. What the decision does indicate is that possession of external sovereignty is not one of the bases upon which member states of federations can claim immunity.

According to Sucharitkul, the case of *Feldman v. Etat de Bahia*, decided in 1908 by the Court of Appeal of Brussels, provides further evidence that international immunity can be enjoyed only by those states enjoying external sovereignty.[20] It was found that the State of Bahia was not entitled to immunity. In this case: 'Attendu que ces Etats [of Brazil], parmi lesquels figure l'Etat de Bahia ici en cause, se disent souverains, mais qu'en somme la souveraineté absolue et complète, au point de vue du droit international, n'appartient qu'aux Etats-Unis du Brézil.'[21]

This clearly supports his contention that member states of federations are amenable to the jurisdiction of Belgian courts even if they are regarded internally as sovereign states. But Sucharitkul does not mention that part of the decision in which the court, speaking of the State of Bahia, said: 'Si l'acte en question rentre dans le cercle des droits et des attributions qui lui sont réservés par la constitution fédérale et par la sienne propre, il a été posé par un Etat souverain, et par suite l'examen et la critique de son opportunité échapperont au contrôle des tribunaux belges.'[22]

The truth, therefore, is that Belgian courts appear ready to admit that political subdivisions of foreign states can, in certain circumstances, enjoy the immunity of a sovereign power even though they are not externally sovereign.[23]

But the leading case upon which Ténékidès, Batiffol and Sucharitkul base their views is that of *State of Céara v. Dorr*. The Court of Appeal of Colmar stated, in this decision, that: 'A State cannot be recognized in international law as sovereign if, whatever the

---

[19] *Feuille Fédérale*, 4 mai 1892; see 26 *AJIL* (1932), supp., 486.
[20] *Pasicrisie Belge*, 1908, part ii, 55; 5 *Revue de droit international privé* (1909), 956
[21] *Pasicrisie Belge*, 1908, part ii, 56.
[22] Ibid., pp. 56–7.
[23] See E. W. Allen, *The position of Foreign States before Belgian Courts*, 1929, p. 18.

extent of its authority in domestic matters, the Constitution to which it is subject recognizes in it no authority to exercise the rights of sovereignty in international relations.'[24] On a further appeal, however, the Court of Cassation held that jurisdictional immunity could be invoked only 'by a state with a separate personality in international public law'.[25] Therefore, in the last resort, the right to immunity of the member state of Brazil was determined not by reference to its external sovereignty, but by reference to its international personality. In other words, if member states of federations were recognized as international subjects, they could claim international immunity; but they could not claim immunity as entities possessing external sovereignty.

In the case of *Molina v. Comision Reguladora del Mercado Henequen*, which concerned a suit brought in New Jersey against a corporation created by the State of Yucatan, Mexico, the argument that member states of federations are not entitled to immunity because they lack external sovereignty was also used. The Court said: 'The members of a federal republic are universally treated as having no independent existence as States in their external relations. Lacking this independence, they lack the very foundation for the right to immunity from judicial process.'[26]

This, however, is not in accord with other American decisions. In 1941, in the joint cases of *Sullivan v. State of Sao Paulo* and *Sullivan v. State of Rio Grande do Sul*, the Circuit Court of Appeals of the United States held that the two defendant states were to be granted immunity.[27] The majority relied upon the similarity between the constitutional structure of the Brazilian federation and that of the United States, concluding that the same immunity should be accorded to the states of each. Since it was well settled in the American practice that the states of the Union were immune from suit, even if they had sacrificed control over foreign affairs, the same treatment had to be extended to the component states of Brazil.[28]

Sucharitkul mentions two more decisions concerning autonomous regions of unitary states. In the first one, the Civil Tribunal of the Seine held that the department of Antiochia—the State of Antiochia in the former federation of Colombia—could legally be

[24] *Annual Digest*, 1927–8, case no. 21; see also *State of Céara v. D'Archer de Montgascon* based more or less on the same facts: *Annual Digest*, 1931–32, case no. 84.
[25] *Annual Digest*, 1931–32, case no. 84.
[26] Hackworth, *Digest of International Law*, ii, 403.
[27] *Annual Digest*, 1941–1942, case no. 50.
[28] The Court referred for that to the case of *Principality of Monaco v. State of Mississippi*, 292 US 313 (1934).

sued before French courts.[29] Referring to the case of *Ville de
Genève v. Consorts de Civry*, the Court declared that what was
true for the Canton of Geneva was *a fortiori* true for the mere
department of Antiochia. The second decision concerns the Basque
autonomous state set up by the Republican Government of Spain
before the civil war.[30] The plea of immunity from jurisdiction
entered by the Spanish authorities on behalf of the Basque
Government was rejected on the ground that the latter was neither
sovereign nor recognized as agent of a sovereign state.

Mention should be made of a last case that is generally over-
looked by those who claim that member states of federations are
not entitled to immunity because they lack external sovereignty.
This is the case of *X v. Prince Lippe-Schaumburg* decided by the
Supreme Court of Hungary in 1875. In this suit, instituted against
Prince Lippe-Schaumburg by a lawyer to collect his fees, the
District Court of Pécs had decided that it had jurisdiction. On
appeal, however, the Supreme Court of Hungary reversed this
decision, declaring that it was against international law that the
court of another state 'should exercise jurisdiction in a personal
action over a reigning foreign sovereign without an explicit declaration of his submission thereto'.[31] Of all the cases examined so far,
this is the only one actually involving a member state of a federation enjoying international personality.[32]

Weighing up the evidence, it appears that political subdivisions
of states cannot claim immunity before the courts of foreign states
as entities possessing external sovereignty. In most of the cases
examined so far, this argument was expressly rejected.[33] In only
one case was it accepted, but this involved a member state which
in fact enjoyed international status.[34] However, if political subdivisions of states cannot claim immunity as entities possessing
external sovereignty, some of the cases mentioned clearly suggest
that they can claim immunity on other grounds. In *Feldman v.
Etat de Bahia* and *Sullivan v. State of Sao Paulo*, internal
sovereignty and not external sovereignty was said to be the decisive
factor. In *Etat de Céara v. Dorr*, the French Court of Cassation

[29] *Crédit foncier d'Algérie et de Tunisie v. Restrépo et département
D'Antiachia, Annual Digest*, 1919–22, case no. 201; 50 *Clunet* (1923), 857.
[30] *Rousse et Maber v. Banque d'Espagne, Annual Digest*, 1935–37, case
no. 67.
[31] See Harvard Law School Research, 26 *AJIL* (1932), Supp., pp. 477–8.
[32] The granting of immunities to the member states of the German Federal
Empire is discussed below, at pp. 140–142.
[33] In *Ville de Genève v. Consorts de Civry, Molina v. Comision Reguladora del Mercado Henequen, Crédit foncier d'Algérie et de Tunisie v.
Restrépo et départment d'Antiochia* and *Feldman v. Etat de Bahia*.
[34] In *X v. Prince Lippe-Schaumburg*.

examined the right to immunity of the Brazilian State in the light of its international personality. Finally, in *Rousse et Maber v. Banque d'Espagne*, the possibility that political subdivisions of states might have to be granted immunity as agencies of sovereign powers was seriously envisaged. All these grounds require detailed analysis.

INTERNAL SOVEREIGNTY

Some international lawyers contend that member states of federations, although they lack external sovereignty, must be granted immunity because they have retained their internal sovereignty. Weiss, for instance, declares that the Cantons of Switzerland and the various states of the American Union do not differ essentially from protected states or vassal states, both groups of states having surrendered external sovereignty but not internal sovereignty.[35] He claims that, since protected states are generally granted immunity, the same treatment must be accorded to member states of federations. Guggenheim apparently agrees with this when he suggests that the immunity enjoyed by the Swiss cantons is similar to that which is enjoyed by protected states or mandated territories.[36] In practice, there is ample evidence to show that protectorates and vassal states have generally been granted immunity in the courts of foreign countries. But whether this was because they had retained their internal sovereignty is another matter.

In the case of *Gouvernement du Maroc et Maspéro v. Laurens et Société Marseillaise de crédit*, a French court held that:

> Part-sovereign States or Protectorates which have retained internal sovereignty, the right of self-government, self-administration and self-legislation, although they lack external sovereignty, which they have surrendered to a protecting State, have the same standing as fully sovereign States and the same immunity from jurisdiction is accorded to them.[37]

This statement, however, does not really reflect the attitude of French courts on this subject. After an exhaustive study of French practice, regarding protectorates, Kiss reaches the following conclusions. First of all, he defines the institution as 'la prise en charge des relations extérieures de l'Etat protégé par l'Etat protecteur et le contrôle de son activité interne, sans, toutefois, que

[35] Weiss, 'Compétence ou incompétence des tribunaux à l'égard des Etats étrangers' 1 *HR* (1923), 521 at 538–9.
[36] Guggenheim, *Traité de droit international*, i, 186, n. 3.
[37] *Annual Digest*, 1929–30, case no. 75; *Sirey*, 1930, ii, 152.

l'on puisse parler de droits de souveraineté existant au profit de l'Etat protecteur',[38] But not satisfied with this, he specifies afterwards that 'une des caractéristiques essentielles de tous les protectorats est la délégation faite par l'Etat protégé à l'Etat protecteur de l'exercice de sa souveraineté extérieure'.[39] Therefore, the true position regarding protected states is not that they lack external sovereignty, but rather that they have delegated the exercise of this sovereignty to the protecting power. Nominally, at least, international protectorates remain fully sovereign states. This view is confirmed by the decision of the International Court of Justice in the *Case Concerning Rights of Nationals of the United States in Morocco*. The Court found that Morocco, under the Treaty of Fez, had remained 'a sovereign State' but had made 'an arrangement of a contractual character whereby France undertook to exercise certain sovereign powers in the name and on behalf of Morocco, and, in principle, all of the international relations of Morocco'.[40]

It follows from this that member states of federations should not really be compared with international protectorates as far as concerns their right to international immunity. International protectorates are sovereign entities whose rights—including the right to immunity—and whose obligations are determined directly by international law. Member states of federations are not directly subordinated to international law. The extent of their rights and duties is fixed essentially by a municipal act, the federal constitution. If they enjoy internal sovereignty, it does not mean that, like international protectorates, they must be granted international immunity.

But it should be pointed out that certain protectorates, which are not directly subordinated to international law, are also granted immunity. British courts, for instance, have repeatedly held that the Native States of India were not subject to their jurisdiction.[41] In fact, however, they were not granted immunity as a matter of international law. The British parliamentary report of the Indian States Committee, which came out in 1929, stated categorically that the relations between the Indian States and Britain were governed, not by rules of international law or ordinary municipal

---

[38] Kiss, *Répertoire français de droit international public*, ii, 572–3.
[39] *Ibid.*, p. 588.
[40] *Case Concerning Rights of Nationals of the United States of America in Morocco*, Judgment of 27 August 1952, *ICJ* Rep. 1952, p. 176 at 188.
[41] *Mighell v. Sultan of Johore* (1894) 1 *QB* 149; *Duff Development Co. Ltd v. Government of Kelantan* [1924] *AC* 797; *Statham v. Statham and Gaekwar of Baroda* (1912) P., 92; *Kahan v. Federation of Pakistan* (1951) 2 *KB* 1003; *Sultan of Johore v. Abubakar Tunku Aris Bendahar* [1952] *AC* 318.

law, but by rules which formed 'a very special part of the constitutional law of the Empire'.[42] Twenty years later, in 1949, Sir Arnold McNair as he then was commented in the following way on the British practice of granting immunity to colonial protectorates:

> There are many decisions of English courts which show that, as a matter of British constitutional law and not of international law, many protected states within the British Empire and their Heads enjoy in British courts a degree of state immunity analogous to, or identical with, that accorded in pursuance of international law to truly foreign independent states and their heads.[43]

In 1958, Kröneck mentioned with approval this opinion of McNair.[44] Similar conclusions were reached again in 1963 by Fawcett, who wrote then that 'the grant of immunity in the British courts from process and execution to rulers of protected states rests upon a constitutional convention and not upon international law'.[45] More recently, in 1966, Brownlie expressed the view that: 'decisions allowing immunity on the ground that an entity is "sovereign" under the law of the forum are not very much in point'.[46] Clearly, one would be mistaken to rely on them in order to establish that member states of federations are entitled to immunity.

Therefore, the argument of Weiss that member states of federations, like protectorates, are internally sovereign and, like them, must be granted immunity is unacceptable. A more cogent argument is that certain decisions dealing with political subdivisions of states clearly state that such entities must be allowed immunity in so far as they enjoy internal sovereignty.

In the case of *Feldman v. Etat de Bahia,* previously referred to, the Court of Appeal of Brussels declared that a member state of a federation acting within its reserved powers was to be considered as a sovereign state and granted immunity.[47] But the Court also said that sovereignty, from the point of view of international law, belonged exclusively to the federation.[48] These two statements are not easily reconcilable. A possible explanation is that the Court felt bound, not as a matter of international law but as a matter of comity, to grant immunity to a member state of a federation

---

[42] British Government Publications, Cmd 3302, 1929, p. 25.
[43] McNair, 'Aspects of state sovereignity', 26 *BYIL* (1949), p. 6 at 37, n. 1.
[44] Kröneck, at p. 97.
[45] Fawcett, *The British Commonwealth in International Law*, 1963, p. 129.
[46] Brownlie, *Principles of Public International Law*, 1966, p. 285.
[47] 5 *Revue de droit international privé* (1909), p. 956; see above, p. 125.
[48] *Ibid.*, p. 957. For a recent discussion of this case, see Suy, 'Immunity of states before Belgian courts and tribunals', 27 *Zeit. für ausl. öff. Recht und Völk.* (1967), 670–2; the author also finds that the decision is not easy to explain.

acting within its constitutional competence. But this cannot be proved. The judgment itself does not indicate why immunity had to be granted to an entity lacking international legal sovereignty and, furthermore, the state of Bahia was refused immunity on the ground that it had not acted as a sovereign entity in the particular circumstances of the case.

In *Sayce v. Ameer of Bahawalpur*, McNair J. relied on a number of English decisions allowing immunity to colonial protectorates as well as on a letter from the Commonwealth Relations Office to declare that the Ameer of Bahawalpur, despite the accession of his state to the Federation of Pakistan, had remained a sovereign ruler entitled to immunity.[49] He also added that the statement of the Commonwealth Relations Office precluded him from considering 'the difficult question of the status of component parts of a federation.'[50] On appeal, his decision was affirmed.[51] This case, however, does not really support the view that there is an international obligation to grant immunity to member states of federations which have retained their internal sovereignty. The admission that the question of the status of component parts of federations was not considered and the reliance put on cases concerning colonial protectorates clearly indicate that immunity was allowed to the Ameer, not so much as a matter of international law, but rather as a matter of British constitutional law.[52]

Turning now to the decisions of American Courts, it is necessary to examine in the first place the case of *Kawananakoa v. Polyblank* which recognized the immunity to suit of the Territory of Hawaii.[53] The case involved the question whether the Territory of Hawaii could be joined as a defendant in a suit on a mortgage by a citizen of the Territory itself. The problem raised clearly had nothing to do with international immunity. But because the Circuit Court of Appeals of the United States relied in another case on the decision in *Kawananakoa v. Polyblank* to grant immunity to the political subdivisions of a foreign state,[54] it is necessary to deal with the latter briefly. The *ratio decidendi* of it appears to be that 'a sovereign is exempt from suit, not because of any formal conception or obsolete theory, but on the logical and practical ground that there can be no legal right as against the authority that makes

[49] 1 *All England Law Reports* (1952), 326.
[50] *Ibid.*, p. 331.
[51] 2 *All England Law Reports* (1952), 64.
[52] See Brownlie, p. 285.
[53] 205 *US* 349 (1907).
[54] See *Sullivan v. State of Sao Paulo, Annual Digest*, 1941–42, case no. 50, 187, discussed below.

the law on which the right depends.'[55] While an interesting theory, it can in no way be used to prove that political subdivisions of foreign states are entitled to immunity. Such a foreign entity can never be 'the authority that makes the law on which the right depends'. Therefore, the theory enunciated in *Kawananakoa v. Polyblank* has no validity in such a case and cannot be taken as a guide to international practice.

Similar remarks also apply to the decision of the Supreme Court in the case of *Monaco v. Mississippi.*[56] The case concerned a motion by the Principality of Monaco for leave to bring suit in the Supreme Court of the United States against the state of Mississippi upon bonds issued by such state. The Court asserted first of all that:

> Behind the words of the constitutional provisions are postulates which limit and control. There is the essential postulate that the controversies, as contemplated, shall be found to be of a justiciable character. There is also the postulate that States of the Union, still possessing attributes of sovereignty, shall be immune from suits, without their consent, save where there has been 'a surrender of this immunity in the plan of the convention. . . .' The question is whether the plan of the Constitution involves the surrender of immunity when the suit is brought against a State without her consent, by a foreign State.[57]

The Court pointed out that the debates in the Convention which adopted the constitution threw no light on the intention of the framers in regard to the matter, although some of the fathers like Madison and Marshall had expressed opinions elsewhere that no such suit could be entertained by the Supreme Court. The eleventh amendment to the Constitution excluded from the jurisdiction of the Court suits brought against one of the states of the Union by citizens of another state or by subjects of a foreign state, but it was silent as to suits brought by a foreign state itself. After a close examination of the nature of the 'constitutional plan', the Court finally reached the unanimous conclusion that it had no jurisdiction to hear the case. It declared:

> We perceive no ground upon which it can be said that any waiver or consent by a State of the Union has run in favour of a foreign State. As to suits brought by a foreign State, we think that the States of the Union retain the same immunity that they enjoy with respect to suits by individuals whether citizens of the United States or citizens or subjects of a foreign State. The foreign State

[55] *Kawananakoa v. Polyblank,* 205 *US* 353.
[56] *The Principality of Monaco v. The State of Mississippi,* 292 *US* 313 (1934).
[57] 292 *US* 322–323.

enjoys a similar sovereign immunity and without her consent may not be sued by a State of the Union.[58]

In the whole judgment there is not one reference to international law. All the arguments in favour of the immunity of Mississippi are taken from the constitutional law of the United States. For that reason, it cannot be accepted as a valid expression of international law.[59]

In *Leubrie v. State of Sao Paulo*,[60] an American court was called upon for the first time to decide whether member states of foreign federations were entitled to international law immunity. The New York Supreme Court had previously denied a motion to vacate an attachment entered against the defendant state's property, the motion being based upon its claims to immunity from suit because it was a foreign sovereign power. The defendant moved to reargue. On this motion for reargument, the United States Attorney appeared and submitted to the Court communications received and submitted to the Department of State from the Government of Brazil concerning this matter. However, he preferred not to express an opinion on the subject, leaving the question to the state Court for determination as a matter of law. The Court adhered to its original decision not to grant immunity to the State of Sao Paulo. It argued that the United States of Brazil possessed 'the entire external sovereignty of all the states within that union in so far as such sovereignty is recognized internationally'.[61] Therefore, the claim of immunity of Sao Paulo which pretended to be a foreign sovereign power, could not be accepted. This was a clear rejection of the argument that internal law sovereignty is a sufficient basis for granting international immunity to political subdivisions of federal States.

A few years later, in *Sullivan v. State of Sao Paulo* and *Sullivan v. State. of Rio Grande do Sul*, a second occasion for deciding whether member states of federations were entitled to international immunity presented itself.[62] These were actions for the recovery of the payment of principal and interest on bonds issued by the defendant states, the actions having been started against the states by the attachment of their New York bank accounts. The defendant states and the Government of Brazil appeared specially and moved to dismiss the complaint and vacate the warrant of attach-

---

[58] 292 *US* 330.
[59] See O'Connell, *International Law*, 1965, ii, 952.
[60] *New York Law Journal*, 30 April 1937, p. 2160 (New York Supreme Court).
[61] *Idem.*
[62] *Annual Digest*, 1941–42, case no. 50.

ment on the basis of their sovereign immunity from suit. While these motions were pending, the Brazilian Ambassador to the United States sent a letter to the Department of State, asserting defendant's immunity from suit and asserting further that the interest of the federal government in the funds was such as to render them immune to attachment. On the request of the Secretary of State, the United States Attorney for the Eastern District of New York submitted to the Court a written suggestion embodying the diplomatic representations of the Brazilian Ambassador to the United States Secretary of State, but expressly disapproving any intention to appear in the suit on behalf of Brazil, the defendants, or of the United States and not in any way vouching for the validity of the claims.

The two cases were heard in the first instance by District Judge Moscowitz. He held that:

> [O]n the facts as outlined by the Brazilian Ambassador, the State of Sao Paulo should be accorded by this court the rights of sovereign immunity. Sao Paulo is akin to a state of the United States which has been recognized as possessing sovereign immunity. While the absence of external sovereignty on the part of the State of Sao Paulo puts this court under no obligation as a matter of international law to accord sovereign immunity to the State of Sao Paulo, yet, as a matter of comity and reciprocal treatment, the court is of the opinion that Sao Paulo should be recognized as possessing sovereign immunity.[63]

On appeal to the Circuit Court of Appeals, the judgment was affirmed. Circuit Judge Clark delivered the majority opinion. He held that the defendant states should be accorded sovereign immunity in their own right. Referring to the decisions in *Kawananakoa v. Polybank, Monaco v. Mississippi* and *Duff Development Co. Ltd v. Government of Kelantan,* he declared that the defendant states were sovereign in the sense defined by those decisions and should therefore possess the immunity which is conceded to a friendly foreign state.[64] He added that the privilege 'would not be open to all foreign political subdivisions, only to those of the kind for which our law itself demands immunity.'[65]

In his concurring opinion, Circuit Judge Hand relied on a different theory. It was his belief that the letter of the State Department clearly indicated that the interest of the Government of Brazil in the matter was of such a character as to entitle the funds to immunity.[66] Apart from that, he could find no other reason to be-

[63] *Ibid.,* p. 184.
[64] *Ibid.,* p. 187.
[65] *Ibid.,* p. 189.
[66] *Ibid.,* p. 190.

lieve that the federal States of Brazil should be granted immunity. In particular, he hesitated to hold that every political subdivision which exercised substantial governmental powers was entitled to immunity. In his view, the decisions cited in the majority opinion did not touch the point and, moreover, as he pointed out, French and Belgian courts had entertained suits against the political subdivisions of a federation.[67]

Can it be concluded from this that member states of federations which have retained their internal sovereignty have a right to immunity in international law. At first sight, the decision of the Circuit Court of Appeals seems to justify this conclusion. However a closer look at what was actually said reveals that this decision was not reached on the basis of international law. The Court did not reject the assertion of the trial judge that there was no international obligation to accord sovereign immunity to the State of Sao Paulo. Nor, in its majority opinion, did it say that immunity had to be granted to the State of Sao Paulo as a matter of international law. The Court simply relied on a number of American and British constitutional law decisions to conclude that the State of Sao Paulo was entitled to immunity. At the end of its judgment, it spoke not so much of a right as of a privilege that would be open only to those foreign political subdivisions of the kind to which American law itself accords immunity. As for Circuit Judge Hand, he did not believe that every political division exercising substantial governmental powers was immune from suit. Thus, it would appear that the State of Sao Paulo and the State of Rio Grande do Sul were accorded immunity as a matter of comity and of reciprocal treatment rather than as a matter of international law.

None of the decisions examined so far really support the claim that member states of federations have a right to immunity in international law proportionate to their internal sovereignty. But there remains a last argument which may be mentioned in favour of this view. This is that the legislation of certain states grants privileges and immunities to the political subdivisions of some other countries.

According to Section 1, Subsection 2, of the Diplomatic Immunities (Commonwealth Countries and Republic of Ireland) Act 1952, Her Majesty's Government in the United Kingdom may by order in Council confer on a person recognized as the chief representative in the United Kingdom of any state or province of any other country to which the Section applies, and on members of the staff of any such person: 'any immunities and privileges which

[67] *Ibid.*, p. 191.

are conferred or may be conferred under the Consular Relations Act 1968'.[68] Among the countries to which the Section applies are the federations of Canada, Australia, India and Nigeria.[69] In 1961 an Order in Council conferred on the Agents General for the States of Australia and the Agents General for the Regions of Nigeria the immunity from suit and legal process and inviolability of archives provided for in Section 1, Paragraph 2, of the 1952 Act.[70] In 1967 another Order in Council granted the same privileges to the Agents General for the Provinces of Canada.[71] But all this, in reality, amounts to no more than diplomatic courtesy.[72] This is evidenced by the fact that the Agents General for the Provinces of Canada were covered by the terms of the 1952 Act only in 1967, after they had been functioning for years.

On the whole, then, it cannot be seriously argued that member states of federations are entitled to immunity because they have retained their internal sovereignty. Some of them, to be sure, are granted the kind of immunity usually accorded only to fully sovereign states; but no state is precluded from according privileges and immunities to political subdivisions of other states.[73]

SOVEREIGN STATE AGENCIES

However, there may be a legal obligation to grant immunity to member states of federations if the latter are in reality agencies of the central government of a foreign state. Pillet was the first one to suggest this possibility in a note appended to the report of the decision in *Ville de Genève v. Consorts de Civry*.[74] He argued that a sovereign state could exercise its sovereignty through various agencies, each of which was entitled to immunity like the sovereign state itself. He showed that this was accepted in the French practice of international law and pondered why a member state of a

[68] Diplomatic Immunities (Commonwealth Countries and Republic of Ireland) Act, 1952, 15–16 Geo. 6 & Eli. 2, ch. 18, Sect. 1, subsect. 2, as amended by Sect. 12 of the Consular Relations Act 1968.
[69] *Ibid.*, Subsect. 6; Nigeria was included later, on becoming independent.
[70] The Commonwealth Countries and Republic of Ireland (Immunities) (Order) 1961, Statutory Instruments, 1961, no. 1194.
[71] The Commonwealth Countries and Republic of Ireland (Immunities) (Amendment) Order 1967, Statutory Instruments, 1967, no. 160.
[72] See Laskin, 'Some international legal aspects of federalism: the Experience of Canada', in *Federalism and the New Nations of Africa*, ed. Currie, 1964, p. 394; see also Patry, 'La capacité internationale des Etats fédérés', in Brossard, Patry and Weiser, *Les Pouvoirs extérieurs du Québec*, 1967, p. 69.
[73] See Harvard Law School, Research in International Law, 'Competence of courts in regard to foreign states', 26 *AJIL* (1932), supp., 451 at 483.
[74] *Sirey*, 1896, i, 225, 226.

federation could not be as much the organ of the sovereign state as an administrative authority created by a unitary of centralized state. In 1938 Rousseau, in his note appended to the case of *Rousse et Maber v. Banque d'Espagne*, equally considered that the Basque Government was entitled to immunity as 'organe exécutif d'une unité administrative décentralisée'.[75]

Pillet's point of view was further developed by Sucharitkul in 1959.[76] The latter examined a number of cases in which autonomous subdivisions of states were granted immunity on the ground that they formed part of the central government of a foreign state. He arrived at the conclusion that it was: 'permissive and, to some extent, obligatory to grant immunity to political subdivisions of foreign States and semi-sovereign States acting as agencies of the central government of a foreign State'.[77] In his view, such political subdivisions were entitled to immunity because they were invested with extensive governmental powers and represented the central government and not because they were endowed with the fullest sovereignty by their own constitution.

More recently, in 1965, O'Connell has written that the question as to whether a given political subdivision of a foreign state was entitled to immunity depended 'upon proof that it is entrusted with a measure of the national sovereign power'.[78] He declared that, inasmuch as the member states of a federation had exclusive and perhaps residual powers, these were 'real elements of national sovereignty' for which they could claim immunity.[79] But he added that such powers had to be of a political as distinct from an administrative character in order to give rise to immunity.[80]

In practice, surprising as it may seem, there are no judicial decisions holding that member states of federations are entitled to immunity as agencies of sovereign states. In *Sullivan v. State of Sao Paulo*, Circuit Judge Hand held that the interest of the Government of Brazil was of such a character as to endow the funds in question with immunity.[81] But his view was not based on the constitutional law of Brazil; it simply reflected the attitude of the Department of State that the issue was important enough for the District Court not to proceed.

In a certain number of cases, however, immunity was granted

---

[75] *Sirey*, 1938, ii, 17, 19.
[76] Sucharitkul, p. 108.
[77] *Ibid.*, p.112.
[78] O'Connell, *International Law*, ii, 951.
[79] *Ibid.*, i, 318.
[80] *Ibid.*, ii, 951.
[81] *Annual Digest*, 1941–42, case no. 50, pp. 189–90.

to autonomous subdivisions of unitary states for the reason that they formed part of the central government of foreign countries. In *Van Heyningen v. Netherland Indies Government*, for instance, Philip J. of the Supreme Court of Queensland declared:

> In my view an action cannot be brought in our courts against a part of a foreign sovereign State. Where a foreign sovereign State sets up as an organ of its government, a governmental control of part of its territory which it erects into a legal entity, it seems to me that that legal entity cannot be sued here because that would mean that the authority and territory of a foreign sovereign would be subjected in the ultimate result to the jurisdiction and execution of this court.[82]

Similarly, in *Isbrandtsen Co. Inc., v. Netherlands East Indies Government et al.*, Coxe, District Judge (SD New York), granted immunity to the respondents upon receipt of a communication from the Acting Secretary of State stating that the Netherlands and the Netherlands East Indies were 'parts of the Kingdom of the Netherlands which is a sovereign state and has in no way given its consent to be sued in this matter in any court in the United States of America',[83] In *Huttinger v. Upper Congo-Great African Lakes Railway Co.*, the Civil Tribunal of the Seine said that it was impossible to deny that the former Independent State of Congo was now an integral part of the Belgian State; therefore, any action directed against the Colony of Congo was directed in reality against the Belgian State.[84] In the *SS Baurdo*, the District Court of Rotterdam stated that a civil court could not take cognizance of an action against a foreign state or one of its subdivisions.[85] Finally, in *Rousse et Maber v. Banque d'Espagne* the Court of Appeal of Poitiers implicitly admitted that it would have granted immunity to the Basque Autonomous Government if evidence had been produced to show that the latter was an agency of the Spanish Government.[86]

In all these cases it was accepted that political subdivisions of states which are in fact agencies of sovereign states have a legal right to immunity. But they do not really indicate when political subdivisions of states should be considered as agencies of sovereign states. In *Van Heynigen v. Netherland Indies Government, Huttinger v. Upper Congo–Great African Lakes Railway Co.*, and the *SS Baurdo*, the attitude adopted was that all territorial subdivisions

---

[82] Supreme Court of Queensland, *State Reports*, Weekly Notes, no. 19, p. 24 (1948).
[83] 75 F. Supp. 48 (S.D. N.Y. 1947).
[84] *Annual Digest*, 1933–34, case no. 65, pp. 172–3.
[85] *Annual Digest*, 1935–37, case no. 73, p. 200.
[86] *Annual Digest*, 1935–37, case no. 67, p. 189.

of states were agencies of sovereign states. But in *Rousse et Maber v. Banque d'Espagne*, the mere fact that an entity was a territorial subdivision of a sovereign state was not accepted as proof that such entity was an agency of that state; the Court of Appeal of Poitiers refused to grant immunity to the Basque Autonomous Government because no evidence was produced to support the claim that it was an agency of the Spanish Government.

In *Sullivan v. State of Sao Paulo*, moreover, Circuit Judge Hand admitted that he did not know of any measure by which to determine how far the functions of a political subdivision justified giving it immunity. He pointed out that if member states of federations had large governmental powers, so had cities; and he implied that he himself would hesitate to grant immunity to these.[87] A few years later, in *Schneider v. City of Rome*, the City Court of New York held that even if the City of Rome was a political subdivision of the Italian Government which exercised substantial governmental powers, this alone was not sufficient to render it immune.[88] Merely because member states of federations exercise important powers, it does not follow that they can claim immunity as agencies of sovereign states.

There is one test, however, which can tell us with exactitude when subdivisions of federal states should be considered as agencies of the central government. It has been seen in a previous chapter that federal governments are responsible for the public contracts of their member states when the latter act as their agents and, by looking at the decisions on this subject, it should be possible to find out when member states actually act as agents of the federal government.

In *Rosenstein v. Etat Allemand*, it was held that the State of Hamburg, having a legal personality of its own, could not by entering into a contract make the German State responsible.[89] Similarly, in the *Florida Bond Cases*, the State of Florida was considered as exclusively responsible for the payment of bonds issued in its own name.[90] But in the *Bolivar Railway Company Case* of 1903, the British-Venezuela Claims Commission found that a federal government had to answer for the obligations contracted by its member states in a situation where 'the relations of the several States to the National Government is of such intricate character, apparently so intimate that it becomes difficult to discriminate

[87] *Annual Digest*, 1941–42, case no. 50. p. 190.
[88] *Annual Digest*, 1948, case no. 40, p. 131.
[89] 1927 *Tribunaux Arbitraux Mixtes*, vii, p. 121, 123.
[90] Moore, *International Arbitrations*, iv, 3594.

rightfully between the two".[91] Thus, to the extent that member states of federations are 'constitutionally made an essential part of the central government',[92] it seems that they must be considered as agents of the latter.

Theoretically, however, such a situation should never arise; for true federalism presupposes the coexistence within a state of a central and of regional governments enjoying a certain independence from each other. As Wheare says, the federal principie is a 'method of dividing powers so that the general and regional governments are each, within a sphere, co-ordinate and independent'.[93] Therefore, member states of a federation which are no more in practice than administrative subdivisions of the central government, are members of a federation in name only. In most federal states, in fact, the general and regional governments do enjoy a certain independence from each other. This probably explains why in none of the decisions concerning the immunity of political subdivisions of federal states was the idea taken up that such entities were entitled to immunity as agents of the central government of a foreign state.[94]

The right to immunity of member states of federations as subjects of international law

The evidence examined so far suggests that component states of federations cannot claim immunity before foreign courts either as sovereign states or as agencies of sovereign states. But then, how can we explain that the individual states of Germany after 1871 still enjoyed in their relations with foreign powers the kind of immunity normally reserved to sovereign states? How can we explain further that Ukraine and Byelorussia nowadays enjoy the privileges and immunities granted to the members of the United Nations and its various agencies? Some international law writers, in an attempt to solve this problem, have asserted that member states of federations are entitled to immunity in so far as they enjoy international personality, a view that has also been expressed by certain municipal courts. It is the purpose of this section to examine this approach.

Following the formation of the German Empire in 1871, the

[91] *British-Venezuela Claims Commission*, 1903, p. 386; 9 *RIAA*, p. 450.
[92] See Sucharitkul, p. 104; the author uses the expression to characterize governmental agencies in general.
[93] Wheare, *Federal Government*, 4th edn, 1963, p. 10.
[94] See above, pp. 123–36.

individual States of Germany were not completely deprived of their right of legation. A certain number of them continued to maintain delegations abroad and receive foreign representatives.[95] Furthermore, individual states would send diplomatic agents to foreign Powers to consider specific matters. What in practice was the status of these agents? Some light may be shed on this question by looking at the agreements signed by them on behalf of their states. In the agreement of 1885 between Bavaria and Russia, for instance, the representative of Bavaria is referred to as 'the Envoy Extraordinary and Minister plenipotentiary of His Majesty the King of Bavaria'.[96] The same expression of 'envoy extraordinary and minister plenipotentiary' is used in agreements between Austria and Bavaria'.[97] and between Mecklenburg-Schwerin and Sweden.[98] Now this expression has always had a special meaning in the diplomatic practice of states. It refers to a particular category of diplomatic agents coming immediately after that of ambassadors.[99] Envoys are one of the four types of public ministers (ambassadors, envoys, ministers resident and chargés d'affaires) who are entitled to the highest degree of diplomatic immunity.[100] Therefore, when the representatives of the German states were referred to as envoys, the implication was that they were diplomatic agents legally entitled to immunity.

The reigning monarchs of the German states were themselves granted immunity as of right. Mention has been made, for instance, of the fact that the Prince of Lippe-Schaumburg was granted immunity by the Supreme Court of Hungary in 1875 on the ground that he was a reigning foreign sovereign.[101] Commenting on this practice, Oppenheim wrote in 1905: 'The reigning monarchs of these member-States are still treated by the practice of the States as heads of Sovereign States, a fact without legal basis if these States were no longer International Persons.'[102] Nowadays, Ukraine and Byelorussia are also granted immunity. The two member Republics of the Soviet Union are represented in a number of inter-

---

[95] In 1872, 7 German States had 18 delegations abroad and 17 of them were receiving 98 foreign delegations; in 1914, 2 individual States maintained 7 representations in other countries and 104 foreign delegations were accredited to the German States: see Baumbach, *Die unmittelbare völkerrechtliche Handlungsfähigkeit der deutschen Einzelstaaten in Vergangenheit und Gegenwart*, 1928, p. 45, note 4.
[96] De Martens, *NRG*, ser. 2, ii, 594.
[97] *Ibid.*, i, 484.
[98] *Ibid.*, xxxi, 572.
[99] See Satow, *A Guide to Diplomatic Practice*, 4th edn, 1957, p. 169.
[100] See *Engelke v. Musman* [1928], A.C. 433 at 449–50.
[101] See above, p. 127.
[102] Oppenheim, *International Law*, 1st edn, 1905, i, 131.

national organizations and their representatives enjoy the same immunities as the representatives of any other sovereign state.[103] Yet, Ukraine and Byelorussia are not sovereign entities. This grant of immunity is only justified by the fact that they are members of the United Nations and of some of its agencies. In other words, they are entitled to immunity only to the extent that they are accepted as subjects of international law.

The early practice concerning the member states of the German Empire attracted numerous comments from publicists. In 1883, for instance, von Sarwey expressed the opinion that the member states of Imperial Germany had to be granted immunity in those states where they had diplomatic representatives.[104] Later, in 1895, following the decision of the Court of Appeal of Paris in *Ville de Genève v. Consorts de Civry*, Audinet remarked that immunity would have to be granted to those member states of federations, such as the individual states of Germany, which still possessed a recognized international personality.[105] The same year, Féraud-Giraud also gave his support to this view.[106] In 1901, Laband acknowledged that even if the member states of Germany and their rulers were no longer sovereign, they were, nevertheless, still treated as if they had retained their sovereignty.[107] In 1913, finally, Karl Windisch explained that such immunity as was granted to the member states of Germany was justified on the grounds that they had retained a limited international personality.[108]

Influenced by these views, a certain number of writers have declared that member states of federations in general are entitled to immunity in so far as they enjoy international personality. Thus, Van Praag wrote in 1915 that immunity had to be allowed to political subdivisions which could deal internationally with foreign powers.[109] Similarly, E. W. Allen concluded her study of *The Position of Foreign States before National Courts* by saying

---

[103] See section 7 (b) of the *International Organizations Immunities Act* 1945 (USA), where it is said that 'representatives of foreign governments in or to international organizations . . . shall be immune from suit . . .': in 40 *AJIL* (1946), Suppl., p. 89. See also Gross, 'Immunities and privileges of delegations to the United Nations', 16 *International Organizations* (1962), 483.

[104] Von Sarwey, *Das Staatsrecht des Königreichs Württemberg*, 1883, i, 40.

[105] Audinet, 'L'incompétence des tribunaux français à l'égard des Etats étrangers et la succession du Duc de Brunswick', 2 *RGDIP* (1895), 391.

[106] Féraud-Giraud, *Etats et souverains, personnel diplomatique et consulaire devant les tribunaux étrangers*, 1895, i, 40.

[107] Laband, *Das Staatsrecht des deutschen Reiches*, 1901, i, 96.

[108] Windisch, p. 34.

[109] Van Praag, *Juridiction et droit international*, 1915, p. 414.

that: 'The entity claiming the immunity need not be a "State" in the traditional sense, but it must be a person of international law.[110] In 1954 Cavaré surveyed the doctrine of international law pertaining to the question of jurisdictional immunity of member states of federations and concluded that: 'La doctrine leur a reconnu l'immunité dans la mesure où ils pouvaient entretenir avec les autres Etats des relations de Droit international public'.[111]

Another writer who holds that member states of federations should be granted immunity when they are accepted by foreign powers as subjects of international law is Kröneck.[112] The author notes first that the doctrine on the subject reveals three points of view: some writers refuse immunity to member states of federations on the grounds that they lack sovereignty, some claim that immunity must be granted to them because they enjoy delegated competence and others believe that immunity must be allowed to political subdivisions of federal states if they are accepted as subjects of international law. There then follows a detailed examination of all the decisions of national courts dealing with the question. Here again, he sees a basic lack of uniformity, some decisions according immunity, others not. But these decisions have also certain common characteristics. None of them, for instance, recognize the idea of a delegation of competence. In most cases, sovereignty and international competence are the criteria used to assess the right to immunity of member states of federations. Sovereignty itself, he finds, is often confused with autonomy, especially in the Anglo-American decisions. Reviewing the evidence, Kröneck argues that no useful purpose is served by trying to prove that member states of federations are entitled to immunity as sovereign entities. In a federal union, only the central state is considered as sovereign. But this, according to him, does not mean that sovereign states and member states of federations have nothing in common. In so far as the latter are accepted as subjects of international law, they are directly subordinated to that law, in the same way as sovereign states. Now, since immunity is granted to those states that are directly subordinated to international law, Kröneck suggests that member states of federations acting as subjects of international law may also be entitled to immunity. Referring to the case of *Etat de Céara v. Dorr*,[113]

---

[110] Allen, *The Position of Foreign States before National Courts, Chiefly in Continental Europe*, 1933, p. 301.
[111] Cavaré, 'L'immunité de juridiction des Etats étrangers', 58 *RGDIP* (1954), 177 at 201.
[112] Kröneck, dissertation, 1958.
[113] *Annual Digest*, 1931–32, case no. 84; *Dalloz*, 1933, i, 196.

where immunity was denied to the State of Céara because it had no separate personality in public international law, Kröneck sees in this decision a confirmation of his view. He therefore concludes that member states are to be granted immunity whenever they are accepted as subjects of international law.

It seems clear that Kröneck is right when he asserts that member states of federal unions cannot claim immunity either as sovereign entities or as agencies of sovereign entities. Although he does not distinguish in this respect between internal and external sovereignty, his conclusion that sovereignty is not the criterion of immunity for member states of federations is entirely borne out by the jurisprudence. As for his suggestion that member states enjoying international personality should be granted immunity, this really rests on one decision linking the immunity of member states of federations to their international status. It is surprising that he does not mention the practice of states relating to the German Federal Empire of 1871 or the present practice concerning Ukraine and Byelorussia.

There remains one last writer to mention. This is W. Rudolf who, in 1966, wrote an article entitled *Internationale Beziehungen der deutschen Länder*.[114] In this article, the author declares without any comments that *ad hoc* representatives sent by the present German states to foreign countries have a legal right to immunity.[115]

Turning now to the decisions of municipal courts, the first case to be considered is that of *Etat de Céara v. Dorr*.[116] In this case, the French Court of Cassation held that jurisdictional immunity could only be invoked by a State with a separate personality in international public law.[117] It added that, whatever its status within the sovereign confederation of the United States of Brazil, it was clear that the State of Céara had no diplomatic representation and no personality of its own in international political relations and that, therefore, it was not entitled to immunity. In a note appended to the report of the case, André Gros commented that the question of the international status of member states of federations was one of positive law, the solution of which had to be found, in each case, in the relevant provisions of the federal constitution. According to him, this was exactly what the court had done.[118]

---

[114] Rudolf, 'Internationale Beziehungen der deutschen Länder', 13 *Archiv des Völkerrechts* (1966), 53.
[115] *Ibid.*, p. 68.
[116] *Annual Digest*, 1931–32, case no. 84; *Dalloz*, 1933, i, 196.
[117] *Annual Digest*, 1931–32, case no. 84, p. 163.
[118] *Dalloz*, 1933, I, p. 196, at 199.

In 1948, in *Dumont v. Etat d'Amazone*, the Civil Tribunal of the Seine repeated the arguments used by the Court of Cassation. It held that the defendant, also a member of the United States of Brazil, had no international personality and was, accordingly, not immune from jurisdiction.[119] Colliard, in a commentary on this case, declared:

> Il importe de souligner que la jurisprudence qui confirme le jugement rapporté n'exclut pas automatiquement, d'une manière générale, du bénéfice du privilège d'immunité tous les Etats-membres des Etats fédéraux. Elle exclut ceux qui sont dépourvus de personnalité internationale, de représentation diplomatique.[120]

However, Colliard himself disapproved of this tendency of French Courts to grant immunity to member states of federations endowed with international personality.

There are no other decisions where the immunity of member states of federations is expressly made to depend on the possession of international personality. However, the case of *Ville de Genève v. Consorts de Civry* can perhaps be considered as supporting this view.[121] Although immunity was linked in that case to the possession of sovereignty, the decisive factor appears to have been the power to exchange diplomatic representatives. Now such power has been possessed in the past by non-sovereign subjects of international law, such as the individual states of the German Federal Empire, and is possessed nowadays by non-sovereign entities such as the member Republics of the Soviet Union. The decision, therefore, can be interpreted to mean that only states with a distinct international personality can claim immunity. This at least is how Audinet interpreted it.[122]

On the whole, then, there are three main reasons for believing that member states of federations acting as subjects of international law are entitled to immunity. First of all, there is the clear tendency of French Courts to consider the right to immunity of such entities in the light of their international status. Secondly, there is the fact that immunity has been enjoyed in the past, and is still being enjoyed by member states of federations endowed with international personality. Finally, this point of view is accepted by numerous authors. It is true that a certain number of writers insist that only sovereign entities are immune from the jurisdiction of foreign

[119] *Annual Digest*, 1948, case no. 44, pp 140–146; *Dalloz*, 1949; Jurisprudence, p. 428.
[120] *Dalloz*, 1949, Jurisprudence, p. 429.
[121] *Dalloz*, 1894, II, 513; affirmed on appeal by the Court of Cassation, *Dalloz*, 1895, I, 344.
[122] Audinet, 2 *RGDIP* (1895).

courts. But when they declare that political subdivisions of states are not entitled to immunity, they often refer at the same time to the lack of international personality of such entities.[123] On balance, it seems fair to assert, then, that member states of federations which are recognized by foreign powers as international subjects must be granted immunity before their courts.

Conclusion

In this chapter, we have seen that political subdivisions of federal states cannot claim immunity before foreign courts either as sovereign states or as agencies of sovereign states; but we have found that they can do so in so far as they are recognized as subjects of international law. This again is entirely in conformity with the general principles of sovereignty, consent and recognition. From an international law point of view, only the federal state is sovereign; therefore, it is logical that the member states of a federation cannot claim immunity as sovereign entities. But a particular federal constitution may grant a limited international competence to the member states and allow them to deal on a basis of equality with foreign powers. If such powers recognize these subdivisions as subjects of international law and accept to deal with them, then the latter would appear to be entitled to immunity.

[123] See above, pp. 123–124.

PART TWO

FEDERALISM AND EVOLVING INTERNATIONAL LAW

CHAPTER 5

THE IMPACT OF THE FEDERAL MODEL ON INTERNATIONAL LAW

In previous chapters, it was seen that traditional international law does not concern itself with the question whether a state is federal or unitary. The distribution of powers between a federal state and its constituent units is held to be a domestic matter with which foreign states are not concerned. Federal states, therefore, are treated exactly like any other sovereign states: they enjoy the same right to immunity and are responsible in exactly the same way. Occasionally, the federal distribution of powers may become relevant from the point of view of international law; such is the case, for instance, when the member states are granted international competence and this grant of competence is acknowledged by third states. But there is nothing extraordinary in this; it is just another application of the principles of consent and recognition. In reality, the federal pattern has not affected the traditional rules of international law.

In the past fifty years, however, international law itself has changed profoundly.[1] Many matters formerly reserved to municipal law have now become proper subjects of international law. New terms such as international constitutional law, international administrative law, international labour law, international criminal law and international economic law have made their appearance. Inevitably, such developments have transformed the relationship between federalism and international law.

It must be remembered that federalism at the origin was intimately linked with economic liberalism. When modern federations first appeared, state intervention in general was condemned. The main concern of central governments at that time was to ensure the free movement of wealth. Treaties were used mainly to make alliances and to deal with commercial and trade relations. As to the powers of the member states, they were confined to local matters; treaties dealing with such matters were simply not envisaged. In those days, the sharing of competence between a

---

[1] See on this subject Friedmann, *The Changing Structure of International Law*, 1964.

federation and its member states could hardly raise serious diffi-culties.[2]

Since then, the intervention of the state has increased in many ways. Nowadays, there are almost no activities which are not some-how regulated by the state. As a result, powers which not so long ago were considered as insignificant—such as those possessed by member states of federations—have now become important. As A. Brady puts it: 'They may have been insignificant in the days of the horse and buggy, but with the advent of a progressive indus-trial society they loomed into conspicuous importance, necessitat-ing ever larger sums of money'.[3] In international relations, a paral-lel movement has taken place. As already stated, matters which fifty years ago were regulated only by national law, or not regula-ted at all, have now become the objects of international obligations. More specifically, matters within the jurisdiction of the member states have become the object of international agreements. For many federations, this was to raise serious problems.

In 1951 an enquiry conducted jointly by Unesco and the Inter-national Institute of Administrative Science sought to find explana-tions for the failure of national governments to discharge promptly and effectively their international obligations. The final report noted a particular difficulty in the case of federal states such as Australia, Brazil, India and the United States, where matters like those dealt with in labour conventions and in Unesco educational programmes fell wholly or partly within the orbit of the unit governments rather than of the federal authorities.[4] But the report did not elaborate on the nature of that difficulty.

International lawyers have been more explicit on this subject. The problem, they believe, is one of basic incompatibility between the federal division of internal sovereignty and the requirements of modern international life. Looper, for instance, asks: 'How is a federal State, a polity with a constitutional division of powers along central-regional lines, to participate in international treaties involving matters which fall within the constitutionally reserved powers of the constituent units?'[5] Unable to find a satisfactory answer, he declares that the federal 'division of sovereignty can-

[2] See Reuter, *International Institutions*, 1958, pp. 197–200.
[3] Brady, 'The modern federation: some trends and problems', in *Back-ground Papers and Reports*, Ontario Advisory Committee on Confederation, 1967, p. 4.
[4] *National Administration and International Organization. A compara-tive study of fourteen countries*, Unesco and the International Institute of Administrative Sciences, 1951, p. 59.
[5] Looper, 'Limitations on the treaty power in Federal States', 34 *New York University Law Review* (1959), 1046–1047.

not stand up to the test of modern international relations'.[6] His view is shared by Sørensen who declares that 'the federal system of government is particularly ill adapted to international co-operation'.[7] For Ghosh, the problem boils down to the following dilemma:

> [E]ither there will be a redistribution of powers between the General and the Regional Governments in these Federal States in accordance with the legal requirements of a growing world community, or there will be an exclusion of the subject-matters within the competence of their constituent units from the jurisdiction of general International Law, with an inevitable set-back to the growth of that law and a gradual erosion of certain principles and purposes of the Charter of the United Nations.[8]

Such remarks are in no way exceptional: they express a certain conviction that federal states are an obstacle to the development of international law.

Yet, in spite of this, federalism has been proposed more and more often in recent years as a model for international integration. Among international lawyers, political scientists, economists and politicians, it has become a recurrent formula for effective organized cooperation between states. Schwarzenberger, for instance, writes that 'the federal pattern is the most clear-cut alternative to power politics'.[9] Friedrich, for his part, suggests 'that federalism holds out the prospect of organizing the world at large as an alternative to world domination'.[10] In 1939, F. A. Hayek declared: 'It is rightly regarded as one of the great advantages of inter-states federation that it would do away with the impediments as to the movement of men, goods and capital between the states, and that it would render possible the creation of common rules of law, a uniform monetary system, and common control of communications'.[11] Finally, such experienced men as Robert Schuman, Spaak, Monnet and others have urged the formation of a European federation as a first step towards global unification.[12]

It may even be argued that there is a federalizing process at work

---

[6] *Ibid.*, p. 1065.

[7] Sørensen, 'Federal States and the international protection of human rights', 46 *AJIL* (1952), 218.

[8] Ghosh, *Treaties and Federal Constitutions: Their Mutual Impact*, 1961, p. 308.

[9] Schwarzenberger, *Power Politics*, 3rd edn, 1964, p. 526.

[10] Friedrich, *Man and His Government. An empirical theory of politics*, 1963, p. 596.

[11] Hayek, 'Economic conditions of inter-state federalism', *The New Commonwealth Quarterly* (1939), p. 131.

[12] See Mitrany, 'The prospect of integration: federal or functional', 4 *Journal of Common Market Studies* (1965), 124.

in international law.[13] But this remains to be proved. In fact, no comprehensive study of the impact of federalism on international law has ever been undertaken. It will, therefore, be the object of the present chapter to determine to what extent and in which direction the federal model is influencing the evolution of international law. A first section will deal with the contention that federalism is an obstacle to the development of international integration; a second section will examine federalism as a model for international integration.

Federalism as an obstacle to international integration

THE PROBLEM OF DIVIDED COMPETENCE IN FEDERAL STATES

It has been said that 'federalism and a spirited foreign policy go ill together'.[14] To a certain extent this is true because federal states, with their division of internal sovereignty, are at a disadvantage in their dealings with foreign powers. On the one hand, they must execute their international agreements as if they were unitary states, their internal division of competence not excusing the non-fulfilment of their international obligations. On the other hand, they cannot afford to ignore the federal division of competence and act as if they were unitary states; in most cases, such a course of action would entail political if not legal complications. Federal states, therefore, must always be careful when they undertake international obligations.[15]

Canada is one of the federations most impeded in the conduct of its foreign relations. Until the end of the First World War, it enjoyed no independent external status. Its external relations were conducted by the British Government acting in most cases on the advice of the Canadian Government. The latter was asked several times whether it wanted to adhere to international agreements dealing with subject matter within the competence of the provinces. Legally, no problem was posed. Under section 132 of the British North America Act, the Parliament of Canada had all the powers

[13] This is the theory of Friedrich: see above; see also McWhinney, *Federal Constitution-Making for a Multi-National World*, 1966, ch. 8.

[14] Wheare, *Federal Government*, 4th edn, 1963, p. 186.

[15] The impact of federal constitutions on the treaty-making policy of federal states has been examined in 1931 by Stoke, *The Foreign Relations of the Federal State*, ch. 9, and more recently by Ghosh, ch. 5. However, the subject has not been exhausted and a new and systematic examination of it might help to provide a better understanding of the nature and extent of this impact.

necessary and proper for performing the obligations of Canada, or of any province thereof, incurred towards foreign countries in treaties between the Empire and foreign states. But even then, there appear to have been political reasons for not invading the fields of competence of the provinces; for quite early after the federation was created, a constitutional practice grew whereby the Canadian Government would not adhere to new treaties where the matter concerned was within the exclusive competence of the legislatures, 'unless it be the desire of all the provincial governments'.[16] Until 1921, for instance, when implementing statutes were finally passed by all the provinces, the Canadian Government refused to adhere to the convention of 1899 between the United States and Great Britain relative to the disposal of real and personal property.[17] It also refused to adhere to the Berne Convention of 1907 for the prohibition of night work of women and the international Convention forbidding the manufacture and sale of matches made with white phosphorus.[18] But then the pressure of world opinion was not what it is now and Canada was not directly responsible for its foreign policy.

After the First World War, these conditions changed. Canada soon became an independent state with full responsibility for its own international relations. In 1920 the Federation was accepted as an original member of the League of Nations. In the same year, Canada became a member of the International Labour Organization, where it came under greater pressure to undertake international obligations on subject matter held until then to belong to the provinces. At first, it hesitated to do so. In 1925 the Supreme Court of Canada was asked for an advisory opinion on the following question:

> Are the legislatures of the provinces the authorities within whose competence the subject-matter of the said draft convention [Draft Convention Limiting the Hours of Work in Industrial Undertakings to eight in the day and forty-eight in the week] in whole or in part lies and before whom such draft convention should be brought, under the provisions of Article 405 of the Treaty of Peace with Germany, for the enactment of legislation or other action?[19]

In answer to this question the Court declared that the matter of labour in industrial undertakings in Canada was primarily within

[16] Keith, *Responsible Government in the Dominions*, 2nd edn, 1928, ii, 920.

[17] *Ibid.*, i, 580, note 1, and ii, 921.

[18] *Ibid.*, ii, 920–1.

[19] *In the Matter of Legislative Jurisdiction over the Hours of Labour* [1925], Supreme Court Reports, 505, 509.

the competence of provincial legislatures, but that Parliament could legislate as to labour in territories not yet organized into, or forming part of, a province and as to labour of servants of the Dominion if these were within the scope of the draft convention. Until 1935 this remained the official position of the Canadian Government.

In 1935, however, after a visit to Geneva as delegate to the League Assembly, Mr Bennet, Prime Minister of Canada, decided to ratify a certain number of labour conventions.[20] In the same year the Dominion Government enacted the necessary legislation to give effect to these conventions. As was to be expected, the validity of this legislation was contested by the provincial governments. The matter went on appeal before the Judicial Committee of the Privy Council. Delivering the judgment in 1937 Lord Atkin declared that the Dominion could not, 'merely by making promises to foreign countries, clothe itself with legislative authority inconsistent with the constitution which gave it birth'.[21] The judgment supported the stand adopted by the provinces and the federal legislation was declared *ultra vires*. For most international lawyers in Canada, the decision came as a shock. A typical reaction of the time is that of Mackenzie who wrote: 'The result of their Lordships' decision seems to be: that for international purposes Canada is no longer a nation, not even a league of nations, but a strange agglomeration in which the parties with power (the Provinces) have no status (internationally), and the party with status (the Dominion) has no power.'[22] As for the Canadian Government, it soon reverted to its former practice of not adhering to labour conventions the subject matter of which was beyond its legislative competence. In 1964 it had ratified twenty conventions out of nearly 120, all of which except the three of 1935 were within its legislative competence. As the Department of External Affairs explained then: 'Canada is a federal country, and the fact that most labour conventions are wholly or partly under provincial jurisdiction has placed obstacles in the way of the Federal Government, up to the present, ratifying many of the 110 Conventions.'[23]

After the Second World War, Canada became a member of the

[20] See Carter, 'Canada in the International Labour Organization', thesis, London, 1939, p. 127. See also Després, *Le Canada et l'Organisation internationale du travail*, 1947, pp. 85–178.

[21] *A.G. of Canada v. A.G. of Ontario*, [1937] A.C. 326 at 352.

[22] MacKenzie, 'Canada: the treaty-making power', 18 *BYIL* (1937), 172 at 175. See also Scott, 'The consequences of the Privy Council decisions', XV *Can. Bar. Rev.* (1937) 485.

[23] Department of External Affairs, Information Service, no. 85, 1964, p. 3; since then however, a few conventions dealing with provincial matters have been ratified with the cooperation of the Provinces. See below, p. 194.

United Nations. As such, it pledged itself to take joint and separate action in cooperation with the Organization to promote:

> a—higher standards of living, full employment, and conditions of economic and social progress and development;
> b—solutions of international economic, social, health, and related problems; and international cultural and educational cooperation; and
> c—universal respect for, and observance of, human rights and fundamental freedoms for all without distinction as to race, sex, language or religion.[24]

But as early as 1948 a Canadian writer had prophesied that the existing constitutional arrangements would prevent the country from fulfilling in a responsible manner the international obligations incurred under the Charter of the United Nations.[25] This was soon shown to be true.

In November 1947 a resolution was submitted to the General Assembly which recommended that member governments encourage the teaching of the United Nations Charter and various aspects of the Organization in their schools and institutions of higher learning. Canada abstained from voting on the resolution. As its delegate explained:

> In Canada, under our system of confederation, there is a federal government and nine provincial legislative assemblies. By our constitution, the government of each province has complete and exclusive jurisdiction and control over educational matters.
> Therefore, everyone will understand that my government could not, if the proposal is adopted, take measures to encourage the teaching of the United Nations Charter, etc. in the schools of Canada.[26]

A year later, in 1948, a similar statement was made regarding the Universal Declaration of Human Rights. Casting his vote in favour of the declaration, in the General Assembly, the Canadian delegate warned that: 'In regard to any rights which are defined in this document, the federal Government of Canada does not intend to invade other rights which are also important to the people of Canada, and by this I mean the rights of the provinces under our federal Constitution.'[27] During the eighth session of the General Assembly, the Canadian representative pointed out that because

---

[24] Article 55.
[25] Angus, 'The Canadian Constitution and the UN Charter', 12 *Canadian Journal of Economics and Political Science* (1946), 127.
[26] See *Canada and the United Nations*, 1947, pp. 235–6. See also Eayrs, 'Canadian federalism and the United Nations', 16 *Canadian Journal of Economics and Political Science* (1950), 172 at 179.
[27] *External Affairs* 1 (Jan. 1949), p. 24.

of the type of subjects dealt with by the Covenants on Human Rights, it would be impossible for Canada, in the absence of a federal state clause, to ratify the Covenants 'short of a drastic overhaul of its basic constitutional arrangements'.[28] The Canadian Government's stand on a federal state clause was reiterated in a statement submitted to the Secretary General and published on 10 March, 1954. It declared that: 'In the absence of a satisfactory Federal State clause, Canada could not become a party to the Covenants, due to the nature of its constitution which divides legislative powers concerning Human Rights between the national parliament and the provincial legislatures.'[29] But no such clause was included in the final draft of the proposed Covenants on Human Rights. As a result, Canada complained, in 1964, that no provision had been made to take into account the constitutional difficulties of federal states such as Canada.[30] Nevertheless, Canada did vote in favour of the final Covenants on Human Rights adopted in 1966 and is presently giving consideration, in consultation with the provinces, to ratifying them.[31]

It is impossible to say how long this process will take; the difficulties are considerable and far from being solved. In February 1968, two years after the Covenants on Human Rights and Fundamental Freedoms were adopted, M. Johnson, the then prime minister of Quebec, declared that the clause included in these Covenants to the effect that their provisions shall apply without limitations or exceptions whatsoever to all constitutive units of federated states was in direct opposition to Canadian constitutional law. 'In no way,' he added, 'can we accept it, for it would result in permitting the federal government to legislate in provincial matters under the cover of international agreements.'[32]

Other examples of caution on the part of the Canadian Government are to be found in its acceptance, in 1957, of the Convention on the Political Rights of Women accompanied by a reservation 'in respect of rights within the legislative jurisdiction of the Provinces',[33] and its refusal so far to adhere to the Convention relating

---

[28] *Canada and the United Nations*, 1953–54, p. 47.
[29] *Canada and the United Nations*, 1953–54, p. 48.
[30] *External Affairs* 14, no. 12 (Dec. 1964), 579.
[31] Gotlieb, *Canadian Treaty-Making*, 1968, p. 80.
[32] *The Government of Quebec and the Constitution*, Office d'information et de publicité du Québec, 1968, p. 86.
[33] See United Nations, *Status of Multilateral Conventions in respect of which the Secretary General acts as Depositary*, 1959, p. XVI–9 (Doc. ST/LEG/3, REV.1). For the text of the Convention, *UN Treaty Series*, vol. 193, p. 135.

to the Status of Refugees of 1951, even though it included a federal state clause.[34]

On one occasion, Canada has found itself in a rather embarrassing position because of its internal division of powers. This happened when the Province of Quebec refused to exempt the personnel of the International Civil Aviation Organization, which has its headquarters in Montreal, from provincial taxes and succession duties. Canada was not a party to the 1947 Convention on the Privileges and Immunities of the Specialized Agencies; in the Headquarters Agreement of 1951 it had undertaken to exempt the Organization and its personnel, as well as national representatives, from federal taxes only.[35] Legally, therefore, Canada was not answerable for the imposition by the Province of Quebec of those various taxes. But this meant that the ICAO itself had to reimburse staff members the amount that they were taxed by the Province. Further difficulties with the Province of Quebec arose over succession duties on an indemnity paid to the widow of an ICAO employee killed while on a mission for the Organization.[36] Preoccupied by this question, the ICAO Assembly adopted in 1955 the following resolution:

> WHEREAS the Assembly has noted the report of the Council in relation to privileges, immunities and facilities within the grant of the Province of Quebec; and
> WHEREAS the Assembly has noted that many approaches made by the Council to the Province on this subject have met with little or no response; and
> WHEREAS the Assembly has noted that in relation to the question of provincial succession duties certain officials of the Province have advised the Organization that legal proceedings might be instituted against it; and
> WHEREAS the Assembly has noted with regret that the attitude of the Province appears to be in conflict with the assurance given ... by the Minister of Trade and Commerce for the Province of Quebec that the Province would extend its full co-operation to the Organization:
> *The Assembly resolves*
> to record its approval of the action taken by the Council in these matters; invites the Council at its discretion:
> (a) to communicate with the Federal Government of Canada and to request that it continue its intercession with a view to securing a solution of the problems pending with the Province of Quebec and,
> (b) to carry out a study in order to determine the cost of maintaining ICAO in those cities which might be most suitable

[34] See *Canada and the United Nations*, 1950 (Department of External Affairs), p. 67; see also Gotlieb, p. 78.
[35] ICAO Doc. 7147 (27 April 1951).
[36] See Cheng, *The Law of International Air Transport*, 1962, p. 41.

as possible headquarters for the Organization;
and directs that a copy of this resolution be transmitted to the
Federal Government of Canada.[37]

Thus, Canada was made to feel at least morally responsible for
the conduct of the Province of Quebec. In 1956 the Federal
Government offered to bear most of the burden of the reimburse-
ments made by ICAO. In the same year, the Government of
Quebec finally accepted to grant the privileges and immunities
which the Organization had been seeking since its establishment in
Montreal.[38]

Canada is clearly at a disadvantage when it comes to participating actively in the development of international cooperation. This
we have demonstrated. However, it would be interesting to specu-
late on Canada's ability, given its division of powers, to join
organizations like the European Communities, which have reached
the most advanced stage of international integration.

Participation in supranational organizations like the European
Communities entails a transfer of legislative powers to an outside
agency.[39] The question arises, therefore, whether, in a federal
country like Canada, this can be done. There is nothing express in
the Canadian constitution about delegation or transfer of legislative powers. However, certain rules have emerged through judicial
practice. Thus it has been held that the federal Parliament and
the provincial Legislatures 'may delegate in certain cases their
powers to subordinate agencies'.[40] But neither of them 'can abdicate their powers and invest for the purpose of legislation, bodies
which by the very terms of the *BNA Act* are not empowered to
accept such delegation, and to legislate on such matters'.[41] In other
words, interdelegation between Parliament and the Legislatures is
prohibited. Why is this so? Essentially it is because the Parliament
of Canada and the Provincial Legislatures 'are created by and
derive their respective legislative jurisdictions from the *British
North America Act*',[42] which means that they cannot modify their

[37] See 10 (5) *ICAO Bulletin* (1955), 16–18.
[38] See 11 (7–8) *ICAO Bulletin* (1956), 27, and Cheng *op. cit.*, p. 42. For
the latest development on this subject, see: Province of Quebec, Order-in-
Council no. 1174 of 20 July 1966, Concerning Certain Fiscal Concessions to
non-Canadian Representatives to the Inter. Civil Aviation Organization:
United Nations Juridical Yearbook, 1966, p. 5.
[39] See the decision of the Court of Justice of the European Communities
in *Costa v. ENEL*, 10 *Recueil de la jurisprudence* (1964), 1143, 1160 (décision 5/64); see also Hay, Cooley and Moorhead, 'Problems of US participation in the European Common Market', 23 *University of Pittsburgh
Law Review* (1962), 595, 647 ff.
[40] *AG for Nova Scotia v. AG for Canada*, [1951] SCR 31 at 44.
[41] *Idem.*
[42] *Ibid.*, p. 53.

jurisdiction without an amendment to this Act. Does it follow then that legislative powers in Canada cannot be delegated to an outside agency? This is a matter that merits further discussion.

In *Attorney-General for Ontario v. Scott* this question was indirectly treated. The problem was whether a Province could confer on a non-resident a right to enforce a duty in the province in accordance with provisions prescribed by the law of England. The Ontario Court of Appeal held that the Ontario Act was void because a Legislature could not 'abdicate and surrender to the legislative body of any foreign State the right to declare concerning the civil rights of a person resident in this Province'.[43] However, the Supreme Court of Canada declared otherwise. It did not conclude that a Legislature could abdicate and surrender legislative powers to a non-Canadian legislative body; on the contrary, Locke J. expressly accepted the argument of the Ontario Court of Appeal that such powers could not be delegated to an outside agency.[44] What the Supreme Court said was that, in the particular instance, no delegation was involved. It would seem, following this case, that present Canadian constitutional law does not authorize the surrender of powers which membership in a supranational organization would require.

Even if it were possible to transfer legislative powers to an outside agency, difficulties would arise in effecting this transfer. Quite obviously, the only powers that the federal government of Canada could surrender by treaty would be its own legislative powers. As already seen, it cannot 'merely by making promises to foreign countries clothe itself with legislative authority' which it does not have.[45] Yet membership in supranational organizations like the European Communities involves the transfer of legislative powers which in Canada are possessed not only by the federal Parliament but by the provincial Legislatures.[46] The Canadian Government could try to convince the provinces to give up part of their legislative competence. But it would have to convince all the provinces, and not only a few of them, to do so; otherwise, it would not really qualify to become a member of a supranational organization. If, moreover, the provinces agreed to a partial transfer of their competence, would this be done through a constitutional amendment or through federal-provincial agreements? If the latter procedure were adopted, would the provinces be bound by such agreements?

---

[43] [1954]*Ontario Reports*, 676, 686; [1954] 4 *DLR* 546 at 551.
[44] (1956) SCR 137 at 152.
[45] See above, p. 154.
[46] See for instance Article 57 of the EEC Treaty, which authorizes the Council to issue directives concerning the mutual recognition of diplomas.

This is an interesting point, for it is far from clear what law would apply in such circumstances and which court would have jurisdiction.[47] These are some of the problems that joining supranational institutions would raise in Canadian constitutional law.

The situation in the United States is quite different. There, as early as in 1796, it was held that a treaty could not be the supreme law of the land, as directed by the constitution, if any act of a state legislature was allowed to stand in its way.[48] In 1880, in *Hauenstein v. Lynham*, a treaty enabling aliens to inherit land within a state was sustained as overturning a law of the state prohibiting such inheritance.[49] Ten years later, in *Geofroy v. Riggs*, the treaty power of the United States was said to extend to all proper subjects of international negotiation,[50] but at the same time it was added that the treaty power probably did not extend 'so far as to authorize what the Constitution forbids, or a change in the character of the government or in that of one of the States, or a cession of any portion of the territory of the latter, without its consent'.[51] In 1920, in *Missouri v. Holland*, it was further decided that a treaty could enable Congress to pass statutes on subjects not otherwise within its delegated powers;[52] but Mr Justice Holmes who delivered the judgment implicitly admitted that the treaty in question should not 'contravene any prohibitory words to be found in the Constitution'.[53] A similar attitude was adopted by Mr Justice Sutherland in *United States v. Curtiss-Wright Export Corp.*, decided in 1936. The latter held that 'the broad statement that the federal government can exercise no powers except those specifically enumerated in the Constitution, and such implied powers as are necessary and proper to carry into effect the enumerated powers, is categorically true only in respect of our internal affairs'.[54] He also added that the power of the federal government over international relations, like every governmental power, had to be exercised 'in subordina-

---

[47] See Moore, 'The federations and suits between governments', 17 *JCLIL*, 3rd ser. (1935), 163 at 170; see also section 30 of the Canadian Exchequer Court Act, Revised Statutes of Canada, 1952, c. 98, which provides for the settlement of inter-provincial disputes as well as disputes between the Dominion and any province that has passed an Act accepting the jurisdiction of the Court. See also Mundell, 'Legal Nature of Federal and Provincial Executive Governments: Some Comments on Transactions between them', 2 *Osgoode Hall Law Journal* (1960–63), p. 56.
[48] *Ware v. Hylton*, 3 Dall., 199.
[49] *Hauenstein v. Lynham*, 100 US 483 (1880).
[50] *Geofroy v. Riggs*, 133 US 258 at 266 (1890).
[51] *Ibid.*, 267.
[52] *Missouri v. Holland*, 252 US 416 (1920).
[53] *Ibid.*, 433.
[54] *United States v. Curtiss-Wright Export Corp.*, 299 US 304, 315–16.

tion to the applicable provisions of the Constitution'.[55] In 1957, in *Reid v. Covert*, Mr Justice Black stressed that:

> It would be manifestly contrary to the objectives of those who created the Constitution ... to construe Article VI as permitting the United States to exercise power under an international agreement without observing constitutional prohibitions. In effect, such construction would permit amendment of that document in a manner not sanctioned by Article V.[56]

Quite obviously, there are constitutional limits on the treaty power of the United States; but those limits are not to be found in the federal division of competence. Therefore, it would seem that in so far as international cooperation is concerned, the United States may be regarded as a unitary state.

Such a conclusion, however, would overlook the political limitations imposed by the federal framework of the United States. The American Government itself, it seems, has always been aware of such limitations. In 1893 the Italian Government proposed to the United States the conclusion of a convention giving the right to free legal assistance in civil and criminal proceedings to Italian citizens in America, as it was accorded to aliens in Italy. The United States refused to accept the proposal 'on the ground that provision was already made by State laws—certainly in some of the States—for suits by aliens as well as by citizens in *forma pauperis*, and that it was not competent for the Federal Government to impose an obligation of that nature on the several States by treaty stipulation'.[57] In 1899, the Department of State declined a proposal of the British Government to negotiate a treaty to prevent discriminatory legislation by the several states of the US subjecting foreign fire insurance companies to higher taxes than domestic companies; the reason given by the Department of State was that the negotiation of such a treaty would probably be futile on account of the indisposition of the people to permit any encroachment upon the exercise of powers of the local legislatures.[58] In 1922, the United States declined to adhere to the Convention for the Suppression of Traffic in Women and Children on the grounds that Congress was not in a position to enact legislation which might impose on the rights of the states.[59] At an inter-

---

[55] *Ibid.*, 319–20.
[56] *Reid v. Covert*, 354 US 1, 17.
[57] Moore, *International Law Digest*, iv, 8.
[58] *Ibid.*, v, 164–5.
[59] See Potter, 'Inhibitions upon the treaty-making power of the United States', 28 *AJIL* (1934) 456, 457.

national conference of American states, in 1928, the United States refused to adhere to a code of private international law; the American Delegation declared that it was unable to approve the project of Dr Bustamente in view of the Constitution of the United States which reserved the regulation of such matters to the states, members of the Union.[60] But it is really with the advent of the International Labour Organization that the full extent of the difficulties which the American Government had to face in the conduct of its foreign relations became clearer.

The representatives of the United States participated very actively in the drafting of the constitution of the International Labour Organization. Against the opinion of the majority, 'they raised, stressed and defended the needs of federalism'.[61] They fought for, and obtained, the inclusion of a federal state clause. However, the United States did not join the Organization until 1934. By that time, the point of view supported by the American delegates in 1919—namely that the US Federal Government could not legally give effect to all the decisions of the International Labour Conference—had become completely untenable. As Manley O. Hudson pointed out then:

> The fact that in the United States general power to legislate with reference to labour conditions is vested in the legislatures of the States, does not impose a necessary limitation on the treaty-making power of the Federal Government, for many treaties of the United States have dealt with matters as to which the federal power is otherwise limited.[62]

The hope of Hudson, and of many other international lawyers, was that the Federal Government of the United States would agree to ratify labour conventions dealing with matters vested in the legislature of the states. But their expectations were not to be fulfilled.

In 1939, five years after the United States had joined the Organization, the Federal Government had ratified only five conventions, none of them concerning subject matters reserved to the competence of the states. In the same year, the Delegation of the United States to the International Labour Conference recommended that a resolution be adopted requesting the Governing Body of the

[60] *Ibid.*, pp. 457–8. This was not the first time that the Government of the United States refused to participate in international efforts to unify rules of private law. For other examples, see Nadelmann, 'Ignored states interests: the Federal Government and efforts to unify rules of private law', 102 *University of Pennsylvania Law Review* (1953–54), 323.

[61] Looper, 'Federal state clauses in multilateral instruments', 32 *BYIL* (1955–56), 162 at 164.

[62] Hudson, 'The membership of the United States in the ILO', *International Conciliation*, no. 309 (1935), p. 120 at 130.

International Labour Office 'to undertake a study of the position of Federal States as regards the ratification of Conventions'.[63] The Government delegate of the United States explained: 'What we ask is the opportunity to do more, rather than less, than the Constitution requires.'[64]

In answer to the American suggestion, the International Labour Review published from 1940 to 1947 a series of articles discussing the situation in various federal countries. The second article, written by David Riesman, concerned the United States. The author concluded that so far as cooperation in international labour conventions was concerned, 'the United States could legally be regarded as a unitary rather than a federal State'.[65] The political issues, he admitted, were both more important and more complex; but the problems raised differed only in degree from those to be found in unitary states.[66] His whole attitude, generally speaking, was one of tempered optimism. But it seems that Riesman misjudged the importance of the political issues. So far, the Government of the United States has consistently refused to ratify labour conventions susceptible of affecting the reserved powers of the states.[67]

Further difficulties arose, after the Second World War, over the United Nations Covenants on Human Rights and Fundamental Freedom. Through the treaty power, Congress could constitutionally do everything that the Covenants required; but serious reservations were expressed as to whether two-thirds of the Senators would ever agree 'to authorize federal enforcement in the whole vast area of human rights'.[68] Acknowledging the need to preserve some kind of sensible boundary between the responsibility of the nation and the responsibility of the states, the American Government asked to have a federal clause included in the Covenants. For the various states members of the Union, however, this was no guarantee that the federal government would not use its treaty power to invade their area of reserved powers. Soon, the treaty supremacy doctrine came to be regarded as a serious threat to the American form of government.

[63] International Labour Conference, 25th session, *Record of Proceedings*, p. 354.

[64] *Ibid.*, p. 355; the resolution was seconded by Canada and unanimously approved: *Ibid.*, pp. 356–8.

[65] Riesman, 'The American Constitution and international labour legislation', 44 *International Labour Review* (1941), 123 at 124–5.

[66] *Ibid.*, pp. 126 and 192.

[67] See International Labour Conference, 49th session, 1965, *Record of Proceedings*, p. 612.

[68] Chafee, 'Federal and state powers under the U.N. Covenant on Human Rights', 1951, *Wisconsin Law Review*, 389 at 472.

Between 1950 and 1952, a series of articles appeared in the *Journal* of the American Bar Association calling attention to the perils seen by their authors in the potentialities of international agreements.[69] In 1952 the House of Delegates of the American Bar Association resolved to recommend to Congress a constitutional amendment restricting the making of treaties.[70] Between 1950 and 1952, similar amendments were also proposed by three state legislatures, three members of the House of Representatives, one federal Circuit Judge and one Senator.[71]

Explaining its proposed amendment to the Senate on 7 February 1952, Senator Bricker declared: 'By misuse of the treaty power, it is possible for the President and the Senate to transfer to Washington all the powers reserved to the States by the Tenth Amendment.'[72] To prevent this, he suggested a change in the Constitution which would leave the treaty power supreme over federal and state law, provided it be implemented by Act of Congress and subject to a limitation against impairment of constitutional rights of citizens and a prohibition against vesting power in an international body.[73] His suggestion, as was to be expected, found a receptive audience among many American lawyers. One of them, commenting on the Bricker amendment, wrote in 1953:

> It is quite apparent that what is needed now in order to preserve the life of the Constitution, and to prevent the gradual destruction, first, of state sovereignty and, then, of national sovereignty by a starry-eyed internationalism or by an insidious Communism, is a reaffirmation of the fundamental limitations of the Constitution upon the law-making powers of the Federal Government.[74]

Other writers used more discernment. Sutherland, for instance, declared:

> To adopt sweeping constitutional changes in a spirit of alarm, or of annoyance at past mistakes of domestic or international policy, is to create certain confusion and delay in our complicated day-by-

[69] Holman, 'Treaty law-making: a blank check for writing a new constitution', 36 *Am. Bar. Ass. Jour.* (1950), 707; Ober, 'The treaty-making and amending powers: do they protect our fundamental rights?', 36 *Am. Bar. Ass. J.* (1950), 715; Fleming, 'Danger to America: the Draft Covenant on Human Rights', 37 *ABAJ* (1951), 816; Deutsch, 'The treaty-making clause: A decision for the people of America', 37 *ABAJ* (1951) 659.
[70] See Sutherland, 'Restricting the Treaty Power', 65 *Harvard Law Rev.* (1952), 1305.
[71] *Ibid.*, pp. 1305–6.
[72] 98 *Congress Rec.*, 925 (1952).
[73] *Ibid.*, p. 921.
[74] Richberg, 'The Bricker amendment and the treaty power', 39 *Virginia Law Review* (1953), 753 at 763. See also Holman, 'Need for a constitutional amendment on treaties and executive agreements', *Washington University Law Quarterly* (1955), 340 at 342.

day foreign affairs, gaining in return only an estimated protection against the supposititious unwisdom of men now unknown, who may come to office years after the amenders have left the scene.[75]

The Bricker amendment in the end was rejected.[76] But as a result of the controversy that the amendment provoked, Secretary of State Dulles announced in 1953 that the United States would not ratify the proposed Covenant on Human Rights.[77]

Nowadays, for political rather than for legal reasons, the United States finds itself in a position similar to that of Canada regarding the conduct of its foreign policy. It is even possible that in certain circumstances, it would be legally prevented from undertaking international engagements. Could the United States, for instance, join a supranational organization like the European Economic Community? Short of a constitutional amendment, this would be very difficult.

There are various reasons for believing that the present constitution of the United States prevents it from joining a supranational organization. However, not all of them are relevant to the federal structure of the United States. Thus it may be argued that a transfer of legislative, executive and quasijudicial powers to the EEC would be impossible because it would be in conflict with the basic constitutional pattern of separate, independent branches of government.[78] But this has nothing to do with the federal organization of the United States; the traditional distinction between the executive, the legislative and the judiciary applies to many unitary states. Lack of judicial review by US courts and due process considerations probably constitute further obstacles to American participation in supranational organizations.[79] But again, such arguments are not specifically related to the federal structure of the United States.

There are also reasons intimately linked to the federal organization of the United States which mitigate against that country joining supranational institutions. It has been argued, for instance, that the treaty power does not extend so far as to authorize 'a change

[75] Sutherland, 'Restricting the treaty power', 65 *Harvard Law Rev.* (1952) 1305, 1337–8.

[76] 100 *Cong. Rec.* 2358 (1954).

[77] See Looper, 32 *BYIL* (1955–56), 197, where the author refers to a letter from Secretary Dulles to Mrs Oswald B. Lord, United States representative on the Human Rights Commission: 28 *Dept. of State Bulletin* (1953), 579–81.

[78] See Hay, *Federalism and Supranational Organizations,* 1966, p. 255; in chapter 6 of his book, the author makes a detailed analysis of the various motives which could prevent the United States from joining a supranational organization. See also Nathanson, 'The Constitution and world government', 57 *North-western University Law Review* (1962), 355.

[79] Hay, *Federalism*, pp. 221–7.

in the character of the government or in that of one of the States'.[80] If the United States were to join a supranational organization like the EEC, there is no doubt that a 'major structural change'[81] would occur in the governmental hierarchy of the country. The various states of the Union would be relegated to a large extent to the rank of mere administrative units, since a good part of their legislative powers would cease to be exercised by them. Such a result, it seems, would be contrary to the injunction in *Geofroy v. Riggs* against 'a change in the character of the government'. Hay argues that it would also be contrary to Article IV of the Constitution which provides that 'The United States shall guarantee to every State in the Union a Republican form of government'.[82] In his opinion, the reference to 'government' in this article requires quite clearly 'the preservation of the states as political entities rather than administrative units'.[83] Admittedly, there is no certitude that the Supreme Court of the United States would accept this. But the view that Congress alone cannot cede state territory[84] and the requirement that any constitutional change must not affect state representation in the Senate certainly support the theory of Hay.[85] It would be most surprising, indeed, if the United States were to become a unitary state without even a formal acknowledgment of the fact in the constitution.

A cursory analysis of the constitutional system of Germany can be deceptive. It seems that the federation and Canada are in exactly the same situation as far as treaty relations are concerned. The mere fact that the federal government is obligated under a treaty with a foreign country does not, in the implementation of the treaty, give it power over subject matters otherwise belonging to the states. Though the principle of 'federal fidelity' (Bundestreue) requires the member states to pay attention to the interests of the federation as a whole, the failure of the Constitutional Court to consider the applicability of this duty in the *Concordat* case makes

---

[80] *Geofroy v. Riggs*, 133 US 267 (1890).

[81] Hay, *Federalism*, p. 241.

[82] *Ibid.*, pp. 241–4.

[83] *Ibid.*, p. 244. See also Ghosh, p. 170, where the author writes: 'It is a strong presumption that it cannot be the intendment of the Constitution to vest unlimited and indiscriminate treaty-making and treaty-implementing power in the General Government to the detriment of the guaranteed autonomy of the Regional Governments'; at p. 176 the author equally refers to Article IV, Section IV.

[84] See on this subject, Moore, *International Law Digest*, v, 174; Hackworth, *Digest of International Law*, v, 13 and the discussions which preceded the Chamizal Convention of 1963 with Mexico (109 *Cong. Rec.* 24851–54 (1963). See also *Texas v. White*, 7 Wallace, 700.

[85] Article V, last clause, of the Constitution.

it clear that only in exceptional circumstances can the federal government invade the exclusive jurisdiction of the *Länder*.[86] In reality, the political structure of Germany is much more centralized than that of Canada. According to Article 73 of the Constitution, the federal government has exclusive power over foreign affairs, defence, foreign trade, citizenship, migration, currency, weights and measures, federal railways, air traffic, post and telecommunications, industrial property, federal civil services law, federal police and statistics for federal purposes. Articles 74 and 75 cover twenty-eight matters concurrently given to the *Bund* and the *Länder*. These include civil and criminal law, welfare-state services, the law relating to economic matters, labour law, agriculture and *Land* law. Now, in all concurrent matters, *Bund* law overrides *Land* law.[87] This means therefore, that the federal government has the power to implement its treaties in almost every matter. Education is the only subject of any real significance left to the exclusive jurisdiction of the member states. But it is precisely education which has caused most difficulty to the federal government.

As early as 1951, Herbert Kraus pointed out that the incapacity of the federal authorities to legislate in relation to educational matters had the effect of considerably limiting its activity in Unesco.[88] Shortly after this the *Land* of Lower-Saxony decided to ignore the *Reich* Concordat of 1933 and to abolish the old system of denominational schools. Naturally, the Vatican protested. A conflict developed between the Federal Government of Germany and the Government of Lower-Saxony and the matter was finally brought before the Constitutional Court. The outcome of the case is well known: the Court came down in favour of Lower-Saxony and the federal government was left with no power to fulfil the international obligation incurred under the Concordat of 1933.[89] What is probably less well known is that the conflict between Germany and the Vatican took a new turn in 1967, when the *Land* Baden-Württemberg also decided to abolish the system of denomi-

---

[86] See McWhinney, 'Comment of the Concordat case', 35 *Can. Bar Rev.* (1957), 842, 843.

[87] GG. Arts 31, 72 (1); see also Sawer, 'Federalism in West Germany', *Public Law* (1961), 26.

[88] Kraus, 'Die Zuständigkeit der Länder der Bundesrepublik Deutschland zum Abschluss von Kulturabkommen mit auswärtigen Staaten nach dem Bonner Grundgesetz', 3 *Archiv des Völkerrechts* (1951–52), 414 at 417; see also Mosler, 'Kulturabkommen des Bundesstaats—zur Frage der Beschränkung der Bundesgewalt in auswärtigen Angelegenheiten', 16 *Zeit. aus. öff. Recht und Völk.* (1955–56), 1.

[89] See *International Law Reports*, 1957, pp. 592, 594.

national schools.[90] As a result the Vatican warned the federal government that if the Concordat was not observed, it might modify the old diocesan borders without the consent of the German authorities and create new dioceses beyond the Oder-Neisse.[91]

Thus, inasmuch as the member states of Germany retain exclusive jurisdiction over certain matters, the federal government cannot act as it would like in the conduct of its foreign policy. However, in view of the extremely large jurisdiction retained by the *Bund*, the problems which might arise are inevitably limited. It is remarkable, for instance, that the federal structure of Germany has not prevented the country from joining the European Communities. The exclusive competence of the *Länder* in such fields as education was not of course threatened by federal participation in these Communities. Neither for that matter, was the position of the *Länder* in the internal federal framework threatened by a move of this sort. Even though German constitutional theory regards the component units of the federation as sovereign states rather than internal administrative units, in actual fact they are more akin to administrative subdivisions.[92] One of the most important functions of the *Länder* is to administer national law and policy in matters reserved to the exclusive jurisdiction of the *Bund* as well as in matters of concurrent jurisdiction. Thus, although the entry of Germany into the European Communities may have affected the powers of the *Länder* in certain fields, it has not really affected their status within the federation. Indeed, it should not have done in view of Article 79 (3) of the Constitution, which expressly guarantees the federal structure of the German State.[93] But this very provision ensures at the same time that the few limitations imposed on the treaty power of the federal government are likely to remain for a long time.

In Switzerland the treaty power is plenary and can be exercised independently of the federal allocation of powers; moreover, the power of the Confederation to implement a valid treaty is not limited in any way.[94] But the federal authorities have always been

[90] *The Guardian*, London, 10 February 1967.

[91] *Ibid.*

[92] For the view that the *Länder* are sovereign states, see Maunz and Durig, *Kommentar zum Grundgesetz, Art.* 20, no. 11; compare with Sawer, p. 26, where the author speaks of administrative federalism in the case of Germany (p. 29). See also Wells, Roger H., *The States in West German Federalism: a study in federal-state relations, 1949–1960*, New York, Bookman Associates, 1961, pp. 51–3.

[93] Hay, *Federalism* ..., pp. 293–5, examines the problems raised by Article 79 (3), but omits to say why this article did not prevent Germany from joining the European Communities.

[94] For a clear statement on this subject, see *Feuille Fédérale*, 1920, v, 457.

respectful of the rights of the cantons. This attitude was strongly reinforced by the constitutional amendment of 1921. This provided that those treaties concluded on behalf of Switzerland which purported to bind the state indefinitely or for more than fifteen years had to be submitted for approval to the people in a referendum before they could come into effect if 30,000 voters or eight cantons demanded it.[95] Indications that the federal authorities are aware of the political limitations imposed by the federal organization of Switzerland are not difficult to find. Until 1931, for instance, they consistently refused to intervene in the field of double taxation. As R. Lenz explains: 'Le Conseil fédéral hésita à imposer des conventions aux cantons dans un domaine où ils étaient souverains aux termes de la Constitution. Ces hésitations étaient plutôt de nature politique que juridique.'[96] As a member of the ILO, Switzerland has ratified labour conventions 'whenever the constitutional powers of the Confederation were well established and when executive measures already adopted made resort to a referendum extremely unlikely'.[97] In fact, its record is not much better than that of other federations.[98] As a member of Unesco it does not appear that Switzerland has been very active in ratifying educational conventions. In 1965 the Organization expressed its hope that Switzerland would celebrate the twentieth anniversary of Unesco by ratifying as many conventions as possible.[99] Thus even in a federation like Switzerland where the treaty power of the central authorities is not limited and where the subject matters reserved to the jurisdiction of the member states are few, a federal structure can still raise difficulties.

Similar remarks also apply to Australia and India. In both countries, the federal government possesses treaty-making and treaty-implementing power, although in Australia the treaty-implementing power of the federal government has only been recognized since 1936 and this in a rather ambiguous manner.[100] Also

[95] Article 89 of the Constitution.
[96] Lenz, *Les Conventions suisses de double imposition*, 1951, p. 13.
[97] Secretan, 'Swiss constitutional problems and the International Labour Organization', 56 *International Labour Review* (1947), 1 at 20.
[98] See Looper, 'The treaty power in Switzerland', 7 *American Journal of Comparative Law* (1958), 189–92.
[99] See Rousseau, 'Influence de la structure fédérale de la Suisse sur la conclusion des traités internationaux élaborés par l'UNESCO', 69 *RGDIP* (1965), 840.
[100] Concerning India, see Looper, 'The treaty power in India', 32 *BYIL* (1955–6), 300. Concerning Australia, see Bailey, 'Australia and the International Labour Conventions', 54 *International Labour Review* (1946) 288 ff; see also Menzies, *Central Power in the Australian Commonwealth*, 1967, ch. 8.

in both countries the federal structure imposes political limitations on what the federal authorities can do with the treaty power.
In the Commonwealth of Australia, the federal government is still
extremely careful 'not to trench upon the State jurisdiction by
exercising its treaty-making power except when absolutely necessary'.[101] Even when the British Government was responsible for
the external relations of the Commonwealth, multilateral conventions dealing with subject matters reserved to the competence of
the states were not signed without their assent. Thus when the
question of the accession of Australia to the Convention for the
International Circulation of Motor Cars was referred to the
premiers of the states in 1910, South Australia and Western Australia dissented and the Commonwealth Government therefore informed the British Government that it did not wish to accede.[102]
Nowadays, the situation is still very much the same. So far as
participation in the International Labour Organization is concerned, for instance, Commonwealth policy regarding ratification
of labour conventions dealing with state subjects was described
in 1959 as being 'to ensure that the law and practice in each of
the states are in accord with Convention requirements and that
each State is agreeable to ratification'.[103] In the United Nations
Commission on Human Rights the representatives of Australia
have always insisted on the inclusion of a federal state clause, even
becoming the leading supporter of such a clause after the United
States had decided not to ratify the Covenants.[104]

As for India, 'its unlimited treaty-power has not intoxicated it
to brush aside the peculiar circumstances and difficulties of the
member-States'.[105] In 1948, for example, the Union Government
expressed doubt about the compatibility of certain provisions of
the Labour Convention relating to Freedom of Association and
Protection of the Right to Organize (no. 87) with the regulations
laid down by the states concerning the right of public officials to
organize.[106] More recently, in the UN Commission on Human
Rights, the Indian Government has appeared as a staunch supporter of a federal clause, siding openly with Australia against such

[101] Ghosh, p. 267.
[102] See Doeker, *The Treaty-Making Power in the Commonwealth of Australia*, 1966, p. 42, n. 81.
[103] *The Parliament and the Commonwealth of Australia. Report from the Joint Committee on Constitutional Review*, 1959 para. 777.
[104] See Looper, 32 *BYIL* (1955–56), p. 197; see also Ganji, *International Protection of Human Rights*, 1962, p. 215, and Doeker, pp. 220–7.
[105] Ghosh, p. 276.
[106] ILO *Report of the Committee of Experts*, 1957, p. 171.

states as Yugoslavia and the Soviet Union.[107] In India as well as in Australia, it is obvious that the federal pattern does not facilitate international cooperation.

Enough evidence has been gathered now to permit a fair appreciation of the nature and extent of the problems facing federal states in the conduct of their foreign relations. It is obvious, in the first place, that the questions involved 'are partly questions of constitutional capacity, partly questions of constitutional appropriateness, which, without necessarily involving insuperable legal difficulties, raises issues of wisdom, of propriety and of balance between the different elements of the federation'.[108] Such difficulties cannot be easily dismissed. The degree of integration reached in a federal state is very often based on a delicate balance between diverging political interests. The true expression of this compromise is to be found in the federal balance of powers. This is why any alteration in this balance requires serious consideration.

On the other hand, it is equally obvious that, 'with the expansion of the area of what may legitimately be made the subject of international negotiation, the treaty power contains the seeds for the virtual destruction of the federation's constituent units'.[109] Therefore, it would seem that a choice must be made at a certain point between preserving the degree of integration already realized in a federal state and the further development of international integration. But such a conclusion ignores the various solutions provided so far to the problem of divided competence in federal states.

THE EXISTING REMEDIES

The existing remedies fall into three main groups. First of all, there are special concessions granted to federal states in bilateral or multilateral agreements and generally termed 'federal state clauses'; they operate exclusively at the level of international law. Then, there are various schemes permitting a plural representation of the federal state in international relations; these involve rules of municipal law as well as of international law. Finally, there are a certain number of purely municipal law arrangements in which reliance is placed on internal cooperation as a means of securing uniform action in external affairs. In the following pages, individual attention will be given to each of these types of solutions.

[107] Looper, 32 *BYIL* (1955–56), 197–9.
[108] Jenks, *Human Rights and International Labour Standards*, 1960, p. 142. See also: Sørensen, 'Federal states and the international protection of human rights', 46 *AJIL* (1952), 195 at p. 207.
[109] Looper, 34 *NY Univ. Law Rev.* (1959), 1045 at 1066.

Federal state clauses

Federal state clauses must be distinguished from territorial application clauses. Both forms of clauses are used in treaties in order to give the signatory state a greater degree of flexibility in the application of the international instrument either to its member state or to its colony. The rationale is that these units often enjoy a large measure of internal autonomy such that treaty-implementing legislation by the signatory power is either impossible or unwise. But here the similarity between the two clauses ends.

The territorial application clause, also called the colonial clause, stipulates either that a treaty will not apply to colonies and dependencies unless the signatory state notifies its intention to the contrary, or that it will apply to such territories unless they are excluded by specific negotiation.[110] The general rule of international law is that a convention will apply to the signatory state and to all territories for the international relations of which it is responsible, unless the contrary can be adduced from the treaty itself or is otherwise established.[111] Federal state clauses, on the other hand, limit, or otherwise affect, the obligations of the signatory federal state with respect to subject matters falling within the jurisdiction of its member states. Thus, the territorial application clause is concerned with the problem of the inclusion or exclusion of non-metropolitan areas in the sphere of application of the treaty; whereas the federal state clause takes into consideration the difficulty of applying to the component parts of a federation an international instrument that deals wholly or in part with subject matters within their exclusive field of jurisdiction. One clause is jurisdictional, the other territorial, and it is unsafe to lump the two together as though they were one.

Unfortunately, the difference between the two types of clauses has not always been made. In a recent book the 1964 Convention on the Choice of Court, prepared by the Hague Institute of Private International Law, is said to contain a provision taking

[110] McNair, *The Law of Treaties*, 2nd edn, 1961, pp. 118–19.
[111] See article 29 of the Vienna Convention on the Law of Treaties. See further the Comments of Sir Humphrey Waldock on the subject in *Yearbook of the International Law Commission*, 1964, ii, p. 13 Among other things, Sir Humphrey raises the interesting problem of the British islands. Prior to 1950, it was customary that all international instruments signed by the United Kingdom applied to the British islands in general. Since the Isle of Man and the Channel Islands enjoy a large measure of autonomy, it is now accepted that United Kingdom treaties do not apply to them unless there be a specific extension. For a description of the constitutional relationship of the Channel Islands and the Isle of Man to the United Kingdom, see Roberts-Wray, *Commonwealth and Colonial Law*, 1966, p. 672 ff.

into consideration the position of federal states.[112] However, the provision in question simply states that 'Any State may, at the time of signature, ratification or accession, declare that the present Convention shall extend to all the territories for the international relations of which it is responsible, or to one or more of them. Such a declaration shall take effect on the date of entry into force of the Convention for the State concerned.'[113] It seems clear that such a provision has no application to a federal state which is made up of member states, without any external territories. If it were to apply, it would lead to the ridiculous result that, for example, Canada could sign a treaty incorporating this provision, refuse to make the necessary declaration and find itself not being bound at all. Obviously, no foreign state would accept such a situation.

Concerning the federal state clause, there exists a fairly large body of literature.[114] However, important aspects of the subject have so far been ignored. Most writers, for instance, seem to be unaware of the extent to which these clauses have been used by federal states: whilst considering their use in multilateral instruments, they appear to ignore their presence in numerous bilateral agreements. Sometimes also, no distinction is established between clauses qualifying the obligation of the federal state in certain matters and clauses excluding purely and simply these matters from the normal application of a treaty. Finally, there is a marked tendency in the studies produced so far to emphasize the defects of the clause at the expense of its more positive aspects. But such criticism of the literature on federal state clauses cannot be properly appreciated without a review of existing practice.

Federal state clauses qualifying the obligations of federal states in respect of matters left to the exclusive competence of their constituent units are not exactly new. As far back as in 1853, for instance, such a clause was included in a consular Convention between the United States and France. Article VII of this Convention read as follows:

[112] See Gotlieb, *Canadian Treaty-Making*, 1968, p. 79; also Castel, 'Canada and the Hague Conference on private international law 1893–1967', 45 *Can. Bar Rev.* (1967), 1 at 29.

[113] Convention on the Choice of Court, art. 19. Final Act of Hague Conference on Private International Law, Tenth Session, 28 Oct. 1964, p. 22.

[114] The most important studies are those of Looper, 32 *BYIL* (1955–56), 162, Sørensen, p. 195; Liang, 'Colonial clauses and federal clauses in UN multilateral instruments', 45 *AJIL* (1951), 108; Bernhardt, 'Föderale Klausel', in Strupp-Schlochauer, *Wörterbuch des Völkerrecht*, i, 548. See also Ganji, pp. 212 ff; Wiebrignhaus, 'Le droit européen face au problème des accords internationaux dans les structures fédératives', 2 *Rivista di diritto europeo* (1962), 240 at 256 ff.

> In all the States of the Union, whose existing laws permit it, so long and to the same extent as the said laws shall remain in force, Frenchmen shall enjoy the right of possessing real and personal property by the same title and in the same manner as the citizens of the United States.... As to the States of the Union, by whose existing laws aliens are not permitted to hold real estate, the President engages to recommend to them the passage of such laws as may be necessary for the purpose of conferring this right.[115]

What is remarkable here is the refusal by the United States to grant a definite right in respect of real and personal property and its undertaking of a more limited obligation to recommend the passage 'of such laws as may be necessary for the purpose of conferring this right'. Similar provisions can be found in a number of other bilateral agreements between the United States and other countries.[116] In the Convention of Establishment of 1959 between France and the United States, for instance, Article IV (2) provides that: 'National treatment accorded under the provisions of the present Convention to French companies shall, in any State, territory or possession of the United States of America, be the treatment accorded therein to companies constituted in other States of America'.[117] Provisions of this kind are due to the fact that 'federal States cannot accord to aliens exactly the same benefits as those enjoyed by their own nationals, each in his own State.'[118]

It was only in 1919, however, that suggestions were made for the inclusion of a federal state clause in a multilateral instrument. This happened in the following circumstances. The British delegates to the Commission responsible for drafting the Constitution of the ILO had submitted a plan which involved for each member state an obligation to ratify all conventions unless the legislature of the state concerned had expressed its disapproval of ratification.[119] But the United States first, and other federal states afterwards, pointed out that labour matters were not within their constitutional jurisdiction and that, therefore, they could not undertake such obligations if a federal state clause was not included. After

---

[115] Malloy, *Treaties, Conventions, International Acts, Protocols and Agreements between the United States of America and Other Powers*, 1910, p. 528 at 531.

[116] See in particular the Treaty of 1854 with the UK, art. IV; the Treaty of Washington (with the UK) of 1871, Art. 27; compare also Article 2 of the Exchange of Notes between the USA and Canada of March 1948, (1951 *UN Treaty Series*, vol. 77), p. 194; see Ghosh, pp. 251 and 263; see also Crandall, *Treaties, Their Making and Enforcement*, 2nd edn, 1916, p. 267. On the interpretation of such provisions, see Bates, *Les traités fédéraux et la législation des Etats aux Etats-Unis*, 1915, p. 108 ff.

[117] (1961) *UN Treaty Series*, vol. 401, p. 75 at 92.

[118] Piot, 'Of realism in conventions of establishment' 88 *Journal du droit international* (1961), p. 39, 71; see also Stoke, pp. 180–2.

[119] See Looper, 32 *BYIL* (1955–56), 164 ff.

a heated discussion, the following clause was finally accepted:

> In the case of a Federal State, the power of which to enter into conventions on labour matters is subject to limitations, it shall be in the discretion of the Government of such State to treat a draft convention to which such limitations apply as a recommendation only, and the provisions of this article with respect to recommendations shall apply in such case.[120]

The main effect of this clause was to place the United States and any other state in a similar position 'on a different footing from and under a lesser degree of obligation than other States in regard to Draft Conventions adopted by the Conference'.[121] But the clause was not devoid of ambiguity. Literally taken, as Looper points out, its language applied to no state that was a member of the Organization, for no ILO member—not even Canada—was 'by reason of federalism subject to limitations of *power* to *make* treaties on labour matters'.[122] Moreover, the clause did not specify which authority in each federal state was to decide whether the power to enter into a particular convention was limited or not. In practice this subjective determination was made by the federal governments themselves. The leading federal states all tended to consider their case as falling within the purview of the federal state clause.[123] By 1939 the number of conventions ratified by them was so low that the International Labour Conference accepted an American suggestion to undertake a study of methods of securing more widespread ratification by federal states.[124]

After the Second World War the whole question of federal states' participation in the ILO held the attention of the Conference Delegation on Constitutional Questions. One of the first moves of the Conference was to invite federal states to cooperate in the search for a better solution to their problems. Various possibilities were examined with them. In the end, it was realized that flexibility and general acceptability offered the best means of securing more widespread ratification by federal states.[125] To meet these requirements, the following clause was adopted, which became Article 19 (7) of the amended Constitution:

> 7. In the case of a federal State, the provisions of this Article shall apply subject to the following modifications:

[120] *Ibid.*, p. 167.
[121] *Ibid.*, p. 167.
[122] *Ibid.*, p. 171.
[123] *Ibid.*, pp. 171–9.
[124] International Labour Conference, 25th session, 1939, *Record of Proceedings*, pp. 354–8.
[125] *Ibid.*, 29th Session, 1946, *Record of Proceedings*, p. 352.

(a) In respect of Conventions and Recommendations which the federal Government regards as appropriate under its constitutional system for federal action, the obligations of the federal State shall be the same as those of Members which are not federal States;

(b) In respect of Conventions and Recommendations which the federal Government regards as appropriate under its constitutional system, in whole or in part, for action by the constituent states, provinces, or cantons rather than for federal action, the federal Government shall:

(i) make, in accordance with its Constitution and the Constitution of the States or provinces concerned, effective arrangements for the reference of such Conventions and Recommendations not later than eighteen months from the closing of the sessions of the Conference to the appropriate authorities of the States or provinces for the enactment of legislation or other action;

(ii) arrange, subject to the concurrence of the State or provincial Governments concerned, for periodical consultations between the federal and the State or provincial authorities with a view to promoting within the federal State co-ordinated action to give effect to the provisions of such Conventions or Recommendations;

(iii) inform the Director of the International Labour Office of the measures taken in accordance with this article to bring such Conventions and Recommendations before the appropriate authorities of its constituent States or Provinces with particulars of the authorities regarded as appropriate and of the action taken by them;

(iv) in respect of each such Convention which it has not ratified, report to the Director of the International Labour Office, at appropriate intervals as requested by the Governing Body, the position of its laws and practice in regard to the Convention, showing the extent to which effect has been given, or is proposed to be given, to any of the provisions of the Convention by legislation, administrative action, collective agreement or otherwise;

(v) in respect of each such Recommendation, report to the Director of the International Labour Office, at appropriate intervals as requested by the Governing Body, the position of the law and practice of the various States or provinces in regard to the Recommendation, showing the extent to which effect has been given, or is proposed to be given, to the provisions of the Recommendation and such modifications of these provisions as have been found or may be found necessary in adopting or applying them.

The new federal state clause differs from the old one in two important respects. First, the test to be applied in order to ascertain when a difficulty arises is no longer limitation of power but appropriateness. This means that 'questions of policy and propriety as well as power' may be taken into consideration in deciding what kind of action should be taken in respect of a particular Convention or Recommendation.[126] Secondly, the alternative duties of the federal state are much more detailed than in the original clause. This, apparently, was considered as the best way of ensuring the gradual extension of the conventions and recommendations to all parts of federal states. On the whole, the clause reflects fairly well the objectives of flexibility and general acceptability sought by those who formulated it. Whether or not their expectations were fulfilled remains to be seen.

Those who expected a rapid and substantial increase in the number of ratifications by federal states were disappointed. In 1955 Looper pointed out that the record of ratifications of ILO conventions by federal states since 1948 was not materially better or worse than the prewar record.[127] But this was to be expected. The process envisaged by the new federal state clause was a gradual one involving the setting up of a complex machinery for cooperation between federal authorities and states authorities. With time, more positive results were obtained. The following remarks made in 1966 by the workers' representatives in the Committee on the Application of Conventions and Recommendations are interesting in this respect. In answer to a suggestion that Article 19 (7) should be deleted as weakening the obligations of federal states by giving them certain privileges, they declared:

> In order to overcome constitutional and other difficulties which might exist the arrangements and periodical consultations provided for under Article 19, paragraph 7, of the Constitution should be carried out and developed as much as possible. It was interesting to note that in certain cases, as in Australia and Canada, it had been possible—following such consultations—to ratify Conventions lying partly within the competence of the constituent units of the federation. Such procedures were to be encouraged, since even if they did not always result in the ratification of a Convention they might result in partial action at least to give effect to Conventions and Recommendations in the federal States. Thus submission of international labour instruments to the competent authorities increases the influence of these instruments even in the absence of formal ratification.[128]

Judging by these remarks, it would seem that the new federal state clause does play a useful role.[129]

[126] Looper, 32 *BYIL* (1955–56), p. 183.
[127] *Ibid.*, p. 184.
[128] International Labour Conference, *Record of Proceedings*, 1966, 50th Session, p. 577.
[129] Since 1964, for example, Canada has ratified three international labour Conventions, the subject matter of which falls partly within provincial jurisdiction and partly within federal jurisdiction. See below, p. 194.

After 1946 it became more usual to see a federal state clause included in multilateral agreements. In 1951, for instance, at the request of Canada, Australia and the United States, the Conference of Plenipotentiaries on the Status of Refugees and Stateless Persons agreed to put the following provisions in the Refugees Convention:

> Art. 41: In the case of a Federal or non-unitary State the following provisions shall apply:
> (a) With respect to those articles of this Convention that come within the legislative jurisdiction of the federal legislative authority, the obligations of the Federal Government shall to this extent be the same as those of Parties which are not Federal States;
> (b) With respect to those articles of this Convention that come within the legislative jurisdiction of constituent States, provinces, or cantons which are not, under the constitutional system of the federation, bound to take legislative action, the Federal Government shall bring such articles with a favourable recommendation to the notice of the appropriate authorities of states, provinces or cantons at the earliest possible moment.
> (c) A Federal State Party to this Convention shall, at the request of any other Contracting State transmitted through the Secretary-General of the United Nations, supply a statement of the law and practice of the Federation and its constituent units in regard to any particular provision of the Convention showing the extent to which effect has been given to that provision by legislative or other action.[130]

What is remarkable in this clause is the introduction of a test couched in an objective form, but depending in practice on the subjective determination of each individual state. There is also the fact that information concerning the implementation of the treaty is to be supplied by the federal state, not at regular intervals, but only at the special request of another contracting party. Similar provisions can be found in a number of other international agreements. Article 11 of the Convention of 1956 on the Recovery Abroad of Maintenance,[131] Article 37 of the Status of Stateless Persons Convention of 1954,[132] Article XI of the 1958 Convention on the Recognition and Enforcement of Foreign Arbitral Awards,[133] and Article IV of the Refugees Protocol of 1966[134] reproduce almost word for word Article 41 of the Refugees Convention of 1951.

The latest development in the field of federal state clauses relates to Article 28 of the American Convention on Human Rights signed at San José on 22 November 1969.[135] The first two paragraphs

[130] See *UN Treaty Series*, vol. 189, p. 137, at 180.
[131] See *UN Treaty Series*, vol. 268, p. 3 at 40.
[132] See *UN Treaty Series*, vol. 360, p. 117 at 156.
[133] See *UN Treaty Series*, vol. 330, p. 3 at 46.
[134] See General Assembly, XXI Session, Supp. no. 11A (A/6311/add.1) Part I.
[135] 9 *International Legal Materials* (1970), 673 at 683–4.

follow the classic formula: the federal government is under an obligation with respect to all matters contained in the Convention over which it exercises legislative and judicial jurisdiction; whereas, with respect to subject matters under the jurisdiction of the member states, its obligations are limited to recommending appropriate action in accordance with the Constitution. However, paragraph 3 provides that 'whenever two or more States Parties agree to form a federation or other type of association, they shall take care that the resulting federal or other compact contains the provisions necessary for continuing and rendering effective the standards of this Convention in the new state that is organized'. This particular provision, proposed by the El Salvador delegation, was specifically adopted to provide for the eventuality of the formation of a Central American federation.[136]

It is interesting to note that clauses answering the particular problems of federal states have also been included in the GATT and EFTA Agreements. Article XXIV (12) of the GATT Agreement reads as follows: 'Each contracting party shall take such reasonable measures as may be available to it to ensure observance of the provisions of this Agreement by the regional and local government and authorities within its territory.' Article 14, paragraph 4, of the EFTA Agreement also refers to cases of member states which 'do not have the necessary legal powers to control the activities of regional and local government authorities or enterprises under their control in these matters' and specifies the relevant undertakings of such member states as being to 'endeavour to ensure' that those authorities or enterprises comply with the provisions of this Article. Commenting on this provision, J. S. Lambrinidis writes:

> On the level of international customary law, if the constitution of a federal or otherwise composite State should prevent its central government ... from exercising control over the disputed activities of its constituent States, the law would refuse to sustain a defence by the central State based on this ground.
>
> Therefore, in the absence of a specific provision regulating responsibilities of Member States with regard to the discriminatory policies of their regional or local authorities or enterprises, Member States would be held responsible for any violation of Article 14 effected by such authorities.[137]

[136] See 'Report of the United States delegation to the Inter-American Specialized Conference on Human Rights', 9 *International Legal Materials* (1970), 710 at 733–4.

[137] Lambrinidis, *The Structure, Function, and Law of a Free Trade Area*, 1965, p. 157; concerning Article *XXIV* (12) of GATT, see Jackson, 'The General Agreement on Tariffs and Trade in United States domestic Law', 66 *Michigan Law Review* (1967), 250, 302–11.

Even though they do not refer expressly to federal states, articles XXIV (12) of the GATT Agreement and 14 (4) of the EFTA Agreement, it is submitted, constitute typical federal state clauses.

Finally, it must be noted that certain federal state clauses included in multilateral instruments modify not so much the substantive obligations of the federal government as the procedure by which the Convention is to be implemented. Thus, Article 16 of the European Convention on Information on Foreign Law concluded at London on 7 June 1968, specifies that 'in Federal States, the functions of the receiving agency other than those under Article 2, paragraph 1 (a) may, for constitutional reasons, be conferred on other State bodies'.[138] In this case, the basic obligation of federal governments to supply information on both their law and procedure in civil and commercial fields as well as on their judicial organization is not affected, but foreign states are agreeable to such obligation being discharged by the member states themselves.

In two particular instances, suggestions that a federal state clause should be included in multilateral agreements were turned down. In 1949, in connection with the draft Convention on the Suppression of Traffic in Persons, a subcommittee of the Sixth Committee of the UN General Assembly refused to consider the problem, referring it back to its parent body.[139] The Sixth Committee itself adopted the principle of a federal state clause, but was unable to agree upon the terms of any proposed clause.[140] Finally, the matter went before the Third Committee who refused to consider the question and adopted the Convention without a federal state clause.[141]

The most important setback occurred in the UN Commission on Human Rights. In the 1947 draft prepared by the Working Group set up for drafting the Convention on Human Rights, the following clause was included:

> In the case of a federal State, the following provisions shall apply:
> (a) With respect to any Articles of this Covenant which the federal Government regards as wholly or in part appropriate for federal action, the obligations of the federal government shall, to this extent, be the same as those of parties which are not federal States;

[138] In force 17 December 1969; text in 9 *International Legal Materials* (1970), 477 at 481.
[139] General Assembly, 4th session, *Official Records*, 6th annex, p. 38 (Doc. A/C. 6/L.88); see also Rosenne, 'United Nations treaty practice', 86 HR (1954), 275 at 377.
[140] General Assembly, 4th Session, *Official Records*, 6th annex, pp. 147, 148.
[141] See Rosenne, p. 377.

(b) In respect of Articles which the federal government regards as appropriate under its constitutional system, in whole or in part, for action by the constituent States, Provinces, or Cantons, the federal government shall bring such provisions, with a favourable recommendation, to the notice of the appropriate authorities of the States, Provinces or Cantons at the earliest possible moment.[142]

During the fifth and sixth sessions of the Commission, however, many objections were raised against this clause. According to some, it left 'too wide a measure of appreciation to the federal government itself, without allowing other governments to call into question the correctness of the decision reached'.[143] For others, the clause had the defect of leaving non-federal states in doubt about the obligations of a federal state and, therefore, in doubt about their own rights in relation to such a state. Several countries considered that federal governments, like other governments, should solve their own internal difficulties. Finally, some states held that such a clause was out of place in covenants on human rights, the universality of which should be assured.[144]

After prolonged discussions, the matter was referred for consideration to the Economic and Social Council, which referred it in turn to the General Assembly. On 4 December 1950 the latter passed a resolution asking the Economic and Social Council

> to request the Commission on Human Rights to study a federal State article and to prepare, for the consideration of the Federal Assembly at its sixth session, recommendations which will have as their purpose the securing of the maximum extension of the Covenant to the constituent units of federal States, and the meeting of the constitutional problem of federal States.[145]

Between 1950 and 1954, more suggestions were examined by the Commission on Human Rights itself and by the Third Committee of the General Assembly.[146] But no agreement was reached on any of the proposals put forward. The only solution left, therefore, was to put the matter to the vote. This took place at the 450th meeting of the Commission. The proposal of the Soviet Union was narrowly adopted by eight votes to seven, with three

[142] UN Commission on Human Rights, Doc. E/CN.4/95 (21 May 1948), p. 35; see also Economic and Social Council, *Official Records*, 6th Session, Supp. 1 (Doc.E/600), p. 29.
[143] See Sørensen, 'Federal States and the international protection of human rights', 46 *AJIL* (1952), 215.
[144] These various objections are examined by Looper, 32 *BYIL* (1955–56), 188–95.
[145] UN General Assembly Resolution 421 C (V).
[146] See the Reports of the fifth, sixth and seventh sessions of the Commission on Human Rights; see also *United Nations Yearbook*, 1953, pp. 384–6.

abstentions. It stated in simple terms that 'The provisions of the Covenant shall extend to all parts of federal States without any limitations or exceptions.'[147] This was a federal state clause only in name. Nevertheless, it became Article 50 of the Covenant on Civil and Political Rights and Article 28 of the Covenant on Economics, Social and Cultural Rights, both Covenants being open for signature and ratification since 1966.[148]

So far, attention has been paid only to federal state clauses qualifying the obligation of the federal state in respect of matters left to the competence of the component states. However, during the seventh session of the Commission on Human Rights, a different type of clause was suggested by the representative of Denmark. This clause read in part as follows:

1. The Government of a federal State may at the time of signature, ratification or accession to this Covenant make a reservation in respect of any particular provision of the Covenant to the extent that the application of such provision, under the constitution of the Federal State, falls within the exclusive jurisdiction of the constituent states, provinces or cantons. The Secretary-General of the United Nations shall inform other States Parties to the Covenant of any such reservation.
2. ...
3. ...
4. ...
5. As long as and to the extent that a reservation made under paragraph 1 remains in force, the government of the federal State may not in relation to other State Parties to the Covenant invoke the relevant provisions of the Covenant.[149]

What is striking in this clause is the possibility offered to federal states of purely and simply excluding certain provisions from the normal application of a treaty. In this way, it was considered, the obligations of federal states would be delimited with precision and they would be prevented from bringing complaints against other parties in respect of obligations not undertaken by themselves. But the Danish proposal was not accepted.

The idea of a reservation clause instead of a qualification-of-obligation clause had been suggested in 1958 by Lauterpacht.[150] Earlier, in 1936, the Government of the Commonwealth of Australia had seriously considered the possibility of ratifying the Convention for the Regulation of Whaling of 1931, subject to 'a

[147] E/CN. 4/L.340/Corr. 1.
[148] General Assembly (XXI), Resolution 2200 A.
[149] E/CN.4/636.
[150] Lauterpacht, *International Law and Human Rights*, 1950, p. 363.

reservation in regard to the territorial waters within the jurisdiction of the States'.[151] It was only in 1953, however, that a federal state actually ratified a multilateral agreement subject to a reservation in respect of certain matters. This was done by Canada and the Agreement in question was the 1953 Convention on the Political Rights of Women. The reservation was couched in the following terms:

> Inasmuch as under the Canadian constitutional system legislative jurisdiction in respect of political rights is divided between the provinces and the Federal Government, the Government of Canada is obliged, in acceding to this Convention, to make a reservation in respect of rights within the legislative jurisdiction of the provinces.[152]

However, in the absence of a provision in the text of the agreement stating explicitly that federal states can ratify subject to reservations concerning rights beyond their legislative competence, it is difficult to assess precisely the effects of Canada's reservation against other state parties to the Convention.[153]

It is more usual to find such reservations included in the text of bilateral agreements. For instance Article VIII of the 1946 Treaty of Friendship, Commerce and Navigation between the United States and China concerning the right to own or dispose of real property, provides that:

> In the case of any State, territory or possession of the United States of America which does not now or does not hereafter permit the nationals, corporations and associations of the Republic of China to acquire, hold or dispose of real and other immovable property upon the same terms as nationals, corporations and associations of the United States of America, the provisions of the preceding sentence shall not apply. In that case, the Republic of China shall not be obligated to accord to nationals...[154]

Reservations have also been made by federal states concerning the practice of professions. In 1928, during the negotiations between

---

[151] Conference of Commonwealth and State Ministers, 26 to 28 August 1936, Proceedings and Decisions of Conference, p. 78.

[152] United Nations, *Status of Multilateral Conventions* (ST/LEG/3, REV. 1), p. xvi—9.

[153] See on this problem: *Reservations to the Convention on the Prevention and Punishment of the Crime of Genocide*, Advisory Opinion (1951), *ICJ Rep.* 1951, p. 15; see also Fitzmaurice, 'Reservations to multilateral conventions', 2 *ICLQ* (1953), 1, and the discussions of the International Law Commission on this subject accompanying the various reports on the Law of Treaties as well as the comments made by States with respect to the final Draft Articles (UN Doc. A/CONF.39/5. vol. i). See also Article 19 of the Convention on the Law of Treaties adopted 22 May 1969 and opened for signature 29 May 1969 (UN Doc. A/CONF.39/27).

[154] *UN Treaty Series*, vol. 25, p. 69, at 104.

the United States and Switzerland regarding the conclusion of a commercial treaty, the Chief of the Division of Foreign Affairs for Switzerland was asked by the United States to explain Article 2 of the Swiss proposal which contained a reservation against the practice of the professions of notary and lawyer in the country. In answer to this request, the following information was given:

> We told you already—and we are in a position to confirm it to you today—that the intention of the federal authorities was merely to confirm on the point the right of the cantons to reserve the practice of these professions to Swiss nationals.... In order to make clear that the reservation which appears in Article 2 of the draft treaty of friendship ... in no way prejudices the solution which is or may be adopted by Cantonal laws, there would be no objections to adding after the words 'professions of notary or of lawyer' the words 'which are not covered by this treaty.'[155]

These negotiations, however, did not result in a perfected treaty. Later, in 1953, the Senate of the United States, in giving its advice and consent to the ratification of a number of commercial treaties, attached a reservation which set forth that the relevant part of these treaties in each case

> shall not extend to professions which, because they involve the performance of functions in a public capacity or in the interest of public health and safety, are State-licensed and reserved by statute or constitution exclusively to citizens of the country and no most-favored-nation clause in the said treaty shall apply to such professions.[156]

The Treaty of Friendship, Commerce and Navigation between the Kingdom of Greece and the United States of America, signed in 1952 but ratified only in September 1954, provided more simply that

> Nationals and companies of Greece shall be accorded within the territories of the USA, and reciprocally nationals and companies of the USA shall be accorded within the territories of Greece, national treatment and most-favoured-nation treatment with respect to engaging in commercial manufacturing, processing, financial, construction, publishing, scientific, philanthropic and professional activities, except the practice of law, dentistry and pharmacy.[157]

In double taxation agreements ratified by the United States,

[155] *Foreign Relations*, 1928, iii, 935.
[156] See Hunt, 'International law: reservation to commercial treaties dealing with aliens' rights to engage in the professions', 52 *Michigan Law Review*, (1953–54), 1184, 1186; see also Wilson, *United States Commercial Treaties and International Law*, 1960, pp. 89–90.
[157] *UN Treaty Series*, vol. 224 (1955), p. 310.

Canada and Australia, it is usual to find a definition of taxes which excludes all state or provincial taxes. In the Convention of 1951 between the United States and Switzerland for instance, Article 1 specifies that:

> The taxes referred to in this Convention are:
> (a) In the case of the USA:
>   The federal income taxes, including surtaxes and excess profit taxes.
> (b) In the case of the Swiss Confederation:
>   The federal, cantonal and communal taxes...[158]

Similarly, Article 1 of the 1957 double taxation Agreement between the Government of Canada and the Government of the Commonwealth of Australia provides that:

> The taxes which are the subject of this Agreement are:
> (a) in Australia:
>   The Commonwealth income tax and social services contribution, including the additional tax assessed in respect of the undistributed amount of the distributable income of a private company.
> (b) in Canada:
>   The income taxes, including surtaxes, imposed by Canada.[159]

It is not surprising that in 1963, when the Fiscal Committee of the OECD submitted its Draft Double Taxation Convention on Income and Capital, Canada and the United States reserved their position on that part of Article 1 which stated that the Convention shall apply to taxes of political subdivisions or local authorities.[160] A similar provision was included in the 1966 Draft Double Taxation Convention on Estates and Inheritances, and again Canada and the United States declared that they would not enter into treaties that would restrict the power of the individual states to impose estate or inheritance taxes on the transfer of property at death.[161] In fact, the latest double taxation agreements ratified by Canada still specify that the taxes subject to the Agreement are those imposed by the federal government only.[162] In the double

---

[158] *UN Treaty Series*, vol. 1279 (1952), p. 227 at 228.

[159] *UN Treaty Series*, vol. 392 (1961), p. 41 at 52.

[160] *Draft Double Taxation Convention on Income and Capital*, Report of the OECD Fiscal Committee, 1963, p. 63.

[161] *Draft Double Taxation Convention on Estates and Inheritances*, Report of the OECD Fiscal Committee, 1966, pp. 19–20, 37.

[162] Agreement between Canada and the United Kingdom, entered into force 23 March 1967; *Canada Treaty Series*, 1967, no. 7; Agreement between Canada and Ireland, entered into force 6 December 1967; *Canada Treaty Series*, 1967, no. 9; Agreement between Canada and Norway, entered into force 24 August 1967; *Canada Treaty Series*, 1967, no. 8.

taxation convention of 1967 between Australia and the United Kingdom, states taxes are also excluded.[163]

Such is the practice concerning federal state clauses. With the above in mind, the following statements may be made. First of all, it must be admitted that they are more frequently used than is generally acknowledged. They are to be found not only in multi-lateral conventions but also in numerous bilateral treaties. Bernhardt's claim that only a few conventions contain such clauses is not borne out by the facts.[164] Secondly, these clauses, despite their inherent weaknesses—inequality of obligations, uncertainty, etc.—appear to play a useful role. In 1952, Professor Sørensen explained in the following terms what he considered to be their main advantage:

> If federal states only have the choice between accepting the Covenant as a whole or not accepting any part of it, they will for constitutional or political reasons, as explained above, most likely decline acceptance. This is highly unsatisfactory from an international point of view, and it may be considered a lesser evil to allow federal states to become parties to the Covenant in respect of those provisions only to which effect can be given by the federal government itself.[165]

This is obviously an important point. But almost as important is the fact that federal clauses do, in many instances, extend the influence of a treaty beyond the area of competence of the federal authorities. This was clearly realized by the workers' delegates in the ILO Committee on the Application of Conventions and Recommendations when they declared, in 1966, that submission of international labour instruments to the competent authorities increased the influence of these instruments even in the absence of formal ratification.[166]

Finally, the reasons which may prompt federal states to ask for the inclusion of a federal state clause in an international instrument should be briefly examined. A distinction is usually drawn between reasons of a political nature and genuine legal reasons,[167] the implication being that in the first case, federal state clauses are not really justified. Such a distinction, it is submitted, may be useful in order to establish with precision the nature of the problem facing a particular federal state, but it does not alter the predica-

---

[163] Cmnd 3484 (UK).

[164] Bernhardt, 'Föderal Klausel' in *Wörterbuch des Völkerrechts* (Strupp-Schlochauer), i, 550.

[165] Sørensen, 46 *AJIL* (1952), 211.

[166] International Labour Conference, *Record of Proceedings*, 1966, 50th Session, p. 577; see above, p. 177.

[167] See for instance Sørensen, 46 *AJIL* (1952), p. 207.

ment which the latter finds itself in when dealing with foreign states. The truth is that a federal state clause is necessary when the factors making for unity in a federation do not permit continual reliance on internal cooperation as a means of solving the problems of the union, and when, at the same time, the factors making for disunity are not sufficient to permit a separate representation of the member states in international affairs. But more must be said about these two other means of solving the problems of federal states.

Separate participation of member states in international affairs

Recently, an international lawyer wrote that to try to solve the difficulties of federal states by the use of a federal state clause was tantamount 'to dodging the true solution which must lie in a conciliation between the requirements of federalism and the direct contact between the constituent States in question and International Law matters constitutionally within their sovereign competence'.[168] According to the same writer, some openings to this effect already existed in a number of important federations.[169] The suggestion that separate participation of member states in international relations may provide a valid solution to the problems of federal states is interesting. But whether federal governments themselves and foreign states are agreeable to this type of solution, is a different matter.

There are currently five federations in which member states are permitted to engage in dealings with foreign countries. These are Germany, Switzerland, the USSR, the United States, and to a lesser extent, Canada. In each of these federations, restrictions of one sort or another are imposed on the exercise of this right. In Germany, for instance, Article 32 (3) of the Basic Law provides that 'in so far as the *Länder* are competent to legislate, they may, with the approval of the Federal Government, conclude treaties with foreign States'. In the USSR, each republic has a general right 'to enter into direct relations with foreign states and to conclude agreements and exchange diplomatic and consular representatives with them'.[170] But Article 14 (a) of the Constitution provides that the jurisdiction of the All-Union Government includes 'the establishment of procedure governing the relations between the Union Republics and other States' and Article 68 (d) states

---

[168] Lador-Lederer, *International Group Protection*, 1968, p. 90.
[169] *Idem.*
[170] Article 18 (a) of the Soviet Constitution.

that the USSR Council of Ministers 'exercises general guidance in the sphere of relations with foreign States'.

In Switzerland, Article 9 of the Constitution declares that the treaties of the cantons with foreign Powers must contain nothing 'repugnant to the federation or to the rights of other cantons'. According to Article 10, 'Official relations between a canton and a foreign government or its representative take place through the intermediary of the Federal Council. Nevertheless, upon the subject mentioned in Article 9 the cantons may correspond directly with the inferior authorities or officials of a foreign State.' Lastly, by virtue of Article 102 (7) the Federal Council has the right to examine the treaties of the cantons with foreign countries and if it finds that they are contrary to the Constitution or infringe on the rights of other cantons, it may refuse to sanction them. In the United States, Article 1, Section 10 of the Constitution declares that 'no State shall enter into any treaty, alliance or confederation'. The same Article further declares that no state 'shall, without the consent of Congress ... enter into any agreement or compact with another State or with a foreign Power'.

In Canada, the Constitution is silent about the right of the Provinces to deal with foreign states. The federal government itself has always claimed that they had no independent treaty-making power. But more recently, it has adopted a policy of allowing arrangements between the Provinces and foreign governments which are subsumed under agreements between Canada and the foreign governments concerned.[171] Thus under the 1965 cultural agreement between Canada and France, direct arrangements between the provinces and France are allowed, provided that reference is made in these to the framework agreement or else that the federal government, through a further exchange of letters with France, gives its specific authorization to them.[172]

The various restrictions imposed on the right of member states to deal with foreign powers well reflect the cautious attitude adopted by all federal states on this subject. In each federation where this right is granted, sufficient powers are retained by the federal authorities to ensure that nothing contrary to the general interest of the federation is done. But, more than that, these authorities have, in practice, discouraged the conclusion of separate international agreements by the member states.

In the United States, a very small number of compacts between

---

[171] See *Federalism and International Relations*, a Canadian Government White Paper prepared by the Honourable Paul Martin, Secretary of State for External Affairs, 1968, pp. 31–2.

[172] *Ibid.*, p. 32; see above p. 60.

the states and foreign jurisdictions have been concluded. In the USSR only Ukraine and Byelorussia have been allowed to maintain diplomatic representation abroad and to sign international treaties, and this to a very limited extent. In Canada, the federal government has waited until recently before granting to the provinces a limited right to deal with foreign states; even then, it does not consider that such dealings involve the acquisition of international rights and duties by the provinces.[173] In Germany and Switzerland, the tendency is definitely towards the federal authorities undertaking in their own name obligations relating to the fields of competence of their component units.[174]

At the national level, then, it is obvious that direct participation of the member states in international affairs is not looked upon with favour. At the international level, the situation is somewhat different. All the evidence points towards a more open attitude on the part of foreign powers on the question of member state participation in international affairs. For the sake of efficiency, foreign powers obviously prefer to deal with one authority engaging the federation as a whole. But when the situation demands it, they are quite willing to deal with the individual member states. As far as membership and participation in international organizations is concerned, they are naturally reticent to transform a conference into a congress of huge proportions by admitting all the member states of federations. But here again, they seem ready to consider special cases.

It is not necessary to enumerate all the treaties which foreign powers have concluded with member states of federations. It is enough to say that they have concluded treaties with the Swiss cantons on matters ranging from double taxation to judicial assistance, and with the German *Länder* on subjects like frontier relations and education.[175] France for its part has concluded two cultural agreements with the Province of Quebec.[176] On rare occasions, foreign states have expressed their preference for dealing with federal authorities rather than with the individual member states. In 1873, for instance, the United States proposed to the Imperial Government of Germany to unify and extend the Bancroft Treaties between the US and the Norddeutscher Bund, Baden,

[173] *Idem.*
[174] *Ibid.,* p. 13. See also Sohn and Shafer, 'Foreign Affairs', in Bowie and Friedrich, *Studies in Federalism,* 1954, p. 257.
[175] See above, chapter 2, pp. 36–47.
[176] See in particular FitzGerald, 'Educational and Cultural Agreements and Ententes: France, Canada and Quebec—Birth of a New Treaty-Making Technique for Federal States?' 60 *AJIL* (1966), 529.

Württemberg, Bavaria and Hesse-Darmstadt to the whole of the Empire; but the proposal was rejected by the Imperial Government.[177] In 1926, Germany, Italy, Austria and Hungary, which were bound by double taxation agreements with the Swiss cantons, in turn suggested to the Swiss Federal Government that a double taxation agreement be concluded and made valid for the whole of the federation.[178] They considered, apparently, that the conclusion of individual agreements with each of the cantons involved too many complications.[179] On the whole, therefore, foreign states seem to be ready to deal with member-states of federations whenever they consider that it is necessary and worthwhile.

Foreign powers tend to adopt a more negative attitude in regard to member state participation in international organizations. In 1919 the American delegation to the Commission on International Labour Legislation proposed that sovereign states members of federal states 'should be placed in the same position as the British Dominions if they possess, as did the States of the United States, special competence with respect to labor legislation'.[180] Later, in the course of the discussions, the American proposal was reintroduced in the following form:

> The British Dominions and India and the several states of a federation of states where the states have reserved in whole or in part their autonomy in respect to labor legislation shall have the same rights and obligations, and in such case the representation at the Conference shall in number have reference to the population and industrial importance of the federation of states, such representation to be fixed by the Conference.[181]

Most states, however, were against the American proposal. The British delegate, Mr Barnes, expressed the view that separate representation for each of the states would render doubtful 'the unity of the United States', and turn the Conference into an enormous Congress.[182] When the question was put to the vote, only the Czechoslovak delegate voted with the United States, while the British Empire, Italy, Japan, Belgium, Poland, and one French delegate, voted against them.[183] On several occasions, the Soviet Union has also asked that separate votes be given to its member

[177] See O'Connell, 'State Succession and the Effect upon Treaties of Entry into a Composite Relationship', 39 *BYIL* (1963), 54 at 73–4.
[178] See Lenz, p. 14, n. 1.
[179] *Ibid.*, p. 13.
[180] See Sohn, 'Multiple representation in international assemblies', 40 *AJIL* (1946), 71 at 76.
[181] *Ibid.*, p. 77.
[182] *Ibid.*, p. 76.
[183] *Ibid.*, p. 77.

republics in different intergovernmental organizations. In 1929, for instance, it proposed that in place of the one vote held by the Union in the Universal Postal Union, six votes should be given to its six constituent republics; but this suggestion was turned down by the other states.[184] A similar demand was made in 1932 in relation to the Telecommunications Union, and it was also refused.[185]

But all this does not mean that foreign powers are not ready in special circumstances to admit individual states of federations as members of international organizations. Until 1935 the German states of Baden and Württemberg were represented on the European Commission of the River Danube. In a Note from the British Foreign Office to the German Embassy in London, dated February 1935, their exact situation in the Commission was explained in the following terms:

> At the time when the Treaty was signed, there were two States of the German Reich (Bavaria, Württemberg) whose territory bordered the Danube and, as stated in a Note from the German Embassy..., under the Constitution of the Reich at that time, the administration and control of rivers fell exclusively within the powers of the States, and not of the Reich... The plurality of German Representatives can be explained only by the fact that the two German States were treated as separate entities.[186]

In this instance, it is clear that the two member states of Germany participated in the work of the Commission because they were truly competent to do so; their participation, indeed, excluded that of the Reich itself.[187] A different situation arose in 1946 when Ukraine and Byelorussia were invited to participate in the work of the United Nations. This move was not prompted by compelling legal reasons. The other member Republics of the Soviet Union are absent from the Organization, and this does not alter the working of the organization. The decision to admit Ukraine and Byelorussia to the United Nations, as already said, was a political one and their participation in the Organization must be seen purely as an exceptional grant of multiple representation to Russia.[188] Nevertheless, this example as well as the one previously given show quite clearly that in special circumstances, foreign powers are ready to accept member states of federations as full participants in international organizations.

What then are the implications of member state participation in

[184] *Ibid.*, pp. 82, 83.
[185] *Ibid.*, p. 96.
[186] League of Nations, XVI *Journal Officiel*, 1935, p. 1666.
[187] *Ibid.*, p. 1664.
[188] See Sohn, p. 71.

international affairs as a means of solving the difficulties of federal states? As far as the existing federal states are concerned, the chances of this technique becoming extensively used are clearly remote. On the one hand, the federal authorities in these states are not particularly taken with the idea of their component units becoming involved in international affairs; on the other hand, foreign states will, as a rule, agree to deal with member states of federations only if they have to. But new federal entities might well come into existence in the future. Inasmuch as they will group together states with very different sociological and cultural backgrounds, one can expect that the member states of these federations will be allowed to maintain limited diplomatic relations with other states. In Bowie and Friedrich's *Studies in Federalism*, the conclusion is reached that in the perspective of a new European Federation, the member states should be allowed to maintain foreign relations and diplomatic services in their own field of competence.[189] The last has not been heard, therefore, of plural representation of federal states in international relations.

Cooperative federalism

After deciding in 1937 that the Canadian Parliament had no power to legislate upon provincial matters for the implementation of a Canadian treaty, the Judicial Committee of the Privy Council concluded:

> It must not be thought that the result of this decision is that Canada is incompetent to legislate in performance of treaty obligations. In totality of legislative powers, Dominion and Provincial together, she is fully equipped. But the legislative powers remain distributed, and if in the exercise of her new functions derived from her new international status Canada incurs obligations they must, so far as legislation be concerned, when they deal with Provincial classes of subjects, be dealt with by the totality of powers, in other words by co-operation between the Dominion and the Provinces.[190]

The idea was not entirely new. Twelve years earlier, a similar theory had been advanced in the United States by Frankfurter and Landis who had explained that the combined legislative powers of Congress and of the several states permitted a wide range of permutations and combinations for governmental action.[191] The idea

[189] Bowie and Friedrich, *Studies in Federalism*, pp. 260–7.
[190] *Attorney-General for Canada v. Attorney-General for Ontario* [1937], AC 326, 353–4.
[191] Frankfurter and Landis, 'The compact clause of the Constitution—a study in interstate adjustments' 34 *Yale Law Journal* (1925) 685, 688.

was further developed in 1938 by J. P. Clark.[192] In the same year, a number of papers presented at a symposium on 'co-operative federalism' appeared in the *Iowa Law Review*;[193] also in 1938, Koenig wrote an article entitled 'Federal and state co-operation under the Constitution', published in the *Michigan Law Review*.[194] This indicates that at the time the Privy Council delivered its decision the idea of cooperative federalism had assumed sufficient importance to be studied by various authors.

After the Second World War, more studies appeared on cooperative federalism.[195] The field of study was extended to cover Australia and Canada.[196] But none of the articles published paid serious attention to federal-state cooperation in the field of external affairs. Yet instances of cooperation in this field are not lacking. Some even go back as far as 1850. They are to be found, moreover, not only in America, Australia or Canada, but also in other federations like Switzerland and Germany. Sometimes cooperation in the field of external affairs has given rise to original and interesting solutions. In the following pages, it is hoped to give some idea of the numerous forms that cooperative federalism in the field of external relations can take.

In a White Paper published in 1968 by the Canadian Government under the title of *Federalism and International Relations*, two chapters are devoted to cooperation as a means of securing uniform action in external affairs.[197] In the first chapter, the main initiatives already taken by the federal government are examined; in the second, possibilities for further action are considered. The paper as a whole provides useful information as to Canada's present attitude to cooperation in the field of external relations.

At the outset it is stated quite clearly that a system 'which would permit the constituent members of a federal union to act autonomously in the foreign affairs field' would not be suitable for

---

[192] Clark, *The Rise of a New Federalism: Federal-States co-operation in the United States*, 1938.

[193] 'A symposium on co-operative federalism', 23 *Iowa Law Review* (1938), 455–518.

[194] Koenig, 'Federal and state co-operation under the Constitution', 36 *Michigan Law Review* (1938), 752.

[195] See among others, Vile, *The Structure of American Federalism*, 1961, ch. 10; Elazar, *The American Partnership; intergovernmental co-operation in the nineteenth-century United States*, 1962; Smiley, 'Public administration and Canadian federalism', *Canadian Public Administration* (1964) 371; Bernard, 'Federalism and Public Administration in Canada: a study in constitutional law and practice', Ph.D. thesis, London 1964.

[196] See Birch, *Federalism, Finance and Social Legislation in Canada, Australia, and the United States*, 1955.

[197] See p. 50, n. 198.

Canada and would 'entail grave consequences for the Canadian federal system'.[198] This is followed by an examination of cooperation in treaty-making and implementation. Here, we learn that it has been the practice of the Canadian Government for some time to consult with the provinces on various questions related to treaty-making and treaty implementation.[199] No fixed patterns have been laid down for these consultations, but the procedures devised are judged to have been successful. As evidence of this, reference is made to the fact that Canada has, since 1964, ratified three international labour conventions, the subject matter of which lay partly within the competence of the provinces, and in December 1965, had acceded to the International Road Traffic Convention.[200] But the federal government admits that this record could be improved.

Among other means open for cooperation, mention is made of three different techniques for giving international validity to agreements involving the provinces. In the first place, there is the so-called 'indemnity agreement'. According to this procedure, a treaty entered into by the federal government on a matter of interest to a province is supplemented by an arrangement with that province whereby the latter undertakes to execute the terms of the treaty and to indemnify the federal government in the event of its failure to do so; naturally, extensive consultations between the federal and provincial authorities take place before the treaty is signed.[201] Such arrangements were worked out with the Province of British Columbia (Columbia River Treaty) and with the Province of Ontario (St Lawrence Seaway). Apart from 'indemnity agreements', there are also '*ad hoc* covering agreements' and 'general framework agreements'. In both cases, the procedure is essentially the same. Through an exchange of notes with the foreign state concerned, the federal government gives its assent to arrangements between a province and a foreign governmental agency. But whereas '*ad hoc* covering agreements' concern only specific arrangements between a province and a foreign country, 'general framework agreements' allow for future arrangements in a given field. The two procedures are said to have been used to validate the educational and cultural *ententes* between the Province of Quebec and France.[202]

Apart from these methods of cooperation in treaty-making and

[198] *Federalism and International Relations*, p. 30.
[199] *Idem.*
[200] *Ibid.*, pp. 31 and 34.
[201] *Ibid.*, p. 31
[202] *Ibid.*, pp. 31–2.

treaty implementation mentioned by the Government of Canada in its White Paper, there are other techniques which merit mention. Since 1917, for instance, joint action has been taken by federal and provincial authorities for the protection of birds subject to the Migratory Birds Convention with the United States.[203] Several provinces incorporate in their game laws the provisions of the federal Migratory Birds Convention Act; moreover, the game and fishery officers of all ten provinces are *ex officio* game officers under the same Act.[204] In a similar way, Section 12 of the Quebec Income Tax Act provides that treaties signed by Canada with other countries with a view to avoiding double taxation apply *mutatis mutandis* to the Act.[205] Referential legislation and the contracting of services are, thus, two other means of achieving cooperation in treaty implementation.

Canadian participation in international organizations is another area in which some degree of coordination between the provinces and the central authority is required. In order to achieve such coordination, the following practices have been developed by the federal authorities. First of all, the provinces are consulted whenever the possibility arises of giving effect to international conventions adopted by specialized agencies such as Unesco or the International Labour organization. Secondly, measures are taken to ensure that the provinces are provided with published documentation on various questions falling within their fields of interest. Thirdly, efforts are made to strengthen provincial participation in Canadian delegations to international conferences. The rule has been established now that 'Canadian delegations to conferences of Specialized Agencies dealing with subjects within provincial jurisdiction should contain members drawn from provincial governments who are nominated by the Federal Government in consultation with the provincial governments concerned'.[206]

So far as new perspectives for cooperation are concerned, the Canadian Government White Paper puts forward two main suggestions. The first suggestion is 'to include ratification of multilateral conventions as a recurring item on the agenda of federal-provincial conferences'. In the second place, it is proposed 'to

[203] The text of the convention will be found in a schedule annexed to the Migratory Birds Convention Act, 1970, *Revised Statutes of Canada*, ch. M–12, p. 5081.
[204] 1970 *Revised Statutes of Canada*, ch. M–12 art. 5 (5); see also *Canada Yearbook*, 1967, p. 50.
[205] See *Statuts Refondus du Québec*, 1964, ch. 69.
[206] *Federalism and International Relations*, p. 5. See also Sabourin, 'La participation des provinces canadiennes aux organisations internationales', 3 *Can. Year Book of International Law* (1965), p. 73 ff.

convene periodic conferences between the Federal Government and the Provinces in order to review past, present and proposed treaties with a view to determining the Provinces' 'interest in Canadian ratification'.[207] As an outgrowth and extension of these arrangements, there is the further suggestion: 'to call meetings of senior federal and provincial officials which could deal with all aspects of consultations with the provinces on foreign affairs problems which engage provincial interests'.[208] With such measures, it is believed, effective cooperation in the field of external affairs could be realised.

However, since 1965, the Federal Government has found it difficult at times to cooperate with the Province of Quebec. As already explained, the Quebec Government adopts the view that it is competent internally as well as externally in its own sphere of jurisdiction. The two agreements signed with France in 1965 were considered by the provincial authorities as Quebec treaties and not as Canadian treaties. They were the first manifestation of Quebec's desire to participate to a limited extent in international relations. In February 1968 the Province was invited to a Conference of ministers of education of French-speaking states in Libreville. Despite the intense opposition of the Canadian Government, Quebec accepted this invitation and sent its Minister of Education accompanied by a delegation of three officials.[209] Immediately following this, the Canadian Government published its White Paper entitled *Federalism and International Relations*. In April 1968 the ministerial meeting of February resumed in Paris. Again, the Province of Quebec participated on an equal basis with other delegations. The Federal Authorities replied with the publication of a supplement to *Federalism and International Relations* entitled *Federalism and International Conferences on Education*, in which they reasserted that delegations to be sent to international conferences should speak, act and vote on behalf of Canada, although there could be a substantial provincial component in them.[210] In July 1968 Quebec, which till then had been willing every year to be represented in the Canadian Delegation to the annual Unesco International Conference on Public Education, refused to participate in the future in such Conferences as part of a Canadian Delegation.[211] Since 1970, admittedly, a certain degree of cooperation

[207] *Federalism and International Relations*, p. 44.
[208] *Ibid.*, p. 45.
[209] *Federalism and International Conferences on Education. A Supplement to Federalism and International Relations*, Hon. Mitchell Sharp, Secretary of State for External Affairs, Canada. 1968, p. 34.
[210] *Ibid.*, p. 50.
[211] *Le Devoir*, Montreal, 24 July 1968, p. 1.

has been achieved, particularly in the field of economic and social aid to developing countries.[212] But in spite of this, the prospects of collaboration between Canada and Quebec in the field of external affairs for the present are unclear.

In the United States, the methods of cooperation between the federal and regional governments have much in common with those existing in Canada. Thus it is not unusual for the federal government to consult the various states before signing international engagements relating to their fields of competence. The best example of this is the United States–Canadian Great Lakes Fisheries Convention signed in 1954 and ratified in 1955.[213] One of the main difficulties precluding the successful conclusion of this convention had been the claim by the states governments of exclusive control over fishery on the Great Lakes. Two previous treaties of 1908 and 1946 had come to nothing because of this.[214] In the fall of 1952 the American Government canvassed the eight Great Lakes states and discussed with them the need for a new treaty.[215] This conciliatory attitude led to positive results and finally the desired convention was signed in 1954.[216]

Other methods of cooperation well known in the United States include the use of state representatives in negotiations with foreign countries and the contracting of services. Thus during the negotiations preceding the conclusion of the Columbia River Treaty, three members of the Senate Foreign Relations Committee from the northwestern states gave constant guidance and encouragement to the discussions.[217] Earlier, in 1918, the Government of the United States had used state agencies for the implementation of the Migratory Birds Convention with Canada by commissioning their game wardens.[218] So far, these deputized state wardens have remained under the supervision of their own state officials and also of the Division of Game and Birds Conservation of the Bureau of Biological Survey, Department of Agriculture.[219]

As far as permanent machinery for cooperation between federal and states Governments is concerned, the United States appears to be more advanced than Canada. First of all, there is a Confer-

---

[212] See above, pp. 62–63.

[213] *UN Treaty Series*, vol. 238 (1956), p. 97.

[214] See Piper, *The International Law of the Great Lakes*, 1967, pp. 38–45.

[215] See Selak, 'The United States-Canadian Great Lakes Fisheries Convention', 50 *AJIL* (1956), 124.

[216] Ghosh, p. 250, also talks of a cooperative effort in this case.

[217] See Deener, ed., *Canada-United States Treaty Relations*, 1963, pp. 59–60.

[218] See *Migratory Birds Convention Act*, 40 *Statutes at Large* (1918), p. 755.

[219] See Koenig, 36 *Michigan Law Review* (1938), 752 at 775–6.

ence of Governors which meets annually to discuss the relations of the various states with the federal government.[220] These meetings present a useful occasion for discussing the interests of the states in particular treaties, the implementing steps necessary in order to ratify these treaties, etc. But, more important than that, there is the office of Special Assistant to the Secretary of State for Liaison with the Governors in the field of foreign affairs. The creation of this new agency was announced by President Johnson in 1967. Speaking to six New England Governors at a conference on 15 May, he declared that the Special Assistant would be 'the link between the President and the Secretary of State and the respective Governors of the States in connection with all matters concerning our relations with other nations'; President Johnson added: 'He will also be an enlightened voice in presenting their [the Governors'] views in connection with imports and exports, in connection with the many problems they have in their States as related to other nations.'[221] Thus in the United States formal liaison arrangements between the federal government and the Governors of the various states have been established.

In Germany cooperation between the *Länder* and the federal government is a constitutional duty. The German Federal Constitutional Court has repeatedly affirmed the existence of an 'unwritten constitutional principle' requiring that the constituent states as well as the federal government observe the interests of the union in the exercise of their legislative powers.[222] In the *Concordat* case, the Constitutional Court went so far as to say that 'particularly in the field of external relations, where the Federal Government is presumed to be competent, the duty of fidelity of the *Länder* towards the Bund is to be taken seriously'.[223] According to J. H. Kaiser, this means that the *Länder* are obliged to cooperate with the federal government whenever a treaty deals with matters reserved to their exclusive competence and cannot be implemented without their cooperation.[224] But the Constitutional Court itself,

---

[220] See Wheare, p. 227. Recently, the Governors' Conference has opened a liaison office in Washington; this was received with pleasure by the Secretary of State Rusk who considered the new office as an important step towards more effective relationships between the States and the Federal Government: See *Department of State News Letter*, June 1967, no. 74, p. 3.

[221] See *Department of State News Letter*, June 1967, no. 74, p. 3.

[222] See *Entscheidungen des Bundesverfassungsgerichts*, 12, 205 at 254 (1961); the same, 4, 115 at 140 (1954); see also Maunz and Durig, *Kommentar zum Grundgesetz*, 1964, Art. 20, annotation 22.

[223] *Entscheidungen des Bundesverfassungsgerichts*, 6, 309 at 362 (1957).

[224] Kaiser, 'Die Erfüllung der völkerrechtlichen Verträge des Bundes durch die Länder. Zum Konkordatsurteil des Bundesverfassungsgerichts', 18 *Zeit. für ausl. und öff. Recht und Völk.* (1957–1958) 526 at 545.

in the *Concordat* case, failed to consider the applicability of this duty of federal fidelity. It is, therefore, not altogether clear to what extent the *Länder* are obliged to cooperate with the central government in implementing federal treaties.

A practical solution to this problem was found in 1957 when the *Länder* and the *Bund* entered into an agreement regarding cooperation in the field of external relations. This agreement, known as the Lindauer Agreement, 'provides that the *Länder* will permit treaty invasion upon their reserved powers under certain specific circumstances'.[225] They undertake more particularly to approve typical clauses included in international agreements dealing chiefly with matters reserved to the exclusive competence of the *Bund*, when it is not certain that such clauses do not fall within their exclusive competence.[226] As for treaties dealing substantially with matters reserved to their exclusive jurisdiction, and more specially cultural agreements, the Lindauer Agreement provides that:

> So far as international treaties in the areas of the exclusive power of the *Länder* shall establish an obligation upon the Federation or the *Länder*, the consent of the *Länder* shall be obtained. This consent shall be submitted prior to the time when the obligation will become binding under international law. In case the Federal Government transmits such a treaty to the *Bundesrat* according to Article 59 (2), GG, it will, at the latest, simultaneously request the consent of the *Länder*. For treaties listed in paragraph 1, sentence 1, the *Länder* shall participate in the preparation of the treaty in good time and in any case prior to the final determination of the treaty text.[227]

Finally, it is agreed that for treaties touching upon the essential interests of the *Länder,*

> (a) the *Länder* will be informed of the proposed conclusion of such treaties in good time so that they may promptly make their own suggestions,
> (b) a standing committee consisting of *Länder* representatives will be established to be at the disposal of the Foreign Office or other competent specialized department of the Federation during the period of the negotiation of international treaties as a discussion participant.[228]

Doubts have been expressed about the legality of the Lindauer

---

[225] Hartman, 'Federalism as a limitation on the treaty-making power of the United States, Western Germany and India', 18 *Western Reserve Law Rev.* (1966), 134 at 151.

[226] Article 2 of the Agreement; the complete text can be found in 20 *Zeit. für ausl. öff. Recht und Völk* (1959–60), 116–17.

[227] Article 3 of the Agreement. The translation is that of Hartman, pp. 151–2.

[228] Article 4 of the Agreement.

Agreement. According to Leisner, such a delegation of competence from the *Länder* to the federal government would be constitutionally invalid.[229] Maunz, on the other hand, prudently suggests that the agreement is to be considered as valid.[230] For the moment, and until the question is referred to the Federal Constitutional Court, it remains essentially a *modus vivendi* between the *Länder* and the federal government which does not affect in any way the division of competence established by the Constitution, but facilitates the task of the Federal Authorities in their dealings with foreign states and at the same time protects the legitimate interests of the *Länder*.[231]

In Switzerland and Australia, cooperation in treaty-making takes the usual form of consultations between federal authorities and member states. Regarding Swiss double taxation agreements, for instance, R. Lenz writes:

> Un organe consultatif officieux, la conférence des directeurs cantonaux des finances, a été créé. Tous les projets de conventions lui sont soumis et le Conseil Fédéral ne contracte aucune obligation internationale sans s'être assuré par cet intermédiaire de l'approbation des cantons. Cette procédure se justifie pour des raisons de politique interne: elle est toutefois l'une des causes de l'évolution très lente du droit conventionnel suisse.[232]

According to A. H. Body, Legal Adviser, Department of External Affairs, Canberra, if an Australian treaty deals with matters of concern to the States of the Commonwealth, the state governments are 'often consulted, and any views which they express are taken into account'.[233] In some instances, as in the case of the International Convention on the Pollution of Sea by Oil, this leads to the introduction of complementary legislation in the Commonwealth and State Parliaments to give effect to the provisions of an international agreement.[234] There is also an Australian Premiers' Conference attended by the Prime Minister of the Commonwealth and the Premiers of the States which meets annually in May.[235] Like the

---

[229] See Leisner, 'A propos de la répartition des compétences en matière de conclusion des traités dans la République Fédérale d'Allemagne', *Ann. fr. dr. int.* (1960), p. 310.

[230] Maunz and Durig, p. 17, n. 80.

[231] See Weiser, 'La conclusion d'accords internationaux par les états fédérés allemands, suisses et autrichiens', in Brossard, Patry and Weiser, *Les Pouvoirs extérieurs du Québec*, 1967, p. 135.

[232] Lenz, p. 31.

[233] See O'Connell, ed., *International Law in Australia*, 1965, p. 56; see also, for more details on consultation of State Governments by the Federal Executive, Doeker, pp. 109–12.

[234] See Doeker, pp. 227–30.

[235] See Wheare, *Federal Government*, 4th edn, 1963, p. 227.

Governors' Conference in the United States, it provides a useful occasion for discussing various problems concerning international relations.[236] In Switzerland, moreover, cantonal agencies are sometimes used for the execution of federal treaties. Thus, Article 4, paragraph 4, of the Convention between France and Switzerland for the construction and utilization of the Bâle-Mulhouse airport at Blotzheim states that. 'Le Conseil d'Etat du canton de Bâle-Ville sera substitué au Conseil Fédéral suisse, suivant des modalités techniques et financières à arrêter entre ces deux autorités, en tout ce qui concerne les obligations qui découlent de la construction et de l'exploitation de l'aéroport.'[237]

On the whole, there is no doubt that cooperation is one of the best ways of solving the problems facing federal states in their external relations. Not only does this procedure provide a means for harmonizing the interests of the federal and state governments, but it also constitutes a guarantee for foreign powers that the treaties concluded will be promptly carried out. However, it is not an easy solution. In Australia, the Report of the Joint Committee on Constitutional Review referred in 1959 to 'the insurmountable difficulties sometimes experienced in obtaining approval of six independent states to a single course of action'.[238] It has already been seen that, in Switzerland, prior consultations with the Cantons in certain matters was one of the main reasons for the slow evolution of Swiss conventional law.[239] In Canada, mention has been made of a basic disagreement between the federal authorities and the Government of Quebec as to the role of the province in international relations.[240] But in answer to this it may be stated that federalism is essentially a compromise between diverging interests and that difficulties in harmonizing these interests are always bound to arise. Such a compromise in itself constitutes a first step towards cooperation. Even the granting of a limited treaty-making power to the member states, from that point of view, may be considered as a form of cooperation.

Indeed, it is this cooperative tendency in federal government which provides the most hopeful prospect for federalism.[241] In the sphere of international relations, this has been clearly per-

---

[236] See for instance the discussions surrounding the signature of the Convention for the Regulation of Whaling, *Conference of Commonwealth and States Ministers* 26–28 August 1936, p. 78.

[237] *Feuille Fédérale*, 1949, ii, p. 757.

[238] *The Parliament of the Commonwealth of Australia. Report from the Joint Committee on Constitutional Review*, 1959, paragraph 777.

[239] See above, p. 200.

[240] See above, pp 59–64

[241] See Wheare, p. 243.

ceived. More and more, federalism is being suggested as a model for international integration. Whether it has contributed anything to the developments of international law, however, remains to be investigated.

Federalism as a model for international integration

In his book *The Changing Structure of International Law*, W. Friedmann writes:

> The quest for international organisation, i.e., for the institutionalisation of human purposes of international concern, is today a vital aspect of international legal order, even though when measured against the needs of mankind it is still in an embryonic phase. Any appraisal of trends and patterns of international organisation in our time must first choose between two basic approaches: the constitutional and the functional approach.[242]

The constitutional approach is described by Friedman as being concerned essentially 'with the distribution of competence between various international organs, with the adjustment of voting powers, the setting up of legislative, administrative and judicial institutions, which will be competent to deal with the various aspects of the organized life of mankind'. As an example of this, he mentions the numerous blueprints for world federations which have appeared in the interwar period. But the constitutional approach, in his view, ignores the basic social factors of international society. Therefore, he favours the functional approach which 'implies the acceptance of the pluralistic character of international society' and centres 'upon the possibilities and the scope of the organisation of specific needs'.[243]

More recently, in *Federal Constitution-making for a Multinational World*, Edward McWhinney raises the question:

> What lessons have the theory and practice of 'classical' federalism to offer for what is perhaps the most striking aspect of international law and relations of the present era of change—the movement (whether on a substantially regional basis or whether more generally transcending geographical, even hemispheric limits) for political, military, economic integration and association along some sort of supra-national lines?[244]

Like Friedmann, however, he rejects the classical federal approach to international organization in favour of a more dynamic approach

[242] Friedmann, p. 275.
[243] *Ibid.*, pp. 275, 277.
[244] McWhinney, p. 112.

that views international law in general, and the law of international organizations in particular, 'as essentially a *process* of adjustment and reconciliation of competing societal interests and expectations as pressed by the main ethnic-cultural and ideological groupings in the present-day World Community'; this he calls 'a *new* federalizing trend'.[245]

Yet, before dismissing classical federalism as a model for international integration, it may be useful to examine whether federal ideas have influenced in any way the theory and practice of international integration. In the following pages, an attempt will be made to clarify this particular point. Subsequently, a critical look will be taken at federalism as a model for international integration, bearing in mind the remarks of Friedmann and McWhinney.

THE IMPACT OF THE FEDERAL MODEL ON THE THEORY AND PRACTICE OF INTERNATIONAL INTEGRATION

Among the earliest projects of reconstruction of the political world there are a certain number which can be distinctly related to federal ideas. In 1462, for instance, King George Podiebrad of Bohemia proposed to King Louis XI of France a plan of federation between the two countries which was to be extended to other princes. In essence, it provided for a permanent council with broad compulsory powers over the federated states, for a federal budget and for a permanent federal tribunal.[246] Some hundred and fifty years later, a project still more ambitious was put forward by the Duke of Sully. In his *Grand Design of Henry IV*, he envisaged a European federation of fifteen relatively equal constituent units with a General Council adjusting territorial issues, settling disputes and determining quotas of military forces.[247] In the eighteenth century, the Abbé de Saint-Pierre suggested that the Christian states of Europe should form a federation for the prevention of a foreign as well as of a civil war. There was to be a permanent senate, one central military establishment for enforcement action and centralized control of all military forces under one commander in chief.[248] In the nineteenth century, Proudhon foresaw a society composed

---

[245] *Ibid.*, pp. 122, 123.
[246] See Lange, *Histoire de l'internationalisme jusqp'à la paix de Westphalie*, 1919, i, 108; see also Hodé, *L'idée de fédération internationale dans l'histoire. Les précurseurs de la société des nations*, 1921, pp. 64–6.
[247] Sully, *Mémoires*, 4 vols, 1638–62; see Lange, i, 434.
[248] Abbé de Saint-Pierre, *Projet pour rendre la paix perpétuelle en Europe*, 1713; see Lange, 'Histoire de la doctrine pacifique, et de son influence sur le développement du droit international', 13 HR (1926), pp. 303–9.

of successive federations at the regional, provincial, national and international level.[249] But it was not until the end of the First World War that politicians and publicists became really interested in federalism as a model for international integration.

In 1923, Count Coudenhove-Kalergi of Vienna published a book entitled *Pan-Europa* in which he stressed the need for a European Union based on the federal model.[250] A few years later, in September 1927, Aristide Briand, Foreign Minister of France, made the following statement before the Tenth Assembly of the League of Nations:

> I think that among the peoples constituting geographical groups, like the peoples of Europe, there should be some kind of federal union. It should be possible for them to get into touch at any time, to confer about their interests, to agree on joint resolutions, and to establish among themselves a bond of solidarity which will enable them, if need be, to meet any grave emergency that may arise. This is the link I want to forge.[251]

At a subsequent meeting of European States Members of the League of Nations, the French Government undertook to draft and circulate a Memorandum on a system of European Federal Union. This document, known as the Briand Memorandum, was sent out on 17 May 1930.[252] Its substance has been summarized as follows:

> Strictly speaking, the plan was not a constitution for a federal union, but rather a series of suggestions to be worked out and developed in future 'constituent conferences'. It envisaged a federal union in which a 'European Conference' composed of representatives of all European members of the League of Nations would be the directing body. A smaller group, consisting of a limited number of members of the conference, was to form the 'executive body'. The powers of neither body were defined in the plan itself, but were to be determined at future meetings of the European Conference. The Memorandum reserved to the States full and complete independence and sovereignty.[253]

The reaction to Briand's Memorandum was mixed. Most states received his suggestions favourably but at the same time expressing reservations.[254] On 11 September 1930 the Memorandum was pre-

---

[249] Proudhon, *Du principe fédératif*, 1863.

[250] Coudenhove-Kalergi, *Pan-Europa*, 1923.

[251] See *Documents on International Affairs*, ed. J. W. Wheeler-Bennett, (1930), p. 61.

[252] *Ibid.*, pp. 61–73, where the full text of the Memorandum is given.

[253] Dangerfield, 'Plans of federation', in Eaton *et al*, *Federation, The Coming Structure of World Government*, 1944, p. 48.

[254] The full text of the Replies may be found in League Document A 46, 1930, vii, pp. 17–66; a Summary is provided in *Documents on International Affairs* (1930), pp. 74–9.

sented to the League of Nations Assembly. Eventually, it was sent back to a Study Commission where no more was heard of it.

By the middle of the 1930s, it was becoming increasingly clear that the League of Nations was failing in its basic objectives. This led to renewed interest in federalism as a means of securing international peace. In 1938 Lionel Curtis proposed that Great Britain, Australia and New Zealand be formed into a federal union to demonstrate the advantages of this form of political association.[255] In the following year, Clarence Streit published his famous book *Union Now*. His basic idea was that of a federation englobing the United States, the United Kingdom, the Commonwealth Countries, the Scandinavian States, France, Belgium, Switzerland and the Netherlands. The central government of this federation was to be given five main rights:

1. The right to grant citizenship.
2. The right to make peace and war, to negotiate treaties and otherwise to deal with the outside world, to raise and maintain a defence force.
3. The right to regulate inter-state and foreign trade.
4. The right to coin and issue money, and fix other measures.
5. The right to govern communications: to operate the postal service, and regulate, control or operate other inter-state communication services.[256]

Apart from that, national life would go on as usual. The same year, a similar system was proposed by Mousley,[257] and a plan for a more restricted union between France and Great Britain by Keeton and Schwarzenberger.[258] In 1939 the New Commonwealth Institute in London gave a series of university extension lectures bearing on federalism and world order.[259]

During the Second World War, more projects for associations of states along federal lines appeared. In 1940 W. Ivor Jennings proposed the building of a European federation upon the union already achieved by the European states engaged in fighting the Axis.[260] The same year, Leslie Buell and Alfred M. Bingham put forward plans of regional federations to be federated later into a world federal union.[261] In 1941 George Catlin suggested a federation of

[255] Curtis, *Civitas Dei: the City of God*, 1938.
[256] Streit, *Union Now*, 1939, p. 241.
[257] Mousley, *Man or Leviathan?*, 1939.
[258] Keeton and Schwarzenberger, *Making International Law Work*, 1939.
[259] See vol. 5, no. 2 of the *New Commonwealth Quarterly* (1939).
[260] Jennings, *A Federation for Western Europe*, 1940.
[261] Buell, *Isolated America*, 1940; Bingham, *The United States of Europe*, 1940.

the United States and Great Britain as a first step towards world federalism.[262] In 1943, Ely Culbertson again proposed a world federation based on regional groupings.[263] In 1944 H. O. Eaton and a number of other writers developed similar ideas in a book entitled *Federation: The Coming Structure of World Government*.[264] All these are only a few of the numerous projects which appeared during the War; but they show quite clearly the extraordinary influence exercised at that time by the idea of an international federation.[265]

Since the Second World War, interest in federalism as a model for international integration has not diminished. In 1946 Winston Churchill made a speech at the University of Zurich in which he invited Europeans to unite.[266] Four years later, in 1950, Robert Schuman made his famous declaration which led subsequently to the formation of the European Coal and Steel Community.[267] In 1953 H. Ripka proposed a federation of Central Europe.[268] In 1954 Edith Wynner put forward a plan for a world federal government.[269] Almost every year since 1945 studies such as those of François Cardis on federalism and European integration and of R. W. G. Mackay on *The United States of Europe* have made their appearance.[270] One of the most recent pleas for European unification comes from J.-J. Servan-Schreiber. In a book which has claimed wide appeal, he argues that a minimum of federalism is essential to the future progress of Europe.[271] Another work which deserves mention is that of Clark and Sohn on *World Peace Through World Law*.[272] What they propose essentially is a farreaching and comprehensive revision of the United Nations Charter. Increased powers would be granted to the General Assembly and the Executive Council and new institutions, such as a World Equity Tribunal, a World Police Force and a World Development Authority, would be created. Strictly speaking, this is a plan for world peace and

---

[262] Catlin, *One Anglo-American Nation*, 1941.
[263] Culbertson, *Summary of the World Federal Plan*, 1943.
[264] Eaton *et al.*, 1944.
[265] See Ledermann, *Fédération internationale et organisation économique mondiale d'après guerre*, 1943; and the same author's, *Fédération internationale*, 1950.
[266] See Tessier *et al*, *Dix ans d'efforts pour unir l'Europe*, 1955, p. 6.
[267] *Ibid.*, p. 65.
[268] Ripka, *A Federation of Central Europe*, 1953.
[269] Wynner, *World Federal Government in Maximum Terms*, 1954.
[270] Cardis, *Fédéralisme et intégration européenne*, 1964; Mackay, *Towards a United States of Europe*, 1961.
[271] Servan-Schreiber, *Le Défi américain*, 1967.
[272] Clark and Sohn, *World Peace Through World Law*, 3rd edn., 1966.

not a federal plan; but in certain important aspects, it reflects federal ideas.[273]

So far, only individual writers have been mentioned. However, to understand fully the influence of federal ideas on the theory of international integration, it is necessary to consider briefly the intensive action undertaken by federalist movements since the end of the First World War.

The oldest federalist movement, in a sense, may be said to be the communist movement itself. Although neither Marx nor Engels paid much attention to federalism as a way of organizing the world, Trotsky and Lenin did express at times various federalist ideas. Attacking the social democrats of the Second International who were coming to the defence of their fatherlands, Trotsky declared in 1914: 'The task of the proletariat is to create a far more powerful fatherland ... the republican United States of Europe, as the foundation of the United States of the World.'[274] A year later, in an article 'On the slogan of the United States of Europe', Lenin wrote: 'The United States of the World (not of Europe alone) is a state form of national unification and freedom which we connect with socialism.'[275] Again, on 31 March 1919, Lenin declared: 'It will not be long and we shall see the victory of Communism in the entire world, we shall see the founding of a worldwide Federal Republic of Soviets.'[276] But by that time already, the problem of federal integration was giving rise to serious ideological discussions among communist theoreticians.[277] After 1924 the issue was shelved; but the idea was never entirely lost. Evidence of this may be found in the following remark made in 1945 by the Yugoslav vice-premier Kardelj: 'We would like the Soviet Union to look upon us as representatives of one of the future Soviet Republics.'[278] Subsequent events have shown that even within the communist camp, national governments are not yet prepared to forsake their independence. Nevertheless, it may be argued with Schwarzenberger that 'world revolution and a world federation of soviet

---

[273] The World Equity Court in particular is reminiscent of federal supreme courts.

[274] Trotsky, *The Bolsheviki and World Peace*, New York, 1918; quoted in Goodman, *The Soviet Design for a World State*, 1960, p. 28.

[275] Lenin, 'Olozunge Soedinënnykh Shtatof Evropy', 25 Aug. 1915, 18 *Sochineniia*, 232; quoted in Tornüdd *Soviet Attitudes Towards Non-Military Regional Cooperation*, 1961, p. 66.

[276] Lenin, 'III Kommunisticheskii Internatsional', 31 March 1919, 24 *Sochineniia*, 194; quoted by Goodman, p. 32.

[277] Tornüdd, pp. 65–8.

[278] The remark is quoted by Modelski, *The Communist International System*, 1960, p. 10, n. 1.

socialist republics are the Communist long-range alternatives to the existing system of world power politics'.[279]

In the West, the most significant of the early movements was launched by Count Coudenhove-Kalergi in 1923. It started with the publication of his book *Pan Europa*, and within two years a number of leading European statesmen and intellectual leaders were committed to the Pan-European ideal. Among the names of those who joined the movement are Herriot, Briand, Freud, Einstein, Claudel, Valery, Thomas Mann, Miguel de Unanumo, Richard Strauss and Kreisler.[280] Coudenhove-Kalergi also met most of the politicians of that time and tried to convince them of the validity of his views.[281] His efforts had little success but the federal ideal itself as a result became more popular.

Federalist movements soon sprouted up in many countries. In 1938 'Federal Union' was founded in Great Britain. The purposes of the organization were (1) to secure support in Great Britain and elsewhere for a federation of free peoples under a common government elected by and responsible to the peoples for their common affairs, with national self-governments for national affairs; (2) to ensure that any federation so formed be regarded as the first step towards ultimate world government; (3) within such a federation to secure peace, economic security for all, and the civil rights of the individual.[282] A Federal Union Research Institute was created and as early as 1940 produced a report dealing with the most important aspects of international federalism. Among the active members of the Institute were Sir William Beveridge, Professor F. A. Hayek, J. E. Meade, Dr W. I. Jennings and many other well-known people.[283] In the United States, a similar movement called 'United World Federalists, Inc.', was created and began publication of a monthly magazine, *The Federalist*.[284] With the Second World War many of the activities of these movements were suspended.

The end of the hostilities brought about not only a renewal of activity among the existing movements, but also the formation of new organizations dedicated to international federalism. In order to understand these developments, it is necessary to make a distinction between movements orientated towards world federalism and movements orientated towards European federalism.

[279] Schwarzenberger, *Power Politics*, 3rd edn., 1964, p. 183.
[280] See Coudenhove-Kalergi, *Crusade for Pan-Europe*, 1943, pp. 102–3.
[281] *Ibid.*, p. 104 ff.
[282] This information is taken from *Federal News*, the official publication of the British federalist movement.
[283] See Federal Union Research Institute, *First Annual Report*, 1939–40, pp. 1–5.
[284] *The Federalist* was first published in 1951.

In September 1946 a meeting was called in Luxembourg by Federal Union of Great Britain and other federalist organizations to discuss the need for a world movement. One year later the World Movement for World Federal Government was founded in Montreux; four hundred delegates from twenty-three countries and fifty-two organizations were present.[285] The policy of the new movement was to work for the creation of world federal government in order to achieve world peace and to unite all organizations seeking the creation of a world federal government. Political action was to be exercised on three different levels; on the government level, the aim was to influence the executive to work towards the transformation of the United Nations Charter into a federal Constitution for the world; on the voters' level, the efforts were to be aimed at arousing a mass demand for federal world government culminating in the submission to all nations of very definite proposals agreed upon at a peoples' world constituent assembly; finally, on the level of elected representatives of the people, the aim was to get fast and direct constitution-making.[286] Among the activities of the organization, there was the publication of international magazines, the exchange of political and educational information, research on various topics relating to international integration, and the organization of a Congress every two years: a youth division was also set up under the name of Young World Federalists.[287] According to the *Yearbook of International Organizations* for 1966–67, the membership of the movement in January 1966 consisted of forty-five affiliated and associated organizations totalling 1,400,000 members in thirty-three countries.[288] The present President is Norman Cousins from the United States, and the Vice-presidents are Prof. P. Brandt Rehberg, Robert Buron, Dr G. Brock Chisholm, The Hon. C. D. Deshmukh, Thor Heyerdahl, Leopold Senghor and Setsuo Yamada.[289] The last congress of the World Association of World Federalists was held in Ottawa, 23–27 August 1970. Guest speakers included the Secretary General of the United Nations, Mr U Thant, the Prime Minister of Denmark,

---

[285] This information was taken from *One World*, April–May 1948, pp. 133–5. The movement later changed its name to that of the World Association of World Federalists.

[286] *Idem.*

[287] More details on the movement may be found in *World Federalist*, its magazine which appears six times a year. For a report on the Eleventh conference, held in Tokio, see Tabata, 'The eleventh World Conference of the World Association of World Federalists, Tokio 1963', 8 *Japanese Annual of International Law* (1964), 30.

[288] *Yearbook of International Organizations* (1966–67), p. 974.

[289] See *World Federalist*, World edition, Sept./Oct. 1970, p. 20.

Mr Baunsgaard, and the Secretary of State for External Affairs of Canada, Mr Sharp. The Congress emphasized not only the urgency of reaching agreement on such topics as arms control and disarmament, but also the necessity of relating urgent matters like the control and use of the seas and seabeds and pollution to an overall programme under the umbrella of the United Nations.[290]

When the World Movement for World Federal Government was created in 1946, it was concurrently decided to form a European federalist union. In Paris, in the same year, the 'Union Européenne des Fédéralistes' was founded and various movements in favour of the United States of Europe became members of it.[291] The object of the UEF—whose name was later changed to 'Mouvement Fédéraliste Européen'—was to work for the creation of a European Federation as first step to world federalism. The best way to realize this objective was considered to be the convocation of a constitutive assembly.[292]

In 1947 the Socialist Movement for the United States of Europe was founded in London. This again was organized on the basis of national sections. The objects of the movement were: the creation of a socialist European federation, the working out of a common socialist position regarding problems of European integration and the elaboration of European solutions to the political and social issues of each state.[293] 1947 also saw the appearance of 'Les Nouvelles équipes internationales', a Christian-Democrat inspired movement whose main objective was the realization of a European political community.[294] In the same year there appeared in France 'Le Conseil français pour l'Europe unie', which grouped together various French personalities believing in a federal Europe; in England, Winston Churchill founded the 'United Europe Movement'.[295]

In 1948 all these various movements agreed to be federated into a single organization, the 'European Movement' (Mouvement européen). The idea was to coordinate their action in order to obtain more effective results. Léon Blum, Winston Churchill, Alcide de Gasperi and Paul-Henri Spaak assumed in turn its presi-

---

[290] *Ibid.*, pp. 6–8. For further references on the subject of world government, see Newcombe, 'Alternative approaches to world government', *Peace Research Reviews*, no. 1 (February 1967).

[291] See Tessier *et al*, pp. 25–6; see also *Le Fédéraliste*, Revue de politique, Septembre–décembre 1966, p. 229.

[292] *Le Fédéraliste*, Sept.–Dec. 1966, pp. 229 ff.

[293] *Le Fédéraliste*, Sept. 1965, p. 114.

[294] *Ibid.*, p. 113.

[295] See Tessier *et al*, p. 8.

dency. Its objective was to promote the political unity of Europe through functional integration.[296]

In 1955 Jean Monnet founded 'Le Comité d'action pour les Etats-Unis d'Europe'. This was a grouping of eminent political personalities whose object was to accelerate the processes of political integration in Europe by taking position on problems arising in the course of this integration.[297] But in 1956 diverging views about how to realize European unity occasioned an important split among European federalists. The European Union of Federalists had always worked under the assumption that the best method for securing the formation of the United States of Europe was the convocation of a constitutive assembly. With the failure of the European Defence Community and the resulting abandonment of the project of European political community, a certain number of people formed the opinion that piecemeal integration was preferable to no integration at all. They formed a new movement, 'L'Action européenne fédéraliste', which, without rejecting the ultimate objective of federal union, adopted a different approach: the immediate object became to favour a progressive transfer of competence from individual states to European organs.[298] Since then no other European federal movement has appeared.

On the whole, the federal approach to world order has achieved a sufficiently articulate and influential body of support to justify the demand that it be taken seriously. But has it influenced the development of international integration? In order to answer this question, it is necessary to examine to what extent present international institutions show federal features. Such features, as already seen, consist essentially in (1) a division of powers, (2) a certain degree of independence between central and regional governments, (3) direct action on the people by the central and regional governments and (4) a constitutional court to preserve the division of powers.[299] By paying attention exclusively to these typical features of federal entities, it should be possible to eschew any charges of 'terminological licence'.[300] This rather strict approach may be construed as an attempt 'of jurists to narrow the focus of federalism',[301] but it is preferable not to mix legal and political concepts. There are certainly important differences be-

[296] *Le Fédéraliste*, Sept. 1965, pp. 112–13.
[297] *Ibid.*, p. 115.
[298] *Ibid.*, p. 112.
[299] See above, ch. 1, pp. 2–6.
[300] Mitrany, 'The prospect of integration: federal or functional', 4 *Journal of Common Market Studies*, 1965, 147, n. 43.
[301] Friedrich, 'Federal constitutional theory and emergent proposals', in Macmahon, ed., *Federalism, Mature and Emergent*, 1955, p. 514.

tween the United Nations, the European Economic Community
and a federal state. Even if they are all part of a federalizing process, the legal characteristics of each are not necessarily the same.
When the European Communities are described 'as closer to federal
structures than other international organizations', for instance, this
is implicitly accepted.[302]

International organizations other than supranational institutions
show in fact very few of the characteristic features of federal states.
It may be argued that Article 25 of the United Nations Charter,
which provides that the members of the UN agree to carry out
the decisions of the Security Council, constitutes a significant re-
nunciation of sovereign powers by all states which are not permanent members of the Council.[303] A similar argument may be
put forward regarding various formulas of weighted voting found
in such organizations as the World Bank, the International Monetary Fund, the International Wheat Council and IMCO. There is,
in these instances, an important departure from the traditional
rules of unanimity and equality of votes,[304] and a certain degree
of independence between central organs and member states is
attained.[305] This probably explains why the most enthusiastic sup-
porters of these weighted voting formulas 'are proponents of world
government'.[306] But apart from this limited operational autonomy
granted to certain technical organizations, there is no other federal
feature possessed by ordinary international organizations. For more
important developments, it is necessary to look 'to the more closely
knit regionally limited European Communities'.[307]

Numerous attempts at classifying the European Communities
have been made in the past. They have been considered in turn
as federations, partial federations, functional federations, international organizations with federal features and international
organizations *sui generis*.[308] But this is a secondary problem. What
is important, for the present purposes, is to ascertain the federal
features of the European Communities and their significance for
the development of international law.

[302] Reuter, *Organisations européennes*, 1965, p. 198.
[303] See Wilcox, 'International confederation. The United Nations and state
sovereignty', in Plischke, ed., *Systems of Integrating the International Community*, 1964, p. 27 at 32.
[304] On the rule of unanimity in international organizations, see the *Mosul
Case—Interpretation of Article 3 of the Treaty of Lausanne*, Advisory
Opinion, 1925, *PCIJ*, Ser. B, no. 12.   [305] Wilcox, p. 40.
[306] McIntyre, 'Weighted voting in international organizations', 8 *International Organizations* (1954), 484 at 493.
[307] Friedmann, p. 286.
[308] See on this question Hay, *Federalism and Supranational Organizations*, ch. 2.

One of the most important features of the European Communities is the strict division of powers on which are based. In *Costa v. E.N.E.L.*, the Court of Justice declared:

> En instituant une Communauté de durée illimitée, dotée d'institutions propres, de la personnalité, de la capacité juridique, d'une capacité de représentation internationale et plus particulièrement de pouvoirs réels issus d'une limitation de compétence ou d'un transfert d'attributions des Etats à la Communauté, ceux-ci [the member States] ont limité, bien que dans des domaines restreints, leurs droits souverains et créé ainsi un corps de droit applicable à leurs ressortissants et à eux-mêmes.[309]

As in federal states, therefore, one must distinguish between the powers retained by the member states and those transferred to the Communities. But in contrast to the division of powers in federal states, in the European Communities there is a division of functions rather than of subject matter. In *De Gezamenlijke Steenkolenmijnen in Limburg v. High Authority*, the Court of Justice of the Communities declared:

> Attendu, en effet, que l'intégration établie par le traité n'est que partielle et qu'en raison des pouvoirs retenus par les Etats membres les entreprises du charbon et de l'acier établies sur leurs territoires respectifs restent soumises à des législations et à des réglementations différentes dont les modalités sont susceptibles d'avantager ou de désavantager l'industrie du charbon ou de l'acier d'un Etat membre relativement aux industries similaires relevant de la juridiction des autres Etats membres ou aux autres industries du même Etat.[310]

Yet the difference is not all important. Even in federal states, matters which, from one point of view, fall exclusively within the federal authority, may, nevertheless, be proper subjects of legislation by the states from a different point of view.[311]

Another characteristic of the European Communities is the degree of independence enjoyed by their central organs vis-à-vis the national governments. When in August 1950 M. Robert Schuman put forward his plan for a European Coal and Steel Com-

---

[309] 10 *Recueil de la jurisprudence* (1964), Case 6/64, p. 1159; see also *Firma Max Neumann v. Hauptzollamt Hof/Saale*, 13 *Recueil de la jurisprudence* (1967), Case 17/67, p. 571 at 589. For further references on this subject originating from national courts of member states of the Communities, see Pescatore, 'L'apport du droit communautaire au droit international public'. *Cahiers du droit européen* (1970), p. 501 at 509–10.

[310] 7 *Recueil de la jurisprudence* (1961), Case 30/59, p. 46; see also Reuter, *Organisations européennes*, p. 216.

[311] See *Provincial Secretary of PEI v. Egan*, [1941] 3 DLR 305 at 309. For an illuminating article on this question, see Lederman, 'Classification of laws and the British North America Act', in *Legal Essays in Honour of Arthur Moxon*, 1953, p. 183 ff.

munity to the Consultative Assembly of the Council of Europe, he said of the proposed High Authority: 'The authority thus set up will be the first example of an independent supranational institution.'[312] The Treaty of Paris of 1952 clearly reflects this intention. The most important institution of the Coal and Steel Community is without doubt the High Authority. Originator of almost all decisions, it is composed of nine persons chosen for their general competence as individuals and who may not receive instructions from any government, party or interest groups. The High Authority acts by majority vote and makes 'decisions', which are binding in all their details; 'recommendations', which are binding so far only as their objectives are concerned and gives opinions, which are merely persuasive.[313] Next in importance to the High Authority comes the Council of Ministers composed of six members representing each government. Its role is to approve or veto certain decisions of the High Authority and, in a number of instances, to make a decision itself.[314] The mode of voting within the Council, therefore, is important. Depending on the situation, decisions are reached by simple majority, two-thirds majority, five-sixths majority or unanimity.[315]. On the whole, 'majority voting dominates the decision-making processes of the ECSC'[316] and provides its central organs with a certain degree of independence from the national governments.

The situation in the European Economic Community and Euratom is slightly different. The executive organ, the Commission, disposes of a limited power of decision of its own but more often is called upon to 'formulate recommendations and opinion' and 'participate in the preparation of acts of the Council and of the Assembly'.[317] The Council, for its part, makes most of the decisions, some of them unanimously, others, especially in the later stages of the transitional period, by a qualified majority.[318] Thus in these two organizations, the central organs enjoy a certain degree of independence from the national governments, albeit not as much as the High Authority of the ECSC.

In practice, however, little use has been made of this independence. Ever since the creation of the ECSC, there was a tendency

[312] Council of Europe, Consultative Assembly, *Official Reports of Debates*, 1950, i, 172.
[313] Art. 14 of the ECSC Treaty.
[314] See Articles 58 (3), 59 (6), 78 (6), 81 of the Treaty.
[315] Articles 22, 28, 32, 95 (4), 98 of the Treaty and Article 4 of the Statute of the Court.
[316] Haas, *The Uniting of Europe*, 1958, p. 46.
[317] See Article 155 of the EEC Treaty.
[318] See Articles 145 and 148 of the EEC Treaty.

on the part of the High Authority and Commissions to defer to the intergovernmental organ even when this was not required by the legal texts.[319] Within the intergovernmental organ itself, moreover, there has been a tendency to act unanimously rather than by majority voting.[320] Following the 1965–66 crisis, it was agreed by the member states of the EEC that the Commission would make appropriate contacts with the national governments before adopting a proposition of particular importance, and that any decision of the Council susceptible of affecting seriously the interests of one or more states would not be made before serious attempts at reaching a unanimous decision. France even requested that no majority decision should be taken; but on this point the other states registered their disagreement.[321] So far as the decision-making process is concerned, therefore, one must acknowledge that the degree of independence foreseen by the European Treaties has not been realized in practice. As Reuter says, 'the juridical construction of European federalism shows advances over the political'.[322]

The third federal feature of the European Communities is the direct action exercised by their central organs over the people of the member states. In *Van Gend and Loos v. Tariffcommissie*, the Court of Justice of the European Communities declared: 'Attendu que l'objectif du traité C.E.E. qui est d'instituer un marché commun dont le fonctionnement concerne directement les justiciables de la Communauté, implique que ce traité constitue plus qu'un accord qui ne créerait que des obligations mutuelles entre les Etats contractants.' After stating that this conception was supported by the preamble of the Treaty and by the fact that the citizens of the member states were called upon to participate, through the European Parliament and the Economic and Social Council, in the functioning of the Community, the Court concluded: 'La Communauté constitue un nouvel ordre juridique de droit international, au profit duquel les Etats ont limité, bien que dans des domaines restreints, leurs droits souverains, et dont les sujets sont non seulement les Etats membres mais également leurs ressortissants.'[323]

[319] Haas, *The Uniting of Europe*, p. 486.

[320] Alting von Geusau, 'Problèmes institutionnels des Communautés européennes', *Cahiers de droit européen* (1966), 227 at 232–3.

[321] Lagrange, 'Le pouvoir de décision dans les Communautés européennes: théorie et réalité', 3 *Revue trimestrielle de droit européen* (1967), 1 at 26–9.

[322] Reuter, 'Juridical and institutional aspects of the European Regional Communities', 26 *Law and Contemporary Problems* (1961), 392.

[323] *N.V. Algemene Transport—En Expeditie Ondermining Van Gend and Loos v. Administration Fiscale Néerlandaise*, 9 *Recueil de la jurisprudence* (1963), Case 26/62, p. 1 at 23.

The last federal characteristic of the European Communities is their constitutional court. In his work on *Federal Government*, Wheare writes that it is essential for a federation 'that some impartial body, independent of general and regional governments, should decide upon the meaning of the division of powers'.[324] In the European Communities, there is such a body. The Court of Justice of the European Communities has, in effect, direct judicial control over acts of the community organs and can annul them on grounds of incompetence.[325] Moreover, it has jurisdiction to find a member state in default of its treaty obligations.[326] In *Fédération charbonnière de Belgique v. Haute Autorité*, this resemblance of the Court to a federal tribunal was acknowledged by the Advocate General. He said in his conclusion: 'Notre cour n'est pas une juridiction internationale, mais la juridiction d'une Communauté créée par six Etats sur un type qui s'apparente beaucoup plus à une organisation fédérale qu'à une organisation internationale.'[327] But the comparison with federal courts must not be pushed too far. As opposed to individuals, enterprises or associations, there is no doubt that the member states of the Communities are given a privileged position in invoking the above-mentioned remedies; the differences that exist, it has been suggested, 'emphasize the "intergovernmental" aspects of the communities'.[328] Besides, it may be

---

[324] Wheare, p. 63; see also Friedrich, *Constitutional Government and Democracy*, 1950, p. 191.

[325] See Articles 33, 35, 36 of the ECSC Treaty, Articles 173, 174 and 184 of the EEC Treaty and Articles 146, 148 and 156 of the Euratom Treaty.

[326] See Articles 141, 142 of the Euratom Treaty. See Articles 88, 89 of the ECSC Treaty, 169 and 170 of the EEC Treaty.

[327] 2 *Recueil de la Jurisprudence* (1955–56), p. 263. The similarity between the Court of the European Communities and a federal court has been noted by a number of writers such as Grieves, *Supranationalism and International Adjudication*, 1969, at pp. 176–7, and Feld, 'The European Community Court: Its Role in the Federalizing Process', 50 *Minnesota Law Review* (1966), 423–42. See also the next footnote.

[328] Mashaw, 'Federal issues in and about the jurisdiction of the Court of Justice of the European Communities' 40 *Tulane Law Review* (1965–66), 21 at 28; see also Bebr, *Judicial Control of the European Communities* 1962, pp. 34–6. But according to J. M. Dehousse, the competence of the Court to give a preliminary ruling on the interpretation of the treaties makes it possible for individuals 'de se prévaloir du texte du traité pour demander et obtenir la non-application d'un texte étatique': see Dehousse, 'Du caractère essentiel de l'organe juridictionnel à pouvoir constitutionnel dans toute structure fédérale et application du principe à la Communauté Economique Européenne', *Annales de la Faculté de droit de Liège* (1965), 305 at 330. The decision of the Court in *van Gend and Loos* perhaps gave this impression; but since then, it has become clearer that such preliminary rulings of the Court are not intended to decide on the conformity of legislation and administrative acts of a state with the Treaties (see *SARL Albatros v. Sopèco*, 11 *Recueil de la Jurisprudence*, (1965) Case 20–64). Indirectly, however, a preliminary ruling by the Court of Justice of the European Communities

pointed out that the powers of the Court 'are oriented more toward review of the acts of the community organs than toward control of member-state interposition'.[329]

On the whole, then, it is clear that the European Communities present many of the characteristic features of federal entities. But they are still far from constituting a federal state. First of all, the powers granted to them are by no means as important as those possessed by the central government of a federal state. As Haas points out, 'the division of functions is heavily weighted on the side of national states.'[330] Secondly, the degree of independence enjoyed by the executive organs of the Communities, especially since the crisis of 1965, can hardly be considered as characteristic of a federal state. Thirdly, and this is the most important factor, the member states of the European Communities have refused so far to merge their international law sovereignty into a new and distinct entity. By mutual agreement, they can dissolve them, and without their individual consent, no important modification to the three treaties can be made.[331]

Between 1952 and 1954, the member states of the European Communities were presented with the opportunity to take a decisive step towards political integration. The Treaty instituting the European Defence Community, signed on 27 May 1952, provided in its Article 38 for the constitution of a permanent organization 'so conceived as to constitute one of the elements of a subsequent federal or confederal structure based on the principle of separation of powers and, in particular, on a bicameral system of representation'.[332] In September 1952 an *Ad hoc* Assembly was constituted to work out a draft treaty for a political community, based on the principles set out in Article 38 of the EDC Treaty. By March 1953 the Draft Treaty embodying the Statute of the European Community was completed. In August 1954, however, the French Parliament refused to ratify the European Defence Treaty and the whole question of political integration had to be shelved.[333] Since

---

may lead to the annulment of a State decision by a national Court; see also Buxbaum, 'Article 177 of the Rome Treaty as a federalizing device', 21 *Stanford Law Review* (1969), 1041–57.

[329] Mashaw, p. 53; see also Hay, 'Federal jurisdiction of the Common Market Court', 12 *American Journal of Comparative Law* (1963), 21 at 37.

[330] Haas, *The Uniting of Europe*, p. 58; see also Catalano, *Manuel de droit des communautés européennes*, 1964, p. 24.

[331] See articles 96 ECSC, 236 CEE and 204 Euratom. See also Hay. 'The European Common Market and the Most-Favored-Nation Clause', *Univ. Pitt. Law Rev.* (1962), p. 680.

[332] See Robertson, *European Institutions*, 1966, p. 19.

[333] See Charpentier, 'Pratique française concernant le droit international public', 1 *Ann. fr. dr. int.* (1955), p. 599.

then, the only change of importance to take place in the European Communities concerns the merger of their executives which was realized in July 1967.[334] But the Six are actively discussing at the moment (1972) the possibility of adopting a common monetary unit, something which, if realized, would almost certainly involve a new step forward in their integration.[335]

So what lessons have the theory and practice of classical federalism to offer for the future of international integration? As already seen, many people, including Friedmann and McWhinney, reject the federal approach to international organization.[336] According to Beloff, indeed, federalism 'confuses things that ought to be clear in people's minds, and renders them less able to appreciate the very striking developments that are taking place in international relations and that are much more important for the future than the talks of federal unions'.[337] For these writers, a more useful approach to world integration is the functional one. It is based on the view that 'in a world of a hundred or more States sovereignty can in simple fact never be dismantled through a formula but only through function, shedding national functions and pooling authority in them'.[338] Functionalists, according to Haas, 'believe in the possibility of specifying technical and non-controversial aspects of governmental conduct, and of weaving an ever-spreading web of international institutional relationships on the basis of meeting such needs'.[339] This, however, does not constitute a rejection of the federalist ideal. In 1948 David Mitrany himself, the chief exponent of the functional approach, admitted that the ultimate goal was still federation.[340] The disagreement concerns rather the immediate goals and strategies of international integration.

In order to illustrate the various approaches to international integration, and the differences that exist between the federal

[334] See Houben, 'The merger of the executives of the European Communities', 3 *Common Market Law Review* (1965), 37; the amending treaty came into force on 1 July 1967, after ratification by France; see 13 *Ann. fr. dr. int.* (1967), 783.
[335] On 24–25 February 1970, a meeting of the Ministers of Finance of the Six was held in order to discuss various aspects of the question. See *Problèmes économiques* (La documentation française), 4 June 1970, no. 1, 170, pp. 18–21; also *European Community*, March 1970, no. 132, pp. 18–19.
[336] See above, pp. 202–203.
[337] Beloff, 'Federalism as a model for international integration', 35 *BYIL* (1959), 188 at 203.
[338] Mitrany, 4 *Journal of Common Market Studies* (1965), 119, 145.
[339] Haas, *Beyond the Nation-State. Functionalism and international Organization*, 1964, p. 6.
[340] Mitrany, 'The functional approach to world organization', 24 *International Affairs* (1948), 350 at 360.

approach and the others, it may be useful to consider the following diagram prepared by L. N. Lindberg and S. A. Scheingold, *Europe's Would-Be Polity*, 1970, p. 8.

GOALS

		Transcend the nation-state	Rebuild the nation-state
STRATEGIES	Political Determinism	Federalists (U.S of Europe)	Nationalists (Confederation)
	Economic Determinism	Neo-functionalists (economic integration)	Functionalists (free trade)

Both nationalists and functionalists, according to the authors, are satisfied for the moment with the traditional form of international relations based on the sovereign equality of states and the rule of unanimity. The only difference between them is that the nationalists put more emphasis on political cooperation whereas the functionalists stress the importance of economic cooperation. The neofunctionalists and the federalists on the contrary favour a system which transcends to some extent the nation-states. Where they differ is in the importance that they give to political institutions. The neofunctionalists are satisfied with a system of economic integration involving a limited delegation of political powers to supranational authorities. The federalists, by comparison, consider that peace and economic progress can only be assured if the nation-states agree to delegate their sovereign power to a new entity, the federal state. But the distance between the two is not so great as to prevent a compromise. If one accepts that federalism is a process (at least from a political point of view), and that any attempt to transcend the nation-states implies to some extent the use of federal techniques, then one is bound to admit that such a compromise is indeed possible. This explains that the setting-up of supranational institutions such as the European Communities appeared to the federalists of 1950–60 as a first and important step in the right direction.

One could go even further and affirm that international integration, as opposed to international cooperation, must necessarily proceed along some sort of federal lines. International cooperation, as already explained, is based on the fundamental principle of the sovereign equality of states and functions according to the rule of unanimity. International integration on the contrary attempts to go beyond the nation-states by using such devices as majority voting and weighted voting. This in turn involves the creation of supranational institutions that act on behalf of all the states concerned at least in a certain number of fields. Such devices may be called federal devices.

So the question in the end is not so much whether classical federalism is bound to influence the development of international integration, as whether there is going to be any international integration at all. The experience of the European Communities tends to indicate that the development of international integration is not something that is *a priori* impossible. This being the case, a new question arises: what sort of impact is international (or federal) integration going to have on the development of international law?

FEDERAL INTEGRATION AND THE FUTURE OF INTERNATIONAL LAW

If the movement towards federal integration continues to develop, this will have farreaching consequences for international law. The experience acquired with the European Communities makes it possible to foresee some of the possible results.

So far as organizations are concerned, it is clear that the full realization of the federal ideal, 'if made on a universal scale, must lead to a world state, and, if made on a regional level, to a federal state'.[341] But this is to take a very long view of the evolution of international society. In the nearer future, more immediate results are to be expected. In 1952 Kunz wrote that the concept of supranational organs as developed in the European Communities was new because it transcended international organization without constituting a federal state.[342] The same idea has been taken up more recently by Hay, who writes:

> The contribution of the Communities to legal science is the breaking-up of the rigid dichotomy of national and international law. The Treaties and the Communities' experience demonstrate that an alternative to the creation of treaty-based obligations for the solution of common problems is the constituting of a *law-*

---

[341] Kunz, 'Supra-national organs', 46 *AJIL* (1952), 690 at 695.
[342] *Ibid.*, p. 697.

maker with authority to prescribe norms which bind their addressees. Thus the focus is neither on the specific substantive provisions nor on the completed federal edifice. The central point is that, *while forming*, the Communities fashion intermediate forms of law which are neither national nor international law. It is municipal law in effect, federal in structure, but not national in origin.[343]

Similar views are shared by Reuter who declares: 'From the scientific point of view, the study of organizations such as the European Communities would show that, in reality, international law and internal law are not at all separated in so absolute a manner as certain German and Italian doctrines have tended to assert.'[344] Therefore one of the first results to expect from further international integration is the appearance of new entities which, as the example of the European Communities shows, will defy all attempts at rigid classification. Such entities will stand midway between traditional international organizations and federal states and will themselves affect the future development of international law.

Already the formation of the European Communities has raised serious doubts about the future usefulness of the most-favoured-nation clause. Many countries are linked by Treaties of Friendship, Commerce and Navigation or by Conventions of Establishment, with various states members of the Communities, which are themselves parties to the General Agreement on Tariffs and Trade. Now the applicable standard in these treaties is usually the most-favoured-nation treatment. But Article 234 (3) of the EEC Treaty implicitly declares that the most-favoured-nation treatment will not be extended to third countries with regard to benefits under the EEC Treaty. This obviously raises a problem.[345]

Customs unions have been recognized for many years as a legitimate exception to most-favoured-nation commitments. Customs Unions exceptions may be found in a number of bilateral and multilateral treaties including GATT.[346] However, it would seem to be

[343] Hay, 'The contribution of the European Communities to International Law', 59 *Proceedings of the American Society of International Law* (1965), 195 at 199.
[344] Reuter, 26 *Law and Contemporary Problems* (1961), 381 at 393; see also on the subject the recent study of Pescatore, 'International law and community law: a comparative analysis', 7 *Common Market Law Review* (1970), 167–83.
[345] See on this subject Hay, 'The European Common Market and the most-favored-nation clause', 23 *University of Pittsburgh Law Review* (1961–62), 661–84; see also the discussions held on the subject of 'Regionalism and international law: the most-favoured-nation clause in a changing world', 54 *Proceedings of the American Society of Int. Law* (1960), pp. 153–94.

wrong to claim that the exception does not need any longer to be expressly stated in international agreements. According to Schwarzenberger:

> In the absence of an express reservation, a State can demand under the most-favoured-nation standard the benefits of exclusive preferential treaties, bilateral or multilateral, between the promissor and third States, such as customs unions which leave the international personalities of the contracting States intact.[347]

In fact, soon after the creation of the EEC, the Soviet Union made it known that it considered itself entitled to the benefits granted by the EEC Treaty vis-à-vis those member states with which it was bound by a most-favoured-nation clause.[348] As far as concerns the Contracting Parties to the General Agreement on Tariffs and Trade, they have refused so far to declare that the EEC member states were entitled to claim the benefits of the customs union exception provided for by Article XXIV of that Agreement. Instead, they have agreed to a kind of *modus vivendi* whereby the member states of the Common Market may proceed with the integration of their economies, but must keep the Contracting Parties informed of practical developments and make available procedures for consultation and complaints as provided for under Articles XXII and XXIII of the General Agreement; moreover, the Contracting Parties reserve under this *modus vivendi* the right to declare the EEC Treaty incompatible with GATT and to take action accordingly.[349]

Another problem that arises in connection with the customs union exception to the most-favoured-nation clause is whether it extends to matters other than trade barriers. To take a practical example, does it cover provisions concerning the right of establishment? According to Hay, there is no legal basis for such an extension of the customs union exception.[350] Yet, in practice all the benefits accruing to the member states of the European Economic Community are excluded from the normal operation of

---

[346] Article XXIV of GATT; regarding bilateral treaties, see the examples mentioned by Hay (see note above) p. 662 ff.

[347] Schwarzenberger, 'The most-favoured-nation standard in British state practice', 22 *BYIL* (1945), p. 96 at 109, n. 5.

[348] See Lacharrière, 'Aspects récents de la clause de la nation la plus favorisée', 7 *Ann. fr. dr. int.* (1961), p. 107 at 110. See also EEC Commission, *Seventh General Report*, par. 311.

[349] See GATT, *Basic Instruments and Selected Documents*, Seventh Supplement (1958), p. 71 ff. See also Lambrinidis, p. 243 ff., and more generally, Allen, *The European Common Market and the GATT*, 1960.

[350] Hay, 23 *Univ. Pittsburgh Law Rev.*, 679.

the most-favoured-nation clause. This raises serious questions as to the continued usefulness of the latter, especially in view of the growing tendency towards regionalism. As outlined in a recent article:

> Ainsi, l'exemple de la C.E.E. est pour beaucoup dans la générali-sation, à travers le monde de la mode des systèmes prérérentiels régionaux. Or il ne fait pas de doute que la généralisation du régionalisme ne transforme considérablement la physionomie du régime de non-discrimination (ou de non-préférence ou de traite-ment de la nation la plus favorisée) à travers le monde.[351]

Hay, for his part, concludes more prophetically that: 'For pro-spective treaties the most-favored-nation clause may then reassert itself on the multi-state regional basis in the form of a "most-favored-*region*" clause.'[352] But already the European Economic Community is concluding commercial agreements with foreign states which include provisions for the granting of reciprocal most-favoured-nation treatment. An example of this kind of agreement is the commercial treaty signed on 19 March 1970, between the European Economic Community and Yugoslavia.[353]

The discussion so far has centred upon the problems raised by the treaties of the member states of the Common Market concluded prior to their entry into the Community. A few words must now be said about the technique developed to ensure that the future com-mercial treaties of the member states do not run contrary to the economic policy of the Economic Community. In July 1960 the Council of the EEC adopted the so-called 'Common Market Clause' which reads as follows: 'Should those obligations under the Treaty establishing the European Economic Community which relate to the gradual establishment of a common commercial policy make this necessary, negotiations shall be opened as soon as feasible in order to amend this present agreement as appropriate.'[354] Such a clause was to be inserted in all future commercial agreements of the member states with third countries. In October 1961 a new decision was adopted which laid down that:

Art.1: La durée des accords relatifs aux relations commerciales

---

[351] X.X.X., 'Evolution de la réglementation internationale en matière de discrimination et de préférences', 9 *Ann, fr. dr. int.* (1963), 64 at 68–9.
[352] Hay, 23 *Univ. Pittsburgh Law Rev.* 684.
[353] For the text of the agreement, see *Journal Officiel*, 13 March 1970, no. L58/1; its official signature is announced in *Journal Officiel*, 24 March 1970, no. L67/15.
[354] Campbell and Thompson, *Common Market Law*, 1962, p. 70; see also Alting von Geusau, 'The external representation of plural interests', 5 *Journal of Common Market Studies* (1967), 426 at 450.

qui seront signés entre les Etats membres et les pays tiers ne peut pas dépasser la durée de la période transitoire d'application du traité...

Art. 2: Dans la limite fixée à l'article 1, les accords ne comportant ni clause C.E.E. ni une clause de dénonciation annuelle ne pourront pas avoir une validité supérieure à un an.[355]

Although clear and simple, these two measures raise a number of theoretical problems. From the point of view of international law, the 'common market' clause can only be interpreted as a *pactum de contrahendo*. In other words, it involves an obligation to negotiate, but not an obligation to reach an agreement.[356] This means in practice that the objectives of the 'common market' clause may not always have been fulfilled; that is, to coordinate the commercial policy of the member states with that of the Economic Community. A second difficulty arises from the decision adopted by the Council in October 1961. It is one thing to assert that commercial treaties concluded by member states which do not include a 'common market' clause or a 'clause de dénonciation annuelle' are valid for only one year; it is quite another thing for the member states which have concluded such treaties to terminate them unilaterally. Under Article 111 of the EEC Treaty, they have undertaken to 'coordinate their commercial relations with third states so as to bring about, by the end of the transitional period, the conditions necessary for putting into effect a common policy in the field of external trade'; there is no doubt that the decision of July 1961 was adopted on the basis of this Article and is, therefore, binding upon them.[357] But it is just as clear that the provisions of the Treaty of Rome cannot affect the rights of third states. If a member state has concluded an agreement with a third party which does not contain a denunciation clause, it cannot terminate it unilaterally. The resulting situation is one of conflict of treaties.

In practice, however, it must be acknowledged that the Council of the European Economic Community has adopted a rather flexible attitude concerning such problems. On a number of occasions, it has granted to various member states a waiver of Article 1 of its decision of 9 October 1961, relating to the duration of commercial agreements with third states. It did so, for instance, on 1 August 1969, concerning an agreement on commercial matters concluded

---

[355] *Journal Officiel*, 4 November 1961, p. 1274/61.
[356] *Railway Traffic Between Lithuania and Poland*, Advisory Opinion, *PJCIJ* (1931), Case A/B 42, p. 116.
[357] Pescatore, 'Les relations extérieures des Communautés européennes', 103 *HR* (1961), 1 at 94.

earlier by France with the Union of Soviet Socialist Republics.[358] In this particular case, the Council took into consideration the fact that 'the fundamental objective of the agreement was not incompatible with the general orientation of the common commercial policy', as well as the fact that the agreement contained a clause which reserved to the contracting parties the right to hold possible consultations arising from their international commitments, provided these consultations did not jeopardize the basic objectives of the agreement.[359] The Council also noted that the agreement in question was essentially an 'umbrella agreement' containing no precise lists of quotas. More recently, the Council has adopted a similar course of action concerning a number of commercial agreements negotiated by the member states of the Community before the end of the transitional period in January 1970.[360]

Bearing in mind Article 113 (1) of the Treaty of Rome which stipulates that 'after the expiry of the transitional period the common commercial policy shall be based on uniformly established principles, particularly in regard to ... the conclusion of tariff and trade agreements', the Commission on 16 December 1969 took a decision concerning the progressive uniformization of all commercial agreements concluded by the member states with third countries and the negotiation of Community agreements.[361] It decided to permit the prolongation of commercial agreements already concluded by the member states with third parties on condition that they do not compromise the common commercial policy of the Community, the decision in each case being taken after consultation between the Commission and the member state concerned. Unless the agreement includes a 'common market clause' or a 'clause de dénonciation annuelle', its prolongation is for a maximum period of one year. Furthermore, any member state finding it desirable to conclude a new commercial agreement with a third country must bring the matter to the Commission which

---

[358] Decision no. 69/265/CEE of 1 August 1969, *Journal officiel*, 15 August 1969, p. L206/33; see also *VIII International Legal Materials* (1969), pp. 1337–1338.

[359] *VIII International Legal Materials* (1970), pp. 1337–8.

[360] Decision no. 70/80/CEE, of 20 January 1970, authorizing the French Republic to conclude a commercial agreement with Bulgaria (*Journal officiel*, 24 January 1970, no. L18/24); decision no. 70/107/CEE, of 26 January 1970, authorizing the Italian Republic to conclude a commercial agreement with Japan (*Journal Officiel*, 30 January 1970, no. L23/23); decision no. 70/140/CEE, of 6 February, 1970, authorizing the French Republic to conclude a commercial agreement with Japan (*Journal officiel*, 14 February 1970, no. L36/28.

[361] Decision 69/494/CEE, of 16 December 1969 (*Journal officiel*, 29 December 1969, no. L326/40).

advises the other member states. Depending on whether or not the agreement in question fulfils the conditions for Community negotiations, the Commission will submit a report to the Council asking authorization to begin such negotiations, or will consult the other member states so as to fix in advance the essential conditions of the agreement to be concluded by the member state which has proposed it in the first place.

What is striking in the procedure elaborated by the Community to ensure that its external commercial policy is not hindered by the member states during the transitional period, and immediately after, is the use of certain techniques traditionally employed in federal states for similar purposes. The 'Common Market Clause' in particular bears a comparison with 'federal state' clauses. The former takes into consideration the lack of absolute competence of the states members of the European Economic Community which are bound under Articles 111 and 113 of the Treaty of Rome to uniformize gradually their external commercial policy and to transfer eventually their competence in this field to the Community itself. Federal state clauses on the other hand take into consideration the lack of internal competence of federal governments in the sphere of jurisdiction belonging properly to the component units. A similar comparison could again be made with regard to the process of consultation used in the Common Market as well as in federal states for harmonizing the interests of the member states with those of the larger group. But what is important in the last resort is the reappearance on the level of supranational institutions of problems characteristic of federal states, and the use of techniques traditionally employed by these states in finding a solution for these problems. Such remarks apply not only to the European Economic Community, but also to the European Coal and Steel Community and Euratom.

In the ECSC and Euratom Treaties, the technique used to coordinate the commercial policy of the member states with that of the Communities is essentially that of consultation. Article 75, Paragraph 1, of the Treaty of Paris provides that the member states will keep the High Authority informed of proposed commercial agreements relating to coal and steel. Under Paragraph 2 of the same Article: 'If a proposed agreement or arrangement contains clauses which would hinder the implementation of the Treaty, the High Authority shall make the necessary recommendations to the State concerned within ten days of receiving notification of the agreement or arrangement; or it may in any other cases give opinions.' Similarly, according to Article 103 of the Euratom

Treaty, the member states undertake to communicate to the Commission any draft agreement or convention with a third party to the extent that such agreement or convention concerns the field of application of the Treaty. If the proposed agreement contains clauses impeding the application of the Treaty, the Commission makes its comments to the state concerned and the latter cannot proceed to ratify the agreement until it has removed the objections of the Commission or complied with a ruling of the Court of Justice as to the compatibility of the proposed clauses with the provisions of the Treaty. But this technique, which is very similar to that employed in federations to ensure that treaties concluded by the member states are in accordance with the general interest, has not been used with too much success in Euratom. So far the member states have only agreed to inform the Commission of their bilateral agreements; the rest of Article 103 has remained a dead letter.[362]

Probing further into the impact of supranational organizations on international law, mention must be made of a certain number of problems that arise in connection with the treaty-making and treaty-implementing powers of the European Communities. To begin with, it must be remembered that the international competence of the Communities is not unlimited. According to Catalano:

> Elle trouve d'abord sa limite naturelle dans les dispositions mêmes des traités, qui définissent le cadre des compétences attribuées à chaque Communauté. En outre, l'article 228 C.E.E., bien que par une formule générale, autorise la Communauté à conclure des accords internationaux seulement dans les hypothèses expressément prévues par les traités. La compétence pour conclure des accords internationaux est expressément limitée par le traité C.E.E.A. aux hypothèses formellement prévues à l'article 101.[363]

This point of view is not shared by every writer on the subject;[364] but there is a general consensus that the external competence of the European Communities is not necessarily co-extensive with their internal competence. This is particularly true in the case of the European Economic Community.[365] Now when it is decided to conclude an international agreement, this division of competence

---

[362] Alting von Geusau, 5 *Journal of Common Market Studies* (1967), pp. 449–50.
[363] Catalano, *Manuel de droit des communautés européennes*, 2nd edn., 1965, p. 172.
[364] See for instance Raux, *Les relations extérieures de la Communauté économique européenne*, 1966, pp. 56–61.
[365] See on this question Pescatore, *HR* (1961), p. 95 ff; Megret, 'Le pouvoir de la CEE de conclure des accords internationaux', *Revue de Marché Commun* (Dec. 1964), p. 529 at 531; Reuter, *Organisations européennes*, p. 393.

between the member states and the Communities gives rise to certain difficulties.

Here, it is necessary to distinguish between various situations. First a situation may arise where the Community organs possess the necessary competence to conclude part of an international agreement, but not the whole of it. In this case, Megret suggests, two different solutions may be envisaged.[366] If the agreement can be made the object of two distinct international acts, the Community organs can sign one, and the member states the other; or if they prefer, there need be only one international act, signed by all of them: then the treaty is termed a 'mixed' agreement. If on the other hand the various parts of the treaty are so intimately connected that they cannot be separated, there is no choice and a 'mixed' agreement must be signed. In practice, the solution adopted in the majority of cases has been that of the 'mixed' agreement. It was first used for the association agreement between the ECSC and Great Britain in December 1964. Subsequently, the procedure was adopted for all other association agreements. In the law of treaties, this constitutes a new development. Second, a situation may present itself where the Community organs are competent to sign an agreement, but do not have the power to implement it; or vice versa, they have the power to implement the agreement, but not the competence to sign it.[367] In such a case, the best answer to the problem is without doubt cooperation. But judging by the experience of federal states, which have been faced with similar difficulties, it remains an open question whether this solution will prevail. The importance of the problem for the future development of international law must not be underestimated.

The European Communities also raise an interesting problem of international responsibility which remains so far a purely theoretical one. Only international lawyers have examined the question and they have been unable to arrive at a clear consensus.[368] Their views range from the acceptance of an exclusive responsibility of supranational organizations for their own conduct to the acceptance of a fundamental responsibility of the member states for such organizations.

The theory that supranational organizations are exclusively responsible for their own conduct was put forward by von der

[366] Megret, p. 535.
[367] *Idem.*
[368] A useful survey of the literature on this subject will be found in von Munch, *Das völkerrechtliche Delikt in der modernen Entwicklung der Völkerrechtsgemeinschaft*, 1963, pp. 274–8.

Heydte in 1953.[369] He argued that a union of states like the European Coal and Steel Community constituted a partial federation and therefore had to answer for its own obligations in the same way as a federal state. His case, however, is not very well taken. In comparing supranational organizations to federations, it must be kept in mind that the relationship between Communities and member states is the reverse of the relationship between federal states and member states; whereas sovereignty, in functional federations, rests with the member states, in political federations it usually rests with the central state.[370] Therefore, the comparison should be that the European Communities are responsible for their conduct in the same way as political subdivisions of federal states.

This also seems to be the view of Wengler,[371] de Visscher,[372] and Heinrich,[373] who claim that supranational organizations are not exclusively responsible for their conduct because third states cannot in practice coerce them into fulfilling their obligations. As already seen, the same argument is often used to assert that federal states are indirectly responsible for the international engagements of their member states. Strictly speaking, however, it is not a legal argument but a purely practical one. As Brownlie says, it follows generally from the reasoning of the International Court in the *Reparation* case that 'the correlative of legal personality and a capacity to present international claims is responsibility'.[374] Therefore, the argument of Wengler, de Visscher and Heinrich must be judged for its practical value. The basic assumption is that third states with claims against the European Communities would find it easier to retaliate against their member states. But would they retaliate against all the member states at the same time, or only against some of them? Would each member be jointly and severally responsible, or responsible instead only for its part? In a non-contractual claim, it would be fairly easy to identify the tort-

---

[369] Von der Heydte, 'Schumann-Plan und Völkerrecht', in *Festschrift für R. Laun*, 1953, p. 117, note 7.

[370] As rightly pointed out by Pescatore, 103 *HR* (1961), p. 217.

[371] See *Actes officiels du congrès d'études de Stresa*, Milan, 1958, vol. iii, 88 (French translation).

[372] *Ibid.*, ii, 43–4.

[373] Heinrich, *Die auswärtigen Beziehungen der europäischen Gemeinschaft für Kohle und Stahl, insbesondere ihr Verhältnis zur OEEC*, 1961, pp. 111–112.

[374] Brownlie, *Principles of Public International Law*, 1966, p. 537; but the same author admits that 'in the case of more specialized organizations with a small number of members, it may be necessary to fall back on the collective responsibility of the member States': at p. 525. Similarly, Reuter in *Organisations européennes*, 1965, p. 392, speaks of a practical rather than legal difficulty.

feasor;[375] but if the claim is for the non-fulfilment of treaty obligations contracted by the Communities, retaliation against some
member states only would be very difficult. Thus, it becomes apparent ultimately that the solution proposed by Wengler, de
Visscher and Heinrich still raises many practical problems.

Another approach also based on practical considerations is that
of Pescatore and Raux.[376] According to this view, the Communities, more particularly the European Economic Community and
Euratom, do not possess the financial resources to reimburse third
states having a monetary claim against them. Faced with such a
claim, it is suggested, the role of the Communities can only be to
assign the financial burden to the individual member states, who
are thus themselves made indirectly responsible.

This approach, however, raises the following problems. In the
first place, it obviously finds no application in the case of non-
monetary claims involving some form of action on the part of the
Communities; the latter in such circumstance are perfectly able to
fulfil their obligations without having recourse to the member
states. This fact, noted by Pescatore,[377] shows clearly that the indirect responsibility of the member states of the European Communities cannot be taken as an absolute rule. In the second place,
it must be acknowledged that the basic assumption upon which
the argument rests is in the process of being eroded. Since 1952
the European Coal and Steel Community has had the power to
borrow or to place a levy on the production of coal and steel which
is paid by enterprises direct to the High Authority.[378] It thus
enjoys an important degree of financial autonomy.[379] In the case
of the European Economic Community and Euratom, it may
have been exact up until now to claim that they were financially
dependent on their member states; but with the adoption of the
financial agreement of December 1969, one is forced to recognize
that by 1975 all the Communities should have become financially
autonomous.[380] The argument of Pescatore and Raux will then
have lost all validity.

[375] See Seidl-Hohenveldern, 'The Legal Personality of International and
Supranational Organizations', 21 *Revue égyptienne de droit international*
(1965), 56–7.

[376] Pescatore, 103 *HR* (1961), 1 at 223–4; Raux, p. 85.

[377] Pescatore, 103 *HR* (1961), 222–3.

[378] Articles 49, 78 of the Treaty of Paris, as amended by Articles 20 (1) of
the 'Merger' Treaty of 8 April 1965.

[379] Pescatore explicitly admits that his reasoning does not apply to the
ECSC: 103 *HR* (1961), 223.

[380] See *Articles et Documents* (La Documentation française), 19 December
1969, no. 0.1987, pp. 21–2; see also *Problèmes économiques* (La documentation française), 4 June 1970, no. 1.170, pp. 8–13.

For Pescatore, however, this argument based on very practical considerations constitutes only a part of a more general approach to the problem of international responsibility in functional federations. Looking at this problem from a strictly legal point of view, he goes on to suggest that the answer to it in the last resort must be found in the legal relationship existing between the Communities and the member states. If the Communities enjoy a certain autonomy in their dealings with foreign states, then they must answer themselves for their own international delicts. He mentions in support of this view the conclusions reached by Eagleton concerning the international responsibility of international organizations in general.[381] In his view, therefore, each case must be considered on its own merits. As far as the European Communities are concerned, he finds that they enjoy enough autonomy to be held responsible for their own conduct. But he adds at the same time that the institutional links between the Communities and the member states are sufficiently close to justify a subsidiary responsibility of the member states. Finally, he admits that non-recognizing states could raise the question of the existence of the Communities with a view to evading their international obligations.[382] He does not say, however, whether the Communities would be responsible vis-à-vis non-recognizing third states.

This particular aspect of the problem of international responsibility in functional federations has received special attention from Seidl-Hohenveldern and von Munch.[383] Their view is that responsibility in functional federations is basically a question of recognition. If supranational organizations are recognized as distinct subjects of international law, then they are exclusively responsible for their conduct. If, on the other hand, they are not recognized the problem is simple: vis-à-vis the non-recognizing state, they have no international existence and so cannot be held internationally responsible. In such cases, the member states themselves are responsible for the conduct of the Organization.

A more radical view is that of F. von Munch.[384] He considers that

---

[381] See Eagleton, 'International organization and the law of responsibility', 76 *HR* (1950), 323.

[382] Pescatore, 103 *HR* (1961), 214. For a more recent exposition of this view by the same author, see Pescatore, 'La personnalité internationale de la Communauté', in *Les Relations extérieures de la Communauté européenne unifiée*, Liège, 1969, p. 77.

[383] Seidl-Hohenveldern, 'Die völkerrechtliche Haftung für Handlungen internationaler Organisationen im Verhältnis zu Nichtmitgliedstaaten', 11 *Öster. Zeit. für öff. Recht* (1961), 497–506; von Munch, *supra* note 368.

[384] Von Munch, 'Internationale Organisationen mit Hoheitsrechten' in *Festschrift für H. Wehberg*, 1956, p. 301 at 323.

member states of supranational organizations always retain a basic responsibility for the conduct of such organizations unless it can be shown that third states have expressly absolved them from all responsibility. Mere recognition of international personality, in his view, is not enough to make these organizations exclusively responsible for their conduct.

The least favourable view to a responsibility of supranational organizations is that of Quadri.[385] According to him, international organizations in general cannot be held internationally responsible for their wrongs because, in practice, it is impossible to outline the extent of this responsibility. However, this argument really takes for granted what it sets out to prove. It minimizes in particular the important role played by such general principles as those of content and recognition in the solution of similar problems.

On the whole, the safest conclusion would seem to be that the problem of responsibility in supranational organizations must be solved by reference to the constitution of the organization and the degree of recognition granted by third states, taking into consideration also the dynamic evolution of the organization itself. But again, it remains to be seen whether this solution will prevail in practice. Further developments on this question are awaited.

Another problem that has been raised in connection with the European Communities is that of their right to immunity in the territories of third states. In the course of its negotiations with the High Authority of the European Coal and Steel Community regarding the conclusion of an association agreement, the Government of the United Kingdom acceded to the request that the High Authority's delegation in London and its own in Luxembourg should be treated alike.[386] In conformity with this engagement, the European Coal and Steel Community Act was passed in 1955.[387] This Act confers the like immunity from suit and legal process as is accorded to the envoy of a foreign sovereign state and his family on the chief representative in the UK of the High Authority of the Community and his family; and a limited immunity from suit, extending only to things done or omitted to be done in the course of the performance of their official duties, on members of his official staff, representatives of the High Authority at meetings in the United Kingdom of Council of the Association and their official

---

[385] Quadri, 'La personnalité internationale de la Communauté', in *Les Relations extérieures de la Communauté européenne unifiée*, Liège, 1969, p. 41.

[386] House of Commons, *Parliamentary Debates*, 5th series, vol. 543 (1955), col. 434.

[387] 4–5 Elizabeth II, Chapter 4.

staff. But was there an obligation to grant immunity to the Organization?

Here, international lawyers are in complete disagreement. In 1957, at the Congress of Stresa where the various legal aspects of the European Coal and Steel Community were examined in detail, W. Wengler stated categorically that the privileges and immunities enjoyed by the representatives of the Community in third states had nothing to do with public international law and were granted to them purely as a courtesy.[388] Ricardo Monaco seems to have shared this view.[389] But Pescatore, for his part, believed that the delegates of the Community in foreign states were entitled to at least some kind of immunity.[390] In 1958, Mathijsen claimed in his own study of the law of the European Coal and Steel Community that the exchanges of legations between the Community and third states were regulated by the rules of international law concerning international immunity.[391] Since then, however, the discussion has tended to centre round the more general problem of the right to immunity of international organizations. The question as to whether the European Communities raise a specific problem of international immunity is still open.

A further topic for discussion is that of the impact of the European Communities on the movement for the unification of law. Since unification of law is one of the methods used in order to avoid a conflict of law problem, it may be useful to begin by a brief explanation of what constitutes a true conflict of law, and how it may be avoided.

A conflict of law problem may be said to arise when the various juridical orders (e.g. countries, provinces, states) involved in a particular factual situation have, as it were, different domestic laws to solve a particular question. As a consequence whereof, a choice of law must be made. To solve a conflict, courts and legislatures have generally resorted to jurisdiction selecting choice of law rules, adopted both on the basis of their own national, social, political and economic interests, and on the basis of general concepts of justice and convenience. However, the task of solving conflict of law problems remains a complicated one, and much attention has been given in recent years to the possibility of avoiding them altogether.

To this end, two basic types of solutions have been proposed.

[388] *Actes officiels du congrès d'études de Stresa*, 1957, iii, 78.
[389] *Ibid.*, pp. 289–90.
[390] *Ibid.*, p. 347.
[391] Mathijsen, *Le Droit de la Communauté européenne du charbon et de l'acier*, 1958, p. 72.

The first possibility is to formulate a uniform code of choice of law rules. This may be done, either by entering into one or more international law agreements having this precise effect, or by the voluntary adoption of private international law rules which are similar in each country. The second solution is even more radical: it consists in uniformizing the various domestic laws of each country. Again, this may be done through the adoption of international law conventions, or through the voluntary modification of each municipal law system. It is in connection with this second type of solutions that the approximation of law provided for in the European Economic Community must be examined.

The provisions of the Treaty of Rome dealing with approximation of law are somewhat unique.[392] Article 3 of the Treaty declares that the activities of the Economic Community 'shall include under the conditions and with the timing provided for in this Treaty ... (h) the approximation of their [member states] respective municipal law to the extent necessary for the functioning of the Common Market'. This general mandate is further detailed by express treaty provisions relating to specific matters[393] and,

> A broad authorization, set forth in articles 100–102, for direct intervention by institutions of the EEC to reconcile the legislative and administrative rules and regulations of Member States when: a.—the existence of a disparity in the legal systems of Member States directly affects the establishment and functioning of the Common Market; b.—an existing disparity in the legislative and administrative provisions of the Member States distorts conditions of competition within the Common Market; or, c.—it is feared that a Member State's enactment or amendment of a legislative or administrative provision may distort conditions of competition in the Common Market.[394]

Without going into the details of these various provisions, it is necessary to point out at least two aspects of this process of harmonization which, for our purposes, merit further discussion.

The first one concerns the fact that the task entrusted to the Community is not the achievement of complete uniformity of law between the member states but simply the elimination of 'the most marked juridical discrepancies through the mutual acceptance of

---

[392] See in general on this subject: Grisoli, 'The impact of the European Economic Community on the movement for the unification of law', 26 *Law and Contemporary Problems* (1961), 418–29; Monaco, 'Le rapprochement des législations nationales dans le cadre du marché commun', 3 *Ann. fr. dr. int.* (1957), 558–68; Stein, 'Assimilation of national laws as a function of European integration', 58 *AJIL* (1964), 1–40.

[393] Such as customs and tariff matters (art. 27), mutual regulation of transport matters (art. 75), matters relating to the free movement of persons, services and capital (art. 54-56-57-58 and 66) and certain fiscal matters (art. 99).

[394] Grisoli, p. 419.

common principles'.[395] This modest objective is perhaps more realistic than any attempts to promote the adoption of farreaching uniform law codes.[396] It has the advantage of preserving to some extent the independence of the states concerned which are not obliged to dismantle their existing system of law. The second point concerns the procedure adopted in order to harmonize the law of the member states. In most cases, intervention by the institutions of the Community takes the form of directives which are binding as to their objectives but leave the member states free to adopt the appropriate means to achieve them. This procedure appears particularly well suited to the basic goal of harmonizing the law of the member states. Whether this goal will in fact be reached, it is too early to say. But if approximation of law does succeed in the European Economic Community, the chances are that it will constitute a basis for further unification of the laws of the member states. If the procedure is also adopted by other regional organizations, then we may be witnessing an important development in the movement for unification of law.

Finally, it remains to say a few words about the possible impact of the Court of Justice of the European Communities on International Law. The first point to stress here is that the Court of Justice of the European Communities differs considerably from an international tribunal. According to Scheingold:

> This treaty [EEC Treaty], as well as those of the Coal and Steel Community and Euratom, are not simple international obligations but constitutional documents. The European Court, for its part, is not an international tribunal but one of the co-ordinate governmental organs of an emerging political system. It is thus the distinctive character of the total community experience which tends to make international law irrelevant for the European Court.[397]

As a result, many writers consider that the decisions of the Court are only marginally relevant to international law. Scheingold again declares: 'Moreover, one must also ask what would be the gains for international law? I submit that they would be negligible, since it would be perfectly natural to attribute the progressive advances

[395] *Ibid.*, p. 426.
[396] This is not to say that 'harmonization' of law is easy or that it is preferable in all cases to unification of law. For an illuminating study of the two systems, see Malintoppi, 'Les relations entre l'unification et l'harmonisation du droit et la technique de l'unification ou de l'harmonisation par la voie d'accords internationaux', in Unidroit, *L'unification du droit/Unification of Law, Year Book 1967–1968*, ii, 43–91.
[397] Scheingold, 'The Court of Justice of the European Communities and the development of international law', 59 *Proceedings of the American Society of International Law* (1965), 190, 191.

of the European Court to the aberrational character of the Community system.'[398] Therefore, it would seem that Community law, in view of its special nature, cannot influence the development of international law.

Yet it would be surprising if the decisions of the Court of Justice of the European Communities were not to exercise in the future a certain influence on international law. Already, the methods and reasoning of the European Court in its interpretation of community law have been examined and compared to the classical criteria of interpretation used by international tribunals.[399] Recently, also, some interesting studies on the elaboration of general principles of law by the European Court of Justice have appeared.[400] Looking into the future, one may even go further. Referring in 1968 to the growing number of *inter se* agreements between the member states of the European Communities, Reuter has compared them to interstate agreements in federal states and suggested that the European Court might well be called upon in a near future to consider the legality of such agreements, in the same way as the Federal Court of Switzerland has been called upon in the past to interpret intercantonal agreements.[401] Were such a situation to arise, there is no doubt that the decisions reached would be considered attentively in international circles.

A last point worth mentioning in connection with the European Court of Justice is the secretness of its deliberations, which is protected through the single opinion rendered by the Court.[402] According to Grieves, 'the apparent success this secretness has had within the Community justifies at least its consideration as a possible reform of the International Court of Justice (where separate opinions can reveal how individual judges voted in a given case)'.[403]

---

[398] *Ibid.*, p. 192–193.

[399] See Chevalier, 'Methods and reasoning of the European Court in its interpretation of community law', 2 *Common Market Law Review* (1964), 21; Monaco, 'Les principes d'interprétation suivis par la Cour de Justice des Communautés Européennes', in *Mélanges Henri Rolin* (1964), 217; McMahon, 'The Court of Justice of the European Communities: Judicial Interpretation and International Organization', 37 *BYIL* (1961), 320.

[400] Lorenz, 'General principles of law: their elaboration in the Court of Justice of the European Communities', 13 *AJCL* (1964), 1; Reuter, 'Les recours de la Cour de Justice des Communautés Européennes à des principes généraux de droit', in *Mélanges Henri Rolin*, 1964, p. 263.

[401] Reuter, 'La Cour de Justice des Communautés Européennes et le droit international', in *Recueil d'études de droit international en hommage à Paul Guggenheim*, 1968, p. 665 at 669.

[402] See 'Protocol on the Statute of the Court of Justice of the European Economic Community', *UN Treaty Series*, vol. 298, pp. 147–59 (arts. 32, 33, 34).

[403] Grieves, Supranationalism and International Adjudication, 1969, p. 150.

Be that as it may, the adoption of the system used in the European Court of Justice would not be surprising, were new regional tribunals to be created in the future.

Conclusion

The object of this chapter has been to examine the impact of the federal model on international law. It has been found first of all that states which have adopted this form of government had to face particular difficulties in the conduct of their foreign relations and could not always contribute, by their effective participation, to the development of international law. It has also been seen that certain solutions have been found to this problem which correspond broadly to the varying stages of internal integration reached within the federations. At the lowest stage of integration, the member states are permitted to deal directly with foreign states, subject to the assent of the federal authorities. At the second stage, external representation of the member states ceases to be a practical solution; but the mechanism of cooperation between the central government and the member states is not sufficiently developed yet to permit the conclusion of farreaching international agreements without the guarantee of a 'federal state' clause. In the final stage, reliance is put exclusively on internal cooperation which is then considered as the best means of coordinating the local interests of the member states with the duties of the federation as a member of the international community.

Cooperation, then, is the underlying assumption of federalism. It is precisely because of this that federalism has been considered for a long time as the most appropriate way of integrating the world community. Since the end of the First World War, more particularly, a vast number of projects of international federations have been put forward and federalist movements have sprouted up in almost every part of the world. But it was not until the 1950s that a first attempt at federal integration was made. With the creation of the European Communities, a new stage in the development of international law has been reached. The dichotomy between national and international law has been broken down for the first time. Not only do the Communities raise new problems for international law, but their extensive practice must also be considered as a possible source of that law. In short, federalism is exercising a growing impact on the development of international law.

CHAPTER 6

THE IMPACT OF FEDERAL LAW ON INTERNATIONAL LAW

In the foregoing chapter, the federal model was shown to exercise, despite its defects, a growing influence on the development of international law. The present chapter will explore the possible contribution that federal law makes to the development of international law. As will be realized, this is a controversial question.

Basically, there are two different ways of looking at this problem. On the one hand, it may be argued that there is a fundamental difference between federal law and international law and that the former cannot contribute anything to the latter. Schwarzenberger, for instance, writes:

> To draw analogies from international law and apply these in the relations between federal States is entirely legitimate. Rules which exist and are helpful even on lower levels of social integration may well be taken for granted on levels of closer social cohesion. To reverse the process, however, means to infer that unorganised or partly organised international society has reached a degree of integration that may be expected only on a federal level.[1]

On the other hand, it may be argued that federal law has already influenced in practice the development of international law. Cowles, for example, asserts that '[t]he decisions of supreme courts of federations have long since proved their value as precedents in international adjudication'.[2] In fact, these two approaches are complementary: the one examines the possibility of using federal law in order to determine the content of international law; the other considers exclusively what has happened in practice.

In the following pages, both approaches are used. First of all, we enquire whether a difference exists between federal law and international law of sufficient significance to justify the conclusion that the former cannot contribute anything to the latter. Then we examine the international practice in order to find out whether federal law has actually influenced international law.

---

[1] Schwarzenberger, *A Manual of International Law*, 4th edn, 1960, i, 105.
[2] Cowles, 'International law as applied between subdivisions of federations', 74 *HR* (1949), 663.

Federal law and international law

THEORETICAL CONSIDERATIONS

It is necessary at the outset to explain what is meant here by federal law. In the present context, the expression refers specifically to the rules that federal courts apply in disputes between member states of federations. In this case, most writers prefer to speak of 'interstate law'. Huber, for instance, writes:

> Interstate law is the law governing the relations between the members of a confederation of states with each other, in so far as they are opposed to each other as states. It is distinguished from international law because its subjects are not sovereigns, but belong to a governed body of a superordinate commonwealth. As opposed to federal state law it is characterized by having for its object not relations of supremacy and subordination between the federation and its members, but relations of co-ordination between the members of the federal state.[3]

Interstate law is a more specific term than federal law and will be retained in subsequent pages. But until evidence to the contrary is forthcoming, it is essential to remember that interstate law, as opposed to international law, is just another part of the municipal law of federal states.

Interstate law, then, is the name for the body of rules that govern the relations between member states of federations. But it may be asked: what kind of relations take place nowadays between states of federations? Certainly, they no longer enter into diplomatic relations.[4] More and more, however, they conclude various kinds of agreements with each other. In many federations, they have a constitutional right to do so. In Switzerland, Article 7 of the Constitution provides that the cantons have the right to conclude agreements (concordats) among themselves with regard to legislative, judicial or administrative matters. In the United States, Article 1, Section 10, declares that a state of the Union may, with the consent of Congress, enter into agreements of compacts with other states. In Australia, Germany and Canada, there are no such constitutional provisions. But agreements between member states of these federations are not unusual.[5]

[3] Huber, 'The intercantonal law of Switzerland (Swiss Interstate Law)', 3 *AJIL* (1909), 62.
[4] See on this subject Laband, 'Les relations diplomatiques et consulaires entre les Etats de l'Empire Allemand', 11 *RGDIP* (1904), 121.
[5] See Schneider, 'Verträge zwischen Gliedstaaten im Bundesstaat', 19 *Veröffentlichungen der Vereinigung der deutschen Staatsrechtslehrer* (1961),

As is only natural, conflicts also arise between member states of federations.[6] These may concern the interpretation or the non-ful-filment of a common agreement, but more often are about boundaries, frontier relations and other similar matters. In these circumstances, recourse must be had to interstate law. The problem then arises of determining what exactly is interstate law.

According to Mallmann[7] it is possible to distinguish three basic approaches concerning the nature of the law that applies in relations between member states of federations. A first group of writers, including Nawiasky and Ross in particular, equates interstate law with international law. For them all the relations taking place between member states of federations are fundamentally international law relations. According to Ross, partial self-governments, such as those of member states of federations, are subjects of international law in so far as they are properly exercising their rights of self-government. In their dealings with other self-governments, they necessarily have to rely on international law.[8] Nawiasky, for his part, argues that the member states of a federation enjoy full sovereignty concurrently with the central Government. Consequently, the relations between the member states themselves must be regulated by international law.[9]

A second group of writers considers that international law has no validity within a state unless it has previously been incorporated or transformed into municipal law. Therefore, the law that applies to the relations between member states of federations can only be municipal law. Among the many writers who hold such a view are Kunz and Berber. The former is very explicit on the subject. He writes: 'In *Wisconsin v. Michigan*, Justice Butler stated that "principles of international law apply also to boundaries between States constituting the United States". But it must be understood that if they do, they apply by force of municipal, not international law.' And goes on to say:

1–85; Schaumann, 'Verträge zwischen Gliedstaaten im Bundesstaat', *ibid.*, pp. 86 ff; Ibrahim, 'The Application of International Law in Disputes between Member States of Federal Unions, with special reference to the United States, Australia and Canada', doctoral thesis, Leiden, 1952; Zimmermann and Wendell, *The Interstate Compact Since 1925*, Chicago, 1951; Zimmermann and Wendell, *The Law and Use of Interstate Compact*, Chicago, 1961; Leach, *Interstate Relations in Australia*, 1965.

[6] To obtain an idea of how often this happens, see Scott, *Judicial Settlement of Controversies between States in the American Union*, 2 vols, 1918–1919; see also Rice, *Law Among States in Federacy*, 1959.

[7] Mallmann, 'Völkerrecht und Bundesstaat', in Schlochauer, *Wörterbuch des Völkerrechts*, iii, 649.

[8] Ross, *A Text-Book of International Law*, 1947, p. 98 ff.

[9] Nawiasky, *Der Bundesstaat als Rechtsbegriff*, 1920, pp. 106 ff and 121.

We must distinguish between what this writer, for purposes of theoretical clarification would call *genuine* international law and international law *by analogy*. The application of international norms in these interstate cases is neither a duty imposed by international law nor has it anything to do with the municipal 'part of the law of the land' rule which envisages only *genuine* international law. It is purely a matter of municipal law to apply in such cases international law *by analogy*.[10]

Berber, on the other hand, makes the following comments regarding the use of international law in interstate disputes:

The municipal judge can naturally, if permitted by the relevant municipal law, borrow rules of international law and apply them to the municipal dispute before him. The municipal judge does not, however, by virtue of this borrowing become an international judge; he does not apply international law, but through his application transforms international law into municipal law, in just the same manner as the international judge in adopting 'general principles of law recognized by civilized nations' does not become a municipal judge, but transforms these principles into international law by his application of them.[11]

According to these two writers then, it is theoretically impossible to equate interstate law with international law.

Finally, there is a third group of publicists who affirm that international law regulates the relations between member states of federations when there are no other principles of law available. Schindler, for instance, writes:

The rules of law for the decision of disputes between cantons are found in the first place in the Federal Constitution and in Federal legislation. But fixed rules cannot always be derived from these sources. However, the Federal Court is bound to decide every cantonal dispute submitted to it. If, therefore, the positive Federal law furnishes no solution, it must be sought upon the basis of the principles on which Federal law is constructed ... In case a solution can not be found in the Federal law, international law is applied.[12]

Manley O. Hudson similarly recognizes that the 'relations of States which compose a federal union may to some extent be governed by principles of international law'.[13] Cowles, for his part, declares that 'when no provision of the United States Constitution is controlling, the principles and rules of international law are applied

---

[10] Kunz, 'International law by analogy', 45 *AJIL* (1951), 329 at 334.
[11] Berber, *Rivers in International Law*, 1959, p. 173.
[12] Schindler, 'The administration of justice in the Swiss Federal Court in intercantonal disputes', 15 *AJIL* (1921), 149 at 159–60.
[13] Hudson, *Cases and other Materials on International Law*, 2nd edn, 1936, p. 49.

by the State and Federal Courts'.[14] Such writers can easily point to decisions of federal courts that support their view. In the *Donauversinkung* case, the Supreme Court of Germany remarked that:

> As the dispute was one of public law between States it was impossible to apply the municipal law of a single State. There were in the Constitution no provisions bearing upon the dispute. In view of this the Court was bound to apply rules of international law the applicability of which, as between members of the German federation, must be recognised, though to a limited extent.[15]

In the case of *Kansas v. Colorado*, the Supreme Court of the United States declared: 'Sitting, as it were, as an international, as well as a domestic, Tribunal, we apply Federal law, state law and international law, as the exigencies of the particular case may demand.'[16] In *Solothurn v. Aargau*, finally, it was stated that where a solution to a conflict between the cantons of Switzerland could not be found in the federal law, international law had to be applied.[17]

THE PRACTICE OF STATES

According to Nawiasky and Ross, international law is to be applied to all disputes between member states of federations. But does this really conform to the practice of federal states? In Switzerland, the Federal Court has recently held, in a case relating to the use of the water power of the intercantonal stretch of the Hongrin River, that:

> Il n'est pas nécessaire de recourir aux principes du droit des gens, comme le font les auteurs de certains avis de droit produits en cause. En effet, à l'intérieur d'un Etat fédératif et dans les limites de la législation qu'il a établie, la situation est différente de ce qu'elle est entre les Etats pleinement souverains. Non seulement la communauté des Etats riverains—également reconnue par le droit des gens—est plus étroite entre les Etats fédérés, mais surtout il existe pour eux un droit positif qui les oblige tous et une juridiction qui est placée au-dessus d'eux tous. L'objet de la loi fédérale sur l'utilisation des forces hydrauliques est précisément de créer, en matière d'utilisation des forces hydrauliques, un régime juridique commun et de rendre possible, du point de vue du fond comme de la compétence, la solution des conflits pouvant surgir entre cantons. Il s'agit donc exclusivement d'interpréter la loi applicable.[18]

[14] Cowles, p. 690.
[15] *Württemberg and Prussia v. Baden, Annual Digest*, 1927–28 (1902), case no. 86, 128, at p. 130.
[16] 185 *US* 125 at 147.
[17] 26, *Recueil Officiel*, i, 450.
[18] *Vaud v. Fribourg*, 78 *Recueil Officiel*, i, 37 (1952).

In Germany, the Supreme Court has resorted to international law only when there was no provision in the Constitution bearing upon the dispute in question.[19] In the United States, the Supreme Court applies federal, state and international law as the exigencies of the particular case may require.[20] Some of its decisions are clearly not based on international law. In *Wyoming v. Colorado*, for instance, the Court concluded that Colorado's objections to the application of the doctrine of appropriation were not well taken.[21] The Court stated:

> Each of these States applies and enforces this rule in her own territory, and it is the one to which intending appropriators naturally would turn for guidance.... Both States pronounce the rule just and reasonable as applied to the natural conditions in that region; and to prevent any departure from it the people of both incorporated it into their constitutions. It originated in the customs and usages of the people before either State came into existence, and the courts of both hold that their constitutional provisions are to be taken as recognizing the prior usage rather than as creating a new rule. These considerations persuade us that its application to such a controversy as is here presented cannot be other than eminently just and equitable to all concerned.[22]

These arguments obviously have nothing to do with international law. It is, therefore, clear that international law does not apply to all disputes between member states of federations.

But what about the view that international law applies directly when there are no other rules of law available? The argument, as already seen, is based on a certain number of cases in which federal courts have admitted using international law when no other legal system could be applied. It may be useful then to examine these cases more attentively. In the *Donauversinkung case*, the Supreme Court of Germany explained that

> a greater restriction on the fundamental principle of sovereignty is reached in the relations of the German states to each other than when two completely foreign states face each other. The general bond between the separate States in spite of their fundamental independence is here expressed particularly strongly, and the concept of community shows itself the stronger. From this arises the obligations of the German states in relation to each other which are not, at least in the same measure, to be drawn from inter-

---

[19] *Württemberg and Prussia v. Baden, Annual Digest*, 1927–28, case no. 86. p. 128.
[20] *Connecticut v. Massachusetts*, 282 *US* 660, 670 (1931). See also Smith, *The American Supreme Court as an International Tribunal*, 1920, p. 57.
[21] 286 *US* 494 (1932).
[22] *Ibid.*, p. 503.

national law which is intended for all states.[23]

In other words, even if the Court had to resort to international law, this did not mean that it could ignore other obligations deriving from the nature of the federal state itself. Its duty was to balance these various obligations in order to find out what conduct was appropriate in the particular circumstances of the case. In *Solothurn v. Aargau*, the Federal Court of Switzerland similarly asserted that even if it was necessary sometimes to have recourse to international law to solve conflicts arising between the Swiss cantons, the confederate relations of the latter could never be disregarded.[24] In *Kansas v. Colorado*, the Supreme Court of the United States went further. It said: 'through these successive disputes and decisions this court is practically building up what may not improperly be called interstate common law.'[25] Now this can only be interpreted to mean that the Supreme Court does not apply international law as such in disputes between the member states of the federation.[26] Otherwise, it would not have talked of 'building up a system of interstate common law'. In fact, what the Supreme Court did do in this case was to deduce, from what it termed a cardinal rule of equality of right underlying all the relations of states to each other, a new concept of 'equitable apportionment' applicable to interstate disputes about rivers. It did not even once refer to international decisions or to the writings of international lawyers.

A last case which shows clearly that international law does not apply as such in disputes between member states of federations is that of *Iowa v. Illinois*.[27] Here, the Supreme Court of the United States stated that:

> The reason and necessity of the rule of international law as to the mid-channel being the true boundary line of a navigable river separating independent states may not be as cogent in this country, where neighbouring states are under the same general government, as in Europe, yet the same rule will be held to obtain unless

[23] *Entscheidungen des Reichsgerichts in Zivilsachen*, vol. 116, Appendix, pp. 18 *et seq*; the translation is taken from Berber, *Rivers in International Law*, p. 176.
[24] *Recueil Officiel*, 26, I, p. 444 at 450 (1900); in his *Traité de droit constitutionel suisse* published in 1967, J. F. Aubert writes: 'Mais ce droit des gens doit être adapté à la situation particulière des cantons. La notion de souveraineté en est totalement absente: les cantons ne sont indépendants ni envers la Confédération, ni même dans leurs relations réciproques; ils doivent plus d'égard à la communauté intercantonale qu'un Etat souverain n'en doit à la communauté internationale', ii, 588.
[25] 206, *US* 46 at 98 (1907).
[26] See Scott 'Kansas v. Colorado Revisited' 52 *AJIL* (1958), 432.
[27] 147 *US* 1 (1893).

changed by statute or usage of so great a length of time as to have acquired the force of law.[28]

If international law had applied directly to this dispute, the Court would not have used the words: 'The same rule will be held to obtain.' Thus it would seem that interstate law and international law are two different things.

This conclusion substantiates the views of Kunz and Berber that international law cannot apply as such to the relations between member states of federations. Their basic argument is that international law has no internal validity unless it has been adopted by the municipal authority and that by the very fact of its adoption it loses its original character to become municipal law. But assuming that this is true—although some writers would not agree[29]—does it necessarily follow that interstate decisions cannot be used as a source of international law? Decisions of municipal courts applying rules of international law in private suits are often treated as precedents contributing to the formation of international law;[30] yet they also transform rules of international law into municipal law. Therefore, it would seem that interstate decisions may also be used for the determination of international law—unless of course it is established that the difference between interstate law and international law is of a greater significance than the difference between international law as applied by municipal courts in private suits and international law as applied by international tribunals in disputes between sovereign states.

In fact, this difference is greater. In decisions of municipal courts applying international law in private suits, the judge ascertains the content of international law on a particular point and applies the findings directly to the case before him. In municipal decisions dealing with interstate disputes, the judge applies not only international law, but also federal law and state law according to the exigencies of the particular case. When he has recourse to international law, he always takes into consideration the fact that the relations between member states of federations differ from those between sovereign states. In the end, the kind of law that he applies is a mixture of various rules and principles that can only be called

[28] *Ibid.*, 10.
[29] Lauterpacht, for instance, declares that this reasoning 'is not accurate, or, at least, not wholly accurate'; see 'Decisions of municipal courts as a source of international law', 10 *BYIL* (1929), 77. '
[30] There are practically no international law writers who do not mention decisions of municipal courts as evidence of the content of international law. But see Parry, *The Sources and Evidences of International Law*, 1965, pp. 9–14 and 94–103.

interstate law. By opposition to international law, it remains strictly federal law.

Federal decisions as a source of international law

It is clearly not advisable to use interstate decisions in order to determine conclusively the content of international law. But whether it follows that interstate law has not influenced the development of international law is another question. In an attempt to shed light on this, we will examine four of the different fields in which it may be claimed that interstate law has influenced the development of international law. These are: boundary matters, matters relating to the economic uses of international rivers, acquisitive prescription and the *clausula rebus sic stantibus*. In each case, we will try to find out to what extent reliance is put on interstate law in the determination of the relevant rules of international law.

BOUNDARY MATTERS

Boundary matters have given rise to numerous decisions in the United States and other federations. Whereas there seems to be no international judicial decisions defining the thalweg or studying the effects of alluvial changes, there are many decisions of federal courts dealing with such problems. Quite naturally, such decisions have attracted the notice of international law writers.

In Green's *International Law Through the Cases*, one of the three decisions mentioned concerning land frontiers is that of the Supreme Court of the United States in *Kansas v. Missouri*.[31] The problem involved there was one of accretion and avulsion. The Supreme Court declared:

> The states are not in dispute about the applicable law. They agree that when changes take place by the slow and gradual process of accretion the boundary moves with the shifting in the main channel's course. Likewise, they agree that a sudden or avulsive change in that course does not move the boundary, but leaves it where the channel formerly had run.[32]

In Schwarzenberger's *Manual of International Law*, reference is also made in the Study Outlines to various decisions of the United States Supreme Court dealing with river boundaries.[33] Similarly,

[31] Green, *International Law Through the Cases*, 1959, p. 375.
[32] 322 *US* 213, 215 (1943).
[33] Schwarzenberger, *A Manual of International Law*, 4th edn, ii, 516.

Elihu Lauterpacht, in 1960, wrote an article on the legal aspects of the Shatt-Al-Arab frontier in which he used American interstate decisions to define the thalweg and to illustrate the rule of international law concerning alluvial changes.[34]

In another article written in 1963 by L. J. Bouchez, the reader is warned that: 'Although decisions of national courts with regard to internal boundaries are not always irrelevant for international boundary rivers, there is no doubt that these decisions as such cannot be considered as standards for the practice of States concerning international boundaries.'[35] Nevertheless, the author does mention incidentally a certain number of American decisions regarding river banks as boundary lines and alluvial changes.[36]

In his 1967 book entitled *The Settlement of Boundary Disputes in International Law*, A. O. Cukwurah adopts a different attitude.[37] For him, the validity of interstate decisions as international law precedents does not leave room for any doubt. Discussing the question of boundaries in lakes, bays and straits, he refers to a decision of the United States Supreme Court and declares: 'The *ratio* enunciated by the United States Supreme Court in the case just cited is not undermined by the fact that it refers to a dispute between two States of the Union.'[38] He also mentions interstate decisions in relation to the following topics: the bed of a river, the thalweg, avulsion, historic title to islands in rivers and the territorial sea of adjacent states.

Colombos himself, in his *International Law of the Sea*,[39] relies heavily on interstate decisions when discussing questions of international rivers. In his view:

> Special importance must be attached, in considering this division of waters, to the decisions of the Supreme Court of the United States in inter-state litigation on boundary rivers. They are of special weight as they are mainly based on the principles of international law and bring out with clearness the practical application of the doctrine of 'equitable apportionment'.[40]

Like Cukwurah, he refers to interstate decisions in relation to such topics as the thalweg, changes in the course of a river by accretion

---

[34] Lauterpacht, 'River boundaries: legal aspects of the Shatt-Al-Arab frontier', 9 *ICLQ* (1960), p. 208 at p. 216.

[35] Bouchez, 'The Fixing of Boundaries in International Boundaries Rivers', 12 *ICLQ* (1963), p. 789 at 801.

[36] *Ibid.*, pp. 792 and 807.

[37] Cukwurah, *The Settlement of Boundary Disputes in International Law*, 1967.

[38] *Ibid.*, p. 70.

[39] Colombos, *The International Law of the Sea*, 6th edn, 1967.

[40] *Ibid.*, p. 227.

or avulsion and the diversion of boundary rivers.[41]

On the whole, one can certainly conclude that the doctrine of international law on boundary rivers is influenced to a certain extent by the decisions of federal courts in interstate disputes. Furthermore, one can also conclude that interstate law has had an influence on the decisions of international tribunals dealing with the same problem. Evidence of this can be found in the 1911 *Chamizal* Arbitration.[42]

According to the Convention of 1910 for the arbitration of this dispute between the United States and Mexico, the arbitrators were to take into consideration various treaties and agreements existing between the two countries, as well as principles of international law.[43] According to the same Convention, moreover, they were to decide 'solely and exclusively' as to whether international title to the Chamizal tract was in the United States of America or Mexico. Now, a previous boundary Convention signed in 1884 provided that:

> The dividing line shall forever be that described in the aforesaid Treaty and follow the center of the normal channel of the rivers named notwithstanding any alterations in the banks or in the course of those rivers, provided that such alterations be effected by natural causes through the slow and gradual erosion and deposit of alluvium and not by the abandonment of an existing river bed and the opening of a new one.[44]

The latter treaty had a retroactive effect and applied to a series of changes which had taken place in the course of one of the rivers, the Rio Grande, between 1848 and 1868. But the two states, having never been able after 1884 to agree on whether the changes which had taken place were slow and gradual or of the avulsive type, signed the 1910 Arbitration Agreement.

The presiding Commissioner and the Mexican Commissioner found that up until 1864, the changes had been slow and gradual but that, in 1864, a sudden and visible change occurred which altered the course of the Rio Grande in a matter of days. Accordingly, they decided to divide the tract into two parts, one going to Mexico, the other to the United States. In dividing the tract, they declared that they were following a precedent laid down by the Supreme Court of the United States in *Nebraska v. Iowa*.[45]

[41] *Ibid.*, pp. 224–27.
[42] 5 *AJIL* (1911), p. 782.
[43] 5 *AJIL* (1911), Suppl., p. 117.
[44] Malloy, *Treaties, Conventions, International Acts, Protocols and Agreements, between the US and Other Powers*, i, 1159–60.
[45] 143 *US* 359 (1892).

It had been held in this case that, up to the year 1877, the changes in the Missouri River were due to accretion, and that in that year the river made for itself a new channel. On these findings, it had been decided that the boundary between Iowa and Nebraska was a varying line in so far as affected by accretion, but that from and after 1877 the boundary had not changed, and had remained as it was before the cutting of a new channel.

The American Commissioner registered a dissenting opinion.[46] Among other things, he declared that he was 'unable to understand the force of the reference in the opinion of the Presiding Commissioner, to the case of *Nebraska v. Iowa* as a "precedent" for dividing the tract in question between the parties.'[47] He added:

> There is an apparent difference between the powers of the Supreme Court of the United States, acting under the provisions of the Constitution of the United States, conferring general and original jurisdiction in controversies between States, on a bill and cross bill in equity to establish a disputed boundary line between two States, and this Commission with powers and jurisdiction strictly limited by the conventions which have called it into being.[48]

According to him, the terms of the 1910 Arbitration Agreement did not envisage a partition of the tract; he therefore recommended that his Government should reject the award.

This conclusion was accepted by the United States Government who pressed for the negotiation of a new boundary convention. The issue remained unsolved until 1963 when a final agreement was announced. In this agreement, Mexico and the United States expressed their desire 'to give effect to the 1911 arbitration award in today's circumstances'.[49]

ECONOMIC USES OF INTERNATIONAL RIVERS

The subject of the economic uses of international rivers is of particular interest in exemplifying the role that interstate decisions can play when there are no international precedents in a particular field of international law. International lawyers have often referred to interstate decisions as subsidiary evidence of international law in this developing sphere and in the *Lake Lanoux Arbitration*, tribute was also paid to the value of such decisions as indirect evidence of international law. But the process is not without danger,

---

[46] 5 *AJIL* (1911), 813.
[47] *Ibid.*, p. 815.
[48] *Ibid.*, p. 815.
[49] See 58 *AJIL* (1964), 336, 337.

as has been pointed out by many publicists. In subsequent pages, we will follow the evolution of the doctrine of international law on this subject, paying particular attention to the influence of inter-state law and considering at the same time the few relevant decisions of international tribunals.

It is interesting to note that Max Huber, the first writer to under-take a systematic examination of the legal problems associated with the use of international rivers, took as the starting point of his enquiry a dispute between two cantons of Switzerland.[50] Not surprisingly, a good part of his research is devoted to Swiss federal law and to intercantonal agreements. But he also has recourse to international law; at least to what he refers to as international law. In fact, he examines the opinion of a number of international law writers, the opinion of the Swiss Federal Court and the practice of the cantons themselves.[51] He reaches the conclusion that a state may not restrict the natural flow of waters running through its territory into other countries.[52]

This conclusion was severely criticized by von Bar in 1911.[53] In his report to the Institut de droit international, he declared that he could not agree with the decision of the Federal Court of Switzer-land holding that a canton had no right to divert more water than usual from a river without the assent of the other cantons. He explained: 'Cela peut être juste et pratique pour les rapports entre cantons. Pour les relations internationales, je ne puis reconnaître à cette régle de décision une valeur exclusive dans tous les cas.' But immediately after that, he added: 'Un jugement antérieur du tri-bunal fédéral ... admet plus justement qu'il y a lieu de distinguer deux choses: les droits de prise d'eau actuellement acquis et les forces hydrauliques non utilisées jusqu'à ce jour.'[54] Finally, von Bar concluded that no state could, by installations erected on its territory, cause a positive and easily recognizable injury to the territory of another state.[55]

The first major work to appear in English on the subject of economic uses of international rivers was that of Smith, published in 1931.[56] It contained some interesting remarks on the relevance of interstate decisions for international law. At the beginning of

[50] Huber, 'Ein Beitrag zur Lehre von der Gebietshoheit an Grenzflüssen', 1 *Zeitschrift für Völkerrecht und Bundesstaatsrecht* (1907), p. 25.
[51] *Ibid.*, p. 214.
[52] *Ibid.*, p. 215.
[53] *Annuaire de l'Institut de droit international*, session de Madrid, 1911, p. 156 at p. 161, note 1.
[54] *Ibid.*, p. 163, note 1.
[55] *Ibid.*, p. 166.
[56] Smith, *The Economic Uses of International Rivers*, 1931.

a long chapter dealing with particular interstate controversies, Smith declared:

> Some of the decisions examined in this Chapter have arisen between the member states of federal systems, and are therefore not international in the strict sense of the word. They have been included because they involve the application of the same principles which are valid as between fully independent States. Indeed, they have a particular value for us, since the submissions of both parties to a common superior has in some cases brought the dispute before a court of law.[57]

In this chapter, however, more attention was attached to the facts of the disputes than to the actual judgments.

Smith dealt more fully with interstate law in the following chapter entitled 'Judicial decisions'. At the outset, he stated:

> So far as I am aware, there are no strictly international decisions touching the problems discussed in this book. But the mutual relations of the member States in a federal union have a quasi-international character, and in determining their respective rights federal tribunals have been compelled to decide according to principles of international law. The purpose of this chapter is merely to present, without comment, such extracts from the judgments as are of interest from the international point of view.[58]

Then he quoted at length from eight decisions of supreme courts of federal states. He also referred to a treaty of 1917 between Württemburg and Bavaria.[59] In his conclusions, he declared that judicial decisions as well as treaty provisions were 'uniformly inconsistent with the theory that the territorial sovereign can do as he pleases with the water upon his own territory'.[60] Consequently, he felt justified to formulate the following principle of international law: 'No State is justified in taking unilateral action to use the waters of an international river in any manner which causes or threatens appreciable injury to the lawful interests of any other riparian State.'[61]

In 1941 an important event took place which was to have serious influence on future discussions concerning international rivers. This was the Award of the *Trail Smelter* Arbitral Tribunal in which it was stated that no state had the right 'to use or permit the use of its territory in such a manner as to cause injury by fumes in or to the territory of another or to the properties or persons therein, when the case is of serious consequence and the injury is established by

[57] *Ibid.*, p. 24.
[58] *Ibid.*, p. 104.
[59] *Ibid.*, p. 182; see also, Martens, *NRG*, 3rd ser., 12, p. 290.
[60] Smith, p. 147.
[61] *Ibid.*, p. 151.

clear and convincing evidence'.[62] In substance, this was very close to what von Bar and Smith had said regarding the use of waters of an international river. Now it is interesting to see on what basis the tribunal reached this conclusion. By virtue of article 4 of the Convention of Arbitration, it was entitled to apply the law and practice followed in dealing with cognate questions in the United States of America as well as international law and practice.[63] In fact, the decision was reached largely on the basis of precedents established by the United States Supreme Court. In referring to these, the Arbitrators declared that it was

> reasonable to follow by analogy, in international cases, precedents established by that Court in dealing with controversies between States of the Union or with other controversies concerning the quasi-sovereign rights of such States, where no contrary rule prevails in international law and no reason for rejecting such precedents can be adduced from the limitations of sovereignty inherent in the Constitution of the United States.[64]

The Arbitrators then examined a number of American interstate decisions. Finally, they found that these decisions, taken as a whole, constituted an adequate basis for the conclusion that 'under the principles of international law as well as of the law of the United States, no state had the right to use or permit the use of its territory in such a manner as to cause injury by fumes'.[65]

After the Second World War the topic of the economic uses of international rivers acquired more and more importance. Discussions appeared first of all in continental studies on international neighbourhood law. Relying on the *Trail Smelter* Award as well as on cases decided between member states of federations, Andrassy undertook in 1951 to demonstrate the existence of an international law of neighbours whose main characteristic was the prohibition against sovereign states using their territory in such a manner as to cause serious prejudice to other states. [66] At the beginning of his work, he explained that international neighbourhood relations existed, not only between sovereign states, but also between semi-sovereign entities such as member states of federations.[67] In the course of his argument he added that interstate decisions came within the subsidiary sources of international law mentioned in article 38 (1,d) of the Statute of the International Court of

[62] *The Trail Smelter Arbitration*, 3 *RIAA* (1941), 1905 at 1965.
[63] See *US Treaty Series*, no. 893; see also 3 *RIAA* p. 1907.
[64] 3 *RIAA*, p. 1964.
[65] *Ibid.*, p. 1965.
[66] Andrassy, 'Les relations internationales de voisinage', 79 *HR* (1951), 73 at 89–94.
[67] *Ibid.*, p. 84.

Justice.[68] When finally formulating general rules of international neighbourhood law, he once again referred to interstate decisions.[69] Thalmann, in contrast, adopted a more cautious attitude. Writing also in 1951 about international neighbourhood law, he declared:

> Great importance is to be attached to American learning and practice in water matters both for present day and especially for future international water laws; but as these are however concerned with the relationships within a federal state the evidentiary value of the decisions in ascertaining currently valid rules of international law will on the other hand be decreased.[70]

But relying on theoretical arguments and on some appropriate instances taken from the practice of states, he nevertheless reached the conclusion that international neighbourhood rights existed, at least in Europe.[71]

In 1952 the Economic Commission for Europe published under the title of *Legal Aspects of Hydro-Electrical Development of Rivers and Lakes of Common Interest* a detailed study of the legal problems associated with the use of international rivers.[72] An important part of this study dealt with judicial precedents. Acknowledging that most of the existing decisions relate to the 'settlement of disputes that have arisen between Federal States of the United States of America, between Cantons of the Swiss Confederation and between certain German *Länder*',[73] the author of the report declared:

> Certain jurists, however, hesitate to attribute real value to these judgments. It seems very dangerous, in their opinion, to transpose into the international sphere rules laid down by certain confederations to govern the relations between their member States. Such relations, whether derived from conventions freely discussed among those communities or from the constitution of the Confederation of which they are members, nevertheless owe their existence to a particular legislative code which may vary from one confederation to another and which, even in its most important passages may be quite different from that in force in other States. There is no doubt that in some cases, the supreme decision of the federal authority has been of a political rather than a legal nature, and has found a compromise solution by 'cutting the cake in half...' The fact nevertheless remains that, in the absence of

[68] *Ibid.*, p. 100–1.
[69] *Ibid.*, p. 111–30.
[70] Thalmann, *Grundprinzipien des modernen zwischenstaatlichen Nachbarrechts*, 1951, p. 134; the translation is borrowed from Berber, *Rivers in International Law*, 1959, p. 175.
[71] Thalmann, *op. cit.*, pp. 58, 79.
[72] UN, Economic Commission for Europe, E/ECE/EP/136 and E/ECE/EP/98. Rev. 1.
[73] *Ibid.*, p. 69.

international case-law proper, the rulings of these courts can make a useful contribution to this study.[74]

These remarks were followed by a complete survey of the various decisions of federal courts dealing with the problem of economic uses of interstate rivers. The author concluded that it was doubtful whether the theory and case law could be of much help in drawing practical conclusions.[75] Nevertheless, some generalizations were attempted. In substance, these reflected the view that a state had the right to develop unilaterally that section of waterway traversing or bordering its territory, insofar as such development did not cause or threaten serious damage to the territory of another state.[76]

Following this Report of the Economic Commission for Europe, the number of studies on the subject of international rivers increased rapidly. In 1953 Georges Sauser-Hall gave a lecture at the Hague Academy which dealt with the legal problems raised by the industrial use of international rivers.[77] He, too, referred to decisions reached between member states of federations; but he specified that such decisions

> ne peuvent être considérés comme l'expression du droit international dans les conflits d'intérêts que suscite l'aménagement hydro-électrique des fleuves internationaux, pour une raison évidente, alors même que les autorités auraient fait appel aux principes du droit des gens; et cette raison est, que dans tous les litiges de droit interne le conflit de souveraineté ne se produit pas à l'état aigu et que la juridiction suprême chargée de les trancher a la possibilité d'adopter des solutions de compromis qui furent d'ailleurs contradictoires.[78]

Sauser-Hall drew attention nevertheless to an underlying principle to be found in all decisions: this was that states cannot divert the course of international rivers if by doing so serious injuries to the interests of other states resulted. This he considered to be the main contribution of interstate law to international law.[79]

In 1954 Professor Clyde Eagleton proposed the subject of economic uses of international rivers to the International Law Association. The following year (1955) he published an article in which he developed his idea and suggested some general principles of law relating to the use of the waters of international rivers.[80]

[74] *Ibid.*, p. 70–71.
[75] *Ibid.*, p. 92–3.
[76] *Ibid.*, p. 211.
[77] Sauser-Hall, 'L'utilisation industrielle des fleuves internationaux', 83 *HR* (1953), 465.
[78] *Ibid.*, p. 516.
[79] *Ibid.*, p. 517.
[80] Eagleton, 'The use of the waters of international rivers', 33 *Can. Bar Rev.* (1955), p. 1018.

The first of these principles was that sovereignty is not unlimited. Lacking cases before international tribunals to prove the existence of such a principle, he turned to 'cases between the quasi-sovereign members of a federal system'. He also referred to a certain number of treaties, and concluded that 'while each state has sovereign control within its own boundaries, in so far as international rivers are concerned, a state may not exercise that control without taking into account the effects upon other riparian states'.[81] The second principle which he proposed was that of equitable apportionment. Again, he relied almost exclusively on interstate decisions to demonstrate the existence of this principle.[82] Yet another principle related to the necessity of prior agreement before undertaking works affecting an international river. But then Professor Eagleton declared: 'Thus far, I could claim that I have been talking existing international law; at this point, I am going off into the *lex feranda*.'[83] Judging by this comment, he was obviously convinced of the relevance of interstate decisions for the determination of international law. For what he claimed to be existing international law was almost entirely based on such decisions.

The same year, a Committee of the International Law Association appointed under the chairmanship of Professor Eagleton to consider the subject of international rivers delivered its first Report.[84] In essence, it was a statement of principles upon the basis of which could be formulated rules of international law concerning the use of waters of international rivers. The Report was accompanied by some interesting comments by individual members of the Association. Those of J. G. Laylin in particular merit attention. He stated, at the outset: 'The most fully developed contribution to the jurisprudence on this subject is that of the Supreme Court of the United States in controversies between the States of the Union. A question may be raised of the applicability of this source of authority, because the cases deal with interstate rather than international disputes.'[85] But relying on the *Trail Smelter* Award, the writings of Smith, Eagleton, Cowles, Sauser-Hall and the Report of the Economic Commission for Europe, he asserted that there was a strong analogy between such decisions and those which might be anticipated from a truly international

[81] *Ibid.*, p. 1020, 1021.
[82] *Ibid.*, p. 1022–23.
[83] *Ibid.*, p. 1024.
[84] International Law Association, *Principles of Law Governing the Uses of International Rivers* (resolution adopted by the Int. Law Association at its Conference held in August 1956 at Dubrovnik, Yugoslavia. Together with Reports and Commentaries submitted to the Association).
[85] *Ibid.*, pp. 2–3 of Laylin's comments.

tribunal. Naturally, the process of analogy in international law was different from 'the process of "analogy" known to civil law-trained-lawyers, according to which an analogous legal principle developed in a context different from that of a given dispute is considered compulsive'.[86] The decisions of the United States Supreme Court, by comparison, acted only 'as a guide' for the solution of specific problems. Using this approach, he reached the conclusion that preventable pollution of water in one state which did substantial injury to another state rendered the former state responsible for the damage done and agreed that 'in general the maxim *sic utere tuo* should be followed by riparian States in all matters concerning the use of the waters of an international river by one or several of them'.[87]

Other interesting comments came from S. M. Sikri. One of his assertions was that there was no basis for considering the maxim *sic utere tuo* as a valid principle applying in this field of international law. Referring to the claim that it was recognized in practically all cases and treaties, he said: 'These cases were not dealing with Sovereign States. These Courts were Municipal Courts dealing with units or States forming one Sovereign State. The problem was different.'[88] And quoting from Hyde, he added:

> As a tribunal possessed of sufficient jurisdiction to prevent or grant relief on account of the diversion of the waters of American Inter-States Streams the Supreme Court of the United States has not been obliged to seek light from the law of nations in enunciating rules that should be applied. Thus it has not sought to explore the problem touching the freedom of a State under that law to divert the waters of a river flowing out of, or constituting the boundary of its territory.[89]

Laylin came back with some comments on Sikri's observations. Against the view that the Supreme Court of the United States 'has not been obliged to seek light from the law of nations', he referred to a number of cases where it was explicitly stated that the relations between the various states were governed largely, if not altogether, by international law.[90] He also referred, as he had done before, to the *Trail Smelter* Award and to the writings of Smith, Eagleton and Cowles.

In 1957 the Arbitral Tribunal in the *Matter of the Use of the Waters of Lake Lanoux* delivered its award.[91] The issue submitted

[86] *Ibid.*, p. 34.
[87] *Ibid.*, p. 30.
[88] *Ibid.*, p. 5 of Sikri's comments.
[89] *Ibid.*, p. 5–6.
[90] *Ibid.*, pp. 4–6 of Laylin's observations on Sikri's comments.
[91] *International Law Reports*, 1957, p. 101.

was whether a change proposed by France in its part of a river system shared with Spain would, if carried out without the prior agreement of Spain, constitute a violation of certain stated treaties.[92] The Tribunal declared at the outset that, in interpreting these treaties, it would take into consideration, not only the spirit in which they had been drawn up, but also 'le droit international commun'.[93] In the Spanish Memorial, various arguments were mentioned in support of the view that prior agreement is mandatory before a riparian may effect a substantial change in the regime of the waters of international rivers and lakes. Among other arguments, the decisions of German, Swiss and American federal courts were reviewed to show that the principle that no substantial change can be brought about by one riparian without the consent of co-riparians, was supported by the opinions of courts which had had to decide analogous questions.[94] France, for its part, argued that the sovereignty of each of the two states on its own territory remained untouched, subject only to the restrictions contained in international agreements in force between them; and according to these instruments, the ability of one state to proceed with works of public utility was not made subject to the prior consent of the other state.[95] The Tribunal found in favour of France. It declared among other things:

> The unity of a basin is sanctioned at the juridical level only to the extent that it corresponds to human realities. The water which by nature constitutes a fungible item may be the object of a restitution which does not change its qualities in regard to human needs. A diversion with restitution, such as that envisaged by the French project, does not change a state of affairs organized for the working of the requirements of social life.

And it went on to say:

> The state of modern technology leads to more and more frequent justifications of the fact that waters used for the production of electric energy should not be returned to their natural course. Water is taken higher and higher up and it is carried even farther, and in so doing it is sometimes diverted to another river basin, in the same State or in another country within the same federation, or even in a third State. Within federations, the judicial decisions have recognized the validity of this last practice (*Wyoming v. Colorado* ... 259 US 419) and the instances cited by

[92] The Treaties of Bayonne of 1856, 1862, 1866 and the Additional Act of 1866; see Hertslet, *The Map of Europe by Treaty*, 1875, iii, 1647.
[93] *International Law Reports*, 1957, p. 121; see also Durelly, 'L'affaire du Lac Lanoux' 62 *RGDIP* (1958), 469 at 481–2.
[94] *International Law Reports*, 1957, p. 112.
[95] *Ibid.*, p. 114.

Dr F. J. Berber, *Die Rechtsquellen des internationalen Wasser-nützungsrechts*, p. 180, and by G. Sauser-Hall, 'L'utilisation industrielle des fleuves internationaux', *Recueil des cours de l'Académie de droit international*, 1953, vol. 83, p. 544; for Switzerland, (see) *Recueil des Arrêts du Tribunal Fédéral*, vol. 78, Part I, pp. 14 et seq.[96]

Since 1957 the number of writers who refer to cases decided between member states of federations when discussing the question of economic uses of international rivers has continued to grow. Some, like R. K. Batstone, admit that this procedure is not to be recommended but nevertheless is helpful as 'an indication of policy and principles'.[97] Other writers are convinced that such decisions constitute valid precedents for the determination of international law. Thus, in a memorandum on the *Legal Aspects of the Use of International Waters*, prepared in 1958 for the US Department of State, W. L. Griffin explains that 'custom being the sum total of the acts of states showing a concordance sufficient to establish a given principle as being accepted as law, the analogy of decision of domestic tribunals should be considered because they are "acts" of states'.[98] He then adds:

> Moreover, there is no reason to believe that the inclusion in article 38 (d) of the Statute of the International Court of Justice of 'judicial decisions' as subsidiary means for determining rules of international law, was meant to refer only to decisions of international tribunals. In addition, there is no reason to believe that opinions of municipal tribunals may not be regarded as the 'teachings' of qualified publicists under article 38 (d).[99]

In a subsequent article on the same subject, written a year later, Griffin again justifies the use of interstate precedents by referring to the *Trail Smelter* arbitration, a typical example 'of the use of national decisions by international tribunals as guides for the determination of international law'.[100]

In the same year, two other writers, Laylin and Bianchi, adopted a similar attitude, relying instead on the *Lake Lanoux Arbitration*.[101] According to them:

[96] *Ibid.*, p. 125.
[97] Batstone, 'The utilization of the Nile waters', 8 *ICLQ* (1959) 523 at 541; see also Wolfrom, *L'utilisation à des fins autres que la navigation des eaux, des fleuves, lacs et canaux internationaux*, 1964, p. 52.
[98] *Legal Aspects of the Use of Systems of International Waters*, Memorandum of the State Department (1958), Senate Document no. 118, 85th Congress, 2nd session, p. 76.
[99] *Idem.*
[100] Griffin, 'The use of waters of international drainage basins under customary international law', 53 *AJIL* (1959), 50 at 66, n. 52.
[101] Laylin and Bianchi, 'The Role of Adjudication in International River Disputes', 53 *AJIL* (1959), 30 at 34–5.

The fact that the decisions of American and other federal courts concern disputes between member States of federations does not impair the analogical value of the principles carved out in such decisions. The fundamental policies to be weighed in passing on matters involving water economics, and the types of factual problems involved are not different essentially in interstate and in international disputes. The existence in the latter cases, of separate sovereignties, not subject to the compulsory jurisdiction of a higher authority, is no more than an obstacle to the growth of international judicial precedents. It renders the analogy the more apposite.[102]

Another writer who holds similar views is C. Bourne. Writing in 1959 on the Columbia River controversy, he mentions in favour of the doctrine of equitable apportionment several decisions of German, Swiss and especially American Courts.[103] He also declares that 'the lawfulness of reasonable diversions under the doctrine of equitable apportionment is supported by such decisions of the United States Supreme Court as *Kansas v. Colorado*'.[104]

There are, however, a sizeable number of writers who strongly deny that interstate law can be used for the determination of international law. In his book entitled *Rivers in International Law*, F. J. Berber examines at length this problem and arrives at the conclusion that interstate decisions have no relevance for international law, except in so far as they reproduce 'general principles of law recognized by civilized nations'.[105] In his view, the underlying principles in international law are 'quite different from those in federal constitutional law'. In the first place, the sanctions of international law such as retorsion, reprisal, etc., do not exist in municipal law. Secondly, the duty of the federal judge is not only to give a legal opinion but includes also 'the task entrusted to the state of keeping the peace in respect of its internal affairs';[106] the order of the federal judge, therefore, will be executed, where necessary, against the member state of the federation. In municipal disputes, finally, 'the judge has to give a solution according to law and equity of the problem disturbing internal order'; in international law, on the contrary, 'the legal question only is to be answered', unless the parties have decided otherwise.[107] In view of these facts, it is clear that the municipal judges who sometimes borrow from international law for the solution of interstate disputes do not really

---

[102] *Ibid.*, p 41.
[103] Bourne, 'The Columbia River Controversy', 37 *Can. Bar. Rev.* (1959), 444 at 458 ff.
[104] *Ibid.*, p. 461.
[105] Berber, p. 177.
[106] *Ibid.*, p. 173.
[107] *Ibid.*, p. 176.

apply international law but instead transform international law into municipal law. Berber then expresses his disagreement with those decisions of federal courts saying that international law is to be applied and the Award in the *Trail Smelter* case, in which by way of analogy use is made of decisions of the American Supreme Court as international law precedents. In support of his belief that there is a clear distinction between federal law and international law, he also refers to Thalmann and Huber and to the judgment of the German *Staatsgerichtshof* in the *Donauversinkung* case.[108] In conclusion, he asserts that the principle of equitable apportionment so often used in disputes between the constituent states of the American Union 'was not drawn from international law and cannot in consequence be introduced into international law by the roundabout way of the alleged application of international law in federal courts'.[109]

J. S. Bains and G. S. Raju are two other writers who, like Berber, refuse to accord any significance to interstate decisions in international matters. The former argues that since international law is the product of sovereign states, 'the rules of law dealing with the disputes among semisovereign states or provinces cannot be accepted as the rules of international law'.[110] The latter, using the argument of Schwarzenberger that federal courts are 'the judicial organ of a much more highly integrated society', declares that the decisions of such courts cannot be treated as 'decisive in determining principles of international law'.[111]

It remains to say a few words about the research undertaken by the International Law Association. At the 50th Conference of the Association, held in Brussels in 1962, the Report of the Committee on the Uses of the Waters of International Rivers was noted and its substance tentatively approved.[112] The report dealt with three topics in particular: procedural rules for settlement of disputes, navigation and water pollution. Concerning water pollution, the following article was proposed: 'Except as may be otherwise provided by convention, agreement or binding custom, a State is required by international law to prevent or to abate pollution originating within its territory of the waters of an international

[108] *Ibid.*, p. 175; but Berber should have said that Huber does use interstate law to clarify the content of international law: see above, p. 250.
[109] *Ibid.*, p. 177.
[110] Bains, *India's International Disputes*, 1962, p. 41.
[111] Raju, 'Principles of law governing the diversion of international rivers', 2 *Indian Journal of International Law* (1952), 370 at 374.
[112] International Law Association, *Report of the Fiftieth Conference*, Brussels, 1962, p. 425.

drainage basin causing substantial injury to a use in the territory of another State'. In support of such a rule, reference was made to the decision of the *Trail Smelter* Arbitral Tribunal and to the various interstate disputes mentioned by this Tribunal.[113] In 1964 the 51st Conference of the Association again accepted provisionally another Report of the Committee on the Uses of the Waters of International Rivers which included more or less the same rule.[114] In 1966, finally, the 52nd Conference of the International Law Association adopted the Helsinki Rules on the Uses of the Waters of International Rivers.[115] Among these rules, there was one which stated that 'each basin State is entitled, within its territory, to a reasonable and equitable share in the beneficial uses of the waters of an international drainage basin'.[116] In the comments attached to the rule, it was explained that in recent water disputes between Bolivia and Chile and between Israel and certain Arab states, the principle of equitable apportionment had been accepted as binding. The important part played by the Supreme Court of the United States in the formulation of this principle was not mentioned. Regarding water pollution, however, reliance was put once more on the *Trail Smelter* Award and on the interstate decisions mentioned therein to declare that a state had a duty to prevent or abate pollution originating within its territory.[117]

Is it to be concluded, in view of all this, that interstate law has positively influenced the development of international law relating to the use of international rivers? It would seem that in order to answer this question, it would be necessary to determine precisely where international law stands on this problem, but this is by no means a simple matter.

There is no general convention regulating the subject of economic uses of international rivers. There is, of course, an extensive network of bilateral treaties dealing with this subject. But after studying these treaties in detail, Berber comes to the conclusion that they do not provide reliable evidence in support of the existence of universal rules of international law in the present context.[118] He acknowledges at best that 'in some parts of Europe rules of customary international law concerning international riparian rights have arisen'[119] which tend to recognize on the whole

[113] *Ibid.*, p. 472–3.
[114] International Law Association, *Report of the Fifty-first Conference*, Tokio, 1964, pp. 162 and 177.
[115] International Law Association, *Helsinki Rules on the Use of the Waters of International Rivers*, 1967.
[116] *Ibid.*, Article IV, p. 9.
[117] *Ibid.*, Article X, pp. 19–21.
[118] Berber, p. 149.

that 'no works likely to have a considerable reaction on the flow of water in the neighbouring country can be erected without the consent of the neighbouring state'.[120]

In some international disputes, as pointed out by the International Law Association, the validity of the principle of equitable apportionment has been accepted without difficulty.[121] But it would seem to be necessary to await events in order to discover whether this principle really becomes a universal rule of international law.

There are very few international decisions pertinent to the subject of economic uses of international rivers. The most important one remains the *Lake Lanoux Arbitration* in which the principle of absolute territorial integrity was explicitly rejected. In coming to its decision, the Tribunal relied, as already seen, on certain precedents relating to disputes between member states of federations. The Tribunal apparently considered that the rejection of the principle of absolute territorial integrity in a highly cohesive society such as a federal state, made it more likely that such a principle had no validity in the less cohesive international society.[122]

The only other decision of any importance for the solution of problems relating to the industrial use of international rivers is the *Trail Smelter* Arbitration. Here, the Tribunal considered that the solution arrived at in disputes between member states of federations could be used by way of analogy for the solutions of disputes between sovereign states, and, on the basis of such decisions, concluded that a state has a duty to prevent or abate pollution originating from its territory.

Turning now to 'the teachings of the most highly qualified publicists of the various nations', the following remarks may be made. There seems to be a substantial majority of international law writers who accept the existence of the principle of restricted sovereignty concerning international waters and who, to support such a view, refer, directly or by way of analogy, to cases decided between member states of federations. On the other hand, there is a minority which considers that there are no universal rules of international law relating to the subject of international rivers. This minority prefers not to recognize the value of interstate decisions. But merely because most writers favour the principle of restricted territorial sovereignty, it does not follow that this reflects the present position of international law.

[119] *Ibid.*, p. 150.
[120] *Ibid.*, p. 155.
[121] See above, p. 261.
[122] See Gervais, 'L'affaire du Lac Lanoux', *Ann. fr. dr. int.* (1960), p. 372 at 398–9.

In effect, the law relating to the uses of the waters of international rivers is undergoing profound changes. In the absence of sufficient evidence, it is difficult to conclude that definite rules have emerged which are universally applicable. In the present stage of development, however, there is no doubt that the solutions reached in disputes between member states of federations have seriously influenced the practice of states, the decisions of international tribunals and the opinion of international law writers. The principle of equitable apportionment and the principle that a state has a duty to prevent pollution originating from within its territory were developed in the first place by federal courts. Similarly, the rejection of the principle of absolute territorial integrity owes much to the attitude adopted by federal courts. Only when such solutions become universally applicable will it be possible to say that federal law has positively influenced the development of international law.

ACQUISITIVE PRESCRIPTION

In determining the law relating to acquisitive prescription, reference is often made to decisions of federal courts as evidence of the existence of certain rules of international law. In 1950, for instance, D. H. N. Johnson relied on Article IV (a) of the British Guiana–Venezuela Arbitration Agreement of 1897 and on a certain number of international decisions as evidence of the existence of acquisitive prescription in international law. In the end, he added: 'Finally, it may be noted that the Supreme Court of the United States has acted upon precisely the same principles in deciding certain disputes between various states of the Union'.[123] More recently (1965) D. P. O'Connell wrote: 'Respecting the disputed boundary in *Louisiana v. Mississippi*, the Supreme Court held that long acquiescence in the assertion of a particular boundary should be accepted as conclusive. This passage in the judgment epitomises the rules respecting the conduct which must be proved of both parties before prescription can be allowed'.[124]

In the argument put by the United States before the Alaskan Boundary Tribunal, in 1903, there is also a lengthy quotation from *Indiana v. Kentucky* in which the Supreme Court of the United States declared that: 'It is a principle of public law universally recognized that long acquiescence in the possession of territory and the exercise of dominion and sovereignty over it, is conclusive of

---

[123] Johnson, 'Acquisitive prescription in international law', 27 *BYIL* (1950), 332 and 342.
[124] O'Connell, *International Law*, 1965, i, 488.

the nation's title and rightful authority'.[125]

But the most noteworthy instance of reference to federal law as proof of the existence of rules of acquisitive prescription in international law is to be found in the *Island of Palmas Arbitration*.[126] In the course of his decision, Max Huber, the Sole Arbitrator, declared:

> The principle that continuous and peaceful display of the functions of State within a given region is a constituent element of territorial sovereignty is not only based on the conditions of the formation of independent States and their boundaries ... as well as on an international jurisprudence and doctrine widely accepted; this principle has further been recognized in more than one federal State, where a jurisdiction is established in order to apply, as need arises, rules of international law to the interstate relations of the States members. This is the more significant, in that it might well be conceived that in a federal State possessing a complete judicial system for interstate matters—far more than in the domain of international relations properly so-called—there should be applied to territorial questions the principle that, failing any specific provision of law to the contrary, a *jus in re* once lawfully acquired shall prevail over *de facto* possession however well established.[127]

THE 'CLAUSULA REBUS SIC STANTIBUS'

Decisions of federal tribunals are often mentioned also as evidence of a rule of *rebus sic stantibus* in international law. In 1928 G. Crusen referred to a number of diplomatic incidents as well as to a decision of the Swiss Federal Tribunal to demonstrate the existence of such a rule.[128] A few years later, in 1934, Chesney Hill undertook a comprehensive study of the question of *rebus sic stantibus*.[129] He examined in turn opinions of writers, general principles of law, decisions of national and international tribunals, statements made by the Permanent Court of International Justice, provisions of multipartite treaties and finally the practice of states. In conclusion, and relying on two decisions of the Swiss Federal Court as well as on other sources, he declared that the doctrine of *rebus sic stantibus* as understood by states was 'based juridically upon the intention of the parties at the time of the conclusion of the treaties'. Relying on the case of *Bremen v. Prussia*, decided by the German Supreme Court in 1925, he added that the doctrine was

---

[125] *Proceedings of the Alaskan Boundary Tribunal*, v, 201–4.
[126] 2 *RIAA*, 829.
[127] 2 *RIAA*, 840.
[128] Crusen, 'Les servitudes internationales', 22 *HR* (1928), 63.
[129] Hill, 'The doctrine of *Rebus sic stantibus* in international law', 9 *The University of Missouri Studies* (1934), no. 3.

limited to perpetual treaties. Finally, he mentioned the case of *Thurgau v. St Gallen* as evidence that 'the party which relies upon the doctrine for release from treaty obligations must invoke the changes within a reasonable time after they have occurred'.[130] More recently (1953) Guggenheim referred to decisions of the Swiss Federal Court with a view to clarifying certain aspects of the doctrine of *rebus sic stantibus* in international law; in these decisions, he explained, rules of international law had been applied by analogy.[131]

In its study of the law of treaties, the International Law Commission has also considered the problem of *rebus sic stantibus* in international law. In the second Report on the Law of Treaties submitted by Sir Humphrey Waldock, the Commission's Special Rapporteur, it is stated that municipal courts 'have not infrequently recognized the relevance of the *rebus sic stantibus* doctrine in international law, though for one reason or another they have always ended by rejecting the application of the doctrine in the particular circumstances of the case before them'.[132] Referring in particular to a certain number of interstate decisions, the Special Rapporteur declared:

> These cases emphasize that the doctrine is limited to changes in circumstances the continuance of which, having regard to the evident intention of the parties at the time, was regarded as a tacit condition of the agreement; that the treaty is not dissolved automatically by law upon the occurrence of the change but only if the doctrine is invoked by one of the parties, and that the doctrine must be invoked within a reasonable time after the change in the circumstances was first perceived. Moreover, in *Bremen v. Prussia*, the German *Reichsgericht*, while not disputing the general relevance of the doctrine, considered it altogether inapplicable to a case where one party was seeking to release itself not from the whole treaty but only from certain restrictive clauses which had formed an essential part of an agreement for an exchange of territory.[133]

But Sir Humphrey himself did not really approve of the expectations-of-parties approach. In his view, to try to give effect to the intentions of the parties ran the risk of further abuse or of limiting the operation of the doctrine too strictly. The real problem, he suggested, was 'to define the relation which the change of circumstances must have to the original intentions of the parties and the extent to which that change must have affected the fulfilment of

[130] *Ibid.*, p. 75, 77.
[131] Guggenheim, *Lehrbuch des Völkerrechts*, 1948, i, 114.
[132] 1963 *Yearbook of the International Law Commission*, ii, 81.
[133] *Ibid.*, p. 81.

those intentions'.[134] In the final Draft Articles on the Law of Treaties adopted by the International Law Commission, in 1966, the attitude adopted was a compromise. Article 59, which dealt with fundamental change of circumstances, appeared 'to be inspired by distrust of the expectations-of-parties approach, though leaving room for giving effect to the intentions of the parties'.[135] Without substantial modification, it has now become Article 62 of the Vienna Convention on the Law of Treaties.

The practice of states offers a last example of reliance put on interstate decisions as evidence of a rule of *rebus sic stantibus* in international law. In 1929, France and Switzerland went before the Permanent Court of International Justice to decide the question of the *Free Zones of Upper Savoy and the District of Gex*.[136] Speaking on behalf of France, Me Paul Boncour declared:

> Si je prends une des études les plus récentes parues sur la matière, le cours du professeur MacNair, de l'Université de Londres, professé en 1928 à l'Académie de Droit International, je constate qu'au tome XXII du Recueil des cours de l'Académie de Droit International, le professeur MacNair signale comme constituant le principal précédent de jurisprudence en cette matière une décision du Tribunal fédéral suisse rendue en 1882 entre les cantons de Lucerne et d'Argovie.[137]

After quoting the relevant part of the decision, Me Boncour concluded:

> Messieurs, quelle jurisprudence accablante, je me permets de le dire très courtoisement et très respectueusement, pour la thèse suisse que cette décision de ce Tribunal fédéral suisse déclarant que, même unilatéralement, un traité peut être dénoncé s'il est intervenu un changement des circonstances qui, d'après l'intention apparente des Parties à l'époque de la création de la servitude, constituaient une condition tacite de son maintien.[138]

But the matter did not rest there. Speaking on behalf of Switzerland, Professor Logoz replied with the following remarks:

> Il est évident qu'on ne saurait assimiler les Etats souverains de la communauté du droit international aux membres autonomes d'un Etat fédératif soumis constitutionnellement à une même juridiction, le Tribunal Fédéral. En droit international, le respect des conventions existantes est encore plus nécessaire.[139]

[134] *Ibid.*, p. 84.
[135] Lissitzyn, 'Treaties and Changed Circumstances (Rebus Sic Stantibus)', 61 *AJIL* (1967), 918.
[136] Permanent Court of International Justice, Series C. No. 17–1, Vol. 1.
[137] *Ibid.*, p. 98.
[138] *Idem.*
[139] *Ibid.*, p. 253.

Then he added:

> Mais si la Cour veut bien transporter sur le terrain international la jurisprudence intercantonale de notre Cour suprême, nous en serons très heureux. Nous nous permettrons de signaler respectueusement encore un autre arrêt, plus récent, du 10 février 1928, rendu entre les cantons de Thurgovie et de Saint-Gall...[140]

Finally, Professor Logoz concluded that the jurisprudence of the Federal Court was in favour of Switzerland rather than of France. But the French argument having failed on facts, the Court did not have to pronounce on the application of the *rebus sic stantibus* doctrine.[141]

Conclusion

The present study has shown that interstate law differs in many respects from international law. In essence, it is a mixture of federal, state and international law. In certain cases, it may happen that the only rules of law available for the solution of a dispute between member states of federations are those of international law; but in resorting to such rules, federal courts have always taken into consideration the confederate relations of the member states. They have also admitted that the compelling recourse to rules of international law is not as obvious in federal states, where the neighbouring states are under the same general government, as in the international society. In view of this, it is concluded that interstate decisions should not be used for the determination of international law.

In practice, however, such decisions have often been used for the determination of international law. In the field of economic uses of international rivers, more particularly, they have influenced to a considerable extent the evolution of international law. In boundary matters, also, they have helped to clarify certain important concepts. On the whole, it is impossible to deny that interstate law has had some impact on international law. Why should this be so, it is more difficult to say.

A close examination of the examples given shows that there is a valid way of using interstate law for the determination of international law. In the *Lake Lanoux* arbitration, the Tribunal, relying on the fact that the principle of absolute territorial integrity had no

---

[140] *Ibid.*, p. 253.
[141] *Case of the Free Zones of Upper Savoy and the District of Gex*, Judgment, 1932 Permanent Court of International Justice, A/B 46, p. 158.

validity in federal states, concluded that such a principle, *a for-tiori*, did not apply in international relations. Similarly, Max Huber, in the *Islands of Palmas* arbitration, considered that if acquisitive prescription still applied to territorial questions in inter-state law, then it applied even more forcibly to the same problems in international law. In these two instances, the reasoning used was that limitations of sovereignty which were not accepted in highly integrated federal societies could not be presumed to exist in the less integrated international society. Such a reasoning, it is sub-mitted, is perfectly valid.

In complete contrast to this, however, is the use made of inter-state decisions in the *Trail Smelter* and the *Chamizail* arbitrations. In these two instances, interstate law was applied by analogy to the solution of disputes between sovereign states. In view of what has been said above about the distinction between interstate law and international law, it is necessary to emphasize that such a process is not justified. Nevertheless, there is an explanation for this. In 1909 Max Huber wrote:

> However, interstate law has not only interest for the federal states but also for other countries, for it shows us a higher system of international law, so to speak: an international law having its sanction not in the loyalty of those bound by custom and treaty and in the *ultima ratio* of war, but in a developed judicial and executive power.... The tendency of contemporary international law is more and more towards an association of states not only on the ground of the administration of common economic interests but also upon that of justice.[142]

Although it is not generally advisable to use interstate law for the determination of international law, the tendency mentioned by Huber seems to point towards a greater influence of interstate law on international law in the future.

---

[142] Huber, 'The intercantonal law of Switzerland (Swiss Interstate Law)', 3 *AJIL* (1909), 62, 63.

CHAPTER 7

GENERAL CONCLUSION

Perhaps the best way to describe the relationship that presently exists between federalism and international law is to depict it as a love-hate relationship. The fundamental tendency of international law is to rely on state sovereignty as a starting point for the solution of most international legal problems. By contrast, federalism tends to divide sovereignty in order to make room for more effective action. The two positions are clearly not reconcilable since each constitutes a danger to the other. But while international law is often blamed for its lack of effectiveness, federalism is criticized for its inability to maintain a real balance of autonomy between central and regional authorities. Therefore, it is not altogether surprising that there should exist this love-hate relationship between federalism and international law.

The basic incompatibility between international law and federalism is illustrated by the fact that the former refuses to concern itself with whether a state is federal or unitary. Both are treated alike. If the federal division of powers becomes relevant from the point of view of international law, this is always in accordance with the fundamental principles of sovereignty, consent and recognition. In short, traditional international law leaves it to sovereign states to organize themselves internally as they see fit, provided the rights of third states are safeguarded under international law. This conclusion comes out most clearly from a study of the three problems usually associated with federal states: those of personality, responsibility and immunity.

Concerning the problem of international personality in federal states, most of the theories based on the concept of sovereignty have been found unsatisfactory. In practice federal states are universally considered as full and sovereign subjects of international law. This does not mean that such states enjoy unqualified sovereignty under municipal law, or that their member states cannot enjoy international personality. In fact, the practice of states shows that the latter can effectively become subjects of international law. This may happen when the federal constitution grants them the right to deal separately with foreign states and such states agree to deal with them. If, however, the constitution is not clear as to the right of the member states to deal with foreign jurisdictions, and if there is no agreement within the federation itself on this point, then it is the duty of foreign states to abstain from intervening in the internal affairs of the federation. This is in accordance with the fundamental principles of sovereignty, consent and recognition.

As sovereign subjects of international law, federal states are responsible, not only for their own acts or omissions, but also for those of their member states, contrary to the international obligations of the federation. If the member states are themselves competent to deal independently with foreign states, and effectively undertake international obligations in their own name, they are directly responsible for the fulfilment of their international engagements. The federal state may, or may not, be held indirectly responsible for such engagements, depending on the degree of independence enjoyed by the member states and the attitude adopted by third powers towards them. But if, in concluding agreements with foreign states, the member states exceed their external competence, the federal government may denounce the agreement which then becomes null and void; if the agreement is not denounced, and the other contracting party has no objection, then the treaty remains in force and both the federal state and the member states are responsible for its execution. Again, this is entirely consistent with the fundamental principles of sovereignty, consent and recognition.

There is no difficulty in establishing that, as a sovereign entity, the federal state is fully entitled to the immunities usually granted to other sovereign states. On the other hand, the possibility of the member states being entitled to immunity as sovereign entities, or as agencies of sovereign entities, must be rejected as not in conformity with the practice of states. However, evidence exists that, to a certain extent, member states may claim immunity in the courts of foreign states if such states recognize them as subjects of international law and accept to deal with them on a basis of equality. The same principles which govern the questions of international personality and international responsibility in federal states again apply here, that is, those of sovereignty, consent and recognition.

Such is the attitude of traditional international law towards federalism. But this attitude was possible so long as international law did not intrude into the fields of activities traditionally reserved, within federations, to the member states. With the widening of the scope of international law, the picture has been significantly altered.

The growth of international law was obviously not to be hindered by the existence of federal states incapable for constitutional reasons of undertaking international obligations in various fields of activities. The only solution that traditional international law offered was to allow direct participation in international affairs of member states, when the sovereign states concerned did not object. But few federations have seized this possibility because of the danger of contradictory action on the international plane. In fact, it is a solution that may play a useful role only in the case of loosely integrated federations.

This meant that a new solution to this problem had to be found. As was perhaps to be expected, when one was found it was in the nature of a compromise solution that did not really solve the problem but rather avoided it. Beginning with the middle of the nineteenth century, federal states included in certain of their treaties provisions that had the effect of limiting, or otherwise affecting, their obligations with respect to subject matters falling within the jurisdiction of their member states. In 1919 this technique was extended to multilateral instruments. Since then it has frequently been used in bilateral as well as multilateral treaties. But the problem with federal state clauses is that they give rise to inequality of obligations between contracting parties. This is clearly unsatisfactory from an international law point of view. On the other hand, they have the merit of allowing federal states to become parties to treaties with respect to those provisions to which effect can be given by the federal government itself. In certain circumstances they even extend the influence of a treaty beyond the area of competence of the federal authorities, to that of the member states. Be that as it may, federal state clauses offer the only example so far of a specific concession being granted to such states in international law. They are necessary when the factors making for disunity within a federation are not sufficient to justify a separate representation of the member states in international affairs, and when the factors making for unity do not permit continued reliance on internal cooperation as a means of solving the external problems of the union.

Ideally, the problem of harmonizing the local interests of member states with the duties of the federation as a member of the international community should be solved through federal state cooperation. From the point of view of foreign states, that is without a doubt the most simple and attractive solution, but it is not an easy solution. Despite numerous attempts made in this direction by federal states, there is much yet to be done. The explanation may be that smooth cooperation between federal and state authorities presupposes a high degree of integration that has not yet been reached in many federations.

Autonomy and cooperation are the underlying assumptions of successful federalism. Precisely because of this, for a long time, federalism has been considered as the most appropriate way of integrating the world community. For the same reason, federal techniques have also been viewed as a valid solution to some of the long-term problems of international law. But more recently such techniques have found their way into international law, and this despite the basic incompatibility which appears to exist between the two systems.

The first significant step in this direction has been the creation of the European Communities. The latter do not yet constitute a federation or even a confederation of states. For instance, the powers granted to the Communities are by no means as important as those possessed by the central government of a federal state, and the degree of independence enjoyed by their executive can hardly be considered as typical of a federal state. But the repartition of competence between the Communities and their member states, and the presence of a Court that acts as a guardian of this division of competence, are two features which are definitely characteristic of a federal state. In short, the European Communities transcend ordinary international organizations without constituting a federal state. At the same time they offer a new model for the development of international law that is distinctly federal in outlook.

What will be the impact of this new development on the future growth of international law? Already the extensive practice of the European Communities makes it possible to foresee some of the eventual consequences. First of all, it would appear that the multiplication of such entities must, sooner or later, lead to the formulation of new concepts of law. For instance, it would not be surprising if the 'most-favoured-nation' clause reasserted itself in the future in the form of a 'most-favoured-region' clause. This would follow logically from the adoption of common commercial policy by supranational organizations. Similarly, the 'national treatment' clause could gradually be replaced by a 'regional treatment' clause as a consequence of a certain degree of harmonization of law within the Communities. A third example would be the appearance of a 'common market' clause that would, for supranational organizations, play the same role as the 'federal state' clause does for federal states.

Another likely consequence would be the formulation of more precise rules of international law concerning the competence, responsibility and immunity of international organizations. Supranational organizations enjoy more autonomy than traditional international organizations; in certain fields their competence even excludes that of their member states. An example of this is the negotiation of commercial treaties by the European Economic Community. Such organizations therefore, may be expected to play a greater role in conventional international law than ordinary international organizations. At the same time, the risks of conflict between them and third states will necessarily increase. It is when such conflicts do arise that more precise rules of international law concerning the competence, responsibility and immunity of international organizations will have to be formulated. Judging by the experience of federal states, the solution to these problems will almost certainly result from the interplay of the principles of sovereignty, consent and recognition.

A greater reliance on courts as a means of settling international disputes is also to be expected. Supranational organizations like the European Communities provide for the judicial settlement of all disputes between their member states that relate to the implementation of the constituting treaty. Controversies between community organs and governments of the member states equally come within the jurisdiction of the adjudicating agency. Considering that membership of a supranational organization normally assumes a place of importance in the external relations of a country, it is only fair to expect that an increasing number of problems will come to be settled by judicial means. If, furthermore, the adjudicating agency adopts a centralizing tendency, then further integration along federal lines may be anticipated.

The federal model appears thus to be exercising a growing influence on the development of international law. But so does federal law itself, albeit by a roundabout way. Occasionally it happens that the only rules of law available for the solution of a dispute between member states of a federation are those of international law. In resorting to such rules, federal courts have always taken into consideration the confederate relations of the member states. So much so that the kind of law that they apply in the last resort is often a mixture of federal, state and international law. In view of this, it may come as a surprise to learn, that in the absence of international case law, the decisions of these courts have made a useful contribution to the development of international law itself. In the field of economic uses of international rivers more particularly, they seem to have had an important impact. In boundary matters also, they have helped to clarify certain important concepts. On the whole, it is impossible to deny that federal law has had some influence on international law, despite the fact that both systems of law are fundamentally different.

They stand, so to speak, at different levels of social integration. The international society of today is a partly organized society. The law that governs it is based on the principle of the sovereign independence of all its members; but at the same time it recognizes the need for a certain degree of coordination. Federal societies, on the contrary, exist at a higher level of social integration. They are built on the idea that matters of common interest must be coordinated at a superior level, while matters of local importance may be left to the exclusive competence of the member states. In a sense, federalism may be seen as a higher system of international law. But as yet it is impossible to say whether international law is definitely moving towards federalism or not. For the moment, there simply exists a love-hate relationship between the two systems.

BIBLIOGRAPHY

1. BOOKS

AIYAR, S. P. *Federalism and Social Changes*, London, Asia Publishing House, 1961.

ALLEN, J. J. *The European Common Market and the GATT*, Washington University Press, 1960.

ALLEN, ELEANOR W. *The Position of Foreign States before National Courts, Chiefly in Continental Europe*, Harvard University Press, 1933.

ANZILOTTI, DIONISIO. *Cours de droit international public*, Paris, 1929.

ASPATURIAN, VERNON V. *The Union Republics in Soviet Diplomacy*, Geneva, Droz, 1960.

AUBERT, JEAN-F. *Traité de droit constitutionnel suisse*, Paris, Dalloz, 1967.

AUSTIN, JOHN. *The Province of Jurisprudence Determined etc.* (*1832*), Library of Ideas, London, Weidenfeld and Nicolson, 1954.

BAINS, J. S. *India's International Disputes*, London, Asia Publishing House, 1962.

BASDEVANT, JULES, ed., *Dictionnaire de la terminologie du droit internationnal*, Paris, Sirey, 1960.

BASU, DURGA D. *Shorter Constitution of India*, Calcutta, Sarkar, 1960.

BATES, LINDELL T. *Les Traités fédéraux et la législation des Etats aux Etats-Unis*, Paris, 1915.

BATIFFOL, HENRI. *Droit international privé*, 4th edn, Paris, Pichou et Durant-Auzias, 1967.

BAUMBACH, MAX. *Die unmittelbare völkerrechtliche Handlungsfähigkeit der deutschen Einzelstaaten in Vergangenheit und Gegenwart*, Göttingen, 1928.

BERBER, F. J. *Rivers in International Law*, London, Stevens and Sons, 1959.

BEBR, GERHARD. *Judicial Control of the European Communities*, London, Stevens and Sons, 1962.

BERNHARDT, RUDOLF. *Der Abschluss völkerrechtlicher Verträge im Bundesstaat. Eine Untersuchung zum deutschen und ausländsichen Bundesstaatsrecht*, Köln-Berlin, Heymanns, 1957.

BINGHAM, ALFRED M. *The United States of Europe*, New York, 1940.

BIRCH, ANTHONY H. *Federalism, Finance and Social Legislation in Canada, Australia and the United States*, Oxford, Clarendon Press, 1955.

BORCHARD, EDWIN M. *The Diplomatic Protection of Citizens Abroad*, New York, 1915.

BOREL, EUGÈNE. *Etudes sur la souveraineté de l'Etat fédératif*, Berne, 1886.

BOWIE, R. R. and FRIEDRICH, C. J. *Studies in Federalism*, Boston, Little, Brown, 1954.

BRIGGS, H. W. *The Law of Nations*, 2nd edn, New York, Appleton, 1952.

BROSSARD, PATRY, and WEISER. *Les Pouvoirs extérieurs du Québec*, Presses de l'Université de Montréal, 1967.

BROWNLIE, IAN. *Principles of Public International Law*, Oxford, Clarendon Press, 1966.

BRUNS, KARL. *Fontes Juris Gentium*, Berlin, Heymanns, 1961.

BUELL, RAYMOND L. *Isolated America*, New York, 1940

CALHOUN, JOHN C. *A Discourse on the Constitution and Government of the United States*, in *The Works of John C. Calhoun*, ed. R. C. Cralle, 1858.

CALVEZ, J. Y. *Droit international et souveraineté en U.R.S.S.*, Paris, Colin, 1953.

CAMPBELL, A. and THOMPSON, D. *Common Market Law, text and commentaries*, London, Stevens and Sons, 1962.

CARDIS, FRANÇOIS. *Fédéralisme et intégration européenne*, Univeristé de Lausanne, 1964.

CASTEL, J. G. *International law: Chiefly as Interpreted and Applied in Canada*, University of Toronto Press, 1965.

CATALANO, NICOLA. *Manuel de droit des communautés européennes*, 2nd edn, Paris, Dalloz et Sirey, 1964.

CATLIN, G. *One Anglo-American Nation: the foundation of Anglo-Saxony as basis of World Federation*, London, Dakers, 1941.

CAVARÉ, LOUIS. *Le Droit international public positif*, Paris, Pedone, 1951.

CHEN, TI-CHIANG. *The International Law of Recognition*, London, Stevens and Sons, 1951.

CHENG, BIN. *The Law of International Air Transport*, London, Stevens and Sons, 1962.

CHENG, BIN. *General Principles of Law as applied by International Courts and Tribunals*, London, Stevens and Sons, 1953.

CLARK, G. and SOHN, L. B. *World Peace Through World Law*, 3rd edn, Harvard University Press, 1966.

CLARK, JANE P. *The Rise of a New Federalism: Federal-States co-operation in the United States*, New York, 1938.

COLOMBOS, C. JOHN. *The International Law of the Sea*, London, Longmans, 1967.

COUDENHOVE-KALERGI, R. N. *Crusade for Pan-Europe*, New York, 1943.

COUDENHOVE-KALERGI, R. N. *Pan-Europa*, Vienna, 1923.

CRANDALL, S. B. *Treaties, Their Making and Enforcement*, 2nd edn, Washington, 1916.

CUKWURAH, A. O. *The Settlement of Boundary Disputes in International Law*, Manchester University Press, 1967.

CULBERTSON, ELY. *Summary of the World Federation Plan: an Outline of a Practical and Detailed Plan for World Settlement*, London, Faber, 1944.

CURRIE, D. P., ed. *Federalism and the New Nations of Africa*, Univ. of Chicago Press, 1964.

CURTIS, LIONEL. *Civitas Dei: the City of God*, London, Macmillan, 1938.

DEENER, DAVID R., ed. *Canada-United States Treaty Relations*, Duke University Press, 1963.

DEENER, DAVID R. *The U.S. Attorneys General and International Law*, The Hague, Nijhoff, 1957.

DESPRÉS, JEAN-PIERRE. *Le Canada et l'Organisation internationale du travail*, Montréal, Fides, 1947.

DICEY, ALBERT V. *Introduction to the Study of the Law of the Constitution*, 7th edn, London, Macmillan, 1908.

DOEKER, GÜNTHER. *The Treaty-Making Power in the Commonwealth of Australia*, The Hague, Nijhoff, 1966.

DÖHRING, ERICH. *Das Gesandtschaftsrecht der deutschen Einzelstaaten unter der Verfassung von Weimar*, Halle, 1928.

DOKA, KARL. *Der Bodensee im internationalen Recht*, Leipzig, 1927.

DONOT, MAURICE. *De la responsabilité de l'Etat fédéral à raison des actes des Etats particuliers*, Paris, 1912.

DUMBAULD, EDWARD. *The Constitution of the United States*, University of Oklahoma Press, 1964.

DURAND, CHARLES. *Les Etats Fédéraux*, Paris, Sirey, 1930.

EATON, H. O. *et al.*, *Federation. The Coming Structure of World Government*, University of Oklahoma Press, 1944.

ELAZAR, DANIEL J. *The American Partnership*, University of Chicago Press, 1962.

ELBEN, OTTO. *Die Staatsverträge Württembergs mit nicht-deutschen Staaten*, Berlin, 1926.

ESCH, OTTO. *Das Gesandtschaftsrecht der deutschen Einzelstaaten*, Bonn, 1911.

FAWCETT, J. E. S. *The British Commonwealth in International Law*, London, Stevens and Sons, 1963.

FÉRAUD-GIRAUD, LOUIS J. D. *Etats et souverains, personnel diplomatique et consulaire devant les tribunaux étrangers*, Paris, 1895.

FRIEDMANN, WOLFGANG G. *The Changing Structure of International Law*, London, Stevens and Sons, 1964.

FRIEDRICH, KARL J. *Constitutional Government and Democracy*, Boston, Mass., Ginn, 1950.

FRIEDRICH, KARL J. *Man and his Government. An Empirical Theory of Politics*, New York, McGraw-Hill, 1963.

GANJI, MANOUCHEHR. *International Protection of Human Rights*, Genève, Droz, 1962.

GÉRIN-LAJOIE, PAUL. *Constitutional Amendment in Canada*, University of Toronto Press, 1950.

GHOSH, R. C. *Treaties and Federal Constitutions: Their Mutual Impact*, Calcutta, The World Press Private, 1961.

GOTLIEB, A. E. *Canadian Treaty-Making*, Toronto, Butterworths, 1968.

GOODMAN, E. R. *The Soviet Design for a World State*, Columbia University Press, 1960.

GREEN, L. C. *International Law Through the Cases*, London, Stevens and Sons, 2nd edn, 1959.

GREENWOOD, GORDON. *The future of Australian Federalism: A Commentary of the Working of the Constitution*, Melbourne University Press, 1946.

GRIEVES, F. L. *Supra-nationalism and International Adjudication*, University of Illinois Press, 1969.

GUGGENHEIM, PAUL. *Lehrbuch des Völkerrechts*. Basel, Verlag für Recht Gesellschaft, 1948–49.

GUGGENHEIM, PAUL. *Traité de droit international public*, Genève, Georg, 1953–54.

HAAS, ERNST B. *The Uniting of Europe: Political, Social and Economic Forces, 1950–57*, Stanford University Press, 1958.

HAAS, ERNST B. *Beyond the Nation-State. Functionalism and International Organization*, Stanford University Press, 1964.

HAENEL, ALBERT. *Studien zum deutschen Staatsrecht*, Leipzig, 1873–88.

HAENEL, ALBERT. *Deutsches Staatsrecht*, Leipzig, 1892.

HAY, P. *Federalism and Supranational Organizations*, University of Illinois Press, 1966.

HEINRICH, ARMIN. *Die auswärtigen Beziehungen der europäischen Gemeinschaft für Kohle und Stahl: insbesondere ihr Verhältnis zur O.E.E.C.*, Bonn, Bouvier, 1961.

HENDRY, JAMES MCL. *Treaties and Federal Constitutions*, Washington, Public Affairs Press, 1955.

HERTSLET, SIR EDWARD. *The Map of Europe by Treaty*, London, 1874-91.

HILL, CHESNEY. *The Doctrine of 'Rebus sic Stantibus' in International Law*, Columbia University Press, 1934.

HODÉ, JACQUES. *L'Idée de fédération internationale dans l'histoire. Les précurseurs de la société des nations*, Paris, 1921.

HUBER, JEAN. *Le Droit de conclure des traités internationaux*, Lausanne, Payot, 1951.

HUDSON, MANLEY O. *International Legislation*, London, Washington and New York, Carnegie Endowment for International Peace, 1931-50.

HUDSON, MANLEY O. *Cases and other Materials on International Law*, 2nd edn, St Paul, Minn., 1936.

HALL, W. E. *International Law*, 8th edn, ed. Pearce Higgins, 1924.

IMLAH, ANN G. *Britain and Switzerland 1845-1860*, London, Longmans, 1966.

INTERNATIONAL LAW ASSOCIATION. *The Effect of Independence on Treaties*, London, Stevens and Sons, 1965.

JELLINEK, GEORGES. *Die Lehre von den Staatenverbindungen*, Wien, 1882.

JENKS, CLARENCE W. *Human Rights and International Labour Standards*, London, Stevens and Sons, 1960.

JENKS, CLARENCE W. *International Immunities*, London, Stevens and Sons, 1961.

JENNINGS, SIR W. IVOR. *A Federation for Western Europe*, Cambridge University Press, 1940.

KEETON, G. W. and SCHWARZENBERGER, G. *Making International Law Work*, London, Peace Book Co., 1939.

KEITH, A. B. *Responsible Government in the Dominions*, 2nd edn, London, 1909.

KELSEN, HANS. *The Law of the United Nations*, London, Stevens and Sons, 1950.

KELSEN, HANS. *Principles of International Law*, 2nd edn, rev. by R. W. Tucker, New York, Holt, Rinehart and Winston, 1966.

KIRCHENHEIM, ARTHUR VON. *Lehrbuch des deutschen Staatsrechts*, Stuttgart, 1887.

KISS, A. C. *Répertoire de la pratique française en matière de droit international public*, Paris, Centre National de Recherche Scientifique, 1962-66.

KLEIN, FRIEDRICH. *Die mittelbare Haftung im Völkerrecht*, Frankfurt/Main, Klostermann, 1941.

KORTE, HEINRICH. *Grundfragen der völkerrechtlichen Rechtsfähigheit und Handlungsfähigheit der Staaten*, Berlin, Grunewald, 1934.

KUNZ, JOSEPH L. *Die Staatenverbindungen*, Stuttgart, 1929.

LABAND, PAUL. *Deutsches Reichsstaatsrecht*, Tübingen, 1912.

LABAND, PAUL. *Das Staatsrecht des deutschen Reiches*, 3rd edn, Tübingen, 1911-14.

LADOR-LEDERER, JOSEPH J. *International Group Protection: aims and methods in human rights*, Leyden, Sithoff, 1968.

LAMBRINIDIS, JOANNES S. *The Structure, Function and Law of a Free Trade Area*, London, Stevens and Sons, 1965.

LANGE, CHRISTIAN L. *Histoire de l'internationalisme jusqu'à la paix de Wesphalie*, Kristiania, Ahchehoug, 1919.

LAPRADELLE, —. *Recueil des arbitrages internationaux Politis*, vol. i (1905), vol. ii (1924).

LAUTERPACHT, HEARST. *Recognition in International Law*, Cambridge University Press, 1947.

LAUTERPACHT, HEARST. *International Law and Human Rights*, London, Stevens and Sons, 1950.

LEACH, R. H. *Interstate Relations in Australia*, 1965.

LEDERMANN, L. *Fédération internationale et organisation économique mondiale d'après-guerre*, Genève, 1943.

LEDERMANN, L. *Fédération internationale*, 1950.

LE FUR, LOUIS E. *L'Etat fédéral et la Confédération d'Etats*, Paris, Marshal et Billard, 1896.

LENZ, RAOUL. *Les Conventions Suisses de double imposition*, Lausanne, Nouvelle Bibliothèque de Droit et de Jurisprudence, 1952.

LINDBERG, L. N. and SHEINGOLD, S. A. *Europe's Would be Polity*, Englewood Cliffs, N.J., Prentice-Hall.

LIVINGSTON, WILLIAM S. *Federalism and Constitutional Change*, Oxford, Clarendon Press, 1956.

LODGE, H. CABOT, ed. *The Federalist: a commentary on the Constitution of the United States*, 1886.

MACKAY, R. W. G. *Towards a United States of Europe*, London, Hutchinson, 1961.

MACMAHON, A. W., ed. *Federalism, Mature and Emergent*, New York, Russell and Russell, 1962.

MCNAIR, LORD. *The Law of Treaties*, 2nd edn, Oxford University Press, 1961.

MARTENS, G. F. DE. *Nouveau Recueil général de traités*, 1843.

MATHIJSEN, PIERRE. *Le Droit de la Communauté Européenne du Charbon et de l'Acier*, The Hague, Nijhoff, 1958.

MAUNZ, THEODOR and DURIG, G. *Kommentar zum Grundgesetz*, Munich/Berlin, Beck'sche Verlagsbuchhandlung, 1964.

MAUNZ, T. *Deutsches Staatsrecht*, 9th edn, 1959.

MAY, R. J. *Federalism and Fiscal Adjustment*, Oxford, Clarendon Press, 1969.

MCWHINNEY, EDWARD. *Federal Constitution-making for a multi-national World*, Leyden, Sigthoff, 1966.

MENZIES, SIR ROBERT G. *Central Power in the Australian Commonwealth*, London, Cassell, 1967.

MILLAR, T. B. *The Commonwealth and the United Nations*, Sydney University Press, 1967.

MODELSKI, J. A. *The Communist International System*, Princeton, The Center, 1960.

MOMMEJA, ANDRÉ. *De l'influence de la forme fédérale dans les relations de droit international*, Bordeaux, Cadoret, 1910.

MONGOLDT, H. VON and KLEIN, F. *Das Bonner Grundgesetz*, 2nd edn, 1964.

MOUSKHELI, MICHEL. *La théorie juridique de l'Etat fédéral*, Paris, 1931.

MOUSLEY, EDWARD O. *Man or Leviathan?: a 20-century enquiry into war and peace*, London, Allen and Unwin, 1939.

MUNCH, INGO VON. *Das völkerrechtliche Delikt in der modernen Entwicklung der Völkerrechtsgemeinschaft*, Frankfurt/Main, Keppler, 1963.

NAWIASKY, HANS. *Der Bundesstaat als Rechtsbegriff*, Tübingen, 1920.

O'CONNELL, D. P. *International Law*, London, Stevens and Sons, 1965.

O'CONNELL, D. P., ed. *International Law in Australia*, London, Stevens and Sons, 1965.

OPPENHEIM, L. *International Law*, 1st edn, London, 1905-06.

OPPENHEIM, L. *International Law*, 8th edn, ed. H. Lauterpacht, London, Longmans, 1955.

PALLEY, CLAIRE. *The Constitutional History and Law of Southern Rhodesia, 1888-1965*, Oxford, Clarendon Press, 1966.

PARRY, CLIVE. *The Sources and Evidence of International Law*, Manchester University Press, 1965.

PIPER, DON COURTNEY. *The International Law of the Great Lakes*, Durham N.C., Duke University Press, 1967.

PLISCHKE, E., ed. *Systems of Integrating the International Community*, Van Nostrand, 1964.

PRAAG, L. VAN. *Juridiction et droit international public,* The Hague, 1915.

PROUDHON, PIERRE J. *Du principe fédératif et de la nécessité de reconstituer le parti de la Révolution*, Paris, 1863.

RALSTON, J. H. *The Law and Procedure of International Tribunals*. Supplement to 1926 revised edition, Stanford University Press, 1936.

RAUX, JEAN. *Les Relations extérieures de la Communauté Economique Européenne*, Paris, Cujas, 1966.

REDSLOB, ROBERT. *Traité de droit des gens*, Paris, Sirey, 1950.

REUTER, PAUL. *International Institutions*, London, Allen and Unwin, 1958.

REUTER, PAUL. *Droit international public*, Paris, Presses Universitaires de France, 1963.

REUTER, PAUL. *Organisations européennes*, Paris, Presses Universitaires de France, 1965.

RICE, W. G. *Law Among States in Federacy*, Appleton, Nelson Publishing, 1959.

RIKER, W. H. *Federalism: origin, operation, significance*, Boston, Little, Brown, 1964.

RIPKA, HUBERT. *A Federation of Central Europe*, New York, 1953.

ROBERTS-WRAY, K. W. *Commonwealth and Colonial Law*, New York, Praeger, 1966.

ROSS, ALF. *A Text-Book of International Law*, London, Longmans, 1947.

SARWEY, OTTO VON. *Das Staatsrecht des Königreichs Württemberg*, Tübingen, 1883.

SATOW, SIR ERNEST M. *A Guide to Diplomatic Practice*, 4th edn, London, 1957.

SCHLESINGER, R. *Federalism in Central and Eastern Europe*, London, Kegan Paul, 1945.

SCHWARZENBERGER, GEORG. *International Law*, 3rd edn, London, Stevens and Sons, 1957.

SCHWARZENBERGER, GEORG. *A Manual of International Law*, 4th edn, London, Stevens and Sons, 1960.

SCHWARZENBERGER, GEORG. *The Frontiers of International Law*, London, Stevens and Sons, 1962.

SCHWARZENBERGER, GEORG. *Power Politics*, 3rd edn, London, Stevens and Sons, 1964.

SCOTT, JAMES B. *Judicial Settlement of Controversies between States in the American Union*, New York, Oxford University Press, 1918–1919.

SERVAN-SCHREIBER, JEAN-J. *Le défi américain*, Paris, Denoel, 1967.

SMITH, HERBERT A. *The American Supreme Court as an International Tribunal*, New York, 1920.

SMITH, HERBERT A. *The Economic Uses of International Rivers*, London, 1931.

SMITH, HERBERT A., ed. *Great Britain and the Law of Nations*, London, P. S. King, 1932-35.

STARKE, J. G. *An Introduction to International Law*, 6th edn, London, Butterworths, 1967.

STOKE, H. N. *The Foreign Relations of the Federal State*, London, Oxford University Press, 1931.

STREIT, CLARENCE. *Union Now*, London, Cape, 1939.

STRUPP, KARL, ed. *Wörterbuch des Völkerrechts und der Diplomatie*, Berlin and Leipzig, 1922-29.

STRUPP, KARL, *Eléments du droit international public*, 2nd edn, Paris, 1930.

STRUPP, K. (ed. by H. J. Schlochauer), *Wörterbuch des Völkerrechts*, 1960–62 (4 vols.)

STUTZEL, FRITZ. *Die völkerrechtliche Handlungsfähigkeit des Einzelstaates im Bundesstaate*, Babemhausen, 1929.

SUCHARITKUL, SOMPONG. *State Immunities and Trading Activities in International Law*, London, Stevens and Sons, 1959.

TESSIER, JACQUES, et al. *Dix ans d'efforts pour unir l'Europe, 1944-55*, Paris, Bureau de liaison Franco-Allemand, 1955.

THALMANN, HANS. *Grundprinzipien des modernen zwischenstaatlichen Nachbarrechts*, Zürich, Polygraphisches Verlag, 1951.

THILO, ULWICH. *Problem des Staats und völkerrechtlicher Stellung Bayerns*, Berlin, 1930.

TOCQUEVILLE, CHARLES A. DE. *De la démocratie en Amérique*, 2nd edn, Paris, 1835.

TORNÜDD, K. *Soviet Attitudes Towards Non-military Regional Co-operation*, Helsingfors, The Societas, 1963.

TRIEPEL, KARL H. *Völkerrecht und Landesrecht*, Leipzig, 1899.

TRIEPEL, KARL H. *Droit international et droit interne*, 1920.

VALK, W. DE. *La signification de l'intégration européenne pour le développement du droit international moderne*, Leyden, Sithoff, 1962.

VERDROSS, ALFRED. *Die Verfassung der Völkerrechtsgemeinschaft*, Wien, 1926.

VILE, M. J. C. *The Structure of American Federalism*, London, Oxford University Press, 1961.

WAITZ, GEORG. *Grundzüge der Politik, nebst einzelnen Ausführungen*, Kiel, 1862.

WHEARE, K. C. *Federal Government*, 4th edn, London, Oxford University Press, 1963.

WELLS, R. H. *The States in West German Federalism: a study in federal-state relations, 1949–1960*, Bookman Associates, 1961.

WHEELER-BENNETT, JOHN W., ed. *Documents on International Affairs*, London, Oxford University Press, 1931.

WILSON, ROBERT R. *United States Commercial Treaties and International Law*, New Orleans, Hauser Press, 1960.

WINDISCH, KARL. *Die völkerrechtliche Stellung der deutschen Einzelstaaten*, Leipzig, 1913.

WOLFROM, MARC. *L'Utilisation à des fins autres que la navigation des eaux des fleuves, lacs et canaux internationaux*, Paris, Pedone, 1964.

WYNNER, E. *World Federal Government in Maximum Terms*, 1954.

YAKEMTCHOUK, ROMAIN. *L'Ukraine en droit international*, Louvain, Centre Ukrainien d'Etudes en Belgique, 1954.

ZIMMERMANN, F. L. and WENDELL, M. *The Inter-State Compact since 1925*, Chicago, The Council of State Governments, 1951.

ZIMMERMANN, F. L. and WENDELL, M. *The Law and Use of Interstate Compacts*, Chicago, The Council of State Governments, 1961.

2. ARTICLES

ACCIOLY, H. 'Principes généraux de la responsabilité internationale, d'après la doctrine et la jurisprudence', 96 *HR* (1959), 353-441.

ALTING VON GEUSAU, FRANS A. M. 'External representation of Plural interests', 5 *Journal of Common Market Studies* (1967), 426-53.

ALTING VON GEUSAU, FRANS A. M. 'Problèmes intitutionnels des Communautés européennes—La procédure de décision', *Cahiers de droit européen* (1966), 227-50.

AMERICAN SOCIETY OF INTERNATIONAL LAW. 'Regionalism and international law: The most-favored-nation clause in a changing world', 54 *Proc. Amer. Soc. Int. Law* (1960), 153-94.

ANDRASSY, J. 'Les relations internationales de voisinage', 79 *HR* (1951), 77-181.

ANGUS, H. F. 'The Canadian Constitution and the U.N. Charter', 12 *Can. J. E. P. S.* (1946), 127-35.

ASPATURIAN, VERNON V. 'The theory and practice of Soviet federalism', 12 *The Journal of Politics* (1950), 20-51.

AUDINET, E. 'L'incompétence des tribunaux français à l'égard des Etats étrangers et la succession du Duc de Brunswick', 2 *RGDIP* (1895), 385-400.

AUFRICHT, H. 'Principles and practice of recognition by international organizations', 43 *AJIL* (1949), 679–705.

BAILEY, K. H. 'Australia and the International Labour Conventions', 54 *International Labour Review* (1946), 285-308.

BAKER, P. N. 'Le statut juridique actuel des Dominions britanniques dans le domaine du droit international', 19 *HR* (1927), 249–491.

BATSTONE, R. K. 'The utilization of the Nile Waters', 8 *ICLQ* (1959), 523-59.

BELOFF, M. 'Federalism as a model for international integration', 35 *BYIL* (1959).

BEREZOWSKI, C. 'Les sujets non souverains de droit international', 65 *HR* (1938), 5-84.

BERNHARDTE, RUDOLF. 'Föderal Klausel' in Strupp-Schlochauer, *Wörterbuch des Völkerrecht*, 548-50.

BIRCH, A. H. 'Approaches to the study of federalism', 14 *Political Studies* (1966), 15-33.

BONENFANT, J.-C. 'Les relations extérieures du Québec', 1 *Etudes Internationales* (1970), 81-4.

BONENFANT, J.-C. 'Les relations extérieures du Québec', 2 *Etudes Internationales* (1970), 84-90.

BOUCHEZ, L. J. 'The fixing of boundaries in international boundaries rivers', 12 *ICLQ* (1963), 789-817.

BOURNE, C. B. 'The Columbia River controversy', 37 *Can. Bar Rev.* (1959), 444-72.

BOWETT, D. W. 'Estoppel before international tribunals and its relation to acquiescence', 33 *BYIL* (1957), 176-202.

BRADY, ALEXANDER. 'The modern federation. Some trends and problems', in *Ontario Advisory Committee on Confederation, Background Papers and Reports* (1967), 1-24.

BRODERICK, MARGARET. 'Associated statehood—A new form of decolonisation', 17 *ICLQ* (1968), 368-403.

BUXBAUM, R. M. 'Article 177 of the Rome Treaty as a Federalizing Device', 21 *Stanford Law Review* (1969), 1041-57.

CALHOUN, J. C. 'A discourse on the Constitution and Government of the United States', in *The Works of John C. Calhoun*, ed. R. K. Cralle, Charleston and New York, Appleton, 1851–81, i, 111–406.

CABRANES, J. A. 'The status of Puerto Rico', 16 *ICLQ* (1967), 531.

CASTEL, J.-G. 'Canada and the Hague Conference on private international law: 1893-1967', 45 *Can. Bar Rev.* (1967), 1-34.

CASTRO-RIAL, J. M. 'Considérations sur la personnalité internationale', 4 *Revue hellénique dr. int.* (1951), 29–39.

CAVARÉ, LOUIS. 'L'immunité de juridiction de l'Etat étranger', 58 *RGDIP* (1954), 177-207.

CHAFEE, ZACHARIAH, JR. 'Federal and state powers under the U.N. Covenant on Human Rights' (1951), *Wisconsin Law Review*: Part I, 385-473; Part II, 623-56.

CHARPENTIER, JEAN. 'Pratique française concernant le droit international public', 1 *Ann. fr. dr. int.* (1956), 792–858.

CHEFFINS, RONALD I. 'The negotiation, ratification and implementation of treaties in Canada and Australia', 1 *Alberta Law Review* (1955-1961): Part I, 312-24; Part II, 410-30.

CHEVALIER, R. M. 'Methods and reasoning of the European Court in its interpretation of community law', 2 *Common Market Law Review* (1964), 21-35.

COLLIARD, C.-A. 'La collectivité autonome en droit international public et dans la pratique de la Charte de l'O.N.U.', *Ann fr. dr. int.* (1958), pp. 8–32.

COWLES, W. B. 'International Law as applied between subdivisions of federations', 74 *HR* (1949), 659–754.

CRUSEN, GEORG. 'Les servitudes internationales', 22 *HR* (1928), 5-79.

DEHOUSSE, JEAN-M. 'Du caractère essentiel de l'organe juridictionnel à pouvoir constitutionnaire dans toute structure fédérale et application de principe à la Communauté Economique Européenne', *Annales de la Faculté de Droit de Liège* (1965), 305-34.

DELISLE, R. J. 'Treaty-making power in Canada', *Ontario Advisory Committee on Confederation, Background Papers and Reports*, 1967, 115-47.

DESPAGNET, F. 'Chronique des faits internationaux', 6 *RGDIP* (1899), 169-229.

DEUTSCH, E. P. 'The treaty-making clause: A decision for the people of America', 37 *ABAJ* (1951), Part I, 659-62; Part II, 712-14.

DOBRIN, SAMUEL. 'Soviet federalism and the principle of double subordination', 30 *The Grotius Society's Transactions* (1945), 260-83.

DOLAN, EDWARD. 'The member republics of the USSR as subjects of the Law of Nations', 4 *ICLQ* (1955), 629-36.

DUDLEY, B. J. 'The concept of federalism', 1 *The Nigerian Journal of Economic and social Studies* (1963).

DURELLY, F. 'L'affaire du lac Lanoux', 62 *RGDIP* (1958), 469-516.

EAGLETON, CLYDE. 'The use of the waters of international rivers', 33 *Can. Bar Rev.* (1955), 1018-34.

EAGLETON, CLYDE. 'International organization and the law of responsibility', 76 *HR* (1950), 323–423.

EAYRS, JAMES. 'Canadian federalism and the United Nations'. 16 *Can. JEPS* (1950), 172-83.

EVATT, HERBERT V. 'The international responsibility of states in the case of riots and mob violence', 9 *Australian Law Journal* (1935), Supp. 9, 9-28.

FELD, WERNER J. 'The European Community Court: its role in the federalizing process', 50 *Minnesota Law Review* (1965-66), 423-42.

FITZGERALD, GERALD F. 'Educational and cultural agreements and ententes: France, Canada and Quebec—birth of a new treaty-making technique for federal states?', 60 *AJIL* (1966), 529–37.

FITZMAURICE, G. G. 'Reservations to multilateral conventions', 2 *ICLQ* (1953), 1-26.

FLEMING, WILLIAM. 'Danger to America: the Draft Covenant on Human Rights', 37 *ABAJ* (1951), 739-42, 794-9, 816-20, 855-60.

FRANKFURTER, F. and LANDIS, J. M. 'The compact clause of the Constitution —a study in interstate adjustments', 34 *Yale Law Journal* (1925), 685-758.

FRIEDRICH, CARL J. 'Federal constitutional theory and emergent proposals', in Macmahon, *Federalism, Mature and Emergent*, New York, Doubleday, 1955, pp. 510-29.

FRIEDRICH, CARL J. 'International federalism in theory and practice', in Plischke ed., *Systems of Integrating the International Community*, 1964, 117-155.

GERVAIS, ANDRÉ. L'affaire du Lac Lanoux, *Ann. fr. dr. int.* 1.

GIROUX, LORNE, 'La capacité internationale des provinces en droit canadien', 9 *Cahiers de droit* (1967-68), 241-71.

GRENON, J. Y. 'De la conclusion des traités et de leur mise en oeuvre au Canada', 40 *Can. Bar Rev.* (1962), 151-65.

GREWE, W. G. 'Die auswärtige Gewalt der Bundesrepublik', 12 *Veröffentlichungen der Vereinigung der deutschen Staatsrechtslehrer* (1954).

GRIFFIN, WILLIAM L. 'The use of waters of international drainage basins under customary international law', 53 *AJIL* (1959), 50-80.

GRISOLI, A. 'The impact of the European Economic Community on the movement for the unification of law', 26 *Law and Contemporary Problems* (1961), 418-29.

GROSS, LEO. 'Immunities and privileges of delegations to the United Nations', 16 *International Organizations* (1962), 483-520.

HAAS, E. 'Abschluss und Ratifikation internationer Verträge', *Archiv des offentlichen Rechts* 78 (1952), 382.

HALSJCZUK, BOHDON T. 'Les Etats fédéraux face au droit international', 13 *Ost. Zeit. öff. Recht* (1964), 307-17.

HAMSON, C. J. 'Immunity of foreign states: the practice of French courts', 27 *BYIL* (1950), 293-331.

HARTMAN, F. L. 'Federalism as a limitation on the treaty-making power of the United States, Western Germany and India', 18 *Western Reserve Law Review* (1966), 134-56.

HAY, PETER. 'The European Common Market and the most-favoured-nation clause', *University of Pittsburgh Law Review* (1962), 661-84.

HAY, PETER. 'Federal jurisdiction of the Common Market Court', 12 *AJCL* (1963), 21-40.

HAY, PETER. COOLEY, THOMAS H. and MOORHEAD, WILLIAM S. 'Problem of US participation in the European Common Market', 23 *University of Pittsburgh Law Review* (1962), 595, 647ff.

HAYEK, F. A. 'Economic conditions of inter-state federalism', *The New Commonwealth Quarterly* (1939), 131-49.

HEAD, IVAN L. 'The legal clamour over Canadian off-shore minerals', 5 *Alberta Law Review* (1966-1967), 312-27.

HEYDTE, F. A. VON DER. 'Schumann-Plan und Völkerrecht', in *Festschrift für R. Laun.*, 1953, Hamburg, 111.

HOLMAN, FRANK E. 'Need for a constitutional amendment on treaties and executive agreements', *Washington University Law Quarterly* (1955), 340-54.

HOLMAN, FkANK E. 'Treaty Law-Making: A Blank Check for Writing a New Constitution', 36 *American Bar Association Journal* (1950), 707-10.

HOUBEN, P. H. J. M. 'The merger of the executives of the European Communities', 3 *Common Market Law Review* (1965-66).

HUBER, MAX. 'Ein Beitrag zur Lehre von der Gebietshoheit an Grenzflüssen', 1 *Zeitschrift für Völkerrecht und Bundesstaatsrecht* (1907), 25-52.

HUBER, MAX. 'The intercantonal law of Switzerland (Swiss Interstate Law)', 3 *AJIL* (1909), 62-98.

HUDSON, MANLEY O. 'The membership of the United States in the ILO', *International Conciliation* (1935), no. 309, 120-35.

HUNT, ALAN R. 'International law: reservation to commercial treaties dealing with aliens' rights to engage in the professions', 52 *Michigan Law Review* (1953-54), 1184-98

JACKSON, J. H. 'The General Agreement on Tariffs and Trade in United States domestic law', 66 *Michigan Law Review* (1967), 250-332.

JOHNSON, D. H. N. 'Acquisitive prescription in international law', 27 *BYIL* (1950), 332-54.

KAISER, JOSEPH H. 'Die Erfüllung der völkerrechtlichen Verträge des Bundes durch die Länder. Zum Konkordatsurteil des Bundesverfassungsgerichts'. 18 *Zeitschrift für ausl. und öff. Recht und Völk* (1957-58), 526-58.

KEITH, B. 'The international status of the Dominions', 5 *Journal of Comparative Legislation and International Law* (third series) (1923), 161-8.

KEITH, K. J. 'Succession to bilateral treaties by seceding states', 61 *AJIL* (1967), 521-46.

KELSEN, HANS. 'Die Bundesexekution, ein Beitrag zur Theorie und Praxis des Bundestaates', in *Festgabe für Fleiner*, Zürich, 1927.

KELSEN, HANS. 'Recognition in international law, theoretical observations', 35 *AJIL* (1941), 605-17.

KENNEDY, W. P. M. 'The office of the Governor-General in Canada', 7 *Univ. Toronto LJ* (1947-48), 474-83.

KÖLBLE, JOSEPH. 'Auslandsbeziehungen der Länder'? *Die öffentliche Verwaltung* (1965), 145-54.

KOENIG, LOUIS W. 'Federal and state cooperation under the Constitution', 36 *Michigan Law Review* (1938), 752-85.

KRAUS, HERBERT. 'Die Zuständigkeit der Länder der Bundesrepublik Deutschland zum Abschluss von Kulturabkommen mit auswärtigen Staaten nach dem Bonner Grundgesetz', 3 *Archiv. des Volk.* (1951-52), 414-27.

KRYLOV, SERGE. 'Les notions principales du droit des gens', 70 *HR* (1947), 411-75.

KUNZ, JOSEPH L. 'Une nouvelle théorie de l'Etat fédéral', 11 *Revue de droit international et de législation comparée* (1930), 835-77.

KUNZ, JOSEPH L. 'Critical Remarks on Lauterpacht's "Recognition in International Law"', 44 *AJIL* (1950), 713-19.

KUNZ, JOSEPH L. 'International law by analogy', 45 *AJIL* (1951), 329–35.

KUNZ, JOSEPH L. 'Supra-national organs', 46 *AJIL* (1952).

LABAND, PAUL. 'Les relations diplomatiques et consulaires entre les Etats de l'Empire Allemand', 11 *RGDIP* (1904), 121-33.

LAGRANGE, MAURICE. 'Le pouvoir de décision dans les Communautés Européennes: théorie et réalité', 3 *Revue trimestrielle de droit européen* (1967), 1-29.

LANGE, CHRISTIAN L. 'Histoire de la doctrine pacifique, et de son influence sur le développement du droit international', 13 *HR* (1926), 175-423.

LASKIN, BORA. 'Some international legal aspects of federalism: the experience of Canada', in *Federalism and the New Nations of Africa*, ed. Currie 1964, pp. 389-414.

LASKIN, BORA. 'The provinces and international agreements', *Ontario Advisory Committee on Confederation, Background Papers and Reports* (1967), pp. 101-13.

LAUTERPACHT, ELIHU. 'River boundaries: legal aspects of the Shatt-Al-Arab frontier', 9 *ICLQ* (1960), 208-35.

LAUTERPACHT, ELIHU. 'The contemporary practice of the United Kingdom in the Fields of International Law—Survey and Comment VII, 6 *ICLQ* (1957), 506.

I AUTERPACHT, H. 'Decisions of municipal courts as a source of international law', 10 *BYIL* (1929), 65-95.

LAYLIN, JOHN P. and BIANCHI, R. L. 'The role of adjudication in international river disputes', 53 *AJIL* (1959), 30-49.

LEDERMAN, W. R. 'Classification of Laws and the British North America Act', in *Legal Essays in Honour of Arthur Moxon*, University of Toronto Press, 1953, pp. 183-207.

LEISNER, WALTER. 'A propos de la répartition des compétences en matière de conclusion des traités dans la République Fédérale d'Allemagne', 6 *Ann. fr. dr. int.* (1960), 291-312.

LEISNER, WALTER. 'The foreign relations of the member states of the Federal Republic of Germany', 16 *Univ. Toronto LJ* (1966), 346-60.

LEWIS, MALCOLM M. 'The international status of the British self-governing Dominions', 3 *BYIL* (1922-23), 21-41.

LIANG, YUEN-LI. 'Colonial clauses and federal clauses in UN multilateral instruments', 45 *AJIL* (1951), 108-28.

LISSITZYN, OLIVER. 'Treaties and changed circumstances (*Rebus sic stantibus*)', 61 *AJIL* (1967), 895-922.

LISSITZYN, OLIVER. 'Territorial entities other than independent states in the law of treaties', 125 *HR* (1968), 1-92.

LOOPER, ROBERT B. 'The treaty power in India', 32 *BYIL* (1955-56), 300-7.

LOOPER, ROBERT B. 'Federal states clauses in multilateral instruments', 32 *BYIL* (1955-56), 162-203.

LOOPER, ROBERT B. 'Limitations on the treaty power in federal states', 34 *New York University Law Review* (1959), 1045-66.

LOOPER, ROBERT B. 'The treaty power in Switzerland', 7 *AJCL* (1958), 178-94.

LORENZ, WERNER. 'General principles of law: their elaboration in the Court of Justice of the European Communities', 13 *AJCL* (1964), 1-29.

LUCIEN-BRUN, JEAN. 'Une nouvelle étape dans le droit concordataire', 11 *Ann. fr. dr. int.* (1965), 113-21.

MACGIBBON, I. C. 'Estoppel in international law', 7 *ICLQ* (1958), 468-513.

MALINTOPPI, A. 'Les relations entre l'unification et l'harmonisation du droit et la technique de l'unification ou de l'harmonisation par la voie d'accords internationaux', in Unidroit, *L'Unification du droit /Unification of Law, Year-Book 1967-68*, ii, 43-91.

MALLMANN, WALTER. 'Völkerrecht und Bundesstaat', in Strupp-Schlochauer, *Wörterbuch des Völkerrechts*, iii, (1962), 640-50.

MASHAW, JERRY L. 'Federal issues in and about the jurisdiction of the Court of Justice of the European Communities', 40 *Tulane Law Review* (1965-66), 21-56.

MCINTYRE, ELIZABETH. 'Weighted voting in international organizations', 8 *International Organizations* (1954), 484-93.

MCKENZIE, NORMAN A. M. 'Canada: The treaty-making power', 18 *BYIL* (1937), 172-5.

MCMAHON, J. F. 'The Court of Justice of the European Communities: judicial interpretation and international organization', 37 *BYIL* (1961), 320-50.

MCNAIR, LORD. 'Aspects of state sovereignty', 26 *BYIL* (1949), 6-47.

MCWHINNEY, EDWARD. 'Comment of the Concordat Case', 35 *Can. Bar Rev.* (1957), 842-8.

MCWHINNEY, EDWARD. 'Canadian federalism, and the foreign affairs and treaty power. The impact of Quebec's quiet revolution', 7 *The Canadian Yearbook of International Law* (1969), 3-32.

MEGRET, JACQUES. 'Le pouvoir de la communauté économique européenne de conclure des accords internationaux', *Revue de Marché Commun* (Déc. 1964), 529-36.

MENZEL, E. 'Die auswärtige Gewalt der Bundesrepublik', 12 *Veröffentlichungen der Vereinigung der deutschen Staatsrechtslehrer* (1954).

MILLER, ARTHUR S. and HOWELL, RONALD F. 'Interposition, nullification and the delicate division of power in a federal system', 5 *Journal of Public Law* (1956), 2-48.

MITRANY, DAVID. 'The functional approach to world organization', 24 *International Affairs* (1948), 356.

MITRANY, DAVID. 'The prospects of integration: federal or functional', 4 *Journal of Common Market Studies* (1965), 119-49.

MONACO, RICARDO. 'Les principes d'interprétation suivis par la Cour de Justice des Communautés Européennes', in *Mélanges Henri Rolin*, Paris, Pedone, 1964, pp. 216-27.

MONACO, RICARDO. 'Le rapprochement des législations nationales dans le cadre du marché commun'; 3 *Ann. fr. dr. int.* (1957), 558-68.

MOORE, JOHN N. 'Federalism and foreign relations', *Duke Law Journal* (1965), 248-321.

MOORE, SIR W. HARRISON. 'The federations and suits between governments', 17 *JCLIL*, 3rd ser. (1966), 163-209.

MOORE, SIR W. HARRISON. 'The Dominions and treaties', 8 *JCLIL*, 3rd ser. (1926), 21-37.

MORIN, JACQUES-Y. 'La conclusion d'accords internationaux par les provinces canadiennes à la lumière du droit comparé', 3 *Canadian Yearbook of International Law* (1965), 127-86.

MORRIS, GERALD L. 'The treaty-making power: a Canadian dilemma', 45 *Can. Bar Rev.* (1967), 478-512.

MOSLER, HERMAN. 'Réflexions sur la personnalité juridique en droit international public', in *Mélanges Henri Rolin*, Paris, Pedone, 1964, pp. 228-51.

MOSLER, HERMAN. 'Kulturabkommen des Bundesstaats—zur Frage der Beschränkung der Bundesgewalt in auswärtigen Angelegenheiten', 16 *Zeit. aus öff. Recht und Völk* (1955-56), 1-34.

MOSLER, HERMAN. 'Die völkerrechtliche Wirkung bundesstaatlicher Verfassung', in *Festschrift für Richard Thomas*, Tübingen, 1950, 129.

MUNCH, VON. 'Internationale Organisationen mit Hoheitsrechten', in *Festschrift für H. Wehberg*, 1956.

MUNDELL, D. W. 'Legal nature of federal and provincial executive governments: some comments on transactions between them', 2 *Osgoode Hall Law Journal* (1960-63), 56-75.

NADELMANN, KURT H. 'Ignored state interests: the federal government and international efforts to unify rules of private law', 102 *University of Pennsylvania Law Review* (1953-54), 323-66.

NATHANSON, NATHANIEL L. 'The constitution and world government', 57 *North-Western University Law Review* (1962–63), 355–82.

NEDBAILO, P. Y. and VASSILENKO, V. A. 'Soviet Union Republics as subjects of international law', *Soviet Yearbook of International Law* (1963), 85-105; English summary: 105-8.

NEWCOMBE, H. 'Alternative approaches to world government', 1 *Peace Research Reviews*, no. 1 (February 1967).

OBER, F. B. 'The treaty-making and amending powers: do they protect our fundamental rights', 36 *ABAJ* (1950), 715-19; 793-96.

O'CONNELL, D. P. 'State succession and the effect upon treaties of entry into a composite relationship', 39 *BYIL* (1963), 54-132.

o'connell, d. p. 'La personnalité en droit international', 67 *RGDIP* (1963), 5-43.

panhuys, van, j. h. f. 'The international aspects of the reconstruction of the Kingdom of the Netherlands in 1954', 5 *Netherlands International Law Review* (1958), 1-31.

patry, a. 'La capacité internationale des Etats fédérés, in Brossard, Patry and Weiser, *Les Pouvoirs extérieurs du Québec*, 1967.

pescatore, p. 'Les relations extérieures des Communautés europénnes', 103 *HR* (1961), —.

pescatore, p. 'La personnalité internationale de la Communauté', in *Les Relations extérieures de la Communauté européenne unifiée*, Actes du troisième colloque sur la fusion des communautés européennes. organisé à Liège les 25, 26 et 27 octobre 1967, Institut d'études juridiques euro-péennes de la Faculté de droit de l'Université de Liège, Liège, 1969.

pescatore, p. 'L'apport du droit communautaire au droit international public', *Cahier du droit européen* (1970).

pescatore, p. 'International law and community law: a comparative analysis', 7 *Common Market Law Review* (1970), 167-83.

pilotti, m. 'Les unions d'Etats', 24 *HR* (1928), 441-546.

piot, alice. 'Of realism in conventions of establishment', 88 *Journal du droit international* (1961), 38-85.

pohl, heirinch. 'Die Zuständigkeitsverteilung zwischen Reich und Ländern im Auslieferungswesen', 14 *Zeitschrift für Völkerrecht* (1927-28), 1-22.

polak, m. v. 'Die Haftung des Bundesstaates für seine Gliedstaaten', 1 *Oster. eit. für öff. Recht* (1946), 382-7.

potter, p. b. 'Inhibitions upon the treaty-making power of the United States', 28 *AJIL* (1934), 456-74.

quadri, r. 'La personnalité internationale de la communauté' in *Les rela-tions extérieures de la communauté européenne unifiée*, Actes du troisème colloque sur la fusion des communautés européennes, organisé à Liège les 25, 26 et 27 octobre 1967, Institut d'études juridiques européennes de la Faculté de Droit de l'Université de Liège, Liège, 1969, 39-74.

quarles, james. 'The Federal Government: as to foreign affairs, are its powers inherent as distinguished from delegated?', 32 *Georgetown Law Journal* (1944), 375-83.

raju, g. s. 'Principles of law governing the diversion of international rivers', 2 *Indian Journal of International Law* (1965), 370-4.

rand, michael c. 'International agreements between Canadian Provinces and foreign states', 25 *University of Toronto, Faculty of Law Review* (1967), 75-86.

reuter, paul. 'Les recours de la Cour de Justice des Communautés Européennes à des principes généraux de droit', in *Mélanges Henri Rolin*, Paris, Pedone, 1964, pp. 263-83.

reuter, paul. 'La cour de justice des Communautés Européennes et le droit international', in *Recueil d'études de droit international en hommage à Paul Guggenheim* (1968), pp. 665-86.

reuter, paul. 'Juridical and institutional aspects of the European regional Communities', 26 *Law and Contemporary Problems* (1961), 381-99.

richberg, donald r. 'The Bricker Amendment and the treaty power', 39 *Virginia Law Review* (1953), 753-64.

riesman, david, jr. 'The American Constitution and international labour legislation', 44 *International Labour Review* (1941), 123-93.

rodgers, raymond s. 'The capacity of states of the Union to conclude international agreements: the background and some recent developments', 61 *AJIL* (1967), 1021-8.

rodgers, raymond s. 'Conclusion of Quebec–Louisiana agreement on cul-tural co-operation', 64 *AJIL* (1970), 380.

rosenne, shabtai. 'United Nations treaty practice', 86 *HR* (1954), II, 281-443.

rousseau, charles. 'Influence de la structure fédérale de la Suisse sur la conclusion des traités internationaux élaborés par l'UNESCO', 69 *RGDIP* (1965), 840-1.

ROUSSEAU, CHARLES. 'Commentaires sur le concordat entre le Saint-Siège et la Basse-Saxe', 69 *RGDIP* (1965), 768-9.

RUDOLF, WALTER. 'Internationale Beziehungen der deutschen Länder', 13 *Archiv. des Völkerrechts* (1966), 53-74.

SABOURIN, LOUIS. 'La participation des provinces canadiennes aux organisations internationales', 3 *Canadian Yearbook of International Law* (1965), 73-99.

SAUSER-HALL, GEORGE. 'L'utilisation industrielle des fleuves internationaux', 83 *HR* (1953), 465-85.

SAWER, G. 'Federalism in West Germany', *Public Law*, 1961, 26-44.

SCHAUMANN, W. 'Verträge zwischen Gliedstaaten im Bundesstaat', 19 *Verofftlichungen der Vereinigung der Deutschen Staatsrechtslehrer* (1961), 86.

SCHEINGOLD, STUART A. 'The Court of Justice of the European Communities and the development of international law', 59 *Proceedings of the American Society of International Law* (1965), 190-212.

SCHINDLER, DIETRICH. 'The administration of justice in the Swiss Federal Court in intercantonal disputes', 15 *AJIL* (1921), 149-88.

SCHNEIDER, H. 'Verträge zwischen Gliedstaaten im Bundesstaat', 19 *Veröffentlichungen der Vereinigung der deutschen Staatsrechtslehrer* (1961), 1-85.

SCHOEN, PAUL. 'Die völkerrechtliche Haftung der Staaten aus unerlaubten Handlungen', 10 *Zeitschrift für Völkerrecht* (1917), 2nd supplement.

SCHWARZENBERGER, G. 'The most-favoured-nation standard in British state practice', 22 *BYIL* (1945), 96-121.

SCOTT, J. B. 'The British Commonwealth of Nations', 21 *AJIL* (1927), 95-101.

SCOTT, ROBERT D. 'Kansas v. Colorado Revisited', 52 *AJIL* (1958), 432-54.

SCOTT, FRANK R. 'The consequences of the Privy Council decisions', 15 *Can. Bar Rev.* (1937), 485-94.

SECRETAN, JACQUES. 'Swiss constitutional problems and the International Labour Organization', 56 *International Labour Review* (1947), 1-20.

SEIDL-HOHENVELDERN, IGNAZ. 'The relation of international law to internal law in Austria', 49 *AJIL* (1955), 451-76.

SEIDL-HOHENVELDERN, IGNAZ. 'Die völkerrechtliche Haftung für Handlungen internationaler Organisationen im Verhältnis zu Nichtmitgliedstaaten', 11 *Oster, Zeit. für öff. Recht* (1961), 497-506.

SEIDL, HOHENVELDERN, IGNAZ. 'The legal personality of international and supranational organizations, 21 *Revue egyptienne de droit international* (1965), 35-72.

SEYDEL, VON. 'Der Bundesstaatsbegriff', 28 *Zeitschrift für die gesammte Staatwissenschaft* (1872), 185-256.

SELAK, CHARLES B., JR. 'The United States-Canadian Great Lakes Fisheries Convention', 50 *AJIL* (1956), 122-9.

SMILEY, DONALD V. 'Public administration and Canadian federalism', *Canadian Public Administration* (1964), 371-88.

SOHN, LOUIS B. 'Multiple representation in international assemblies', 40 *AJIL* (1946), 71-99.

SOHN, LOUIS B. and SHAFER, PAUL. 'Foreign affairs', in Bowie and Friedrich, ed., *Studies in Federalism*, 1954, 236-95.

SØRENSEN, MAX. 'Federal states and the international protection of human rights', 46 *AJIL* (1952), 195-218.

SØRENSEN, MAX. 'Principes de droit international public', 101 *HR* (1960), 1-251.

STANFORD, J. S. 'United Nations Law of Treaties Conference: first session', 19 *Univ. Toronto LJ* (1969), 59-68.

STANFORD, J. S. 'The Vienna Convention on the Law of Treaties', 20 *Univ. Toronto LJ* (1970), 18-47

STARKE, J. G. 'Imputability in international delinquencies', 19 *BYIL* (1938), 104-17.

STEIN, ERIK. 'Assimilation of national laws as a function of European integration', 58 *AJIL* (1964), 1-40.

STEINBERGER, HELMUT. 'Constitutional subdivisions of states or unions and their capacity to conclude treaties. Comments on Art. 5, para. 2 of the ILC's 1966 Draft Articles on the Law of Treaties', 27 *Zeit. aus. off. Recht und Volk.* (1967), 411-28.

SUTHERLAND, ARTHUR. E., JR. 'Restricting the Treaty Power', 65 *Harvard Law Review* (1952), 1305-38.

SUY, ERIK. 'Immunity of states before Belgian courts and tribunals', 27 *Zeit, für aus. öff. Recht und Völk.* (1967), 660-92.

SZABLOWSKI, G. J. 'Creation and implementation of treaties in Canada', 34 *Can. Bar Rev.* (1956), 28-59.

TABATA, SHIGEJIRO. 'The eleventh World Conference of the World Association of World Federalists, Tokio, 1963', 8 *Japanese Annual of International Law* (1964), 30-43.

TÉNÉKIDÈS, C. G. 'L'immunité de juridiction des Etats étrangers', 5 *RGDIP* 3rd series (1931), 607-32.

TRUDEAU, ANDRÉ. 'La capacité internationale de l'Etat fédéré et sa participation au sein des organisations et conférences internationales', 3 *Revue Juridique Thémis* (1968), 223-76.

VERDROSS, ALFRED V. 'Theorie der mittelbaren Staatenhaftung', 21 *Zeit. für öff. Recht* (1941), 283-309.

VERDROSS, ALFRED V. 'Règles générales du droit international de la paix', 30 *HR* (1929), 275-507.

VERDROSS, ALFRED V. 'Die Völkerrechtssubjektivität der Gliedstaaten der Sowjetunion', 1 *Oster. Zeit. für öff. Recht* (1946), 212-8.

VERDROSS, ALFRED V. 'Theorie der mittelbaren Staatenhaftung', 1 *Öster. Zeit für öff. Recht* (1946), 389-423.

VISSCHER, CHARLES DE. 'Observations sur l'effectivité en droit international public', 62 *RGDIP* (1958), 601-9.

VISSCHER, PAUL DE. 'La Communauté européenne du charbon et de l'acier et les Etats membres', in *Actes Officiels du congrès international d'études sur la Communauté européenne du charbon et de l'acier.* Milan-Stresa, 31 mai-9 juin 1957, Milan, Giuffré, 1958, ii, 9-85.

WARBRICK, COLIN. 'Off-shore petroleum exploitation in federal systems: Canadian and Australian action', 17 *ICLQ* (1968), 501-13.

WEINFELD, ABRAHAM C. 'What did the framers of the Federal Constitution mean by 'Agreements or Compacts?', 3 *University of Chicago Law Review* (1936), 453-64.

WEISER, ELIZABETH. 'La conclusion d'accords internationaux par les Etats fédérés allemands, suisses et autrichiens', in Brossard, Patry and Weiser, *Les Pouvoirs extérieurs du Québec*, Presses de l'Université de Montréal, 1967, pp. 101-62.

WEISS, ANDRÉ. 'Compétence ou incompétence des tribunaux à l'égard des Etats étrangers', 1 *HR* (1923), 525-51.

WENGLER, W. 'La communauté, les pays tiers et les organisations internationales', in *Actes Officiels du congrès international d'études sur la Communauté européenne du charbon et de l'acier*, Milan-Stresa, 31 mai-9 juin 1957, Milan, Giuffré, 1958, iii, 69-124 (French translation).

WIEBRIGNHAUS, HANS. 'Le droit européen face au problème des accords internationaux dans les structures fédératives', 2 *Rivista di diritto europeo* (1962).

WILCOX, FRANCIS O. 'International confederation. The United Nations and state sovereignty', in Plischke, *Systems of Integrating the International Community*, 1964, 27-66.

'X.X.X.' 'Evolution de la réglementation internationale en matière de discrimination et de préférences', 9 *Ann. fr. dr. int.* (1963), 66-77.

ZORN, P. K. L. 'Neue Beiträge zur Lehre vom Bundesstaat', *Hirth's Annalen des deutschen Reiches* (1884), pp. 453-83.

3. PUBLIC DOCUMENTS

Annuaire du Québec/Quebec Yearbook.
Canada Yearbook.
Canada and the United Nations.
Canadian Treaty Series.
Conference of Commonwealth and State Ministers, 26-28 August 1936 (Australia).
Congressional Records (US).
Council of Europe, Consultative Assembly, Official Reports of Debates.
Department of State Bulletin (US).
Department of State Newsletter (US).
Documents of the International Telecommunications Conference at Atlanta City, 1947.
Education Weekly, A Department of Education Bulletin (Quebec).
European Economic Community, Journal Officiel.
External Affairs (Canada).
Federalism and International Relations, Honourable Paul Martin, Secretary of State for External Affairs, Queen's Printer, Ottawa, Canada, 1968.
Federalism and International Conference on Education, A Supplement to Federalism and International Relations, Honourable Mitchell Sharp, Secretary of State for External Affairs, Queen's Printer, Ottawa, Canada, 1968.
Feuille Fédérale (Switzerland).
GATT, *Basic Instruments and Selected Documents.*
HACKWORTH, GREEN H. *Digest of International Law.* 8 vols. Washington: Government Printing Office, 1940-44.
House of Commons, *Parliamentary Debates* (UK).
ICAO Bulletin.
International Labour Conference, *Record of Proceedings.*
International Law Association, *Principles of Law governing the Uses of International Rivers* (Resolution adopted by the Int. Law Assocn. at its Conference held in August 1956 at Dubrovnik, Yugoslavia).
LEAGUE OF NATIONS, *Acts of the Conference for the codification of International Law,* 1930, Minutes of the 3rd Committee (L.N., 1930, 17).
LEAGUE OF NATIONS, *Conference for the Codification of International Law. Bases of Discussion,* 1924, (Doc. C. 75, M. 69).
LEAGUE OF NATIONS, *Official Journal.*
LEAGUE OF NATIONS, *Treaty Series.*
MALLOY, WILLIAM M., comp. *Treaties, Conventions, International Acts, Protocols and Agreements between the United States of America and other Powers,* 1776-1909. Washington: Government Printing Office, 1910.
MOORE, JOHN BASSETT. *A Digest of International Law.* 8 vols. Washington: Government Printing Office, 1906.
OECD, Fiscal Committee, *Draft Double Taxation on Estate and Inheritances,* 1966.
OECD, Fiscal Committee, *Draft Double Taxation Convention on Income and Capital,* 1963.
Official Opinions of the Attorneys General of the United States. Department of Justice, 1852 to present.
Official Reports of the debates of the House of Commons of Canada.
Ontario Advisory Committee on Confederation, Background Papers and Reports, 1967.
Papers Relating to the Foreign Relations of the United States.
Quebec Constitutional Conference Continuing Committee of Officials,

Working Paper on Foreign Relations. Notes prepared by the Quebec Delegation, February 5, 1969.

Recueil des Décisions. Tribunaux Arbitraux Mixtes. Paris: Librairie de la société de Recueil Sirey, 1922.

Reichsgesetzblatt (Germany).

Statutory Instruments (UK).

Status refondus du Québec, 1964.

The Government of Quebec and the Constitution, Office d'information et de publicité du Québec, 1968.

The Parliament and Commonwealth of Australia, Report from the Joint Committee on Constitutional Review, 1959.

The Revised Statutes of Canada.

UK *Cmd, Cmmd* (British Government Publication).

UNITED KINGDOM. Advisory Commission on the Review of the Constitution of the Federation of Rhodesia and Nyasaland, *Report,* Cmnd 1150, HMSO, 1960.

UNITED NATIONS. Commission on Human Rights. Doc. E/CN.4/95 (1948).

UNITED NATIONS. Conference on the Law of Treaties, First Session, Vienna, 26 March-24 May 1968, Official Records (Doc. A/CONF. 39/11).

UNITED NATIONS. Conference on the Law of Treaties, Second Session, Provisional Summary Record of the Eighth Plenary Meeting, Vienna, 26-29 April 1969 (Doc. A/CONF. 39/SR. 7 and SR. 8).

UNITED NATIONS. *Economic Commission for Europe.* Committee on Electric Power. *Legal Aspects of the Hydro-Electric Development of Rivers and Lakes of Common Interest.* E/ECE/EP 136 and E/ECE/EP 98. Rev. Geneva, 1952.

UNITED NATIONS. Economic and Social Council, *Official Records.*

UNITED NATIONS. General Assembly, *Official Records.*

UNITED NATIONS. *Juridical Yearbook.*

UNITED NATIONS. *Status of Multilateral Conventions in respect of which the Secretary General Acts as Depositary,* 1959 (Doc. ST/LEG/3, REV.1).

UNITED NATIONS. Secretary General, *Preparatory Study Concerning a Draft Declaration on the Rights and Duties of States* (Doc. A/CN.4/2).

UNITED NATIONS. Secretary General, *Survey of International Law in relation to the Work of Codification of the International Law Commission.* Memorandum Submitted by the Secretary General, United Nations, General Assembly, International Law Commission, 1949 (Doc. A/C.N.4/1/Rev.1).

UNITED NATIONS. *Treaty Series.*

UNITED NATIONS. *Yearbook.*

UNESCO and the International Institute of Administrative Sciences, *National Administration and International Organization. A Comparative Study of 14 Countries.*

UNITED STATES OF AMERICA. *Constitution of United States Annotated.* Senate Document 39, 88th Congress, 1st Session (1963).

UNITED STATES OF AMERICA. Hearings, Senate, Sub-committee of Committee on Foreign Relations, *the Great Lakes Basin,* 84th Congress, 2nd Session, 1956.

UNITED STATES OF AMERICA. Senate, *Legal Aspects of the Use of Systems of International Waters,* Document No. 118. 85th Congress, 2nd Session, 1958.

UNITED STATES OF AMERICA. *Statutes at Large.*

UNITED STATES OF AMERICA. *Treaty Series.*

USSR Academy of Sciences, *International Law.*

Yearbook of the International Law Commission.

4. UNPUBLISHED MATERIAL

BERNARD, 'Federalism and Public Administration in Canada: a study in Constitutional practice', Ph.D. thesis, University of London, 1964.

BEISSWINGERT, 'Die Einwirkung bundesstaatlicher Kompetenzverschiebungen auf völkerrechtliche Verträge under besonderer Berücksichtung der deutschen Entwicklung', dissertation, Münich, 1960.

CARTER, 'Canada and the International Labour Organization', 1919-1938, M.Sc. thesis, University of London, 1939.

HALLMAYER, 'Die völkerrechtliche Stellung der deutschen Länder nach dem Bonner Grundgesetz', dissertation, Tübingen, 1954.

IBRAHIM, 'The Application of International Law in Disputes between Member States of Federal Unions, with special reference to the United States, Australia and Canada', doctoral Thesis, Leyden, 1952.

KRÖNECK, 'Die völkerrechtliche Immunität bundesstaatlicher Gliedstaaten vor ausländischen Gerichten', dissertation, Münich, 1958.

SCHWARZENBACH, 'Staatsverträge der Kantone mit dem Ausland', thesis, Zürich, 1926.

TABLE OF CASES

Page references to the text are in bold type

AUTHOR INDEX

GENERAL INDEX